OPEN SOURCE SYSTEMS

IFIP – The International Federation for Information Processing

IFIP was founded in 1960 under the auspices of UNESCO, following the First World Computer Congress held in Paris the previous year. An umbrella organization for societies working in information processing, IFIP's aim is two-fold: to support information processing within its member countries and to encourage technology transfer to developing nations. As its mission statement clearly states,

> *IFIP's mission is to be the leading, truly international, apolitical organization which encourages and assists in the development, exploitation and application of information technology for the benefit of all people.*

IFIP is a non-profitmaking organization, run almost solely by 2500 volunteers. It operates through a number of technical committees, which organize events and publications. IFIP's events range from an international congress to local seminars, but the most important are:

• The IFIP World Computer Congress, held every second year;
• Open conferences;
• Working conferences.

The flagship event is the IFIP World Computer Congress, at which both invited and contributed papers are presented. Contributed papers are rigorously refereed and the rejection rate is high.

As with the Congress, participation in the open conferences is open to all and papers may be invited or submitted. Again, submitted papers are stringently refereed.

The working conferences are structured differently. They are usually run by a working group and attendance is small and by invitation only. Their purpose is to create an atmosphere conducive to innovation and development. Refereeing is less rigorous and papers are subjected to extensive group discussion.

Publications arising from IFIP events vary. The papers presented at the IFIP World Computer Congress and at open conferences are published as conference proceedings, while the results of the working conferences are often published as collections of selected and edited papers.

Any national society whose primary activity is in information may apply to become a full member of IFIP, although full membership is restricted to one society per country. Full members are entitled to vote at the annual General Assembly, National societies preferring a less committed involvement may apply for associate or corresponding membership. Associate members enjoy the same benefits as full members, but without voting rights. Corresponding members are not represented in IFIP bodies. Affiliated membership is open to non-national societies, and individual and honorary membership schemes are also offered.

OPEN SOURCE SYSTEMS

IFIP Working Group 2.13 Foundation on Open Source Software, June 8-10, 2006, Como, Italy

Edited by

Ernesto Damiani
University of Milan, Italy

Brian Fitzgerald
CSIS, University of Limerick, Ireland

Walt Scacchi
University of California, United States

Marco Scotto
Free University of Bolzano-Bozen, Italy

Giancarlo Succi
Free University of Bolzano-Bozen, Italy

 Springer

Open Source Systems
Edited by E. Damiani, B. Fitzgerald, W. Scacchi, M. Scotto, and G. Succi

p. cm. (IFIP International Federation for Information Processing, a Springer Series in Computer Science)

ISSN: 1571-5736 / 1861-2288 (Internet)
ISBN: 10: 1-4899-8537-9
ISBN: 13: 978-1-4899-8537-8
ISBN: 10: 0-387-34226-5 (eBook)
Printed on acid-free paper

9 8 7 6 5 4 3 2 1
springer.com

Preface

Early research studies on open source software (OSS) development often betrayed a mild surprise that loosely coordinated networks of volunteers could manage the design and implementation of highly complex software products, successfully tackling many non-trivial project management problems.

In the past few years, a wider research community has become increasingly aware of the tremendous contribution that open source development is making to the software industry, business and society in general. Software engineering researchers are exploring OSS specifically with respect to development tools and methodologies, while organizational scientists and economists are keen on understanding how open sources brought large communities of people, who are seldom acquainted, to help each other effectively.

Being ourselves involved in a number of open source projects, we could directly witness how the creation of new knowledge within OSS developments may have very different motivations and consequences from work done under traditional intellectual property rights regimes like patents, copyrights and trade secrets. Much research work is needed to move from collecting anecdotal evidence to a rigorous scientific study of the OSS phenomenon; as researchers, however, we cannot refrain from remarking that the OSS reward system, based on peer review and discussion, is much closer to the system used for rewarding scientific research than to some corporate practices.

We believe this book to be an important step in the direction of a fuller understanding of the OSS phenomenon. It collects the proceedings of the Second International Conference on Open Software (OSS2006) held in Como, Italy, from June 8th to June 10th, 2006. OSS 2006 was the foundation conference of the IFIP TC2 WG 2.13 on Open Source Software, and attracted many researchers from all over the world interested in how OSS is produced, in its huge innovation potential in many different application fields and in OSS innovative business models. The 20 full papers of this volume were selected via a rigorous refereeing process among more than 100 submissions; 12 additional submissions, in view of their interest, were selected for publication in a more concise form.

We hope that these contributions, while attaining full scientific rigor, can still give the reader an idea of the lively interdisciplinary debate of OSS 2006.

Acknowledgments

We gratefully acknowledge the contribution of the other OSS 2006 conference officials: Kevin Crowston, Scott Hisham, Paolo Pumilia and Barbara Scozzi. Also we would like to thank the OSS 2006 international program committee and the board of reviewers for their valuable help in selecting the papers.

Como, Italy
June 2006

Ernesto Damiani [1]
Brian Fitzgerald [2]
Walt Scacchi [3]
Marco Scotto [4]
Giancarlo Succi [5]

---

[1] DTI, University of Milan - via Bramante 65, Crema (CR), Italy
damiani@dti.unimi.it

[2] CSIS, University of Limerick, Limerick, Ireland
Brian.Fitzgerald@ul.ie

[3] Institute for Software Research, Donald Bren School of Information and Computer Sciences, University of California, Irvine, US
wscacchi@ics.uci.edu

[4] Center for Applied Software Engineering, Free University of Bolzano-Bozen, Italy
Marco.Scotto@unibz.it

[5] Center for Applied Software Engineering, Free University of Bolzano-Bozen, Italy
giancarlo.succi@unibz.it

Organization

Conference Officials

General Chair:	Brian Fitzgerald	CSIS, University of Limerick, Ireland
Program Chair:	Walt Scacchi	University of California, Irvine, US
	Giancarlo Succi	Free University of Bolzano-Bozen, Italy
Program Co-Chair:	Marco Scotto	Free University of Bolzano-Bozen, Italy
Organising and Workshop Chair:	Ernesto Damiani	University of Milan, Italy
Tutorial Chair:	Scott Hissam	Carnegie Mellon University, US
Publicity Chair:	Barbara Scozzi	Polytechnic of Bari, Italy
Panel Chair:	Kevin Crowston	Syracuse University, US
Social and Industrial Liaison:	Paolo Pumilia	'Open Culture' Committee
Web Master:	Alberto Colombo	University of Milan, Italy
	Fulvio Frati	University of Milan, Italy

Program Committee

Pierpaolo Andriani	Durham University, UK
Hala Annabi	University of Washington, US
Tiziana Arcarese	European Commission
Graham Attwell	University of Bremen, Germany
Megan Conklin	Elon University,US
Paul A. David	University of Stanford, US
Francesco Di Cerbo	University of Genoa, Italy
Nicolas Ducheneaut	PARC, US
Mahmoud Elish	King Fahd University, Saudi Arabia
Joseph Feller	University College Cork, Ireland
Rishab Aiyer Ghosh	MERIT, Netherlands
Il Horn Hann	University of Southern California, US
Jim Herbsleb	Carnegie Mellon University, US
Firoz Kaderali	Fern University, Hagen, Germany
Stefan Koch	University of Economics and BA, Austria
Derrick G. Kourie	University of Pretoria, South Africa
Sandeep Krishnamurthy	University of Washington, US
Jean Pierre Laisne	ObjectWeb, France
Karim Lakhani	MIT, US
Martin Michlmayr	University of Cambridge, UK
David Parnas	University of Limerick, Ireland
Giuseppina Passiante	University of Lecce, Italy
Witold Pedrycz	University of Alberta, Canada
Andrea Prencipe	Universita' "G. D'Annunzio", Pescara, Italy
David Rine	George Mason University
Maria Alessandra Rossi	University of Siena, Italy
Barbara Russo	Free University of Bolzano-Bozen, Italy
Glen Sagers	Florida State University
Alexander Schatten	TU Wien, Austria
Marco Scotto	University of Genoa, Italy
Barbara Scozzi	Polytechnic of Bari, Italy
Alberto Sillitti	Free University of Bolzano-Bozen, Italy
Katherine Stewart	University of Maryland, US
Alexandra Tödt	University of Cologne, Germany
Sergiy Vilkomir	University of Limerick, Ireland
Jesus Villasante	European Commission

Board of Reviewers

Sponsors

"*The Competence Center Open Source aims to be a node to create a network which connects the Open Source and Free Software competences in South Tyrol*".

CoCOS (**www.cocos.bz**) is an Interreg IIIA project supported by the Office for Innovation, Research, Development and Cooperation in South Tyrol, the BIC Südtirol, the CAN Südtirol, the Free University Bozen - Bolzano, and the University of the Italian Switzerland.

ENGINEERING INGEGNERIA INFORMATICA

Engineering Ingegneria Informatica (**www.eng.it**) plays a primary role in Italy in the Information Technology. It operates in all software production segments all the way up to strategic consulting services. Engineering Ingegneria Informatica is active in the finance sector, telecoms, industry and services, central and local public administration, defence, healthcare and utilities engineering, together with other 12 major European IT players, is the promoter of the NESSI European Technology Platform under the auspices of the European Commission.

Engineering's approach to Open Source

Engineering's approach to system integration carries out the definition of innovative architectural solutions and the realization of complex projects. Engineering enables enterprises to benefit from its experience and knowledge in the selection, integration, validation and support "best of breed" components, including its open source solutions:

SpagoBI: a complete suite for the development of Business Intelligence projects in an integrated environment. It has the potential of covering the full range of analytical aspects, such as the data and metadata organization, static reporting and dynamic control suite with dashboard components. For more details: http://spagobi.eng.it

Spago: The Java Enterprise Wide Framework for the development of web and multi-channel applications in enterprise environments. It implements the MVC architectural pattern to realize distributed multi-tier applications, based on modular components, and integration services towards external infrastructures. For more deatils: http://spago.eng.it

ASSOCIAZIONE ITALIANA PER IL CALCOLO AUTOMATICO

AICA (Associazione Italiana per il Calcolo Automatico, **www.aicanet.it**) is the most important Italian association of IT professionals. Established in 1961, AICA is a non-profit association whose main goal is the development, among its members and the wider national community, of all scientific, practical, economic and social aspects of computer science. AICA provides a cooperation opportunity to the three main actors of the IT world: universities and scientific research centers producing theoretical and methodological knowledge, public and private users exploiting this knowledge for their practical purposes, and, finally, developers and suppliers of IT services and products. AICA promotes both the professional growth of computer scientists and the diffusion of computer literacy among the broader population. The vision underlying AICA manifold activities puts Italy's IT sector in the framework of international experiences and initiatives. AICA is federated with IFIP, the International Federation of Information Processing, and CESIP, the Council of European Professional Informatics Societies.

List of Contributors

Paul J. Adams
University of Lincoln, UK
padams@lincoln.ac.uk

Hala Annabi
The Information School, University of
Washington, US
hpannabi@u.washington.edu

Claudio Agostino Ardagna
University of Milan, Italy
ardagna@dti.unimi.it

Andres Baravalle
University of Sheffield, UK
andres@dcs.shef.ac.uk

Amit Basu
Cox School of Business, SMU, US
abasu@smu.edu

George Becker
Nerim.net
gbecker@nerim.net

Evangelia Berdou
London School of Economics and
Political Science, UK
e.berdou@lse.ac.uk

Andrea Bonaccorsi
DESA-University of Pisa, Italy
bonaccorsi@sssup.it

Marc Bourgois
Eurocontrol Experimental Center,
France
marc.bourgois@eurocontrol.int

Daniel Brink
University of Cape Town, South
Africa
BRNDAN011@mail.uct.ac.za

Sarah Chambers
University of Sheffield, UK
sarah@dcs.shef.ac.uk

Megan Conklin
Elon University, US
mconklin@elon.edu

Grahame S. Cooper
University of Salford, UK
g.s.cooper@salford.ac.uk

Kevin Crowston
School of Information Studies,
Syracuse University, US
crowston@syr.edu

Jean-Michel Dalle
Université Pierre et Marie Curie
(Paris 6), France
jean-michel.dalle@upmc.fr

Ernesto Damiani
University of Milan, Italy
damiani@dti.unimi.it

Vincenzo D'Andrea
University of Trento, Italy
dandrea@dit.unitn.it

Paul A. David
Stanford University &
Oxford Internet Institute, US
pad@stanford.edu

Adriaan de Groot
Quality Team, KDE e V.
groot@kde.org

Giuditta De Prato
University of Bologna, Italy
deprato@spbo.unibo.it

Ignatios Deligiannis
Aristotle University of Thessaloniki,
Greece
igndel@it.teithe.gr

Matthijs den Besten
Université Pierre et Marie Curie
(Paris 6), France
matthijs.denbesten@lamsade.
dauphine.fr

Ludovic Denoyelle
ARIST Bourgogne, France
l.denoyelle@bourgogne.cci.fr

Francesco Di Cerbo
DIST - University of Genova, Italy
Francesco.DiCerbo@unige.it

Pierluigi Di Nunzio
Polytechnic of Torino, Italy
pierluigi.dinunzio@polito.it

Tharam S. Dillon
University of Technology, Sidney,
Australia
tharam@it.uts.edu.au

Gabriella Dodero
University of Genova, Italy
dodero@disi.unige.it

Anne Sophie Farizy
ARIST Bourgogne, France
s.farizy@bourgogne.cci.fr

Daniele Favara
DIST - University of Genova, Italy
Daniele.Favara@gmail.com

Attilio Fiandrotti
Polytechnic of Torino, Italy
fiandro@initd.org

Ulrich Frank
University Duisburg-Essen, Germany
ulrich.frank@uni-due.de

Fulvio Frati
University of Milan, Italy
frati@dti.unimi.it

Fabrice Galia
Université Panthéon-Assas (Paris II),
France
galia@u-paris2.fr

G.R. Gangadharan
University of Trento, Italy
gr@dit.unitn.it

Mehmet Gençer
Istanbul Bilgi University, Turkey
mgencer@cs.bilgi.edu.tr

Giorgos Gousios
Athens University of Economics and
Business, Greece
gousiosg@aueb.gr

Thierry Grison
L2EI - Université de Bourgogne,
France
thierry.grison@u-bourgogne.fr

Jungpil Hahn
Purdue University, US
jphahn@mgmt.purdue.edu

Il-Horn Hann
University of Southern California, US
hann@marshall.usc.edu

Jean-Luc Hardy
Eurocontrol Experimental Center,
France
jl.hardy@eurocontrol.int

Robert Heckman
School of Information Studies,
Syracuse University, US
rheckman@syr.edu

Federico Iannacci
London School of Economics, UK
F.Iannacci@lse.ac.uk

Sebastian Küugler
Quality Team, KDE e V.
sebas@kde.org

Tommi Kärkkäinen
University of Jyväskylä, Finland
tka@mit.jyu.fi

Stefan Koch
Vienna University of Economics and
Business Administration, Austria
stefan.koch@wu-wien.ac.at

Timo Koponen
University of Kuopio, Finland
timo.koponen@uku.fi

Jussi Koskinen
University of Jyväskylä, Finland
koskinen@cs.jyu.fi

Eric Leclercq
L2EI - Université de Bourgogne,
France
eric.leclercq@u-bourgogne.fr

Edvin Lindqvist
University of Skövde, Sweden
edvin.lindqvist@his.se

Brian Lings
University of Skövde, Sweden
brian.lings@his.se

Björn Lundell
University of Skövde, Sweden
bjorn.lundell@his.se

Kazuaki Maeda
Chubu University, Japan
kaz@acm.org

Angelo Raffaele Meo
Polytechnic of Torino, Italy
meo@polito.it

Monica Merito
DESA-University of Pisa, Italy
merito@sssup.it

Jae Yoon Moon
Hong Kong University of Science and
Technology, Hong Kong
jmoon@ust.hk

Gabriella Moroiu
Carleton University, Canada
gmoroiou@scs.carleton.ca

Beyza Oba
Istanbul Bilgi University, Turkey
boba@bilgi.edu.tr

Thomas Østerlie
Norwegian University of Science
and Technology, Norway
thomas.osterlie@idi.ntnu.no

Bülent Özel
Istanbul Bilgi University, Turkey
bulento@bilgi.edu.tr

Erika Piffero
University of Genova, Italy
erika.piffero@gmail.com

Lucia Piscitello
DIG-Polytechnic of Milan, Italy
lucia.piscitello@polimi.it

Salvatore Reale
Siemens S.p.A., Italy
salvatore.reale@siemens.com

Francesco Rentocchini
University of Bologna, Italy
francesc.rentocchini@studio.
unibo.it

Jeffrey Roberts
Carnegie Mellon University, US
jroberts@andrew.cmu.edu

Llewelyn Roos
University of Cape Town, South
Africa
RSXLLE001@mail.uct.ac.za

Bruno Rossi
Free University of Bolzano-Bozen,
Italy
bruno.rossi@unibz.it

Cristina Rossi
DIG - Polytechnic of Milan, Italy
cristina1.rossi@polimi.it

Francesco Rullani
Sant'Anna School of Advanced
Studies, Italy
rullani@sssup.it

Barbara Russo
Free University of Bolzano-Bozen,
Italy
barbara.russo@unibz.it

Marinette Savonnet
L2EI - Université de Bourgogne,
France
Marinette.savonnet@u-bourgogne.fr

Andrew Schofield
University of Salford, UK
a.j.schofield@pgt.salford.ac.uk

Marco Scotto
Free University of Bolzano-Bozen,
Italy
Marco.Scotto@unibz.it

Barbara Scozzi
Polytechnic of Bari, Italy
bscozzi@poliba.it

Alberto Sillitti
Free University of Bolzano-Bozen,
Italy
Alberto.Sillitti@unibz.it

Gregory L. Simmons
University of Ballarat, Australia
g.simmons@ballarat.edu.au

Sandra Slaughter
Carnegie Mellon University, US
sandras@andrew.cmu.edu

Sulayman K. Sowe
Aristotle University of Thessaloniki,
Greece
sksowe@csd.auth.gr

Ioannis Stamelos
Aristotle University of Thessaloniki,
Greece
stamelos@csd.auth.gr

Knut Staring
University of Oslo, Norway
knutst@ifi.uio.no

Stefan Strecker
University Duisburg-Essen, Germany
stefan.strecker@uni-due.de

Giancarlo Succi
Free University of Bolzano-Bozen,
Italy
giancarlo.succi@unibz.it

Marie-Noëlle Terrasse
L2EI - Université de Bourgogne,
France
marie-noelle.terrasse@
u-bourgogne.fr

Ola Titlestad
University of Oslo, Norway
olati@ifi.uio.no

Vehbi Sinan Tunahoğlu
Istanbul Bilgi University, Turkey
vst@cs.bilgi.edu.tr

Timo Tuunanen
University of Jyväskylä, Finland
timtuun@jyu.fi

Jean-Paul Van Belle
University of Cape Town, South
Africa
jvbelle@commerce.uct.ac.za

Dieter Van Nuffel
University of Antwerp, Belgium
dieter.vannuffel@ua.ac.be

Kris Ven
University of Antwerp, Belgium
kris.ven@ua.ac.be

Jan Verelst
University of Antwerp, Belgium
jan.verelst@ua.ac.be

Tullio Vernazza
DIST - University of Genova, Italy
Tullio.Vernazza@unige.it

Michael Weiss
Carleton University, Canada
weiss@scs.carleton.ca

James Weller
University of Cape Town, South
Africa
WLLJAM005@mail.uct.ac.za

Ann Westenholz
Copenhagen Business School,
Denmark
aw.ioa@cbs.dk

Chen Zhang
Purdue University, US
zhang153@mgmt.purdue.edu

Ping Zhao
Carleton University, Canada
pzhao@connect.carleton.ca

Gregorio Robles
Universidad Rey Juan Carlos, Spain
grex@gsyc.escet.urjc.es

Jesus M. Gonzalez-Barahona
Universidad Rey Juan Carlos, Spain
jgb@gsyc.escet.urjc.es

Katia Lupi
DISI - University of Genova, Italy
katia.lupi@gmail.com

Keisuke Inoue
Syracuse University, US
kinoue@syr.edu

James Howison
Syracuse University, US
jhowison@syr.edu

Contents

Part IV Introduction of OSS in Companies and PAs

Part V Empirical Analysis of OSS

Part VI Case Studies and Experiments

Part VII Impact of OSS on Social Networks

Part VIII Posters

Part I

Foundations and Rationale
of Open Source software

On the Weickian Model in the Context of

Open Source Software Development:

Some Preliminary Insights

Federico Iannacci
Department of Information Systems, London School of Economics,
Houghton Street, London WC2A 2AE United Kingdom (UK),
F.Iannacci@lse.ac.uk
WWW home page: http://personal.lse.ac.uk/iannacci/

Abstract. Despite being regarded as a path-breaking model of organising, Weick's Enactment-Selection-Retention (ESR) model has been labelled too abstract a model find any practical applications. This paper attempts to show that exploration-oriented open source projects represent valuable case studies where Weick's ESR model can be applied. By taking the Linux case study as a case in point, it is argued that a qualitative analysis of micro interactions (i.e. double interacts) might reveal broad organising patterns. Preliminary implications in terms of coordination and knowledge making processes are discussed in the final section.

1 Introduction

Despite being regarded as a path-breaking model of organising (Tsoukas 1998), Weick's Enactment-Selection-Retention (ESR) model has been labelled too abstract a model to find any practical applications (Aldrich 1999, Harrison 1994). Commenting on Weick's ESR model, Aldrich (1999: 56), maintains, for instance, that "some theorists argue that organizational actors essentially create the context to which they react, thus creating a closed explanatory loop. Not every theorist goes that far, but the concept of enactment –that actions precede interpretation and interpretations create a context for action- places heavy demands on anyone conducting research on why people and organizations behave as they do". By the same token, Harrison (1994: 252- 253) remarks that "valuable as this perspective may be, it is important to recognize that interdependence is never manifested or experienced in quite such abstract terms. Weick's model is an important conceptual tool for understanding how coherent patterns of organization emerge from ongoing sequences of interlocked behaviours, but it retains an unreal, skeletal quality because most of the cultural, situational, and historical contexts associated with these processes have been stripped away… Thus Weick's model is essentially a framework without specific content".

The purpose of this paper is to show that a minimalist approach to organising as advocated by Weick's ESR model can go a long way in terms of explaining the interaction patterns emerging within exploration-oriented open source projects in general and the Linux kernel development in particular. My argument unfolds in the

Please use the following format when citing this chapter:

Iannacci, F., 2006, in IFIP International Federation for Information Processing, Volume 203, Open Source Systems, eds. Damiani, E., Fitzgerald, B., Scacchi, W., Scotto, M., Succi, G., (Boston: Springer), pp. 3-8

following fashion: section two introduces Weick's ESR model in the context of open source software development, section three elaborates on the research methodology, section four identifies a few patterns characterising the Linux kernel organising process and, finally, section five highlights some preliminary insights stemming from my analysis of the Linux case study.

2   On Weick's ESR model in the context of open source software development

Weick's ESR model offers a compelling rationale for understanding why interdependence is a processual accomplishment within any social settings (Harrison 1994). Due to the lack of self-sufficiency, individuals engage in interlocked communicative behaviours to meet their goals. Each individual needs the instrumental communicative act of another individual to perform his consummatory act. However, the enactment of these interlocked behaviours produces equivocality because people utter words that can plausibly be interpreted in two or more ways: the crux of organising then consists of reducing equivocality (i.e. misunderstanding) by means of sensible communication cycles so as to achieve a situation where shared understanding is attained[1].

According to the ESR model, organising is a "consensually validated grammar for reducing equivocality" (Weick 1979: 3) because people literally need to share the same representation (i.e. cause map) of the words they have uttered to act collectively regardless of their individual goals (Weick 1979).

At this level of abstraction, Weick's model seems to have no bearing on technology unless one takes technology to stand for "intensive technology" (Thompson 1967) which feeds back on the social endeavour of organisational actors by constantly disrupting their activities through equivocal displays (Cf. Weick 1979: 22). Hence, for sake of clarification, I take enactment to stand both for social construction of technology and bracketing. By social construction of technology I mean a process whereby developers engage in social interactions to generate software artefacts which were not out there initially; by bracketing, otherwise, I intend to refer to a process whereby the equivocal displays stemming from the emergent technological construct are punctuated and made sense of. In addition, I take selection to stand for numerous decision premises (March and Simon 1958) that serve as assembly rules, that is shared criteria whereby only a subset of social interactions is chosen out of the pool of all communication cycles. Finally, I take retention to stand

---

[1] Equivocality stands for a situation where given an output message (e.g. a word being uttered or written), there are multiple perceived inputs (i.e. meanings that might have generated that output message) or vice versa (i.e. given an input there are many associated outputs). See Weick (1979: 179-187) on this point. For sake of simplification, in this paper I take equivocality and ambiguity to be synonyms. I also take knowledge and information to be synonyms.

for the stock of knowledge or information retained from the past that can be brought to bear on present decisions. The ESR model so described is outlined below:

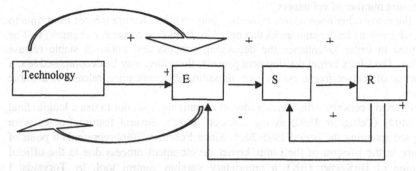

Fig. 1. The ESR Model in Open Source Software Development. Adapted from Weick (1979)

Note that while selection credits the past on the basis of stored memory rules, that is rules stored from past knowledge, enactment discredits the past because it relies on playful behaviours that relax the rules by treating memory as an enemy (March 1988), thus fostering exploration of the space of possibilities. This, in turn, implies that the social construction of technology and, therefore, social interactions are only partially shaped by the stock of past knowledge (i.e. the system's memory) to the extent that developers resort to shared procedures to select subsets of interaction cycles. According to Weick (1979), a system that is simultaneously crediting and discrediting its past is a self-stabilising system because it is able to balance the antithetical pressures deriving from flexibility (i.e. exploration) and stability (i.e. exploitation).

3 On the research methodology

The case study is a research strategy which focuses on understanding the dynamics present within single settings (Eisenhardt 1989). This paper examines the Linux case study to pinpoint broad interaction patterns that apply to the category of exploration-oriented open source projects of which Linux is representative (Nakakoji et al. 2002)[2].

Linux is a Unix-like operating system started by Linus Torvalds in 1991 as a private research project. Between 1991 and 1994 the project size burgeoned to the point that in 1994 Linux was officially released as version 1.0. It is now available free

---

[2] Nakakoji et al. (2002) contend that exploration-oriented projects, including the Linux kernel, aim at pushing the frontline of software development collectively through the sharing of innovations. Contributions made by the community at large exist as feedback and are incorporated only if they are consistent with the ideas of the project leader.

to anyone who wants it and is constantly being revised and improved in parallel by an increasing number of volunteers.

Like many other open source projects, Linux exhibits feature freezes from time to time whereby its leader announces that only bug fixes (i.e. corrective changes) will be accepted in order to enhance the debugging process and obtain a stable release version. The Linux kernel development process, therefore, may be decomposed into a sequence of feature freeze cycles each signalling the impending release of a stable version.

Given my concern with Weick's idea of organising, I set out to use a longitudinal case study (Pettigrew 1990) as my research design. Several feature freezes were analysed spanning the period 1995-2005. Since February 2002 represents a point of rupture in the lifespan of the Linux kernel development process due to the official adoption of BitKeeper (BK), a proprietary version control tool, by Torvalds, I analysed with particular focus the events surrounding the October 2002 feature freeze, the first freeze exhibiting the parallel adoption of two versioning tools, namely BK and CVS (i.e. the Concurrent Versions System)[3]. In analysing such events, I decomposed each thread into sets of two contingent responses between two or more developers, thus taking Weick's (1979) double interact as my unit of analysis.

4 An overview of the Linux kernel organising process

I have claimed above that the ESR model may be viewed as a way of conceptualising the organising process where the collective brackets the equivocal displays stemming from the emergent software construct (i.e. enactment), filters such raw data (i.e. selection) and, finally stores them in various storage devices as knowledge or information (i.e. retention). Put differently, the Linux collective (Shaikh and Cornford 2005) may be conceptualised as an organisational mind of sorts where loosely-coupled developers engage into a set of interactions by following specific decision premises that are collectively shared as assembly rules (i.e. procedures, instructions or guides used to organise the process). Thus, every instance of organising consists of sets of interaction cycles or double interacts and assembly rules whereby such cycles are assembled together and sequenced to create knowledge (Iannacci 2003). But what are the assembly rules that the Linux kernel developers follow?

The longitudinal analysis of the interaction cycles occurring on the Linux Kernel Mailing List (i.e. LKML) and other mailing lists suggests that two rules are followed by developers, namely[4]:

a) Rule of enhancement: select those interaction cycles that enhance the quality of the data inputs. The Linux kernel developers enact their programming skills by

---

[3] Note that, in early April 2005, Torvalds has replaced BK with Git, a GPL-tool that like BK does not rely on a single, centralised repository and maintains a similar workflow for incorporating new patches. See: http://www.linux.org/news/2005/04/21/0012.html

[4] This list of rules is by no means exhaustive since other rules might well apply (Cf. Weick 1979: 114).

following standardised patch submission procedures, as well as standardised bug reporting formats[5]. Standardisation enhances the quality of the data flows and makes them more amenable to sense-making processes occurring across space and time. Consider, for instance, the following patch submitted during the October 2002 feature freeze:

>*On 5 Oct 2002, Maksim (Max) Krasnyanskiy wrote:*
> > *Patch #2:*
>*Why is it so hard to just read the "submitting patches" thing.*
I did. Long time ago though :)
>*Don't bother to email me if you can't be bothered to read how to*
>*submit patches. People do it all the time, and I'm not interested in*
>*fetching compressed patches from web-sites etc.*
Sorry about that. I knew you were gonna pull this stuff from BK any way[6].

Since compressed patches are more equivocal than patches submitted the regular way, Torvalds is explicitly asking developers to follow the pre-defined procedures.

b) Rule of personnel: select those interaction cycles that are manned by the most experienced and, therefore, most trustworthy people. To solve the issue of scalability (i.e. "Linus does not scale"), a loosely-coupled social structure has emerged over time whereby Torvalds interacts with a select number of developers, the so called "Trusted Lieutenants", who, in turn, interact with a few trustworthy people, thus creating a complex attentive system tied together by trust (Weick and Roberts 1993). Without trust developers should expend time and effort to verify the reliability of the patches received. Trust operates as an equivocality-reducing mechanism that ensures reliable performance.

5 Concluding remarks

Despite the obvious limitation concerning the generalisability of findings stemming from a single case study, Weick's ESR model can contribute some original ideas to the study of the open source software development process. Not only does Weick's ESR model shed some light on the delicate issue of coordination by showing that coordination (i.e. organising) accounts for stability in a turbulent context where developers can follow their localised interests in a loosely-coupled fashion; it also helps conceptualise the knowledge-making process considering that the raw data stemming from the emergent source code are transformed into information or knowledge on the basis of collectively-shared assembly rules. Further research should

---

[5] Note that the argument developed above refers to manual rather than automated procedures.
[6] Source: http://www.ussg.iu.edu/hypermail/linux/kernel/0210.0/2396.html. Note that this is a double interact because we have two contingent responses, namely Torvalds' response to Krasnyanskiy's initial message marked with a single arrow (>) and Krasnyanskiy response to Torvalds, the original message being marked with a double arrow (>>).

be devoted to the study of equivocality considering that electronic contexts compound the sense-making problem due to the lack of social context cues.

References

Aldrich, H. E. (1999) *Organizations Evolving*, Sage Publications, London, Thousand Oaks.

Eisenhardt, K. M. (1989) "Building Theories from Case Study Research", *Academy of Management Review,* **14 (4),** pp. 532-550.

Harrison, T. M. (1994) "Communication and Interdependence in Democratic Organizations", *Communication Yearbook 17,* pp. 247-274.

Iannacci, F. (2003) "The Linux Managing Model", *First Monday 8/12; Address: http://www.firstmonday.org/issues/issue8_12/iannacci/index.html, Accessed on 03/12/03.*

March, J. G. (1988) "The Technology of Foolishness" in *Decisions and Organizations,* (March, J. G. ed.) Basic Blackwell Ltd, Oxford.

March, J. G. and H. A. Simon (1958) *Organizations,* John Wiley & Sons, Inc., New York.

Nakakoji, K., Y. Yamamoto, K. Kishida and Y. Ye (2002) "Evolution Patterns of Open-Source Software Systems and Communities". in *International Workshop Principles of Software Evolution,* pp. 76-85,

Pettigrew, A. M. (1990) "Longitudinal Field Research on Change: Theory and Practice", *Organization Science,* **1 (3),** pp. 267-292.

Shaikh, M. and T. Cornford (2005) "Learning/Organizing in Linux:: A Study of the 'Spaces in Between". in *The 27th International Conference on Software Engineering (ICSE 2005). Open Source Application Spaces: 5th Workshop on Open Source Software Engineering,* St. Louis, Missouri, USA, pp. 57-61,

Thompson, J. D. (1967) *Organizations in Action,* Mc Graw-Hill Book Company, New York.

Tsoukas, H. (1998) "Introduction: Chaos, Complexity and Organization Theory", *Organization,* **5 (3),** pp. 291-313.

Weick, K. E. (1979) *The Social Psychology of Organizing,* Addison-Wesley Publishing Company, Menlo Park, California.

Weick, K. E. and K. Roberts (1993) "Collective Mind in Organizations: Heedful Interrelating on Flight Decks", *Administrative Science Quarterly,* **38 (3),** pp. 357-381.

Acknowledgements:
I wish to thank Maha Shaikh and the two anonymous reviewers for their helpful comments. Obviously, I am to blame for any conceptual mistakes.

Conceptual Modelling as a New Entry in the Bazaar: The Open Model Approach

Stefan Koch[1], Stefan Strecker[2], and Ulrich Frank[2]

[1] Institute for Information Business, Vienna University of Economics and BA
stefan.koch@wu-wien.ac.at
[2] Information Systems and Enterprise Modelling, University Duisburg-Essen
{stefan.strecker|ulrich.frank}@uni-due.de

Abstract. The present contribution proposes to transfer the main principles of open source software development to a new context: conceptual modelling; an activity closely related to software development. The goal of the proposed "open model" approach is to collaboratively develop reference models for everyone to copy, use and refine in a public process. We briefly introduce conceptual modelling and reference models, discuss the cornerstones of an open modelling process, and propose a procedure for initiating, growing and sustaining an open model project. The paper concludes with a discussion of potential benefits and pitfalls.

1 Introduction

Open source software development [5] is currently the prime example for collaborative development processes by geographically dispersed participants. Similar joint efforts have emerged in collaborative writing and publishing (i e open content [23]), and in other areas [32] such as open hardware, and open education [16]. Recent research on open source projects has identified fundamental principles common to many collaborative development processes [30], e.g. the named credit and anti-forking norm [35], which seem to carry over to collaborative processes with outcomes other than source code. However, further research is still required to determine possible boundaries for this, and the necessary preconditions that have to be met in an area to make this transfer successful.

The present contribution proposes to apply the main principles behind open source software development to *conceptual modelling*, an activity closely related to software development [9]. The goal of the proposed "open model" approach is to develop *reference models* for everyone to copy, distribute, use, and refine with the collaboration of a large number of participants in a public process. Its consequential objective is to encourage the development of software based on these models as well as the models' use for research and teaching purposes.

Transferring the principles of open source software development to conceptual modelling is of interest for both practical and scientific reasons. The use of tried and tested reference models promises several advantages over "reinventing the wheel"-approaches, e.g. (i) reduced time and effort in software design, (ii)

Please use the following format when citing this chapter:

Koch, S., Strecker, S., and Frank, U., 2006, in IFIP International Federation for Information Processing, Volume 203, Open Source Systems, eds. Damiani, E., Fitzgerald, B., Scacchi, W., Scotto, M., Succi, G., (Boston: Springer), pp. 9-20

use of the knowledge of domain experts, and (iii) facilitation of integration and reuse (cf. Sec. 2). From a research point of view, an open model approach provides an opportunity to research whether and how the principles of open source software development processes carry over to other contexts in general [32] and to modelling in particular. Starting from the observation that the absence of modelling activities in open source software development has been recognized as problematic, e.g. [38, 24, 42], an open model approach also serves as a testbed for investigating the effects of conceptual modelling and open models on open source software development.

An ideological argument refers to the freedom of models: If it is accepted that information needs to be freely accessible [33, 23], this should also pertain to the models behind any software, even more so than the software's documentation, given that the models are of much higher importance. For example, problems with a large code base becoming effectively closed due to high complexity might be overcome at least to some degree when the underlying models are accessible. Even if SAP would release the source code of R/3, or Microsoft the code of Windows or Office, these large software systems would be difficult to understand without the underlying models. Releasing the appropriate models would be of even greater importance than the release of source code. Given a free and open model, alternative implementations of the same functionality will be easier to produce. Other examples are the Netscape/Mozilla or OpenOffice projects, which experienced difficulties in setting up a community.

In this paper, we briefly introduce conceptual modelling and reference models (Sec. 2), discuss the cornerstones of an open modelling process (Sec. 3.1), and propose a procedure for initiating, growing and sustaining an open model approach (Sec. 3.2). We will also discuss both benefits and pitfalls (Sec. 4), and conclude with a summary and future work (Sec. 5).

2 Prospects of conceptual modelling

2.1 Bridging the gap

On a conceptual level, models represent abstractions of real-world phenomena relevant to a certain modelling task (conceptual models) [9]. *Conceptual models* are aimed at providing representations of software systems that are accessible not only to modellers and software developers, but also to domain experts and prospective end users. For this reason, they focus on general concepts commonly used within a certain domain abstracting from technical aspects.

By allowing for various abstractions, e.g. data abstraction, object abstraction, and process abstraction, they contribute to the reduction of complexity and risk. On the other hand, they take into account certain characteristics of implementation-level languages. Thus, conceptual models help to overcome the notorious cultural chasm between developers and end users [20]. At the same time, they support the communication among software developers, thus contributing to more efficient coordination in software development projects.

Furthermore, conceptual models are the instrument of choice to prepare for integrating applications by defining common concepts for a set of applications. Also, abstracting from technical details renders conceptual models better suited for reuse than source code.

2.2 Reference models as silver bullets

The design of high quality conceptual models suited to guide the development of large systems is a challenging task that requires outstanding expertise as well as a thorough and costly analysis. This motivates the development of *reference models*. A reference model is a conceptual model that comes with the claim to suit not just one system, but a whole range of systems, e.g. a generic process model for contract processing in the insurance industry. The claim pertains to two aspects. On the one hand, reference models are intended to provide appropriate generalisations of existing domains. On the other hand, reference models are aimed at delivering blueprints for good system design. Thus, reference models are descriptive and prescriptive at the same time. Reference models are a reification of a very attractive vision: They promise higher quality of information systems at less cost. However, adapting reference models for actual system implementation often requires significant adaptations for a specific application.

The development of reference models currently takes place mainly in academia and in large software companies. Reference models distributed as part of commercial packages, e.g. Enterprise Resource Planning (ERP) software such as SAP R/3, have been adopted in practice. Their development process is typically a closed-shop effort on part of a software or consulting company, e.g. SAP, with the respective copyright and patent issues attached.

Academic research has produced several modelling languages and associated reference models in recent years, e.g. [31, 10]. Conceptual models in general and reference models in particular have been a focus in information systems (IS) research [41]. Research on reference models and modelling languages is commonly subsumed in the field of enterprise modelling [4, 2].

With regard to the tremendous benefits to be expected from high quality reference models, it seems surprising that there is only a small number of reference models available [6]—despite the remarkable amount of work on reference models in academia. However, these models usually suffer from two deficiencies. Firstly, they remain in a prototypical state—due to limited resources available in single research projects. Secondly, they fail to be deployed in practice. While the second shortcoming can in part be contributed to the first one, it is also caused by the lack of effective mechanisms to disseminate research results.

A recent survey on internet-based reference modelling [39] has shown that only very little information on reference models is available on-line and that most models are either published in part or entirely in print publications if at all. The study implies that discussion about and construction of reference models hardly ever is an open process and concludes that the internet offers potential for further distributed, collaborative efforts to develop reference models.

Reference models seem to be an ideal subject for an open, community-driven development process. The modelling process necessitates a higher level of abstraction than programming. Its overall complexity allows for the involvement of a diversity of participants ranging from developers to users to domain experts and reviewers, among others. Following Raymond [30], a larger number and a greater diversity of eyeballs on a modelling task is required to conceive high quality conceptual models. Note, however, the differences between conceptual models and source code. It is likely that the number of eyeballs on models will be less than those on code if only due to the fact that evaluating a reference model to suggest improvements requires different skills and interests. The transparency of a conceptual model fosters the coordination of the various contributions. An open model project would not only allow for bundling academic resources. Rather, it could serve as a common medium for organizing the exchange between academia and practice, thus fostering its acceptance and deployment. With respect to the division of labour, a reference model could be used as a common reference in various disciplines. On a higher level of abstraction, for instance, business experts could analyse and eventually redesign business processes, while software experts could focus on the design of supporting information systems. Hence, reference models could support cross-disciplinary cooperation and contribute to the coherent integration of state-of-the-art knowledge from multiple disciplines.

3 Conceptual modelling as an open process

3.1 Cornerstones of the open model process

In the following, we assume that it is possible to initiate, grow and sustain collaborative processes with outcomes other than source code based on the fundamental principles behind open source software development. Distributed modelling processes are a particular instance of such collaborative processes, in particular, reference modelling processes in which stakeholders in the process collaborate to develop reference models. Therefore the following cornerstones of open source development need to be adopted to the open model approach:

Appropriate licence. An appropriate model licence is required to ensure that everyone is allowed to copy, distribute, use and modify the model (open model) [33, 29]. The licence should explicitly allow for the model's use in proprietary software development to promote its adoption and deployment in practice, while aiming for widest possible range of participants [34].

Roles and stakeholders. The open modelling process should be designed to facilitate contributions from practitioners (e.g. domain experts, business analysts) and academics (e.g. researchers, students) alike. The role of practitioners is twofold: While they can and should participate in the modelling task itself, they serve as the most important form of quality assurance and review. Most often, they will be in the best position to judge the relevance and correctness of business processes modelled against business requirements and practice. Based on common elements in open source team structures, we identify the following roles in an open modelling process:

- Maintainer: The maintainer is responsible for either the whole model or a distinct sub-model. Whether several maintainers are introduced, or become necessary, depends both on the size of the domain, and the success of the initiative. Depending on the organisational model chosen, this can be either an owner/maintainer, benevolent dictator, or trusted lieutenant [30], deciding on whether a submission is accepted, when a new official version is released etc., or, if a democratic structure is adopted, mostly an administrative position. These positions will be filled by people who have demonstrated long-term and high quality commitment, so that their authority is accepted by the others.
- Modeller: The position of a modeller is analogous to the commiter in open source software development, in that he has the right to perform changes to the model. The right to do this directly is normally linked to several prior submission that have successfully passed quality control.
- Contributor: Any person can fill the role of contributor, and propose changes to the model. These need to be passed over to a modeller or maintainer, in order to pass quality control and be accepted. If this is done several times, a contributor might advance to modeller position.
- Reviewers: As in software development, quality assurance is an important task in an open model project. Open source projects employ several mechanisms to this end [45], with extensive peer review as the most prominent example. In an open model project, an official position of reviewer might be established. Naturally, everyone filling up another role might become reviewer, e.g. any modeller could automatically be assigned this additional role. The most important task is to review any proposed changes to the model, and to decide according to relevance and quality. Practitioners are very much suited for this role in order to provide feedback from their experience.
- End users: Anybody can become an end user of an open model. Of special interest are those who become active participants, by either reporting problems or suggesting ideas, or by submitting changes to the model directly.

As empirical research on open source software development teams has shown, in most projects a small inner group forms [25, 19], surrounded by a larger number of contributors, and an even greater number of participants not directly involved in programming, but other tasks like bug reporting. A similar structure might appear in an open model project. It should also be noted that both structure and processes in open source software projects have been found to change over time in accordance with the needs and the evolution of the product, which in turn is of course shaped by the community [43]. In an open model initiative, both team organisation and processes should, therefore, be flexible enough to be adapted to changing needs should they arise.

Motivation and incentives. A key success factor pertains to establishing convincing incentives for participation in order to attract participants and to reach a critical mass of contributors. The question of motivation has been extensively researched in the area of open source software development [21, 12, 14, 15] showing that several different possible motivational factors both intrinsic and extrinsic are relevant. For an open community to work effectively, it is necessary to establish convincing incentives for all participants.

A key incentive to support open source projects originates from the joy of programming and the rewarding experience of creating an artefact that works and is recognized by peers. Conceptual models will usually not be executable, but peer-recognition as reputation mechanism still applies. In fact, most motivational factors are likely to carry over to open models, with the exception of those directly related to coding. On the other hand, people might also gain intrinsic motivation from modelling, though a common perception is that programmers do not like this activity. It remains to be seen whether and how developers perceive the value of open models and the participation in open modelling processes. Nevertheless, the development of models can be very appealing: It is a challenging task, hence, offering reputation for those who submit sustainable contributions. Also, as a blueprint for multiple systems, an open model is rewarding its designers with the practical relevance of their work. However, it is not sufficient to rely on these incentives only. There is need for additional incentives for all groups involved in the development of a reference model.

A researcher's contributions to a reference model could be acknowledged as a substantial academic achievement—similar to a publication. In order to evaluate such a contribution adequately, some sort of a review process would then be required, for example an adapted version of the democratic votes as used in the Apache project [7]. Incentives for practitioners seem hard to establish at first. However, the demand for system architectures and other forms of blueprints from practitioners points to their recognition of the value of reference models. It would also be possible for participants to pursue related business models, for example by providing related services like consulting or implementations.

There are also several explanations for the viability and stability of open source software development, including a reputation-based gift culture [30, 44], a craftsman-model with programming as an immanent good [30, 36] or economic models [22] like the cooking-pot market [11], as an inverse tragedy of the commons [30] or as user innovation networks [40]. Again, all of these might be used to argue the stability of an open model initiative.

Parallelisation of work. Maybe the most important characteristic of open source software development is the strong parallelisation of work, especially software testing, using a large number of participants (*"Given a large enough beta-tester and co-developer base, almost every problem will be characterized quickly and the fix obvious to someone."* [30]). In order to reduce duplicate work, to ensure motivation and to keep the participants' interest, fast release cycles (*"Release eary, release often"* [30]) are necessary. For an open model initiative, this point is also of relevance. As modelling involves creativity and a higher level of abstraction than programming, innovative contributions are even more required. The main question is whether the parallelisation of work is possible. To ensure this, the following preconditions need to be met: (i) appropriate tools for this cooperation, i.e. a model versioning system as described below, (ii) a modelling language supporting appropriate modularity as described below, and (iii) a modelling task extensive enough to bring several people to bear, which is why especially reference modelling is put to the center of this proposal.

Modularity. Achieving a modular design is seen as an important precondition to be able to parallelise large amounts of work on an artefact [26, 28, 8, 1]. Otherwise, costs for coordination and communication would grow exponentially and would negate benefits from higher headcount. Also in open modelling, this precondition is likely to exist. Therefore an appropriate modelling language is necessary that allows for modularity, especially on several levels of abstraction.

Collaboration tools. As most participants in open source software development teams are distributed around the globe without personal contact, communication and collaboration are achieved by appropriate tools, especially mailing lists, source code versioning systems, bug reporting and management and others. This also constitutes a precondition for the parallelisation of work. For an open model approach, comparable tools are needed. While for most communication needs the same tools like mailing lists can be employed, a substitute for source code versioning systems like CVS [8] or SVN might be needed. Although many models can be reduced to a text-based representation, for example using appropriate XML-schemas, models are by nature more visually oriented. Therefore a versioning system which explicitly supports visual inspection of models and especially changes to models would be important. We are not currently aware of a free product that fulfills these criteria, but such a tool should be implemented, probably in the context of a first such project.

3.2 Procedure for implementing an open model project

From having identified the cornerstones of an open model process as described above, several necessary decisions and steps can be derived for the implementation of such an initiative.

1. Choosing an appropriate licence: An appropriate licence should allow for several effects to take place. On the one hand, it should be as free and open as possible to ensure the highest possible number of participants [34], while avoiding ideological debates. On the other hand, using the model as a base for commercial implementations should not be impossible. Therefore, the licence would certainly need to conform to the Open Source Definition [29], while GPL-compatibility, i.e. being copyleft [33], might be problematic. Whether an existing licence from the field of documentation, e.g. creative commons, fulfills these prerequisites and could be adopted, or whether a new licence needs to be defined is still to be determined.

2. Choosing a suitable reference model domain: The domain of the reference model to be developed should also be chosen so as to attract a large number of participants, for whom the domain's problems are *"scratching an itch"* [30]. Also the scope should be large enough to allow for a sufficient number of people to work on the model.

3. Choosing appropriate abstractions: Models of business processes have shown to be a suitable abstraction for understanding a domain. They can be associated with further abstractions such as information models, e.g. object models or resource models. Therefore, it seems reasonable to focus on business process models as a common reference for all participants and as an instrument to integrate additional abstractions.

4. Choosing corresponding modelling languages and tools: Developing business process models, object models and other abstractions requires the selection of appropriate modelling languages. These decisions have to take into account the availability of corresponding tools, which are almost mandatory in order to cope with model complexity, to allow for automated syntax and integrity checks as well as for automated transformation into other representations such as implementation-level languages. The modelling languages themselves should support modularity and extensibility, e.g. to define business processes on several levels, which have been shown to be critical success factors in open source development [28]. Also, far spread knowledge in the chosen languages would increase the number of possible participants. In addition, storage and management of explanations, discussions and reasonings for the documented models and any change to them must be provided.

5. Design the appropriate processes: The necessary processes especially regarding decision making, i.e. new releases, conflict resolution [37] and the release management [17] should be designed. This also includes accounting for the participants' motivations by setting up appropriate incentive schemes.

6. Preparing the necessary infrastructure: As detailled above, the necessary infrastructure for coordination and communication needs to be set up. This includes standard tools like mailing lists or bug tracking, but especially versioning might need further enhancements to existing systems. A survey of reference models and reference modelling on the internet [39] has shown that the internet is hardly ever used to provide reference models. This reluctance is a problem, and will have to be overcome.

7. Delivering a plausible promise in form of a first prototype: To start the community building process, an initial set of open models needs to be released to the interested public. This prototype should give a plausible promise that an interesting initiative is starting, and that joining it would be wortwhile.

8. Continuously evaluating processes, products and community: During the lifetime of the initiative, all aspects will need to be monitored. This includes the processes and the community, where appropriate methods for analysing open source software projects e.g. regarding concentration measures or evolution could be adopted [13].

4 Discussion

From an academic point of view, reference models are appealing, because their claim for general validity makes them resemble scientific theories. Taken the complexity of some domains, reference models could serve as a medium to coordinate research in large teams. Thus, they could serve as object and objectivation of research in IS.

The evaluation of conceptual models is a challenging task - both with respect to quality assurance and from an epistemological perspective [9]. Due to their claim for excellence, this is even more the case for reference models. The concept of truth is only of limited use for evaluating them, since they are usually aimed at intended systems or future worlds. Hence, a discoursive evaluation is the only remaining option. This requires not only the participation of researchers, domain experts, prospective users, but also an open culture of critique and construction. An open model community could provide for that and hence contribute to a multi-perspective evaluation of reference models that is difficult to achieve as long as reference models are subject of single research projects only. Therefore, any model should be accompanied with reasonings about the model, changes to the model and discussions about these.

Reference models could also serve as a subject for teaching, e.g. in IS or Computer Science. Students could study and enhance reference models in order to get a differentiated, but still abstract imagination of application domains, of which a reference model provides the relevant concepts. Therefore, it could serve as a foundation for the development of application level standards ("business language") or enterprise level ontologies [3, 18]. A reference model represents the body of knowledge of the participating disciplines. It also includes best practices and therefore can be regarded as a blueprint for knowledge management as well.

Finally, open source software development itself might benefit from the establishment of open models. The absence of modelling activities has been a center of critique on open source software development, e.g. [38, 24, 42], and has been held responsible, among others, for insufficient documentation, lost possibilities for reuse or missing information for effort estimations. Therefore, open source software projects are prime candidates for experiencing positive effects of open model projects, and vice versa, as any open model project would benefit from one or more open implementations being pursued.

The main challenge for an open model initiative is to reach a critical mass of participants to start a sustainable open process. This will hinge mostly, besides the necessary infrastructure being in place to reduce transaction costs, on the motivation of potential participants. In this paper, we have discussed possible incentives for several groups, but if these fail in practice, the project might not get off the ground. While not the only factor, the question whether people can be found in large enough quantities for which modelling poses an interesting, challenging and therefore in itself rewarding activity remains to be seen.

5 Summary and future work

In this paper, we have proposed to adopt the principles of open source software development for the collaboration of geographically dispersed project participants and their joint efforts to another context: conceptual modelling. The goal of the proposed "open model" approach is to develop reference models for everyone to copy, use, refine and later implement with the collaboration of a large number of participants in a public process.

To this end, the cornerstones of open source development need to be adopted, and in some cases adapted. This led to a list of decisions and steps to be considered for implementing such an initiative. The important next step would be to verify the viability of the open model process in the light of a real-world example, i.e. preparing the set-up of such a project. Following [27], it seems prudent to create a technological infrastructure which facilitates exchange of ideas and models among interested parties, i.e. to make discussions and models available to the open source community and the public at large. Especially for the first project, initial funding for preparing the infrastructure, especially an open "model versioning system", and also for developing a prototype is required. Also, it is necessary to educate relevant groups of prospective participants. We intend to pursue the proposed approach and found an open model initiative. After all, we are convinced that such an initiative would yield substantial benefits, both in itself, and as an academic field study.

References

1. Terry Bollinger, Russel Nelson, Karsten M. Self, and Stephen J. Turnbull. Open-source methods: Peering through the clutter. *IEEE Software*, 16(4):8–11, July/August 1999.
2. Nikunj P. Dalal, Manjunath Kamath, William J. Kolarik, and Eswar Sivaraman. Toward an integrated framework for modeling enterprise processes. *Communications of the ACM*, 47(3):83–87, 2004.
3. Jos de Bruijn, Dieter Fensel, Uwe Keller, and Rubn Lara. Using the web service modeling ontology to enable semantic e-business. *Communications of the ACM*, 48(12):43–47, 2005.
4. Dursun Delen, Nikunj P. Dalal, and Perakath C. Benjamin. Integrated modeling: the key to holistic understanding of the enterprise. *Communications of the ACM*, 48(4):107–112, 2005.
5. Joseph Feller and Brian Fitzgerald. *Understanding Open Source Software Development*. Addison-Wesley, London, 2002.
6. Peter Fettke and Peter Loos. Systematische Erhebung von Referenzmodellen - Ergebnisse einer Voruntersuchung. Working Papers of the Research Group Information Systems & Management 19, University of Mainz, Mainz, Germany, 2004.
7. Roy T. Fielding. Shared leadership in the Apache project. *Communications of the ACM*, 42(4):42–43, April 1999.
8. Karl Fogel. *Open Source Development with CVS*. CoriolisOpen Press, 1999.

9. Ulrich Frank. Conceptual Modelling as the Core of the Information Systems Discipline — Perspectives and Epistemological Challenges. In *Proceedings of the Fifth America's Conference on Information Systems (AMCIS 99)*, pages 695–697, Milwaukee, 1999. Association for Information Systems (AIS).

10. Ulrich Frank. Multi-Perspective Enterprise Models as a Conceptual Foundation for Knowledge Management. In *Proceedings of the Thirty-Third Annual Hawaii International Conference on System Sciences*. IEEE CS Press, 2000.

11. Rishab Aiyer Ghosh. Cooking pot markets: an economic model for the trade in free goods and services on the Internet. *First Monday*, 3(3), March 1998.

12. Rishab Aiyer Ghosh. Understanding free software developers: Findings from the floss study. In Joseph Feller, Brian Fitzgerald, Scott A. Hissam, and Karim R. Lakhani, editors, *Perspectives on Free and Open Source Software*, pages 23–46. MIT Press, 2005.

13. Michael Hahsler and Stefan Koch. Discussion of a large-scale open source data collection methodology. In *Proceedings of the Hawaii International Conference on System Sciences (HICSS-38)*, Big Island, Hawaii, 2005.

14. Alexander Hars and Shaosong Ou. Working for Free? Motivations for Participating in Open-Source Projects. *International Journal of Electronic Commerce*, 6(3):25–39, 2002.

15. Guido Hertel, Sven Niedner, and Stefanie Hermann. Motivation of software developers in open source projects: An internet-based survey of contributors to the Linux kernel. *Research Policy*, 32(7):1159–1177, 2003.

16. Kei Ishii and Bernd Lutterbeck. Unexploited resources of online education for democracy - why the future should belong to OpenCourseWare. *First Monday*, 6(11), November 2001.

17. Niels Jorgensen. Putting it all in the trunk: Incremental software engineering in the FreeBSD project. *Information Systems Journal*, 11(4):321–336, 2001.

18. Ejub Kajan and Leonid Stoimenov. Toward an ontology driven architectural framework for b2b.' *Communications of the ACM*, 48(12):60–66, 2005.

19. Stefan Koch. Profiling an open source project ecology and its programmers. *Electronic Markets*, 14(2):77–88, 2004.

20. Sari Kujala. User involvement: a review of the benefits and challenges. *Behaviour & Information Technology*, 22(1):1–16, January–February 2003.

21. Karim R. Lakhani and Robert G. Wolf. Why hackers do what they do: Understanding motivation and effort in free/open source software projects. In Joseph Feller, Brian Fitzgerald, Scott A. Hissam, and Karim R. Lakhani, editors, *Perspectives on Free and Open Source Software*, pages 3–22. MIT Press, 2005.

22. Josh Lerner and Jean Tirole. Economic perspectives on open source. In Joseph Feller, Brian Fitzgerald, Scott A. Hissam, and Karim R. Lakhani, editors, *Perspectives on Free and Open Source Software*, pages 47–78. MIT Press, 2005.

23. Lawrence Lessig. *The Future of Ideas: The Fate of the Commons in a Connected World*. Random House, New York, 2001.

24. Steve McConnell. Open-source methodology: Ready for prime time? *IEEE Software*, 16(4):6–8, July/August 1999.

25. Audris Mockus, Roy T. Fielding, and James D. Herbsleb. Two case studies of Open Source software development: Apache and Mozilla. *ACM Transactions on Software Engineering and Methodology*, 11(3):309–346, 2002.

26. Alessandro Narduzzo and Alessandro Rossi. The role of modularity in free/open source software development. In Stefan Koch, editor, *Free/Open Source Software Development*, pages 84–102. Idea Group Publishing, 2004.

27. David M. Nichols and Michael B. Twidale. The Usability of Open Source software. *First Monday*, 8(1), January 2003.
28. Tim O'Reilly. Lessons from open-source software development. *Communications of the ACM*, 42(4):32–73, April 1999.
29. Bruce Perens. The open source definition. In Chris DiBona, Sam Ockman, and Mark Stone, editors, *Open Sources: Voices from the Open Source Revolution*. O'Reilly and Associates, 1999.
30. Eric S. Raymond. *The Cathedral and the Bazaar: Musings on Linux and Open Source by an Accidental Revolutionary*. O'Reilly and Associates, 1999.
31. August-Wilhelm Scheer. *Business Process Engineering: Reference Models for Industrial Enterprises*. Springer-Verlag, Berlin, Germany, 2nd edition, 1994.
32. Clay Shirky. Open source outside the domain of software. In Joseph Feller, Brian Fitzgerald, Scott A. Hissam, and Karim R. Lakhani, editors, *Perspectives on Free and Open Source Software*, pages 483–488. MIT Press, 2005.
33. Richard M. Stallman. *Free Software, Free Society: Selected Essays of Richard M. Stallman*. GNU Press, Boston, Massachusetts, 2002.
34. Katherine J. Stewart, Tony Ammeter, and Likoebe Maruping. A preliminary analysis of the influences of licensing and organizational sponsorship on success in open source projects. In *Proceedings of the Hawaii International Conference on System Sciences (HICSS-38)*, Big Island, Hawaii, 2005.
35. Katherine J. Stewart and Sanjay Gosain. The Impact of Ideology on Effectiveness in Open Source Software Development Teams. Working paper, Department of Decision and Information Technologies, University of Maryland, 2005. Forthcoming in MIS Quarterly. http://www.smith.umd.edu/faculty/kstewart/ResearchInfo/KJSResearch.htm.
36. Linus Torvalds. FM interview with Linus Torvalds: What motivates free software developers? *First Monday*, 3(3), March 1998.
37. Ruben van Wendel de Joode. Managing conflicts in open source communities. *Electronic Markets*, 14(2):104–113, 2004.
38. Paul Vixie. Software engineering. In Chris DiBona, Sam Ockman, and Mark Stone, editors, *Open Sources: Voices from the Open Source Revolution*. O'Reilly and Associates, 1999.
39. Jan vom Brocke. Internetbasierte Referenzmodellierung – State-of-the-Art und Entwicklungsperspektiven. *Wirtschaftsinformatik*, 46(5):390–404, 2004.
40. Eric von Hippel. Open source software projects as user innovation networks. In Joseph Feller, Brian Fitzgerald, Scott A. Hissam, and Karim R. Lakhani, editors, *Perspectives on Free and Open Source Software*, pages 267–278. MIT Press, 2005.
41. Ron Weber. *Ontological Foundations of Information Systems*. Coopers & Lybrand, Melbourne, 1997.
42. Greg Wilson. Is the open-source community setting a bad example? *IEEE Software*, 16(1):23–25, January/February 1999.
43. Yunwen Ye, Kumiyo Nakakoji, Yasuhiro Yamamoto, and Kouichi Kishida. The co-evolution of systems and communities in free and open source software development. In Stefan Koch, editor, *Free/Open Source Software Development*, pages 59–82. Idea Group Publishing, 2004.
44. David Zeitlyn. Gift economies in the development of open source software: anthropological reflections. *Research Policy*, 32(7):1287–1291, 2003.
45. Luyin Zhao and Sebastian Elbaum. Quality assurance under the open source development model. *The Journal of Systems and Software*, 66:65–75, 2003.

Evolution of Open Source Communities

Michael Weiss, Gabriella Moroiu, and Ping Zhao

Carleton University, School of Computer Science, 1125 Colonel By Dr, Ottawa, Ontario K1S 5B6, Canada weiss@scs.carleton.ca

Abstract. The goal of this paper is to document the evolution of a portfolio of related open source communities over time. As a case study, we explore the subprojects of the Apache project, one of the largest and most visible open source projects. We extract the community structure from the mailing list data, and study how the subcommunities evolve, and are interrelated over time. Our analysis leads us to propose the following hypotheses about the growth of open source communities: (1) communities add new developers by a process of preferential attachment; (2) links between existing communities are also subject to preferential attachment; (3) developers will migrate between communities together with other collaborators; and (4) information flow follows project dependencies. In particular, we are concerned with the underlying factors that motivate the migration between communities, such as information flow, co-worker ties, and project dependencies.

1 Introduction

There is much anecdotal evidence that open source communities grow according to a preferential attachment mechanism [13]. However, there is not much empirical analysis to demonstrate this phenomenon. Most work on open source communities centers on either static aspects of a community (such as its topology at a given time) [9, 14, 15], or describes the evolution of the community in a qualitative manner [16, 8, 4]. The interaction between communities over time (eg the migration of developers) has also not received sufficient attention.

Our goal in this paper is to document the evolution of a portfolio of related open source communities over time. As a case study, we explore the subprojects of the Apache project, both for reasons that this is a highly visible group of open source communities, but also because a wealth of data is being collected on the Apache project site that allows deep insight into the dynamic project structure. In particular, we rely on mining the project mailing lists. Another reason that made this choice conducive was the availability of the Agora [10] tool for extracting information from the Apache project mailing lists.

The paper is structured as follows. Section 2 describes the methodology followed to extract the community structure and various indicators (such as developer rank) from the mailing list data. In Section 3, we show how the various subcommunities of the Apache project evolve, and are interrelated over

Please use the following format when citing this chapter:

Weiss, M., Moroiu, G., and Zhao, P., 2006, in IFIP International Federation for Information Processing, Volume 203, Open Source Systems, eds. Damiani, E., Fitzgerald, B., Scacchi, W., Scotto, M., Succi, G., (Boston: Springer), pp. 21-32

time. We state our findings in the form of four hypotheses, and provide evidence in their support. Finally, Section 4 presents our concluding remarks.

2 Community Structure

Our goal is to track the evolution of open source communities with time. Communities form around open source projects. They are groups of developers who share a common interest in the project, and who regularly interact with one another to share knowledge, and collaborate in the solution of common problems [16]. Communities are at the core of what is described in [3] as Collaborative Innovation Networks (COINs), highly functional teams characterized by the principles of meritocracy, consistency, and internal transparency. As shown in [16], an open source community co-evolves with its associated project. A project without a community that sustains it is unlikely to survive long-term.

Members of an open source community play different roles, ranging from project leaders (maintainers) and core members (contributors) to active and passive users [13, 14, 16]. Project leaders are often the initiators of the project. They oversee the direction of the project, and make the major development decisions. Core members are members who have made significant contributions to a project over time. Active users comprise occasional developers and users who report bugs, but do not fix them. Passive users are all remaining users who just use the system. Core members can further be subdivided into creators (leaders) communicators (managers), and collaborators [3].

Large open source projects such as GNU, Linux, or Apache comprise many subprojects, not of all of which are strongly connected to one another. They are not associated with a single, homogenous community, but rather an ecology [5] of (sub-)communities is formed around these subprojects. However, they share a common governance, (the Apache Foundation, in the case of the Apache project), and often produce artefacts shared among all projects (such as the Jakarta Commons in the Apache project). The idea of an ecology should convey mutual dependencies between many of the projects and cross-project collaboration, but also competition for resources among projects.

Figure 1 shows the current portfolio of projects in the Apache project and their relationships. It depicts the communication patterns between projects, as determined from the project mailing lists. This diagram was generated by an extension of the Agora [10] tool, which reuses its data extraction and core visualization routines, but adds project and module dependency views (based on JDepend [6]), and significant capabilities for pruning by strength of the communication links and filtering by date, as well as statistical analysis.

The structure of a community can be inferred from the interactions between developers on the mailing list of the associate project. We analyze the communication patterns between developers, and order developers by the strength of their communication links. For each developer we tally the number of inbound

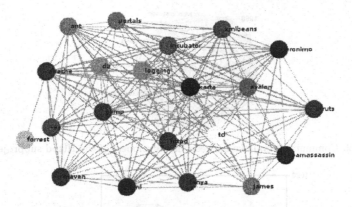

Fig. 1. Portfolio of projects in the Apache project and their relationships

and outbound messages.[1] The project leader is considered the developer with the highest number of inbound messages, as this indicates how frequently this developer is consulted by others. It is, therefore, also a measure of the developer's reputation. The same metric is used in [3] to identify creators, the members who provide the overall vision and guidance for a project.

For the purposes of our analysis, we limit our attention to the group of core developers. According to a previous study of the Apache project [11], most of the contributions are made by the top 15 developers in a project. These are considered the core developers. As noted in [3], a typical core group starts out with 3 to 7 members, and grows to 10 to 15 members, once the community is established. Using the pruning feature of our extended Agora tool, we retrieved the core developers for every subproject of the Apache project. The structure of a community obtained can be visualized as a network of developers.

Fig. 2 shows the community structure of the Httpd subproject based on the messages exchanged over the 01/1999 to 12/1999 time frame.[2] It can be observed that the core group is a nearly fully connected network in which every member communicates directly with every other member. Our database consists of 24 projects and 253 unique core developers. Fig. 3 plots the cumulative number of projects P and developers N for the period of 1997–2004.

---

[1] The algorithm for extracting topological data from the message set in the Agora tool is is based on the concept of "reply": when a person sends a message in reply to another message, a link is created in the graph. To eliminate noise messages that are not replied to are excluded from the extracted data [10].

[2] The color intensity of the links indicates the strength of a communication link.

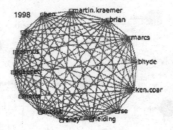

Fig. 2. Communication links between the developers of the Httpd subproject

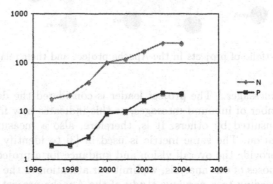

Fig. 3. Cumulative number of projects and developers in the Apache project

3 Tracing Community Evolution

To trace the evolution of a community we took snapshots of its membership at regular intervals. Here, we chose a one year period, but we plan to study the evolution of the Apache communities over smaller time periods in the future. For each period we retrieve the list of core developers ordered by their number of inbound messages, as noted above. The extracted information is captured in a spreadsheet similar to Figure 4 with the nicknames of the core developers for each community and time period. Notably, the top row indicates the project leaders, as inferred from the data. A Perl script translates the spreadsheet data for further processing into a set of Prolog facts. This provide a knowledge base that we can analyze in a flexible manner using the Prolog reasoning engine.

3.1 Growth by Preferential Attachment

Based on this data, we established several hypotheses about the growth of open source communities. Our initial hypothesis that open source communities grow by a process of preferential attachment [9], or selection through professional attention [13] was adopted from the literature. It can be stated as follows:

1997	1998	1999	2000	2001	2002	2003	2004
				donaldp	bloritsch	bloritsch	mcconnell
				bloritsch	peter	mcconnell	niclas
				paul_hamman	paul_hamman	leosimons	bloritsch
				mail	leo.sutic	niclas	leo.sutic
				peter	nicolaken	aok123	dev
				leo.sutic	leosimons	noel	jira
				mcconnell	mcconnell	leo.sutic	cziegeler
				mirceatoma	proyal	alag	aok123
				colus	leif	steve	farra
				charles	craferm	farra	leosimons
				jeff	jeff	nicolaken	noel
				giacomo	noel	cziegeler	develop
				ulim	stefano	holiveira	lsimons
				leif	paulo.gaspar	leosimons	jhawkes
				proyal	cziegeler	paul_hamman	exterminatorx

Fig. 4. Sample of the extracted data (core members of the Avalon subproject)

Hypothesis 1 *The more developers a community has already, the more new developers it will attract (also known as "rich gets richer" phenomenon).*

In support of this hypothesis, we first determine the degree distribution $P(k)$. As shown in Fig. 5, the distribution follows a power law. This indicates that the communication network of the Apache community is scale-free. Such networks contain relatively few highly connected nodes, while the majority of nodes are only connected to few other nodes. This leads to a typical core-periphery structure, as observed for many open source communities.

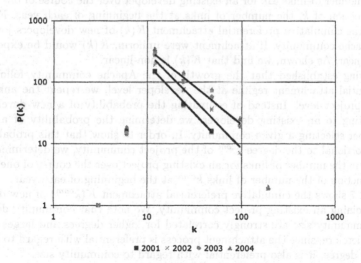

■ 2001 × 2002 ♦ 2003 ▲ 2004

Fig. 5. Developer degree distribution shown with logarithmic binning

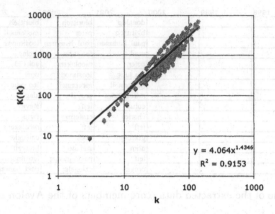

Fig. 6. Cumulative preferential attachment $K(k)$ of new developers

One common mechanism to explain the growth of a scale-free network is preferential attachment [1], as captured by the hypothesis. Preferential attachment implies that, as the network evolves, nodes will link to nodes that already have a large number of links. To verify that the network of the Apache community follows a preferential attachment rule, we determine the probability that a new developer is connected to an existing developer with degree k.

As described in [1], this probability can be estimated by plotting the change in the number of links Δk for an existing developer over the course of one year as a function of k, the number of links at the beginning of each year. Fig. 6 shows the cumulative preferential attachment $K(k)$ of new developers joining the Apache community. If attachment were uniform, $K(k)$ would be expected to be linear. As shown, we find that $K(k)$ is non-linear.

Having established that the growth of the Apache community follows a preferential attachment regime at the developer level, we repeat the analysis at the project level. Instead of estimating the probability of a new developer connecting to an existing developer, we determine the probability of a new developer selecting a given community. In order to show that this probability is proportional to the degree k^{com} of the project community, we determine the change in the number of links for an existing project over the course of one year as a function of the number of links k^{com} at the beginning of each year.

Fig. 7 shows the cumulative preferential attachment $K(k^{com})$ of new developers joining an existing project community. We note that community degree and community size are strongly correlated for higher degrees and larger sizes [12]. Therefore, since the attachment process is preferential with regard to community degree, it is also preferential with regard to community size.

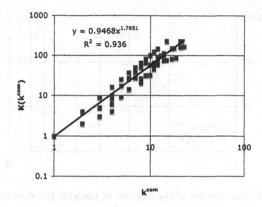

$$y = 0.9468x^{1.7651}$$
$$R^2 = 0.936$$

Fig. 7. Cumulative preferential attachment $K(k^{com})$ of new developers

3.2 Interaction and Migration between Projects

As much as the influx of external developers is a key characteristic of open source communities that distinguishes them from other types of networks, it is not the only factor that affects community evolution. As has been noted by [1, 12], the internal interaction between projects also affects the structure and dynamics of a community. Interaction comprises the flow of information, work products, and developers. We will look at each of these aspects below.

Information Flow Information is shared between projects through common developers who act as bridges between the projects. In [4], these developers are considered the "glue that maintains the whole project together, and the chains that contribute to spread information from one part of the project to another".

Hypothesis 2 *The more developers a community shares with other communities, the more developers from other communities will interact with it.*

Fig. 8 shows that the distribution of projects per developer follows a power law. That means that while most developers participate in only few projects, some are active in many projects at the same time. These well-connected developers act as network hubs and facilitate inter-project information flow.

Fig. 9 shows that the number of shared developers grows according to a preferential attachment rule. We obtain this result by plotting the cumulative change $\Delta(k_1^{com} k_2^{com})$ for each pair of projects as a function of $k_1^{com} k_2^{com}$. This estimates the probability that a project with degree k_1^{com} will establish a link with another project with degree k_2^{com}. As shown, the growth is non-linear.

Migration To determine the migration behavior we look at pairs of projects, and test, for each pair P and Q, whether a developer participates in project P is one year and in project Q during the next one, but she is not already a member

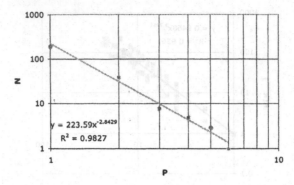

$$y = 223.59x^{-2.8429}$$
$$R^2 = 0.9827$$

Fig. 8. Distribution of the number of projects per developer

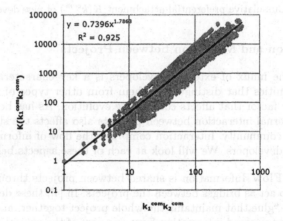

$$y = 0.7396x^{1.7863}$$
$$R^2 = 0.925$$

Fig. 9. Cumulative internal preferential attachment $K(k_1 k_2)$ between projects

of project Q in the current year.[3] Fig. 10 shows the developer migration from 2003 to 2004. Each row contains the number of developers migrating from a given project to any of the other projects during the following year. Note that "pool" is not a project, but indicates the influx of new core developers.

Many of these developers migrate to new projects, of which they form the core to which new developers attach themselves. As projects are spun off from existing projects, developers tend to migrate with community members they closely associate with. We should expect the effect to be most pronounced, if the leader of one project moves on to a new project: this would create an even stronger pull for other core developers to join the new project. Thus, we surmise that developer *reputation* also plays a critical role in migration decisions.

---

[3] This is an example of a rule that we can easily model and evaluate in Prolog. However, space does not allow us to describe the details of this modeling step.

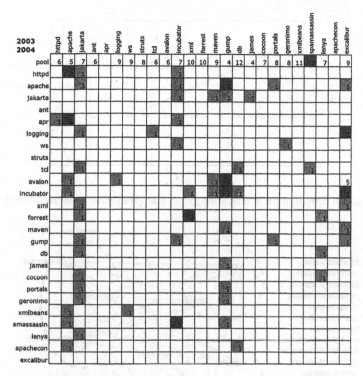

Fig. 10. Migration between projects from 2003-2004

Hypothesis 3 *Developers will migrate between communities with their collaborators, that is, other developers with which they have strong ties.*

Fig. 11 plots the distribution $P(s)$ of group size s. It can be seen to observe a power law. This supports the hypothesis. While many developers will migrate in small groups, some well-connected developers will move in large groups, which provide the support for a new project. Our data supports that most new projects include at least one large group migrated from another project.

As an example, consider the migration into the Excalibur project shown in Fig. 12. The Excalibur project receives its main contribution from the Avalon project. A drill-down into the underlying data reveals that the current leader of the Avalon project (bloritsch), as well as the future leader of the Excalibur project (leosimons) are among those developers. The leader of the Avalon project brings with him four co-workers from that project.

Project Dependencies Sharing of work products takes the form of shared modules. It can be observed in different ways, eg from the developer attributions in a code repository as in [4], or from an analysis of the import statements in the source code. Our extensions to Agora includes a module dependency view, which

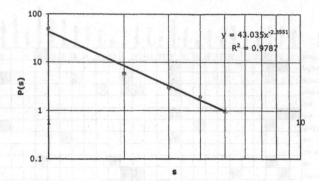

Fig. 11. Distribution of migration group size (transition from 2003-2004)

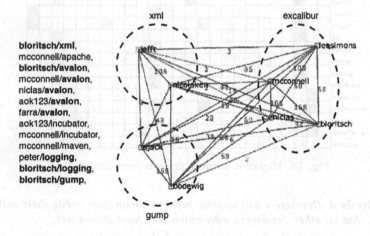

Fig. 12. Migration to the Excalibur project between 2003 and 2004

presents information extracted from the project source code using JDepend [6] as a graph. Links in the graph indicate module dependencies.

Hypothesis 4 *Information flow follows project dependencies.*

While we have not yet extracted dependency information on all subprojects in the Apache project, we have analyzed project dependencies for specific cases, as triggered by observations made during our analysis of information flow or developer migration. As an example of the kind of analysis, we can perform with Agora, Fig. 13 shows the dependencies between the Agora, Forrest, and XML projects (top), and corresponding information flow (bottom). It can be seen that there is one core developer bridging the Avalon and Forrest communities, and that the Forrest and XML projects share three core developers.

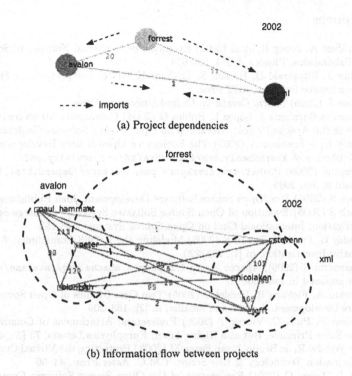

(a) Project dependencies

(b) Information flow between projects

Fig. 13. Project dependencies between the Agora, Forrest, and XML projects in 2002

4 Conclusion

In this paper, we stated a set of hypotheses about the evolution of open source communities. As a first step of the empirical validation of these hypotheses, we presented our initial results exploring the communities formed around the various subprojects of the Apache project. To this end we extended a tool (Agora) developed by a member of the Apache project with project and module dependency views, and pruning and date filtering capabilities, as well as statistics.

We then extracted information about the core developers of each community over an eight year time period (1997–2004). This data allowed us to explore the hypotheses in some detail through various cases, where we documented the migration behavior of developers between selected project communities. We also built an exploratory tool in Prolog for rapidly modeling and testing new hypotheses about the extracted data. We were able to identify different factors that underlie the preferential attachment mechanism of community evolution, including information flow, co-worker ties, and project dependencies.

References

1. Barabasi A, Jeong H, et al (2002) Evolution of the Social Network of Scientific Collaborations, Physica A 311, 590-614
2. Feller J, Fitzgerald B, Hissam S, Lakhani K (2002) Perspectives on Free and Open Source Software, MIT Press
3. Gloor P (2006) Swarm Creatitity, Oxford University Press
4. Gonzalez-Barahona J, Lopez L, Robles G (2004) Community Structure of Modules in the Apache Project, Workshop on Open Source Software Engineering
5. Healy K, Schussman A (2003) The Ecology of Open Source Development, Unpublished, www.kieranhealy.org/files/drafts/oss-activity.pdf
6. JDepend (2006) Project, www.clarkware.com/software/JDepend.html, last accessed in Jan 2006
7. Koch S (2005) Free/Open Source Software Development, Idea Publishing
8. Koch S (2005) Evolution of Open Source Software Systems – A Large-Scale Investigation, International Conf on Open Source Systems, 148-153
9. Madey G, Freeh V, Tynan R (2005) Modeling the F/OSS Community: A Quantitative Investigation, in [7], 203–220
10. Mazzocchi S (2006), Apache Agora 1.2, people.apache.org/~stefano/agora/, last accessed in Jan 2006
11. Mockus A, Fielding R, Hersleb J (2005) Two Case Studies of Open Source Software Development: Apache and Mozilla, in [2], 163–209
12. Pollner P, Palla G, Viczek T (2006) Preferential Attachment of Communities: The Same Principle, But at a Higher Level, Europhysics Letters, 73 (3), 478–484
13. van Wendel R, de Bruijn J, van Eeten M (2003) Protecting the Virtual Commons, Information Technology & Law Series, T.M.C. Asser Press, 44-50
14. Xu J, Madey G (2004) Exploration of the Open Source Software Community, NAACOSOS Conf, no page numbers
15. Xu J, Gao Y, et al (2005) A Topological Analysis of the Open Source Software Development Community, Hawaii International Conf on System Sciences, 1–10
16. Ye Y, Nakakoji K, et al, The Co-Evolution of Systems and Communities in Free and Open Source Software Development, in [7], 59–82

Part II

Tools and Infrastructures for OSS development

Retrieving Open Source Software Licenses

Timo Tuunanen[1], Jussi Koskinen[2], and Tommi Kärkkäinen[3]

1,3 Department of Mathematical Information Technology, University of
Jyväskylä, P.O. Box 35, 40014 Jyväskylä, Finland,
timtuun@jyu.fi, tka@mit.jyu.fi
2 Department of Computer Science and Information Systems, University of
Jyväskylä, P.O. Box 35, 40014 Jyväskylä, Finland, koskinen@cs.jyu.fi

Abstract. Open Source Software maintenance and reuse require identifying and
comprehending the applied software licenses. This paper first characterizes
software maintenance, and open source software (OSS) reuse which are
particularly relevant in this context. The information needs of maintainers and
reusers can be supported by reverse engineering tools at different information
retrieval levels. The paper presents an automated license retrieval approach
called ASLA. User needs, system architecture, tool features, and tool evaluation
are presented. The implemented tool features support identifying source file
dependencies and licenses in source files, and adding new license templates for
identifying licenses. The tool is evaluated against another tool for license
information extraction. ASLA requires the source code as available input but is
otherwise not limited to OSS. It supports the same programming languages as
GCC. License identification coverage is good and the tool is extendable.

1 Introduction

The relative amount of the costs of *software maintenance and evolution* activities has
traditionally been 50-75% of the software life-cycle, in case of successful systems
with long lifetime [12]. Moreover, according to some studies [21] the relative amount
is increasing, so the importance of this subarea can hardly be over-emphasized.
According to *Lehman's first law* [11] software must be continually adapted or it will
become progressively less satisfactory in "real-world" environments. Many *software
systems* have been very large investments, and they contain invaluable business logic
and knowledge. Therefore, there is a need to reuse their components.

Component-based software reuse is one way to reduce the problems of software
system maintenance. Adaptation of the components, however, can be relatively
demanding. For example, the applied *software licenses* need to be taken into account
when designing support for reuse. *Reverse engineering* is the main automated general
approach for retrieving relevant information for supporting maintenance, reuse and
comprehension of large-scale programs. Most of the reverse engineering tools provide
abstracted views of system components and their interrelations. This supports the tool
user to make right choices and decisions concerning potentially reusable components.

The paper is organized as follows. Section 2 shortly describes the general central
problems of software maintenance and nature of reverse engineering approaches.
Section 3 describes specific characteristics and problems of OSS maintenance and
reuse. Section 4 describes an automated reverse engineering approach and its

Please use the following format when citing this chapter:

Tuunanen, T., Koskinen, J., and Kärkkäinen, T., 2006, in IFIP International Federation
for Information Processing, Volume 203, Open Source Systems, eds. Damiani, E.,
Fitzgerald, B., Scacchi, W., Scotto, M., Succi, G., (Boston: Springer), pp. 35-46

implementation, called *ASLA* (Automated Software License Analyzer), for retrieving relevant license information from source code modules. Short description of the approach has been accepted to the software maintenance community's conference: CSMR 2006 [22]. This paper considerably extends that earlier paper, especially by addressing the issue of license retrieval from OSS perspective, and by providing a more detailed description of ASLA. The tool users are mainly component engineers, software reusers, and software maintainers. The approach and its implementation are not restricted to OSS. However, OSS is a natural setting for developing and testing the approach. OSS is a good source of reusable components, and provides many licenses and their versions. Tool user needs, system architecture, tool features, and tool evaluation are presented. Finally, Section 5 draws the conclusions.

2   Reverse Engineering

Maintaining and reusing large-scale software systems is demanding especially if documentation is inadequate or misleading. While solving maintenance problems, maintainers have information needs [10]. One of the main problems is the identification and comprehension of relevant pieces of programs, and their dependencies. Reverse engineering tools extract that information from the source code and store it into a program database. The extraction is usually achieved by calling a parser component, implemented according to the well-established conventions of compiler construction [1].

Five-level classification of the information retrieval features of reverse engineering tools is provided in [10]. That classification will be later applied in the evaluation part of this paper (Section 4.4). The levels of the model are:

L1.   Formation of basic internal data structures (such as abstract syntax trees).
L2.   Formation of higher abstraction level access structures (such as call graphs).
L3.   Visualization of access structures.
L4.   Information request and retrieval mechanisms.
L5.   Navigation mechanisms.

Typical features of the main reverse engineering tools are compared in [10]. There are also some other relevant related studies based on structural program analysis and text and documentation analysis, as listed in [9, Appendix 1, Categories 1-3].

3   Characteristics of Open Source Software

Definitions for OSS-related terminology are provided in [19]. OSS community provides a rich base of potentially reusable software. Unlike the more traditional closed source software (CSS), OSS can be freely accessible, used, modified, and redistributed. OSS development has been studied based on a sample of 406 projects [5]. Most used languages were C, C++, Perl, and Java. Despite the large number of

OSS projects, development effort has focused on a few large projects, such as *Linux*, *Mozilla*, and *Apache* [14].

One important aspect in OSS development is the need for greater maintainability. Based on the analysis of almost 6 million LOCs it was concluded [20] that OSS development will produce legacy systems in much the same way as CSS development. It is stated that 20% of the components will produce about 80% of the maintainability problems. Therefore, the problem-prone modules need to be identified. An empirical study of key success factors in software reuse in general based on 24 projects has been conducted [15]. Reusing OSS neither differs much from reusing other kind of software. Therefore, results received from supporting OSS-development should be quite generalizable to CSS also.

One important problem for partial reuse is that there are over 50 different versions of OSS licenses as listed by Open Source Initiative [19]. GPL is the most common license [5]. License information concerning the dependency of different modules provides the key metainformation for partial reuse. Component-based white-box reuse of OSS is natural, e.g., since license information is typically bound to modules. It is clear that good tool support reduces the reuse and comprehension problems. Reuse can be supported by identifying reusable component candidates, simplifying the license identification, and providing abstracted views of the relevant components and their interrelations.

4   The License Retrieval Approach

There is a clear need for software reuse oriented license analysis. It can be made more effective by automated license identification of source code files by using text searching techniques and by providing information about file dependencies. In this section we present *ASLA*, which is our license retrieval approach for this purpose.

4.1   User Needs

OSS reuse can be classified into two different approaches: Using the whole software package as-is and modifying it and using part of the software packages as part of another program. Both cases introduce three main user needs as presented below.

4.1.1 Identifying Dependencies

There is a huge amount of code for different platforms and not all source code is used in certain platform in large OSS packages such as *Linux* kernel [13]. Therefore, user needs to know what source files are used in a particular environment. When build process outputs are identified the information can be used for component identification. This can give some clues about reusable components inside a larger software package and becomes useful when considering partial reuse. Licenses behave differently depending on what part of software is dependent on other parts of the software. Therefore, the user must also know what libraries are linked to the program and recognize the dependencies between all objects in order to make reliable license analysis.

4.1.2 Identifying Licenses in Each Source File

OSS is distributed under one or more licenses. Unfortunately all OSS licenses are not compatible with each other and they pose different restrictions so that each source code file must be checked separately. It is vital, at least from the commercial perspective, to check that licenses of a software package are in order to avoid any legal consequences.

4.1.3 Adding New License Templates

In most cases programmers who write OSS use the predefined templates [18] to indicate the use of certain license. Unfortunately this is not the case in all software packages. In many cases license of the source code is indicated in a way that is not known in advance. Therefore, there is an obvious need to add new search criteria for licenses as part of the license analysis.

4.2   System Architecture

Fig. 1 shows the system architecture in UML-notation. *ASLA* employs three open source programs: *GCC* [7] [8], and modified versions of *ld* (linker) and *ar* (archive builder) that are based on *GNU binutils* [4] (version 2.15.97). Any version of *GCC* compiler which supports environment variable $DEPENDENCY_OUTPUT can be used.

ASLA is implemented in *Linux* operating system using Java programming language (version 1.5.0_01). *GCC* supports compilation of many programming languages, which are supported by *ASLA* also. Only requirement is that dependency information files (DIFs) produced by *GCC* are available. *Ar* and *ld* are modified in a way that these programs write similar DIFs about dependencies of the libraries as *GCC* does for the source code files and compiled objects. DIFs form the program database. It contains the information about compiled and linked objects and their dependencies. DIFs serve as a basis for data integration between these four programs. *ASLA* reads the DIFs, analyzes licenses of files listed in them, creates a dependency map based on them and visualizes the information.

Fig. 2 presents the contents of *ASLA* user interface after analysing *gaim* [6] (version 1.2.1), which is an open source instant message client. It is used as the main example case in this paper. The left panel of the figure shows hierarchically the analyzed file structure. The modules can be selected from it and opened to the right panel for viewing their contents.

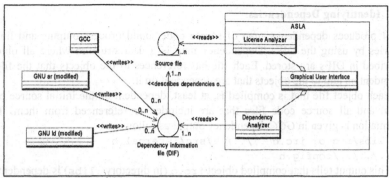

Fig. 1. ASLA's system architecture

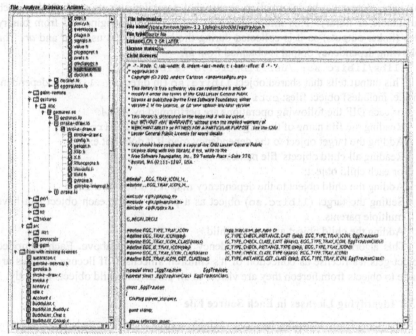

Fig. 2. ASLA after dependency and license analysis of *gaim*

4.3   Features

The implemented features of *ASLA* as described below are based on the user needs
introduced earlier.

4.3.1 Identifying Dependencies

ASLA produces dependency map of source code, build process outputs and linked libraries by using the DIFs. Dependency map is a data structure where all objects described in DIFs are stored. Each file has references to the objects that the file is dependent on and to the objects that are dependent on it.

Each object file that is compiled is, at least, dependent on the initial source code file(s) and all source code files that are included or referenced from them. This information is given in *GCC* dependency output as follows:

```
.libs/irc.o: irc.c ../../../src/internal.h
../../../config.h ...
```

This output tells that compiled object irc.o (in directory .libs) is dependent on (i.e. includes) source files: irc.c, internal.h and config.h etc.

To identify what compiler outputs (and source code files) are included in the software, there must be information about what compiler outputs are linked to each executable or library. This information can not be reverse engineered from binary files (linker outputs) so it is collected during the build process using *ld* and *ar*. The following dependency output is obtained from *ld*:

```
.libs/libirc.so: /usr/lib/crti.o .libs/irc.o
```

This output tells that shared object libirc.so (in directory .libs) is dependent on (i.e. includes) object files: crti.o and irc.o.

For each DIF the following operations are performed by *ASLA*:

- Reading the file name of the target object (for example libirc.so).
- Adding the target object to the dependency map if it does not exist.
- Reading all child objects' file names.

For each child object:

- Adding the child object to the dependency map if it does not exist.
- Setting the target (libirc.so) object as a parent object; each object can have multiple parents.
- Adding the child object as parent's child.

This algorithm produces the dependency map described above. Each compiled object gets it's license as collection of it's children's licenses. If license changes are made to objects from hereon they are visible to all parent and child objects instantly.

4.3.2 Identifying Licenses in Each Source File

ASLA automatically identifies licenses of single source code files. This is achieved by using license templates that are compiled into regular expressions (in BNF) as described below.

Most simple open source licenses, such as BSD or MIT are usually written in the beginning of the source code file. Another way to indicate the license of the source code is to reference the license from the source code. This technique is used for example in GPL and LGPL licenses [18].

In the source code file one can either find a simple notification such as: For license information: see file COPYING, or a defined template text that indicates the license of the source file. COPYING is the typical name of the license file in OSS.

Fig. 3. ASLA after adding a new license template for *gaim*

Identifying licenses of source files that contain pre-defined template or full license text is fairly simple relying on finding the predefined text from source code file. This approach, however, requires that all unnecessary source code characters (such as comment characters) are removed and different white space characters are allowed between words.

Many programmers modify the predefined texts slightly and there are also many different versions of licenses published. For example LGPL was previously called *GNU Library general public license* and nowadays it is called *GNU Lesser general public license*. Therefore, there are many slightly different texts within source code indicating the same license. Hence, their recognition requires more sophisticated text searching techniques. Especially, regular expressions can be used for allowing white space characters, alternative words and undefined characters.

For example, *ASLA*'s license search template for LGPL (version 2 and 2.1) is the following:

```
...   GNU  (Library)|(Lesser)   General   Public   License   as
published by the Free Software Foundation; either version 2.*,
...
```

This is compiled into a regular expression:

```
...\s*GNU\s*(Library)|(Lesser)\s*General\s*Public\s*License\s
*as\s*\s*published\s*by\s*the\s*Free\s*Software\s*Foundation;\s
*either\s*version\s*2.*,\s etc.
```

This is interpreted as follows: "0..n white spaces", "GNU", "0..n white spaces", "Library or Lesser", ... , "version", "0..n white spaces", "2", "0..n any character", "," ...

Unfortunately license of every single source code file can not be reliably identified and, therefore, user must have a possibility to identify licenses also manually. Such feature is supported by *ASLA*. First way to do manual identification is to apply license of the separated license file for all source files in subdirectories of the directory where the file is found. This technique is useful in a situation where license file is meant to cover all files in subdirectories but source files themselves do not include any reference to the used license.

Another way to do manual license identification is to manually check all unidentified source files. This is aided by *ASLA* that lists all source code files that were unidentified separately. To reduce the number of unidentified licenses and need for manual license identification with other software packages the tool user is able to add new license templates.

4.3.3 Adding New License Templates

ASLA offers two different ways to introduce new license identification templates. First way is to create new text file into the directory where existing license template files are saved. File format for new template contains the license name on the first line of the file and template text in regular expression form on the following lines. Another way is especially usable. User is able to select a text in a source file and use that text as a license identification template (Fig. 3). In this case *ASLA* forms the regular expression automatically.

4.4 Evaluation

In this section *ASLA* is evaluated against *LIDESC* [17], which is another license information extractor. *ASLA* and *LIDESC* have many similarities but the focus areas and applied techniques have their differences. *ASLA* is targeted especially for component engineers, and other reuse and maintenance personnel. The approach is extendable and designed to be used for analyzing existing software packages. An especially rich base of possibly reusable software is OSS packages. *ASLA* itself has also been implemented based on reusable OSS components.

As an example of used source code we consider *gaim* which includes total of 506 source files. 437 (86%) of them were used in the selected test environment (*Linux*). *ASLA* does not require any makefile modications to produce DIFs. Existing software packages can be analyzed as they are. In *LIDESC* all source files must be compiled using defined compiler flags. The user must manually modify all makefiles or define the parameters in *autoconf* [3] scripts. From user perspective this is probably not the preferred approach, especially, when analyzing large potentially reusable software packages.

4.4.1 Identifying Dependencies

DIFs contain information of dependencies, which is the basis for forming basic level data structures. This corresponds to level L1 of tool features as presented in section 2. Both *ASLA* and *LIDESC* naturally form internal data structures.

Information contained in the DIFS in *ASLA* is collected and combined in order to create higher abstraction level access structures (level L2). This is done by the *ASLA* dependency analyzer when creating the dependency map based on the DIFs. Features of this level are not convincingly reported for *LIDESC*.

The dependency map is visualized by *ASLA* in tree form (level L3). *LIDESC* does not support this level. The information visualized in *ASLA* is useful both in full and partial reuse of software packages. For partial reuse, compiled objects that have no parent objects are potential reusable components. For example, in Fig. 4 all files with extension .so (shared library objects) are such compiled objects.

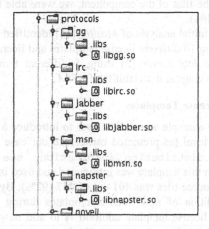

Fig. 4. ASLA's tree for showing the potentially reusable components (*gaim*)

In case of full reuse, the *ASLA* tree format introduces the dependencies of the different parts of the software and indicates how licenses of the compiler outputs are collected from the source files. Neither *ASLA* nor *LIDESC* provide real navigation capabilities (level L5), which could be useful in case of complex dependencies, although *ASLA*'s file tree can be browsed and direct access to the files is provided.

4.4.2 Identifying Licenses in Each Source File

Information requests (level L4) are supported in *ASLA* based on regular expressions. Therefore, the approach adapts well into "real world" of varying OSS packages. *LIDESC* is implemented in a similar way but is based in this regard on exact match of license identification string in the source file. Due to alternative word matching, and ability to handle undefined characters and different commenting styles, *ASLA* provides more flexibility. It handles the identification of modified and different versions of licenses without need to introduce new identification templates for each different license version.

The license identification coverage of *ASLA* against *LIDESC* can be further compared with our *gaim* example case. On our initial analysis we were able to identify license of 315 source files out of 437 (72%) using 7 different license search templates. The reason of the moderate identification ratio was that one *gaim* component did not contain any references to used licenses in source code. To reach the same result using the exact matching technique of *LIDESC* would have required at least 20 unambiguos license identification strings.

Manual license identification, which is not supported by *LIDESC*, complements the license analysis in our example case of *gaim*. By applying the license found in the file COPYING, which was explained earlier and which can be found on top directory of the component, to the files of the component, we were able to identify licenses of 350 files out of 437 (80%).

Moreover, *ASLA*'s initial analysis of *Mozilla* [16] identified licenses of 5654 files out of 5871 (96%) using 10 different license templates and licenses of 283 files out of 301 (94%) of *Apache http server* [2] using 5 different templates. These results illustrate both good coverage and scalability of *ASLA*.

4.4.3 Adding New License Templates

Final step in our *gaim* example was for the user to introduce a new license template during the license retrieval (as presented earlier). In our case it was the following: For copying and distribution information, see the file "mit-copyright.h". When this template was introduced and used in the analysis the final number of identified source files was 401 out of 437 (92%). By comparison *LIDESC* does not support addition of new license templates during the license retrieval. Another way of new license template addition is to add new file entry to license template directory. This offers more versatile but more complex way since the template must be in BNF. *LIDESC* applies a similar approach. However, in that case the license must be in a specifically formatted text file and it must be added using specific seven step process as described in *LIDESC* documentation.

5   Conclusions

This paper has presented a license retrieval approach and its implementation called *ASLA*. It is targeted at retrieving software license information from source code modules. At general level it has been motivated by the characteristics, problems and needs of OSS development, maintenance and component reuse. License retrieval and comprehension is especially important for effective component reuse. It can be concluded that *ASLA* addresses an important problem. *ASLA* has been tested and compared to *LIDESC*, which is another known license information extractor. *ASLA* provides promising results regarding the coverage of identified licenses, and supported information retrieval levels as compared to *LIDESC*. *ASLA* uses regular expressions and dependency information files (DIFs). The approach was found sufficiently effective, and can be applied to several programming languages. Incorporation of new licenses is uncomplicated by using the license templates. The applicability of the approach is neither restricted to OSS. Further research avenues include studies regarding information abstraction and visualization, e.g. architectural views, handling of the even more complex cases of license determination in case of multiple applied licenses, and system efficiency optimizations.

References

1.   Aho, A.V., Sethi, R., Ullman, J.: *Compilers - Principles, Techniques, and Tools*. Addison-Wesley (1986)
2.   APACHE HTTP Server Project. http://httpd.apache.org/ (accessed 25.9.2005)
3.   Autoconf. http://www.gnu.org/ software/autoconf/ (accessed 13.9.2005)
4.   GNU Binutils. http://www.gnu.org/ software/binutils/ (accessed 13.9.2005)
5.   Capiluppi, A., Lago, P., Morisio, M.: Characteristics of Open Source Software Projects. Proc. 7th European Conference on Software Maintenance and Reengineering (CSMR 2003) 317-330. IEEE Computer Soc.
6.   Gaim: A Multi-Protocol Instant Messaging (IM) Client. http://gaim.sourceforge.net/ (accessed 19.9.2005)
7.   GCC: GNU Compiler Collection. http://gcc.gnu.org (accessed 13.9.2005)
8.   GCC 4.0.1 Manual. http://gcc.gnu.org/onlinedocs/gcc-4.0.1/gcc/. Free Software Foundation (2005) (accessed 13.9.2005)
9.   Koskinen, J.: Automated Transient Hypertext Support for Software Maintenance. Jyväskylä Studies in Computing 4 (2000). Univ. of Jyväskylä, Jyväskylä, Finland
10. Koskinen, J., Salminen, A., Paakki, J.: Hypertext Support for Information Needs of Software Maintainers. Journal of Software Maintenance and Evolution: Res. and Pract. 16, 3 (2004) 187-215
11. Lehman, M., Perry, D., Ramil, J.: Implications of Evolution Metrics on Software Maintenance. Proceedings of the International Conference on Software Maintenance - 1998 (ICSM 1998) 208-217. IEEE Computer Soc.
12. Lientz, B., Swanson, E.: Problems in Application Software Maintenance. Communications of the ACM 24, 11 (1981) 763-769
13. The Linux Kernel Archives. http://www.kernel.org (accessed 13.9.2005)

14. Mockus, A., Fielding, R., Herbsleb, J.: Two Case Studies of Open Source Software Development: Apache and Mozilla. ACM Transactions on Software Engineering and Methodology 11, 3 (2002) 309-346
15. Morisio, M.: Success and Failure in Software Reuse. IEEE Transactions on Software Engineering 28, 4 (2002) 340-357
16. Mozilla. http://www.mozilla.org/ (accessed 19.9.2005)
17. Nordquist, P., Petersen, A., Todorova, A.: License Tracing in Free, Open, and Proprietary Software. Journal of Computing Sciences in Colleges 19, 2 (2003) 101-112
18. Opensource Org.: The Approved Licenses. http://www.opensource.org/ licenses/ (accessed 16.9.2005)
19. Perens, B.: The Open Source Definition. http://www.opensource.org/ docs/definition.php. Open Source Initiative (2005) (accessed 13.9.2005)
20. Samoladas, I., Stamelos, I., Angelis, L., Oikonomou, A.: Open Source Software Development Should Strive for Even Greater Code Maintainability. Communications of the ACM 47, 10 (2004) 83-87
21. Seacord, R., Plakosh, D., Lewis, G.: Modernizing Legacy Systems: Software Technologies, Engineering Processes, and Business Practices (2003). Addison-Wesley
22. Tuunanen, T., Koskinen, J., Kärkkäinen, T.: ASLA: Reverse Engineering Approach for Software License Information Retrieval. Accepted to CSMR 2006.

Beyond Low-Hanging Fruit: Seeking the
Next Generation in FLOSS Data Mining

Megan S. Conklin

Elon University, Department of Computing Sciences, Elon, NC 27244
mconklin@elon.edu,
WWW home page: http://www.cs.elon.edu

Abstract. This paper will discuss the motivations and methods for collecting quantitative data about free, libre and open source (FLOSS) software projects. The paper also describes the current state of the art in collecting this data, and some of the problems with this process. Finally, the paper outlines the challenges data miners should look forward to when trying to improve the usefulness of their quantitative data streams.

1 Introduction

It is surprisingly difficult to obtain and compare timely, quantitative data in order to answer even simple questions about the free/libre/open source software (FLOSS) world: How many open source projects are there? How many developers? How many users? How much does each developer contribute? Which projects are dead, which are flourishing? Which projects are popular? How are development teams structured, and which team structures are the most successful?

FLOSS project teams are self-organized, widely-distributed geographically, and use many different programming languages and software development methodologies. Teams are organized in an ad hoc, decentralized fashion. Projects can be very hard to track, and changes can be difficult to follow. Because developers primarily use the Internet for communication, and because they are organized around the idea that anyone can join a team, it is usually easy to get data about FLOSS project teams, but difficult to rely upon or standardize this data.

This is in direct contrast to the way proprietary projects are most often structured. Empirical software engineering researchers have, in the past, typically used metrics from a single company or a single proprietary project. This data was collected systematically and distributed in a tightly controlled manner, consistent with the proprietary nature of the software being developed.

Whereas data analysis about proprietary software practices was primarily a problem of scarcity (getting access and permissions to use the data), collecting and analyzing FLOSS data becomes a problem of abundance and reliability (storage, sharing, aggregation, and filtering of the data). To this end, this paper discusses the motivations and methods for collecting FLOSS data, contrasting these with traditional software engineering methods. We then outline some challenges data miners should look forward to when trying to improve the usefulness of their quantitative data streams.

Please use the following format when citing this chapter:

Conklin, M.S., 2006, in IFIP International Federation for Information Processing, Volume 203, Open Source Systems, eds. Damiani, E., Fitzgerald, B., Scacchi, W., Scotto, M., Succi, G., (Boston: Springer), pp. 47-56

2 Motivations

2.1 Importance of Metrics in Software Engineering

The collection and aggregation of real-world and historical data points are critical to the task of measurement in software engineering. Interesting measures of the software process can vary depending on the goals of the research [1], but they could include things like the number of errors in a particular module, the number of developers working in a particular language or development environment, or the length of time spent fixing a particular code defect [2]. Software engineering metrics can be used to avoid costly disasters [3], efficiently allocate human and financial capital [4], and to understand and improve business processes.

There are hundreds of these examples in the software engineering literature about how important metrics are for studying proprietary projects, but where are the metrics and measurements for studying FLOSS development practices? We know that FLOSS projects are fundamentally different from proprietary projects in several important ways: they are primarily user-driven as opposed to driven by a hierarchically-organized, for-profit corporation [5]. These user-programmers work in loosely defined teams, rarely meet face-to-face, and coordinate their efforts via electronic media such as mailing lists and message boards [1]. These are all fundamentally different arrangements than the way proprietary software is traditionally developed.

2.2 Importance of Metrics in FLOSS

Recognizing this unique separation between proprietary and FLOSS software engineering traditions, and building on a strong foundation of measurement in software engineering literature, there are then several compelling reasons to collect, aggregate, and share data about the practice of FLOSS software development. First, studying FLOSS development practices can be useful in its own right, in order to educate the larger research and practitioner communities about an important new direction in the creation and maintenance of software [6]. FLOSS researchers have noticed that many of the practices of FLOSS teams are not well-understood [7, 8] or, when they are, they seem to directly oppose traditional wisdom about how to build software [9]. At the very least, this situation indicates something interesting is afoot, and in the best case will foreshadow an important methodological shift for software development.

Additionally, the lessons learned through studying FLOSS development teams are applicable to many other fields. Much research has been conducted on the economic [10, 11] and policy aspects of FLOSS development, especially as the reason for various licensing choices [12] or about their implications for intellectual property [13–16]. Additional research has been conducted on the motivations of FLOSS developers [11, 17, 18], which is an interesting question to consider since these developers are working without pay. There are also implications for other types of distributed teams and computer-mediated group work [19, 20], such as gaining a better understanding of the role of face-to-face meetings in highly distributed work teams, or analyzing the leadership hierarchies that work best for distributed teams.

3 Difficulties

FLOSS data appears to be highly available, and appears easier to access for research than proprietary data. While this means that it is possibly more appealing to use than proprietary data, FLOSS data has its own very long list of collection difficulties.

3.1 Questions of Accessibility

Researchers who wish to test a quick hypothesis about the use of a particular software module, or who wish to study adoption rates of various programming languages know that, in theory, they should have access to this information via FLOSS project data, since the code is free and open to everyone. Therefore, it is no longer necessary to find a corporation willing to provide researchers access to their development databases and source code control systems. Much of the FLOSS project data is stored inside large, public source code repositories such as [21–24]. However, the difficulties in gathering FLOSS data from these repositories in an automated fashion are numerous and on-going [25, 26]. Gaining control over this "free" and "open" data is actually a hugely inefficient process for a researcher. If each isolated research team is taking on this tedious responsibility of gathering the same data, this will quickly result in redundancy in the collection effort, which prolongs and denigrates the data analysis effort.

3.2 Questions of Accuracy and Reproducibility

Another significant problem with isolated researchers attempting to collect and analyze FLOSS data is one of validation and reproducibility of results [27]. There are numerous examples in the FLOSS literature that reflect on this general problem with collecting, validating, and reproducing data and results. Some studies have addressed their difficulties with collecting data by limiting their studies to a single public repository, and then to draw on samples that are easy to collect, but which were created for entirely different purposes [28, 29]. In addition, the demands of traditional publication may mean that the data collection methodologies are not fully described. This makes them impossible to reproduce, which slows down the compounding effects [30] started by good research [31]. The tradition of scientists working together to solve a hard problem [32] is an important tradition to continue, but how is this to happen if each isolated research team must start from square one?

3.3 Questions of Quantity

In software engineering data analysis, this massive project cross-referencing and metadata creation is a problem probably unique to FLOSS. Rarely would empirical software engineers studying proprietary systems need to study hundreds of disparate project teams stored in dozens of unique data models (repositories) with thousands of data attributes. The amount of raw data available for collection in FLOSS software is greater than that of proprietary software by orders of magnitude, both in terms of project team counts and in developer counts. For each developer and each project there are thousands of additional attributes that can also be mined for interesting insights.

However, much of the FLOSS research to date closely emulates the research methods used to study proprietary software: the research follows a single project and extrapolates some lesson or advancement which can then be applied to other projects. Examples include [33–36, 18]. Some other projects have used surveys or other instruments to collect information about a small number of FLOSS projects. For example, [37] was based on a survey of 684 developers on 287 FLOSS projects. [7] was based on ethnographic research principles, and involved a dozen software projects in four different research areas. [38] studies four open source projects all related to the same coordinating company. [10] studied four different open source projects, some of which also appear in other studies [35, 36]. [39] surveys 81 developers working on an unspecified number of open source projects. The 2000 Orbiten data [40] includes 12706 (identifiable) developers and 3149 projects. Within the corpus of previously published FLOSS literature, the Orbiten project data can be considered large. However, we know that these numbers represent less than 3% of the total activity in FLOSS development [27].

3.4   Questions of Reliability

Another problem with relying on published-but-proprietary data sources for research is that type of data can disappear. For example, the Orbiten project mentioned above is no longer in active development. Though the original article [40] links to a web site intended to provide both the software and the data, this site is no longer operational. A researcher wishing to duplicate or validate the methods of Orbiten would be at a loss to do so. Thus, there is really no way to build upon or extend the metrics published in the original article (i.e. further this valuable FLOSS research). Using FLOSS development methodologies such as project handoff [11,16] would have reduced this tendency for information to exist only in one place.

4   Future Challenges

As an answer to these goals described above and expressed by the FLOSS research community, the FLOSSmole project [41] was designed to be accessible, accurate, reproducible, compatible, comprehensive, and reliable [27, 42]. In its current state, FLOSSmole serves the greater FLOSS research community by providing a collection of software tools (database schemas, code libraries, scripts, source code) that mines code repositories and provides the resulting data and summary analyses as open source products. The project is hosted on Sourceforge [24], a public, open-source code repository. The code, data, and schemas are all open-sourced and free for other researchers to use and modify. FLOSSmole has been successful in its role as a basic data gathering and reporting tool for research.

However, FLOSSmole and other quantitative FLOSS data gathering projects could be better; in this section we propose improvements to the data-gathering community research infrastructure. Though we have FLOSSmole in mind while writing, these ideas are based on general ideas, and could therefore be applied to many other projects designed to collect and aggregate quantitative FLOSS data.

4.1   Exploit Low-Hanging Fruit

The primary activity of our community data repository is to collect and store data. In FLOSSmole, we currently pull data from two open source code repositories (also called "forges"), and have historical data from a third repository. These forges represent the low-hanging fruit of FLOSS data: even though there is relative difficulty [26] involved in getting data from the forges, they are still the easiest places to get large amounts of data quickly. So, one of the most important things we can provide the community is to pull data from a broader range of forges. There are dozens of independent open source forges that host important projects, but we do not currently collect this significant quantity of data. This also represents a step in the right direction for promoting collaboration and sharing between communities and between development efforts and research groups.

Moreover, as FLOSS researchers in the true spirit of collaboration, we should expect our data to become the low-hanging fruit for other projects. The SWIK project [43], an independent effort by programmers at Sourcelabs, is a wiki-based database of open source projects. Each open source project has an entry in the Swik system, and Swik users can annotate and tag each project page with keywords or descriptors. This entire project was created in one month, using data made public by FLOSSmole. Swik is a great example of why it is important to make data easily accessible. Developers and researchers should be able to find, interpret and use quantitative data quickly and painlessly. However, despite how easy it is to download FLOSSmole data, it is not as easy to query the database or interpret results. FLOSSmole data is available to the research community in two formats: massive text ("raw") database dumps, and summary reports. There is also a nice query tool. But the most important thing the research community has asked us for is for more reporting tools (better visualizations, more graphs/charts, an online, interactive graphing tool), and for fuller descriptions of the data we are making available (more metadata). Both of these items would go a long way to improving the usability of the data in our community data repository.

4.2   Seek High-Hanging Fruit

In the same way that FLOSS development is a collaborative process, FLOSS research is also collaborative at its nature. Thus, any FLOSS data repository will need to integrate both donated data sets and historical research data. We occasionally have access to data from now-defunct projects, and from previously published FLOSS research studies – both of these sources of data are valuable for historical analyses, and may be able to be integrated into the existing (and active!) community database. Even if this donated or historical data were complete, clean, and well-labeled, integrating it could still be problematic: different repositories store different data elements, different forges can have projects with the same names, different developers can have the same name across multiple forges, the same developer can go by multiple names in multiple forges. In addition, forges have different terminology for things like developer roles, project topics, and even programming languages.

What is the best way to extract knowledge from published research? What is the best way to express the quantitative knowledge in a domain and integrate multiple sources of this knowledge? How will we create sufficient metadata about each data source so that the results can be used together? Can any of this be done in an automated fashion? What query tools should be used so that the user can fully explore both data sets? These are big questions with no easy answers; these are the rare and exceptional fruits, located higher up in the tree.

Assuming we are able to successfully meld multiple data sources and create this richer, more interesting multi-repository structure, we must also consider privacy issues. There is some vigorous debate in the research community about breaching developer privacy in a large system of aggregated data like ours [44]. For example, if we aggregate several code repositories and are now able to show in a colorful graph that Suzy Developer is ten times more productive than Bob Coder, does this violate Bob's privacy? If we can show that Suzy's code changes are five times more likely to cause errors than Bob's, does that violate Suzy's privacy? The next generation of community repositories like FLOSSmole should have the ability to hash the unique keys indicating a developer's identity. This effort will have to be researched, implemented, and documented for our community.

5   Conclusions

This paper first reviews why quantitative data is useful in software engineering, including some ways in which the FLOSS and proprietary software data gathering processes are different. Next we point out some common problems with the FLOSS data gathering process. Finally, we pass on the benefit of our experience creating FLOSSmole by posing questions about what the next steps should be for creating a truly valuable and transformative community data repository.

Reflecting on our initial successes creating data repositories for quantitative FLOSS data, it is clear that simply gathering public repository data (the "low-hanging fruits" of FLOSS data collection) is interesting and useful, but not sufficient. This type of data does not capitalize on some of the most interesting aspects of FLOSS movement: its focus on collaboration, its respect for individual privacy issues. In order to provide truly meaningful and useful data, we must reach beyond these low-hanging fruits.

6   References

1. R.E. Park, W.B. Goethert, and W.A. Florac. (1996) Goal Driven Software Measurement – A Guidebook. CMU/SEI-96-BH-002. Carnegie Mellon U. 1996.

2. E. Yourdon, E. *Decline and Fall of the American Programmer* (Prentice-Hall: Englewood Cliffs, New Jersey, 1993).

3. J.-M. Jezequel and B. Meyer, Design by contract: The lessons of Ariane, *Computer* **30** (1),129-130 (1997).

4. F. Brooks, *The Mythical Man-Month*, rev ed. (Addison-Wesley: Reading, Massachusetts, USA, 1995).

5. E. von Hippel, Innovation by user communities: Learning from open-source software. *Sloan Management Review* (Summer). 82-86 (2001).

6. J. Feller, Thoughts on Studying Open Source Software Communities. In *Realigning Research and Practice in Information Systems Development: The Social and Organizational Perspective*, edited by N.L. Russo, et al. (Kluwer Academic Publishers, Dordrecht, 2001).

7. W. Scacchi, Understanding the requirements for developing Open Source Software systems, *IEE Proc. on Software*, **149** (1). 24-39 (2002).

8. E. von Hippel, Exploring the Open Source Software Phenomenon: Issues for Organization Science. *Organization Science* **14** (2), 209-223 (2003).

9. J.D. Herbsleb and R.E. Grinter, Splitting the organization and integrating the code: Conway's law revisited. In *Proc. of the Intl Conf. on Soft. Eng.* (1999).

10. J. Lerner, and J. Tirole, (2002). Some simple economics of open source, *Journal of Industrial Economics* **L**, 197-234 (2002).

11. E. Raymond, *The Cathedral and the Bazaar*. (O'Reilly, Sebastopol, CA, 1999).

12. L. Rosen, *Open Source Licensing: Software Freedom and Intellectual Property Law* (Prentice Hall, Upper Saddle River, New Jersey, 2004).

13. C. DiBona, S. Ockman, and M. Stone, *Open Sources: Voices from the Open Source Revolution* (O'Reilly, Sebastopol, CA, 1999).

14. B. Kogut, and A. Meitu, Open-source software development and distributed innovation, *Oxford Review of Economic Policy* **17**, 2. 248-264 (2001).

15. J. Lerner, and J. Tirole, The open source movement: Key research questions, *European Economic Review* **45**, 819-826 (2001).

16. S. Weber, *The Success of Open Source* (Harvard U. Press, Cambridge, 2004).

17. L. Torvalds, FM interview with Linus Torvalds: What motivates free software developers? *First Monday* **3**(3) (March, 1998).

18. Y. Ye and K. Kishida, Toward an understanding of the motivation of open source software developers. In *Proc. of the 25th Intl. Conf. on Soft. Eng.* (2003).

19. K. Crowston, H. Annabi, J. Howison, and C. Masango, Effective work practices for Soft. Eng.: Free/libre/open source software development, *WISER Workshop on Interdisciplinary Soft. Eng. Research* (2004).

20. K. Crowston, H. Annabi, J. Howison, and C. Masango, Effective work practices for FLOSS development: A model and propositions, *Proc. of the Hawai'I Intl. Conf. on System Science* (2005).

21. Bugzilla. Apache Foundation, (March 1, 2006); http://issues.apache.org/bugzilla/

22. Freshmeat (March 1, 2006); http://www.freshmeat.net

23. Savannah (March 1, 2006); http://savannah.nongnu.org/

24. Sourceforge (March 1, 2006); http://www.sf.net

25. D.M. German, Mining CVS repositories: The Softchange experience. In *Proc. of the Workshop on Mining Software Repositories* (2004).

26. J. Howison and K. Crowston, K. (2004). The perils and pitfalls of mining Sourceforge. In *Proc. of the Workshop on Mining Software Repositories* (2004).

27. M. Conklin, J. Howison, and K. Crowston, K. Collaboration Using OSSmole: A Repository of FLOSS Data and Analyses, *Proc. of the Workshop on Mining Software Repositories* (2005).

28. S. Krishnamurthy, Cave or community? An empirical examination of 100 mature open source projects, *First Monday* **7**(6), (June, 2004).

29. I. Samoladas, and I. Stamelos, Assessing free/open source software quality. TR Aristotle University of Thessaloniki, Thessaloniki, Greece. 2003 (unpublished).

30. K.S. Louis, L.M. Jones and E.G. Campbell, Sharing in science. *American Scientist* **90** (4), 304-307 (2002).

31. D.R. Krathwohl, *Methods of Education and Social Science Research: An Integrated Approach* (Longman: New York, 1998).

32. R.K. Merton, *Social Theory and Social Structure*, (Free Press: New York, 1968).

33. M.S. Elliott and W. Scacchi, Communicating and Mitigating Conflict in Open Source Software Development Projects. *Projects and Profits* **10**(4), 25-41 (2004).

34. D.M. German, Decentralized open source global software development, the GNOME experience. *J. of Soft. Process: Imp. and Practice*, **8** (4), 201-215 (2004).

35. S. Koch and G. Schneider, Results from software engineering research into open source development projects using public data, *Diskussionspapiere zum Tät igkeitsfeld Informationsverarbeitung und Informationswirtschaft*, 22, (2000).

36. A. Mockus, R.T. Fielding, and J. Herbsleb, A case study of open source software development: The Apache server. In *Proc. of the 22nd Intl. Conf. on Soft. Eng.*, 263-272 (2000)

37. K. Lakhani and R.G. Wolf, Why hackers do what they do: Understanding motivation effort in free/open source software projects. WP 4425-03. Sloan School of Management, MIT, 2003 (unpublished).

38. K. Nakakoji, Y. Yamamoto, Y. Nishinaka, K. Kishida, and Y. Ye, Evolution patterns of open-source software systems and communities. In *Proc. of the Intl. Workshop on Software Evolution* (2002).

39. A. Hars and S. Ou, Working for free? - Motivations of participating in open source projects. In *Proc. of the 34th Hawaii Intl. Conf. on System Sciences*, (2001).

40. R.A. Ghosh and P.P. Prakash, The Orbiten free software survey. *First Monday* **5**(7), (July, 2000).

41. FLOSSmole Project (March 1, 2006); http://ossmole.sf.net

42. J. Howison, M. Conklin, and K. Crowston, OSSmole: A Collaborative Repository for FLOSS Research Data and Analyses. In *Proc. of the First Intl. Conf. on Open Source Systems* (2005).

43. Swik (March 1, 2006); http://swik.sourcelabs.com

44. G. Robles, Developer identification methods for integrated data from various sources. In *Proc. of the Intl. Workshop on Mining Software Repositories* (2005).

Call for Quality: Open Source Software Quality Observation

Adriaan de Groot[1], Sebastian Kügler[1], Paul J. Adams[2], and Giorgos Gousios[3]

[1] Quality Team, KDE e.V. {groot,sebas}@kde.org
[2] University of Lincoln padams@lincoln.ac.uk
[3] Athens University of Economics and Business gousiosg@aueb.gr

Abstract. This paper describes how a Software Quality Observatory works to evaluate and quantify the quality of an Open Source project. Such a quality measurement can be used by organizations intending to deploy an Open Source solution to pick one of the available projects for use. We offer a case description of how the Software Quality Observatory will be applied to the KDE project to document and evaluate its quality practices for outsiders.

Keywords

Open Source software, software quality evaluation, static code analysis

1 Introduction

The software development process is well known as a contributor to software product quality, leading to application of software process improvement as a key technique for the overall improvement of the software product. This can be said for any form of software development. Within the Open Source paradigm, the leverage of software quality data can be as useful for the end users as it is for the developers.

From the perspective of a potential *user* of a piece of Open Source software (OSS), it can be very difficult to choose one of a myriad solutions to a given problem. There are often dozens of Open Source solutions which "compete" for users and development resources. They may differ in quality, features, requirements, etc. By making the quality aspects of a given project explicit, it becomes easier for the user to choose a solution based on the quality of the software. Here the Software Quality Observatory (SQO) can play a useful role in quantifying the quality of processes employed by a given OSS project.

With ever increasing numbers of projects and developers on SourceForge (www.sourceforge.net), it is clear that the OSS paradigm is of interest to those wishing to contribute to the creation of software. By using scientifically obtained software quality data, such as that which the Software Quality Observatory will produce, it may be possible to encourage similar growth within the OSS user community.

Please use the following format when citing this chapter:

de Groot, A., Kügler, S., Adams, P.J., and Gousios, G., 2006, in IFIP International Federation for Information Processing, Volume 203, Open Source Systems, eds. Damiani, E., Fitzgerald, B., Scacchi, W., Scotto, M., Succi, G., (Boston: Springer), pp. 57-62

2 The Benefits of Software Quality Observation

As participation has grown in Open Source development over the past decade, so too has the user base of the software grown. Increasingly OSS is being viewed as a viable alternative to proprietary (closed source) software, not just by technically-aware developers, but also by non-developers. European research projects, such as COSPA (www.cospa-project.org/) and CALIBRE (www.calibre.ie), have raised awareness of OSS development through specific targeting of public administration bodies and industrial organisations, especially small and medium enterprises (SMEs).

As the OSS paradigm makes progress within these organisations any potential software procurer is tasked with some important questions which, currently, cannot be answered with any real assurance:

- Many OSS projects are very similar. How do we choose between them? Which is the most appropriate system for the company's IT infrastructure?
- How can we distinguish the "good" and "bad" projects?
- How can we reason about the quality of a software product in order to trust its future development?

Unfortunately these organisations often have nothing more than word-of-mouth on which to base their judgments of OSS products. With 109,707[1] projects currently hosted on SourceForge it is understandable that products of excellent quality may be overlooked. It is possible to supplement the word-of-mouth tradition with some rudimentary data that is available from hosting sites: download numbers, project activity etc. Unfortunately this data is easily skewed and can present a product in an inaccurate manner.

Quality can be a very subjective measure of many aspects of a system in combination: suitability for purpose, reliability, aesthetic etc. Software quality is formally defined by the ISO/IEC 9126 standard as comprised of six characteristics, but no measurement techniques are defined. It has been suggested that the external quality characteristics of a software system are directly related to its internal quality characteristics. It is therefore possible to evaluate the quality of software through its source code and a of project by considering other data sources intimately related to the project's code such as bug-fix databases or mailing lists.

In the long run it is crucial to OSS developers and their projects to know *quantitatively* what the quality of their product is. The volunteer nature of OSS makes "managing" such a project to include quality control a matter of motivating volunteers to behave in ways consistent with improving quality[2]. By fully understanding their software quality, OSS developers are able to promote and improve their products and process. It is also crucial in helping end-users making informed decisions about software procurement.

---

[1] Data from the FLOSSMole Project, 02/12/05.

3 Why SQO of Open Source Software differs from that on Closed Software

There are two aspects that play a role for quality assessment of software, the quality of the product itself and the quality of the product team. The main differences between quality assessment (QA) of Open Source software and QA of closed source software naturally relate to the availability of the source code and the transparency of the development process. Third party quality assessment is facilitated by the availability of the source code and the openness of the development process.

Quality assessment of OSS software is usually much more transparent than that of closed source software, at least to quality observers on the "outside" [2]. Most OSS projects use an Open Source tool-chain to create their software. Those tools, compilers for example, have considerable influence on the quality of the products and therefore need to be taken into account when assessing the quality of a piece of software. Furthermore, discussion about quality issues often happens in public, on mailing lists and message boards, which adds transparency. Third-party quality assessment of closed source software involves guessing in most cases.

The number of open bugs might give another impression of the quality of a product. This number is to be taken with a grain of salt since the number of bugs might indicate that there is a lot of testing, or that there are a lot of people reporting bugs. The type of bugs, response times and their frequency is important. Merely counting the number of bugs reveals more about the community behind the product than about the product itself.

The number of code check-ins gives a good idea of the activity level of the development of the product. Products that receive a lot of attention from developers are likely to be fixed faster than products that have been abandoned. A product can be very actively developed, but that might also indicate that it is unstable and many changes are being made which increase the amount of effort needed to assess and maintain a certain level of quality.

Assessing the product team is another aspect where quality assessment of OSS products differs from QA on closed source software. The term *Product Team* refers to all participants in the project, engineers, documentation team, translators, and of course QA people [3]. In closed software products, the number and skill level of developers is usually kept secret by the company, the number of participants in an OSS project can at least be estimated by educated guessing, based on commit logs and the source code itself.

The size of the team is an important issue to examine the longevity of the product, and thus the chance to have the product supported in the future. The *Open Source Maturity Model* (OSMM) [2] uses team size explicitly as a numeric indicator of quality.

4 The Software Quality Observatory

The automated analysis of source code as a quality measurement is not a new concept. In recent years, the growth of OSS development has provided a wealth of code in which new techniques can be developed. Previous work in this area is often based in metric analysis: statement count, program depth, number of executable paths or McCabe's cyclomatic complexity [5] for example. In their work using on metric-based analysis Stamelos et al. [7] observed good quality code within Open Source. Other techniques, such as neural networks [4] are not only capable of evaluating code, but also in predicting future code quality.

The Software Quality Observatory aims to provide a platform with a pluggable architecture as outlined in figure 1 for software development organisations that will satisfy four objectives:

- Promote the use of OSS through scientific evidence of its perceived quality.
- Enhance software engineers' ability to quantify software quality.
- Introduce information extraction, data mining and unsupervised learning to the software engineering discipline and exploit the possible synergies between the two domains using novel techniques and algorithms.
- Provide the basis for an integrated software quality management product.

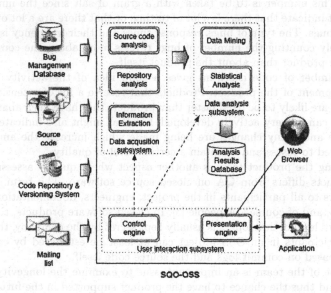

Fig. 1. A schematic representation of the proposed system

SQO-OSS is based around three distinct processing subsystems that share a common data store. The data acquisition subsystem processes unstructured project data and feeds the resultant structured data to the analysis stages. The user interaction subsystem presents analysis results to the user and accepts input to affect the analysis parameters. The components of the data acquisition subsystem are responsible for extracting useful data for analysis from the raw data that is available from the range of sources within software development projects. Metric analysis of source code is well-known and an important aspect of this system. Repository analysis will perform examine the commit behaviour of developers in response to user requests and security issues. The information extraction component will extract structured information from mailing lists and other textual source in order to feed higher-level analyses.

The data mining component will use structured information from project sources to predict the behaviour of the project with respect to quality characteristics and classify projects according to their general quality measurements. The statistical analysis component will apply statistical estimation models in order to predict events in the development life-cycle that can have an impact on the product's quality.

5 The SQO and KDE

The KDE project (www.kde.org) is one of the largest desktop-oriented projects in the world. Its scope encompasses the entire desktop (i.e. end-user use of a computer, including web-surfing, email, office applications, and games). It is a confederation of smaller projects all of which use a single platform (the KDE libraries) for consistency. The project has some 1200 regular contributors and many hundreds more translators. The source code has grown to over 6 million lines of C++ in 10 years of "old-school" hacking.

KDE's quality control system has traditionally been one of "compile early, compile often." By having hundreds of contributors poring over the code-base on a wide range of operating systems and architectures, bugs were usually found quickly. Certainly most glaring deficiencies are quickly found, but more subtle bugs may not be.

In terms of formalized quality control, there is a commit policy which states when something may be committed to the KDE repository [1], but this does not rise much above the level of "if it compiles, commit it." Only recently has a concerted push been made for the adoption of unit tests within the KDE libraries. Adoption of the notion of *writing* unit tests has been enthusiastic, but there are questions of coverage and completeness. Automated regression testing is slowly being implemented, but here the lack of a standardized platform for running the tests hampers the adoption of those automated tests.

Documentation (user and API) quality has become an issue, and quality measurements are now done regularly. User interface guidelines have been formulated, but not enforced. Once again, there is an effort underway to measure (deviations from) the interface guidelines. This produces discouraging numbers, and has not yet been successfully automated in a large scale manner.

The KDE project expects the Software Quality Observatory to extend and enhance the quality measurements which it has begun to implement, in order to guide the actions of the KDE developers. Whether the availability of quality metrics for the code base has an effect on the "average" volunteer developer remains to be seen — experiences with the existing tools suggests that fixing bugs found by automatic techniques does not score high on the "fun" chart for developers. For the core KDE developers (of which there are perhaps 100) the existence of the quality metrics produced by the SQO may guide their efforts in bug fixing and yield more productive code freezes prior to release.

6 Conclusions

Software quality observation has long been performed as a crucial element in software process improvement. However, established methods of quality observation have mostly focused on source code and overlooked other available data sources e.g. mailing lists or bug fix data[6].

Many OSS projects, such as KDE, have established processes for the maintenance of software quality. However, these can only be of limited use when then actual quality of the product is still unknown. By scientifically evaluating the quality of a software *product* and not the *process*, software engineers can leverage this knowledge in many ways. By providing this quality evaluation the SQO-OSS system will allow engineers to make informed choices when addressing their development process and allow them to better maintain quality in the future. The developers and their supporting organisations can also use this evaluation to promote their product. This is especially crucial within the OSS world, where there is a wealth of choice.

Ultimately, the SQO-OSS system will aid OSS developers to write better software and enable potential users to make better informed choices.

References

1. KDE Developer's Corner. KDE commit policy. On http://developer.kde.org/.
2. Bernard Golden. *Succeeding with Open Source*. Addison-Wesley, 2005.
3. Lewis R. Ireland. *Quality Management for Products and Programs*. Project Management Institute, 1991.
4. R. Kumar, S. Rai, and J. L. Trahan. Neural-network techniques for software-quality evaluation. In *Proceedings of the Annual Reliability and Maintainability Symposium*, 1998.
5. T. McCabe. A complexity measure. *IEEE Transactions on Software Engineering*, 2(4):308–320, 1976.
6. Diomidis Spinellis. *Code Quality: The Open Source Perspective*. Addison-Wesley, Boston, MA, 2006.
7. Ioannis Stamelos, Lefteris Angelis, Apostolos Oikonomou, and Georgios L. Bleris. Code quality analysis in open source software development. *Information Systems Journal*, 12(1):43–60, January 2002.

Part III

Knowledge Management in OSS

Towards an Ontology for Open Source Software Development

Gregory L. Simmons[1] and Tharam S. Dillon[2]

1 School of InformationTechnology and Mathematical Sciences, Univeristy of Ballarat, Australia, WWW home page: http://uob-community.ballarat.edu.au/~gsimmons

2 Faculty of Information Technology, University of Technology Sydney, Australia, WWW home page: http://staff.it.uts.edu.au/~tharam/

Abstract. Software development is a knowledge intensive process and the information generated in open source software development projects is typically housed in a central Internet repository. Open source repositories typically contains vast amounts of information, much of it unstructured, meaning that even if a question has previously been discussed and dealt with it is not a trivial task to locate it. This can lead to rework and confusion amongst developers and possibly deter new developers from getting involved in the project in the first place. This paper will present the case for an open source software development ontology. Such an ontology would enable better categorization of information and the development of sophisticated knowledge portals in order to better organize community knowledge and increase efficiency in the open source development process.

1. Introduction

Open source software (OSS) development provides an alternative model of development to commercial systems developed by or for a single corporate entity. In this model of development, a variety of developers carry out development and distribute the source code associated with the product. This allows for incremental improvement by others or development of complementary products that can seamlessly interoperate with the open source products.

Open source projects can be broadly characterized by their distributed development, loose management practices and their uncertain requirements [1, 2], these are considered briefly below:

- Distributed development teams: Open source developers are potentially drawn from a global pool of talent using the Internet; developers do not typically meet face to face. Rather the development community for any one project is centered on a public World-Wide-Web site and communication conducted using mailing lists and discussion forums.

Please use the following format when citing this chapter:

Simmons, G.L., and Dillon, T.S., 2006, in IFIP International Federation for Information Processing, Volume 203, Open Source Systems, eds. Damiani, E., Fitzgerald, B., Scacchi, W., Scotto, M., Succi, G., (Boston: Springer), pp. 65-75

- Loose management: There are no time constraints in an open source project and no mechanism to insist that functionality is implemented. Management is less concerned with utilizing resources efficiently and more concerned with which contributions should be committed to the product and which should be discarded.
- Uncertain requirements: Open source projects are constantly evolving with developers choosing to contribute what they think the product needs rather than the solution to any problem they are assigned, requirements are therefore elicited rather than assigned.

The community around an open source software project usually interacts through asynchronous textual modes of communication, such as email and threaded discussions, which are logged in publicly browsable World-Wide-Web repositories. The merits of proposed changes, requirements for the product, any problems are all debated in the open and archived along with the source code for the product.

Open source repositories serve to advertise the product, document its use, provide help to end users of the product, capture feature requests and bugs from users and developers, support developer collaboration and provide the entry point for new developers to accustom themselves with the project. Repositories are also the means by which users and developers upload and download the product in source and binary form. It is therefore not surprising that these repositories typically contain vast amounts of information.

The information contained within an open source repository serves as a record of the community knowledge accumulated throughout the development process and as such represents an artefact of vital importance. It is therefore unfortunate that the current open source software repositories in widespread use provide little support in terms of their ability to structure information so that it is meaningful to different types of user. Much of the information contained within open source repositories is unstructured, meaning that even if a question has previously been discussed and dealt with it is not a trivial task to locate it, leading to rework, confusion amongst developers and possibly deterring new developers from getting involved. Ankolekar, Herbsleb and Sycara [3] sum up this problem succinctly "there is a need to get the right information to the right person for the current task, and to present it in an understandable, usable way".

One approach to better understand and organize the structure of information from a particular domain is to use ontologies. Ontologies explicitly define a structure of concepts from a particular domain and their relationships to one another. Next generation (semantic) World-Wide-Web applications rely on meaningfully annotated content and often use ontologies to define their annotation vocabulary; with access to the underlying ontology we understand how to process the annotated content, and we have a basis for organizing the information into a meaningfully navigable hierarchy of terms.

The remainder of this paper is organized as follows. Section 2 presents a short description of ontologies and why they can be useful in open source software development. Section 3 introduces an ontology to describe open source software development. Section 4 discusses how such an ontology could be applied by proposing a software architecture for semantic portal development. Finally section 5 presents a brief discussion and conclusion.

2. Ontologies

Gruber [4] defines an ontology as "explicit formal specifications of the terms in the domain and relations among them". An ontology includes definitions of basic concepts in a domain and relations among them, these definitions are expressed in a machine-interpretable way allowing for the development of artificially intelligent applications. More importantly ontologies denote a shared conceptualization, for the ontology to be useful its specification must be one that is accepted in its use by domain experts.

Ontologies broadly contain Instances, Classes and Properties. Classes represent important concepts of the domain (these classes may be arranged in a taxonomy indicating superclass-subclass relationships between classes), properties represent a type of association between the domain concepts (which may or may not have restrictions) and instances represent an observed instance of a concept.

For example: An ontology about animals may state that a subclass of the concept Domestic-Animal called Domestic-Dog requires the properties color, breed, age and name. Furthermore you can place restrictions on concepts governing what definitions are legal or not, for example Domestic-Dog could have a restriction stating that all instances are quadrupeds therefore preventing any two-legged Domestic-Dog subclasses being defined. There may then be many instances of a Domestic-Dog, each describing a different four-legged animal such as the bull terrier known as Max and the retriever known as Rover, who both belong to the class Domestic-Dog.

Noy and McGuinness [5] provide five reasons for the development of an ontology:

1. To share common understanding of the structure of information among people or software agents
2. To enable reuse of domain knowledge
3. To make domain assumptions explicit
4. To separate domain knowledge from the operational knowledge
5. To analyze domain knowledge

Ontologies have been developed to describe everything from pizza[3] to wine [5] to cataloguing artefacts from a museum as displayed by the Museum of Finland website[4].

---

[3] http://www.co-ode.org/ontologies/pizza/2005/10/18/
[4] http://museosuomi.cs.helsinki.fi/

2.2 Open source development – A case for ontologies?

Despite its popularity a number of challenges exist with the potential to reduce the perceived benefits of open source development. One key issue for open source development is its scalability with its high dependence on source code as project documentation and its lack of formal documentation.

"Complexity and size effectively close source code for system programming projects like OSes compilers after, say, 100K lines of code without good higher level documentation or participation in the project from its early stages. This "binarization" of source code in large system programming projects may mean that there is little strategic importance to keep the source code of system programs closed after it reaches a certain level of maturity."[6]

Another issue facing open source development is the scarcity of developers, a number of authors [7-9] has noted a Pareto distribution in the size of the number of developers participating in open source projects with the majority of projects having only one developer and a much smaller percentage with larger, ongoing involvement.

There is also a high degree of conceptual dissonance exhibited between open source projects, development models, licensing, source-code structure, terminology all differ markedly from project to project. The badge open source might suggest a collection of homogeneous projects but the reality is quite different and projects can differ quite markedly from the apparent bazaar style development in the Linux project as documented by Raymond [10] to the Extreme Programming influenced development evident in the Zope project [1].

It would seem obvious that a common understanding of how to the structure of information in open source repositories is something desirable. A common vocabulary could help reduce conceptual dissonance and provide budding contributors with easier access to information about a project than is possible at present. If a potential developer could easily access information about the source-code structure, the tools employed, the development model and the software license easily then perhaps the "binarization" of source code becomes less of a problem and developers would find it easier to join a development effort mid-stream.

In order to better organize the information generated in an open source project we need a conceptual framework that promotes agreement on how information should be organized, without losing any of the flexibility of allowing people to express and view parts in their own familiar expression language. Understanding the meaning of shared information on the web can substantially be enhanced if the information is mapped onto a domain ontology.

An open source software development ontology would encompass diverse, complex, domain knowledge, technology and skills. It will ensure a common ground for distributed collaboration and interactions. It is envisaged that such an ontology could be used as a basis for better organizing the community knowledge contained within open source repositories by providing the backbone for next-generation semantic open source development portals/repositories [11, 12]

3. An open source development ontology

This section presents the top level of a preliminary Open Source Development Ontology (OSDO). The OSDO would provide definitions of relevant classes and properties providing a unified vocabulary and structure for open source development. Each open source project would take the ontology and create instances reflecting the individual circumstances for that project. For example one project might contain the instance CVS for the class Version-Control whilst another project might have the Version-Control instance Subversion.

As with all ontologies the OSDO is a work in progress and the authors welcome any feedback. Due to space limitations it is not possible to present the entire ontology, rather the base concepts are presented along with some restrictions to demonstrate how the ontology could be reasoned with. A full version of the ontology is available from the author's website[5].

3.1 Ontology design

When designing a new ontology one needs design principles to guide development and provide a basis for evaluation, Gruber [13] identifies five design principles which should guide the development of ontologies:

1. Clarity – does the ontology effectively communicate its intended meaning?
2. Coherence – is the ontology logically consistent? "If a sentence that can be inferred from the axioms contradicts a definition or example given informally, then the ontology is incoherent."
3. Extendibility – ontologies should be designed in a way that allows for the definition of new terms for special uses without needing to redefine existing terms.
4. Minimum Encoding Bias – ontologies should be designed at the "knowledge level" rather than committing the ontology to a particular implementation language and its specific limitations.
5. Minimal Ontological Commitment – ontologies should make as few claims as possible about the domain being modeled without sacrificing the usability of the ontology.

3.2 Overview of the ontology

The first activity to be performed in any engineering activity is to decide upon the system's purpose and its intended uses, ontology engineering is no different in that we begin with specifying a number of *competency questions*, and *scenarios of use* [14].

---

[5] http://uob-community.ballarat.edu.au/~gsimmons

By establishing a series of competency questions we can determine the ontology's scope, and its applicability, competency questions also provide a means to evaluate an ontology.

An open source ontology designed with the intention to better organize community knowledge would need to be able to answer questions like; who performs the different tasks? how are the tasks performed? what tools are used? and so on. The following key competency questions can be identified:

1. What output is produced?
2. What activities are performed?
3. Who is responsible for performing the different activities?
4. What procedures need to be followed?
5. What tools are used?

These questions are by no means exhaustive but as they are used to initially scope the ontology and may be revised if later found to be missing. Once the scope of the ontology and its competency questions are identified relevant concepts and relations should be identified. This task can initially be performed using a *top-down* approach, where the most general concepts are identified and then broken down into specializations, or a *bottom-up* approach, which begins by defining specific concepts and groups them into related classes.

Using the competency questions as input, a top-down approach is used to discover the base classes (concepts). Table 1 presents the resultant six base classes for the OSDO along with their respective descriptions.

Table 1: OSDO Base Classes

Class	Description
Participant	Any person who uses or contributes to the project. Some participants may remain anonymous such as those that download and use the product but do not contribute in any other way.
Role	Represents in what capacity a participant was acting when they performed an activity in the project. There are some roles that may be assumed by any participant whilst only certain participants may assume other roles.
Activity	Any action that results in a contribution to the project or where the projects resources have been used in some way.
Procedure	Any established and well defined behaviour for the accomplishment on some activity.
Artefact	Any storable input to or output from an activity.
Tool	Any software resource used by a procedure in order to accomplish some activity.

Once defined these classes can be represented in a formal ontology language (such as RDF, DAML+OIL or OWL). We have chosen to implement our ontology using OWL-DL [15] as it is a dedicated ontology language with large-scale semantic web community support. The ontology was constructed in OWL using the Protégé[6] application.

The full ontology specification in OWL is omitted from this paper for sake of brevity but an example is provided as a means of illustration providing the OWL definition for the "Participant" class (Table 2).

Table 2 - OWL Definition

```
<owl:Class rdf:about="#Participant">
    <owl:disjointWith rdf:resource="#Role"/>
    <owl:equivalentClass>
        <owl:Restriction>
            <owl:onProperty>
                <owl:ObjectProperty rdf:ID="assumes"/>
            </owl:onProperty>
            <owl:someValuesFrom rdf:resource="#Role"/>
        </owl:Restriction>
    </owl:equivalentClass>
    <owl:disjointWith rdf:resource="#Procedure"/>
    <owl:disjointWith rdf:resource="#Tool"/>
    <owl:disjointWith rdf:resource="#Artefact"/>
    <owl:disjointWith rdf:resource="#Activity"/>
</owl:Class>
```

The base classes are further defined through a series of *property restrictions*. Restrictions are used to restrict the individuals that may belong to a class and enable us to *reason* with the ontology [16]. For example the class Participant is restricted with the existential restriction:

∃ *assumes Role*

This states that any individual of the Participant class *assumes* at least one Role. Restrictions can be used to express complicated logic. The following restrictions define an Activity (a1) to be *preactivity* of Activity (a2) iff (a1) *produces* an Artefact (s) which (a2) *requires*.

[6] http://protege.stanford.edu/

> $(\forall a, s) \ (produces(a, s) \rightarrow activity(a, *) \wedge artefact(s) \ )$
>
> $(\forall a, s) \ (requires(a, s) \rightarrow activity(a, *) \wedge artefact(s) \ )$
>
> $(\forall a1, a2) \ (preactivity(a1, a2) \leftrightarrow (\exists s) \ requires(a2,s) \wedge produces(a1,s) \ )$

Once appropriate restrictions are defined for each of the base classes, defining sub-classes for each of Role, Activity, Procedure, Artefact and Tool can further extend the ontology. For example Role can be further broken down into either a *Consumer* or a *Contributor*. Consumers typically use the product but do not actively contribute to its development (other than promoting the product through its very use) and may often be anonymous; contributors however contribute directly to the product through source code development, project support, documentation, administration and so on. The Contributor role can therefore be broken down into a number of further specialized classes.

4. Putting it to work – An ontology driven architecture

Whilst ontologies are useful things in themselves, their real power can only be realized when applied to a broader application framework. In the case of the OSDO our motivation was to better organize open source project repositories. It is proposed that the OSDO could provide the basis for the development of a semantically aware project repository (or portal).

A number of semantic portals have been described in the literature including SEAL [11] and OntoViews [12]. In this section we propose an architecture (depicted in Figure 6) for a semantic portal based on the SEAL project.

The architecture consists of the following components:

- Semantic database – provides storage of semantic content and inferencing capabilities.
- Semantic query – querying facilities that exploit the inferencing capabilities of the semantic database and provides facilities such as semantic ranking.
- RDF generation – a facility to enable remote applications to interact at the RDF level.
- Template services –form generation for user input based on the reference ontology.
- Navigation – provides semantic linking and a dynamically generated portal structure.
- Annotation / Parsing – all new content is parsed against the reference ontology and semantically annotated before being stored in the database.

Each of the components of the architecture with the exception of the Annotator/Parser is present and well described in the SEAL project. To adopt a semantic portal for use in an open source project the addition of some form of automatic/semi-automatic annotation is a necessity because of the high likelihood of developers rejecting the requirement to manually annotate their contributions.

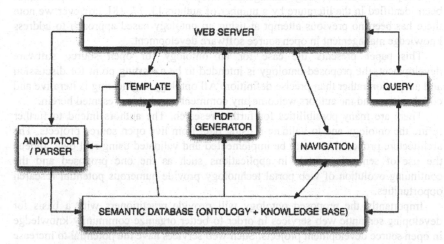

Figure 1: Ontology Driven Architecture

Take for example a bug report. Typically bugs are entered using a web form that requires the user to enter a bug description in free form text (perhaps a binary dump or screen shot) and some metadata (which may or may not be optional). The free form text can be parsed to identify terms known to the ontology and annotated accordingly whilst the metadata could be checked for consistency using the inferencing capabilities of the semantic database and if consistent annotated before being stored in the database for future reference. The problem of identifying duplicate bug reports and resolving incorrectly classified reports has been identified previously in the literature [17], semantically annotated bug reports could suggest possible duplicates via semantic query and ranking mechanisms thus aiding in this (largely manual) time consuming task. Semantic annotation could also allow bug reports could also be automatically emailed (or stored in a pigeon hole) to the responsible module maintainer or allow developers to identify a relevant discussion from a mailing-list archive, there are numerous possibilities for such a system.

5. Conclusion

Software development is well established and well understood in practice. However, distributed open source software development spread over multiple sites using open software for collaboration is a new challenge. The challenge is to develop a conceptual meta-model that will provide the architecture for the collaboration of distributed software teams and better supports the software development.

The problem of knowledge management in open source software development has been identified in the literature by a number of authors [3, 17, 18], however we note there has been no previous attempt at using an ontology based approach to address knowledge management in open source software development.

This paper presents the case for an ontology for open source software development, the proposed ontology is intended to be a starting point for discussion and adaptation rather than precise definition. All ontology engineering is iterative and collaborative and the authors welcome any comment on what is presented herein.

There are many possibilities for further research. The authors intend to further refine the ontology and to validate it using data from live open source projects. The architecture proposed needs to be implemented and validated using real data. Indeed the use of semantic portals in applications such as the one proposed and the continuing evolution of web portal technology provide numerous potential research opportunities.

Importantly the proposed ontology will provide practitioners with a basis for developing semantic web services in order to better organize community knowledge in open source development projects. Such web services have the potential to increase the efficiency of open source development and to make open source projects more accessible to those developers who would like to contribute to a project but are discouraged by the high barriers to entry.

References

1.   Simmons, G. and T.S. Dillon. *Open Source Development and Agile Methods.* in *The 7th IASTED International Conference on Software Engineering and Applications.* 2003. Marina del Rey, CA, USA: ACTA Press.

2.   Simmons, G. and T.S. Dillon. *A Critical Comparison of Agile Methods and Open Source Development through a Case Study.* in *International Conference on Software and Systems Engineering and their Applications.* 2003. Paris, France.

3.   Ankolekar, A., J. Herbsleb, and K. Sycara. *Addressing Challenges to Open Source Collaboration With the Semantic Web.* in *Taking Stock of the Bazaar: The 3rd Workshop on Open Source Software Engineering, the 25th International Conference on Software Engineering (ICSE).* 2003. Portland OR, USA.

4.   Gruber, T.R., *A Translation Approach to Portable Ontology Specification.* Knowledge Acquisition, 1993. 52(6): p. 1111-1133.

5.   Noy, N.F. and D. McGuinness, *Ontology Development 101: A Guide to Creating Your First Ontology,* S.K.S. Laboratory, Editor. 2001, Stanford Knowledge Systems Laboratory.

6.   Bezroukov, N., *A Second Look at the Cathedral and the Bazaar.* First Monday, 1999. 4(12).

7.   Hars, A. and S. Ou. *Working for free? - Motivations of participating in Open Source Projects*. in *The 34th Hawaii International Conference on System Sciences*. 2001.

8.   Hunt, F. and P. Johson. *On the Pareto Distribution of SourceForge Projects*. in *Open Source Software Development Workshop*. 2002. Newcastle, UK.

9.   Madey, G., V. Freeh, and R. Tynan. *The Open Source Software Development Phenomenon: An Analysis Based on Social Network Theory*. in *American Conference on Information Systems*. 2002. Dallas, TX.

10.   Raymond, E.S., *The Cathedral & the Bazaar*. 2 ed. 2001, Sebastápol, CA: O'Reilly.

11.   Maedche, A., et al., *Semantic portal - the SEAL approach*. 2001, Institute AIFB, University of Karlsruhe, Germany.

12.   Mäkelä, E., et al. *OntoViews - A Tool for Creating Semantic Web Portals*. in *The Semantic Web - ISWC 2004*. 2004. Hiroshima, Japan: Springer.

13.   Gruber, T.R., *Towards principals for the design of ontologies used for knowledge sharing*. Internation Journal of Human-Computer Studies, 1995. **43**: p. 907-928.

14.   Gruninger, M. and M.S. Fox. *Methodology for the Design and Evaluation of Ontologies*. in *IJCAI-95 Workshop on Basic Ontological Issues in Knowledge Sharing*. 1995. Montreal.

15.   McGuinness, D.L. and F.v. Harmelen, *OWL Web Ontology Language Overview*. 2004, W3C.

16.   Falbo, R.A., C.S. Menezes, and A.R. Rocha. *Using Ontologies to Improve Knowledge Integration in Software Engineering Environments*. in *World Multiconference on Systemic, Cybernetics and Informatics / 4th International Conference on Information Systems Analysis and Synthesis*. 1998. Orlando, USA.

17.   Gasser, L., et al. *Understanding Continuous Design in F/OSS Projects*. in *International Conference on Software and Systems Engineering and their Applications*. 2003. Paris, France.

18.   Scacchi, W., *Understanding Requirements for Developing Open Source Software Systems*. IEE Proceedings - Software, 2002. **149**(1): p. 24-39.

From Individual Contribution to Group Learning:
the Early Years of Apache Web Server

Hala Annabi[1], Kevin Crowston[2], Robert Heckman[2]
1 University of Washington, The Information School
Box 352840, Seattle, WA 98195-2840
(206) 616-8553, hpannabi@u.washington.edu
2 Syracuse University, School of Information Studies
Syracuse NY 13244, (315) 443- 1676
crowston@syr.edu, rheckman@syr.edu

Abstract. Open Source Software (OSS) groups experience many benefits and challenges with respect to the core group's effectiveness. In order to capitalize on the benefits and minimize the challenges, OSS groups must learn not only on the individual level, but also on the group level. OSS groups learn by integrating individual contributions into the group's product and processes. This paper reports on the characteristics of the learning process in OSS groups. The study utilized an embedded single case study design that observed and analyzed group learning processes in the Apache Web server OSS project. The study used learning opportunity episodes (LOE) as the embedded unit of analysis and developed and utilized three content analytic schemes to describe the characteristics of the learning process and the factors affecting this process.

1 Introduction

Open Source Software (OSS) groups, by their very nature (distributed, often voluntary, and having a potentially large number of submitted bug reports and fixes from outside of the core-development team) experience many benefits and challenges with respect to the core group's effectiveness. Since OSS teams are distributed, they have access to a larger pool of experts, have better load balancing, and are able to train developers (Grinter, Herbsleb, & Perry, 1999). However, the geographical distance between the members challenges the groups in the following ways: miscommunication, problems in product and process management, coordination difficulties, low self-efficacy, low self-sufficiency, and knowledge management problems (Bélanger & Collins, 1998; Carmel & Agarwal, 2001; Herbsleb & Montra, 2001; Jarvenpaa & Leidner, 1999; Kraut, Steinfield, Chan, Butler, & Hoag, 1999). These challenges are especially critical in the case of software development where communication and coordination are paramount. Large scale software development requires knowledge from multiple domains, thinly spread among different developers (Curtis et al. 1988). Thus this is an environment requiring a high degree of knowledge integration and coordination of efforts on the part of multiple developers (Brooks

Please use the following format when citing this chapter:

Annabi, H., Crowston, K., and Heckman, R., 2006, in IFIP International Federation for Information Processing, Volume 203, Open Source Systems, eds. Damiani, E., Fitzgerald, B., Scacchi, W., Scotto, M., Succi, G., (Boston: Springer), pp. 77-90

1975). This is of particular importance for OSS teams as contributions come not only from the core developers but from all the co-developers and active users as well.

Accordingly, to minimize the negative effects mentioned above, OSS core groups must learn effective communication and coordination practices suitable to their new environment. In their study of distributed cross-functional teams, Robey et al. (2000) suggest that to be successful, distributed groups must learn. This learning has to occur on both the individual and group levels (Senge 1990; Lin and Lin 2001). However, research and practitioner communities know little about the processes of learning suitable for distributed teams (Orlikowski, 2002; Robey et al. 2000). Thus it is important to first understand the learning processes of distributed groups. According to Maier, et al. (2001), "Knowledge about the process, or the know how, of learning facilitates corrections that simulate or accelerate learning" (pg. 16).

The study had two objectives. The first was to address the gap in the literature and develop a theoretical approach to study learning process distributed groups. The second was to describe the learning processes in OSS groups and identify factors that enhance or impede this process. This paper will report on the second objective.

2   Learning in OSS Groups

To study learning in OSS groups, we draw on Huber's definition of learning: "An entity learns if... the range of its *potential behaviors is changed*" (Huber, 1991). The term behavioral potential recognizes the fact that not all outcomes of learning will be observable immediately in behavior. Rather, they will only be observable if and when appropriate circumstances arise. For example, airline pilots train to handle emergencies, but are rarely called upon to exhibit these behaviors.

To conceptualize a group's behavioral potential, we draw on Grant's (1996) knowledge-based view of the firm. In this view, a group is a structure for integrating the knowledge of its members. A group creates coordination mechanisms, such as rules and routines to economize on communication, knowledge transfer and learning (Grant 1996). In this view, rules and routines structure how members coordinate their tasks efficiently and effectively. Therefore, changes in the behavioral potential of a group will be observable in changes in these rules and routines (Hayes and Allinson, 1998).

Argyris and Schön (1978) and Brown and Duguid (1991) suggest that for a group to create or change rules and procedures it is key that its members have shared understanding or shared mental models. Shared mental models, as defined by Cannon-Bowers et al. (1993), "are knowledge structures held by members of a team that enable them to form accurate explanations and expectations for the task, and in turn, to coordinate their actions and adapt their behavior to demands of the task and other team members" (pg 228). The importance of shared mental models comes from the fact that for rules and routines to be effective coordination mechanisms, they have to be interpreted consistently on the group level. Without shared mental models individuals may interpret tasks differently based on their backgrounds (Dougherty, 1992). Shared mental models are manifested in common language, communication patterns, and consistency in interpreting and executing the rules.

In summary, we define group learning as *the process by which group members share knowledge and information and integrate it into the group's implicit and explicit rules, leading to changes in the behavioral potential of the group.* Group learning is operationalized as changes in explicit and implicit rules. We focused on changes in rules and procedures as specific indicators of explicit rules, and on changes in shared mental models as specific indicators of implicit rules. The following are the specific research questions of the study:

> RQ1: What are the characteristics of group learning process in OSS groups?
> More specifically:
> RQ1a: How do OSS groups change rules and procedures?
> RQ1b: How do OSS groups change shared mental models?
> RQ2: What are the factors that impede or enhance group learning?

3   Research Framework

In order to guide data collection and analysis, we integrated the definition of group learning, and concepts from multiple area of study including organizational learning (OL), group research, shared mental models (SMM), and asynchronous learning networks (ALN) to develop an initial theoretical framework. The initial framework was modified and refined as more data was analyzed. We represent the learning process of a group in terms of the input-process-output framework illustrated in figure 1. The model includes group structure, organizational level, and group design inputs. These inputs affect the nature of learning opportunity episodes (LOE) (triggers, process and outcomes) in the group which include the group learning process. The learning process results in group and individual learning. The framework indicates that outcomes of learning recursively affect group structure inputs.

Input Variables:

Input variables in this model include organizational context and group design variables as suggested by both Hackman (1986) and Gladstein (1984). Group structures include rules, shared mental models, and role structure. Group structure input variables are affected by outcomes of the learning process. Organizational context represented by corporate participation, which was controlled for in this case study (one case with no corporate participation). Additionally, the framework included group design variables, represented by group composition and task to illustrate effects of members' skills and knowledge and how it may influence the group process. This is also influenced by nature of task.

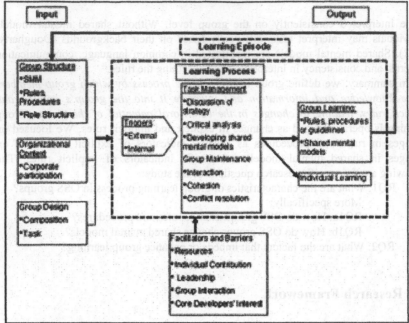

Figure 1 Refined Theoretical Framework for Learning Process in OSS Groups

Learning Opportunity Episodes (LOE):

The theoretical framework conceptualized group learning using an episodic view to bound the phenomenon as suggested by Miles and Huberman (1994). A *learning opportunity episode (LOE) is a group event that occurs over time as a result of a learning trigger. It may or may not lead to changes in the behavioral potential of the group.* The framework suggests that input variables affect group LOEs that include learning triggers and learning process, and that episodes may or may not lead to learning.

Learning Triggers:

Walton and Hackman (1986), propose that all groups must satisfy a number of important group functions (social; interpretive, task, agency, and regulative). If any of the group functions are not met, or can be met more effectively or efficiently, the group has an opportunity to learn. We refer to this opportunity as a learning trigger. As described in the results section below, an important finding of this study was a better understanding of the nature and impact of different types of learning trigger. At this point we will briefly note that learning triggers differed in terms of the type (internal or external) and focus (product or process). Internal triggers occur within the core group (e.g. errors, inconsistent interpretations). External triggers come from the external environment or the core (e.g. new technology, user requests).

Group Learning Process:

Learning is the process by which the group's potential behavior changes. We conceptualized the learning process in terms of *task management* and *group maintenance* functions. Figure 1 indicates that task management includes three aspects of group behaviors discussion of strategy, critical analysis, and developing shared mental models. Group maintenance behaviors included interaction, cohesion, and conflict resolution behaviors.

Facilitators and Barriers

Research question 3 identifies factors that impede or enhance group learning process. We included factors identified in out empirical analysis in the framework as the facilitators and barriers to LOE. These factors include resources, leadership, individual contribution, group interaction, and core developers' interests. Space does not permit a detailed presentation of these factors in this version of the paper.

Process Output

The focus of this study was on changes in rules as an explicit indicator of learning, and changes in shared mental models as an implicit indicator of learning. Observation of these outcomes was used to assess whether or not a particular episode resulted in group learning. Another outcome of group learning identified in the conceptual framework is individual learning. Due to the retrospective nature of this study, individual learning was beyond the scope of this study.

4   Methodology

This study employed a qualitative case study design to better understand the phenomenon of learning in a work setting as suggested by Miner and Mezias (1996). As Yin defines it, a case study is "an empirical inquiry that investigates a contemporary phenomenon within its real-life context; when the boundaries between phenomenon and context are not clearly evident; and in which multiple sources of evidence are used" (Yin, 1984, pg. 23). More specifically, we employed a single embedded case study design, based on theoretical sample strategy for case selection. The case for this study is the Apache httpd Project. The embedded unit of analysis LOE defined earlier.

Theoretical selection criteria in this study were group size and group effectiveness. We selected a group having more than seven core developers, a lower-limit sample as suggested by Hare (1976). The literature suggested that learning leads to effectiveness (Maier et al., 2001). This increases our chances for observing learning, the research selected an effective group previously identified as successful in the OSS literature: Apache Web Server.

A continuation of the httpd server developed by Rob McCool and the National Center for Supercomputing Applications (NCSA) "the Apache HTTP Server Project is an effort to develop and maintain an open-source HTTP server for modern operating systems" (Apache.org). After McCool left NCSA in 1994 eight of the developers started collaborating via private e-mail in 1994 and in early 1995 established a Web presence and mailing list to continue their development effort. The Apache Web server has been the most widely used Web server on the Internet since 1996, holding 64% market share in 2003 according to Netcraft Web Server Survey (http://news.netcraft.com). We observed the Apache httpd project between its inception (February 1995) and the first stable release, Apache 1.0 (December 1995); tracking the group movement from alpha to beta to stable.

We chose to bound the learning process using LOE as suggested by Miles and Huberman (1994). Behavioral potential is manifested in changes in explicit rules (from which we focused on changes in rules and procedures) and implicit rules (from which we focused on shared mental models). We considered a LOE to have no change if one month passed without a direct response to that trigger (the average between LOE times four). Explicit learning outcome was measures by identifying a change in rules or procedures in the group. Implicit learning outcome was measured by identifying group shared mental models evident in change in the code, change in agreement or course of behavior.

Figure 2 illustrates the nature of the LOE. An LOE can be selected by identifying learning triggers, indicators of learning process, or identifying explicit changes to rules. Once any of these elements was identified as being part of the LOE the related interaction messages and documentation were collected. The interaction data was analyzed using Atlas-ti, and the documentation was reviewed.

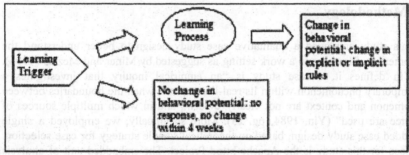

Figure 2 Learning Opportunity Episodes

4.1   Data Collection and Analysis

The study collected data surrounding each LOE from multiple related sources including interaction data, documentation, and primary and secondary source interviews. Interaction and documentation data was publicly available on Apache.org. The study also included one e-mail interview with a core developer and secondary interviews with and articles written by core developers.

We used three content analytic schemes to analyze group interaction data from mailing list. One scheme analyzed group learning process, the second the learning triggers, and the third LOE. Interviews and documentation served to corroborate findings from interaction data. The content analysis process followed Miles and Huberman's (1994) interactive model. We started the data analysis using initial content analytic schemes, but modified these schemes as new indicators emerged. Intercoder reliability tests were conducted and modifications made to the content analytic schemes until the various coders reached acceptable intercoder agreement (Baker-Brown et al., 1990) (LOE scheme (containing learning triggers scheme): 89.6% agreement; learning process: 91% agreement.)

5   Results and Discussion

The Apache group had no formal role structure, procedures, or guidelines to guide group membership, rules for task management, coding style and structure, system requirements or work plans at the start of the project in February of 1995. Individuals interested in the project joined a mailing list (new-httpd@hyperreal.com) where members contributed ideas, code, bug report and bug fixes based on needs and interests. During the period of observation, 6,649 messages were posted to the mailing list, and the group produced 38 versions of Apache as a result of 236 of patches, bug fixes, bug reports, and documentation. Figure 3 displays activity level (number of postings in the mailing list), project's stage of development and major releases overtime.

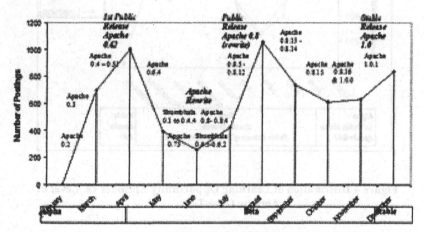

Figure 3 Group Activity in Mailing Lists over Time

Messages posted to the mailing list came from eight core developers and 46 active (co-developers) and occasional (active users) contributors[1]. Code submissions were made by the eight core developers and 24 co-developers and active users. During this period of observation we identified 178 LOE

Due to space limitations, in remainder of this section we will present selected findings that illustrate the nature of learning opportunity episodes, and the events that trigger them.

1. Group learning requires interaction

Figure 4 suggests that the distribution of LOE is correlated with the distribution of level of activity over time (number of LOE was scaled up in figure 4). This further suggests that level of group activity is important for group learning. Periods marked by limited group activity (interaction between the group members) are also associated with periods of fewer learning opportunities. A significant example of this occurred in the period between May and July. During this period, the level of group activity (measured by the number of postings to the mailing list) suggested that there was little group activity taking place. However, documentation and the content of the messages revealed that individuals were independently developing code. These individuals

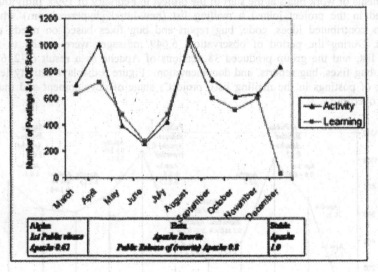

Figure 4 Distribution of Learning Opportunity Episodes vs. Level of Activity Over Time

[1] Note: the number of co-developers and active users is estimated based on our analysis of messages in learning-opportunity episodes and not the total number of messages during this period

might have learned and gained insight about the code, but the group did not learn as a result of individual knowledge. In fact, the group witnessed the least number of learning opportunity episodes during the period. Not until the group started to interact again to integrate the individual contributions did the group learn. To integrate the individual contributions, the group developed new shared mental models and coordinating mechanisms, as evident in the increase of learning in July.

2. A majority of learning opportunities had a product focus

In our analysis we discovered that learning opportunities had a focus on either developing the group *product* (e.g. writing code and documentation), developing *processes* for producing the product (e.g. contribution guidelines, voting procedures), or developing *both* product and process. Table 1 indicates that 72% of the episodes focused on developing the product. In comparison, 56% of episodes are focused on the process. This suggests that the group activities are less focused on developing processes and more focused on developing the product.

Table 1 Focus and Type of Learning Opportunity Episodes

Focus of Episode (Product vs. Process)	Type of Learning (Shared Mental Models or Rules)			Total: focus of episode
	SMM	Rule	Both	
Process	11	21	18	50
Product	64	4	11	79
Product and Process	10	0	39	49
Total: Type of Learning	85	25	68	178

3. Some opportunities produced no learning

As presented in table 2, of the 178 episodes collected, 150 led to change in behavioral potential and 28 led to no change. Most group activities provided opportunities for developing shared mental models of product and process. It is no surprise that 91% of episodes leading to learning resulted in developing shared mental models as indicated in table 2. Only 9% of learning outcomes strictly developed rules and guidelines. Developing rules and guidelines is present in 38% of episodes leading to learning. However, it is important to note that even the episodes that only lead to changes in rules displayed SMM behaviors as will be discussed later in this paper.

Table 2 Learning Outcomes

Outcome	Number	Percentage of Total Number of Episodes	Percentage of Episodes that Led to Learning
No learning	28	16%	0%
Change in shared mental model	93	51%	62%
Change in rule	14	8%	9%
Change in both rule and shared mental model	43	25%	29%
	178		

4. Product-focused episodes produce different learning than process-focused episodes

Product- focused episodes appeared to have different learning outcomes than do episodes focused on process or both process and product. Process-focused episodes, for example, have a higher probability in leading to no learning (32%) than product-focused episodes (11%) or both process and product-focused episodes (6%). This suggests that the group is more likely to ignore learning triggers that are process-focused and respond to triggers that are product-focused. Also, process-focused episodes are more likely to lead to both shared mental models and rules (33%) than product-focused episodes (13%).

Table 3 Learning Opportunity Episodes Focus and Learning Outcomes

Focus of Episode (Process or Product)	Learning Outcome				Total of focus of episode
	No Learning	Shared Mental Models	Rule	Both Rules and Shared Mental Models	
Process	16	10	10	14	50
Product	9	63	2	5	79
Product and Process	3	20	2	24	49
Total Learning Outcome	28	93	14	43	178

5. The majority of learning triggers were internal

We identified a total of 13 different types of internal and external triggers (table 4). In the 178 LOE 75% of the learning triggers were internal and 25% were external. External learning triggers were more likely (23%) to lead to no learning than internal learning triggers (13%). Internal triggers are more likely (88%) to generate complex learning episodes. This suggests that this group was less attentive to learning stimuli generated by users on the periphery.

Table 4 Frequency of Learning Triggers

Learning Trigger	Indicator	Number	Percent
External		44	25%
	User need or request*	13	7%
	New technology*	3	2%
	External expectation/ requests *	11	6%
	Offer to contribution or new member (Grant, 1996)	6	3%
	Error*	11	6%
Internal		134	75%
	Misrepresentations or gaps in understanding*	29	16%
	Conflict (Gladstein)	0	0%
	Lack of resources (Hackman)	0	0%
	Error (Argyris & Schön, 1978)	25	14%
	Share information of code and product status*	35	20%
	Efficacy of the process (Anderson et. al.)	17	10%
	Innovation in the process*	16	9%
	Innovation in the product*	12	7%

6. The group devised its own learning mechanism

An important learning trigger was the mechanism developed by the group to share information on code and product status. This mechanism was developed to ensure every member had the same understanding. A member, (often a release coordinator) would provide the group with a summary of the code and the patches with the intention of generating a discussion to clarify understanding. Other members contributed information to correct errors or omissions provided in the summary. This was an important mechanism for learning, as it addressed shared mental models about the code and about who is doing what, as well as providing grounds for deciding on to-do lists and timelines. This trigger generated 20% of all learning episodes (the largest percentage for any one learning trigger) and 35% of complex episodes

(episodes focusing on both product and process, and both shared mental models and rules).

6   Conclusion

This study had both theoretical and pragmatic implications. The theoretical implications of this research raised new insights into the study of learning in distributed work groups, and addressed several issues concerning the definition, content, outcome and process of learning in these groups. Extending what prior research suggests (Simon, 1991; Grant 1996)), the study discovered that individual learning is not sufficient to change group behavior. It must be integrated into group process and product for learning to occur. This integration is accomplished through an information intensive process that relies heavily on building shared mental models.

We also discovered that learning episodes were more likely to be triggered when the group was focused on its primary mission: (that of writing code) than when it was focused on working processes. This may not be surprising, given that in voluntary organizations such as open-source projects, many important group functions (e.g. role, status) are dependent on the action of writing code. A result that is perhaps more surprising, given claims about the egalitarian and democratic nature of open-source communities, is the fact that learning triggers originating in the periphery of the community where less active users reside were less likely to be attended to by the core. These findings suggest that deeper investigation of the social dynamics of open-source projects may reveal surprising results. Project leaders and management of distributed groups in general, may use findings from this study to improve the management and design of their groups.

References

Argyris, C. and Schön, D. (1978) *Organizational Learning,* London: Addison-Wesley.

Baker-Brown, G., Ballard, E., Bluck, S., De Veries, B., Suedfeld, P., & Tetlock, P. (1990). *Coding Manual for Conceptual/Integrative Complexity*: University of British Columbia University of California, Berkeley

Bélanger, F., & Collins, R. (1998). Distributed Work Arrangements: A Research Framework. *The Information Society, 14*(2), 137–152.

Brooks, F. P., Jr. (1975). *The Mythical Man-month: Essays on Software Engineering.* Reading, MA: Addison-Wesley

Brown, J. S., & Duguid, P. (1991). Organizational Learning and Communities-of-Practice: Toward a Unified View of Working, Learning, and Innovation. *Organization Science, 2*(1), 40–57.

Cannon-Bowers, J. A., & Salas, E. (1993). Shared Mental Models in Expert Decision Making. In *Individual and Group Decision Making*, Castellan, N.J. (Ed.). Lawrence Erlbaum Associates: Hillsdale, NJ, 221-246.

Curtis, B., Krasner, H., & Iscoe, N. (1988). A field study of the software design process for large systems. *CACM, 31*(11), 1268–1287.

Dougherty, D. (1992). Interpretive Barriers to Successful Product Innovation in Large Firms. *Organization Science, 3*(2), 179–202.

Grant, R. M. (1996). Toward a knowledge-based theory of the firm. *Strategic Management Journal, 17*(Winter), 109–122.

Gladstein, D. (1984). Groups in Context: A model of task group effectiveness. *Administrative Science Quarterly, 29*(4), 499-517

Grinter, R. E., Herbsleb, J. D., & Perry, D. E. (1999). The Geography of Coordination: Dealing with Distance in R&D Work. In *Proceedings of the GROUP '99 Conference* (pp. 306–315). Phoenix, Arizona, US.

Hackman, J. R. (1986). The design of work teams. In J. W. Lorsch (Ed.), *The Handbook of Organizational Behavior* (pp. 315–342). Englewood Cliffs, NJ: Prentice-Hall.

Hayes, J. and Allison, C. (1998) Cognitive Style and the Theory and Practice of Individual and Collective Learning in Organizations, *Human Relation,* 51(7).

Herbsleb, J. D. & Moitra, D. (2001). Global Software Development. *IEEE Software* (March/April), 16–20.

Huber, G.P. (1991). Organizational Learning: The contribution processes and the Literatures. *Organization Science.* 2(1): 88-115.

Jarvenpaa, S. L., & Leidner, D. E. (1999). Communication and trust in global virtual teams. *Organization Science, 10*(6), 791–815

Kraut, R. E., Steinfield, C., Chan, A. P., Butler, B., & Hoag, A. (1999). Coordination and virtualization: The role of electronic networks and personal relationships. *Organization Science, 10*(6), 722–740.

Lin, F. & Lin S. (2001) A Conceptual Model for Virtual Organizational Learning, *Journal of Organizational Computing and Electronic Commerce,* Vol. 11(3), Pg. 155-178.

Maier, G.W., Prange, C. and Rosenstiel, L. 2001, Psychological Perspective of Organizational Learning, in M. Dierkes, A. Berthoin Antal, J. Child, and I. Nonaka (eds.), *Handbook of Organizational Learning and Knowledge*, New York, Oxford Press, 14-34.

Miles, M. B., & Huberman, A. (1994). *Qualitative Data Analysis: An Expanded Sourcebook.* Thousand Oaks, CA: Sage

Miner, A.S. and Mezias, S.J. (1996), Ugly Duckling No More: Pasts and Futures of Organizational learning, *Organization Science,* 7(1): 88-99.

Orlikowski, W. J. (2002). Knowing in Practice: Enacting a Collective Capability in Distributed Organizing. *Organization Science, 13*(3), 249–273

Robey, D., Khoo, H. M., & Powers, C. (2000). Situated-learning in cross-functional virtual teams. *IEEE Transactions on Professional Communication* (Feb/Mar), 51–66.

Senge, P. (1990). *The Fifth Discipline: The art and practice of the learning organization.* London: Random House.

Simon, H. A. (1991). Bounded Rationality and Organizational Learning. *Organization Science, 2*, 125-134

Walton, R. E., & Hackman, J. R. (1986). Groups Under Contrasting Management Stratedies. In P. S. G. a. Associates (Ed.), *Designing Effective Work Groups* (pp. 168-201). San Francisco, CA: Jossey-Bass.

Yin, R. (1984). *Case Study Research*. Beverly Hills, CA: Sage Publications Inc.

The role of mental models in FLOSS development work practices[a]

Kevin Crowston[1] and Barbara Scozzi[2]

1 Syracuse University, Syracuse (USA), crowston@syr.edu
2 Politecnique of Bari, Italy, bscozzi@poliba.it

Abstract. Shared understandings are important for software development as they guide to effective individual contributions to, and coordination of, the software development process. In this paper, we present the theoretical background and research design for a proposed study on shared mental models within Free/Libre Open Source Software (FLOSS) development teams. In particular, we plan to perform case studies on several projects and to use cognitive maps analysis to represent and compare the mental models of the involved members so as to gauge the degree of common knowledge and the development of a collective mind as well as to better understand the reasons that underlie team members actions and the way common mental models, if any, arise.

1. Introduction

This paper examines the role of shared mental models in work practices, i.e., the way people coordinate, communicate, learn and make decisions, and the way such models emerge within Free/Libre Open Source Software (FLOSS) development teams. The difficulties of distributed software development are emphasized in the literature on software development and distributed teams ([1]; [2]). The lack of a common organizational setting or functional background can make socialization, communication and coordination processes difficult, so reducing team performance and increasing the need for explicit coordination and learning among members ([3]; [4]). Languages and cultural differences can lead to misunderstanding, reducing the effectiveness of communications ([5]; [6, p.1]). Furthermore, because teams rely on computer-mediated communication, it can be difficult for members to develop the informal relationships and communications necessary to address interpersonal issues [7] . However, the case of FLOSS development presents an intriguing counter-example. Effective FLOSS development teams somehow profit from the advantages and evade the challenges of distributed software development [8].

To understand the origin of work practices, we focus specifically on the role of mental models (e.g., conceptions of the project, other team members, users, competitors or programming standards) that guide team members' behaviours and shape their actions. In this paper, we present the theoretical background and research design for a proposed study on shared mental models. The goals of the study are 1) finding evidence for the existence of shared mental models that shape team work practices and

[a] This research was partially supported by NSF Grants 03-41475, 04-14468 and 05-27457. Any opinions, findings, and conclusions or recommendations expressed in this material are those of the authors and do not necessarily reflect the views of the National Science Foundation.

Please use the following format when citing this chapter:

Crowston, K., and Scozzi, B., 2006, in IFIP International Federation for Information Processing, Volume 203, Open Source Systems, eds. Damiani, E., Fitzgerald, B., Scacchi, W., Scotto, M., Succi, G., (Boston: Springer), pp. 91-97

2) trying to assess how such models arise. The study is part of a larger research project aimed to identify the dynamics through which self-organizing distributed teams develop and work.

2. Theory: Mental models and software development

Shared mental models, as defined by Cannon-Bowers and Salas [9, p. 228] "are knowledge structures held by members of a team that enable them to form accurate explanations and expectations for the task, and in turn, to coordinate their actions and adapt their behavior to demands of the task and other team members". Research suggests that shared mental models help improve performance in face-to-face [10] and distributed teams [11]. Shared mental models can enable teams to coordinate their activities without the need for explicit communications ([12]; [13]). Without shared mental models, individuals from different teams or backgrounds may interpret tasks differently based on their individual backgrounds, so making collaboration and communication difficult [14]. The tendency for individuals to interpret tasks according to their own perspectives and predefined routines is exacerbated when working in a distributed environment, with its more varied individual settings.

Studies have identified the importance of shared understanding for software development ([15]; [16]). Curtis et al. [7, p.52], note that "a fundamental problem in building large systems is the development of a common understanding of the requirements and design across the project team." They go on to say that, "the transcripts of team meetings reveal the large amounts of time designers spend trying to develop a shared model of the design". The problem of developing shared mental models is likely to particularly affect FLOSS development, since FLOSS team members are distributed, have diverse backgrounds, and join FLOSS teams in different phases of the software development process ([17]; [18]). In short, shared mental models are important as guides to effective individual contributions to, and coordination of, the software development process.

Based on [19], we identify socialization, conversation and recapitulation as the means through which shared mental models are built. First, new members joining a team learn how they fit into the process being performed through socialization, e.g., by following a "joining script" [20]. Members need to be encouraged and educated to interact with one another so as to develop a strong sense of "how we do things around here". Barley and Tolbert [20 p. 100] similarly note that socialization frequently "involves an individual internalizing rules and interpretations of behaviour appropriate for particular settings". Second, conversation is critical in developing shared mental models. It is difficult to build shared mental models if people do not talk to one another and use common language. Meetings, social events, hallway conversations and electronic mail or conferencing are all ways in which team members can get in touch with what others are doing and thinking (interestingly though, many of these modes are not available to FLOSS teams). Finally, [19] stress the importance of recapitulation. To keep shared mental models strong and viable, important events must be "replayed", reanalyzed, and shared with newcomers. The history that defines who we are and how we do things around here must be continually reinforced, reinterpreted, and updated.

Most of the existing studies on shared mental models remain conceptual, though a few empirical studies in this area have investigated the relationship between team or organizational factors and the presence of shared mental models. However, while increasing attention has been lately devoted to the topics of knowledge creation, knowledge sharing and learning within the FLOSS development teams, (e.g. [22], [13]; [23]) to our knowledge no other studies have yet looked in detail at shared mental models for FLOSS development. For example, [23] focus on how knowledge is created and shared based on a case study, the KDE project. However, the study does not specifically examine which process aspects/practices are/are not shared and how extensive the sharing process is. [13] try to assess the importance of shared mental models for project coordination, but do not directly investigate the presence of shared mental models. Our project will therefore address this gap in the literature.

3. Research methodology

In this section, we describe the research methodology we will be adopting for the study. To achieve our goal, we plan to perform case studies on several FLOSS projects. In order to ensure that we are studying team large enough to have interesting work dynamics, we have selected projects with more than seven core developers. Different FLOSS projects are being examined and the attendant team members contacted. All the team members of the projects willing to take part to the study will be interviewed.

Interviews will be based on a semi-structured protocol designed to identify how team members interpret their role and the other members' roles, how they act and the reasons for their behaviours, eventual tacit norms and practices and the way such practices have arisen. To address the first set of concerns, the interview protocol will be organized in the following sections.

- *Developer demographics.* Descriptive data about developers, such as areas of expertise, formal role, years with the project, other projects in which they participate as well as perception of their role and other members' role in the project.
- *Project rules and norms.* Any explicitly stated norms or rule as perceived by developers.
- *Project environment and constraints.* The environment in which the team operates, constraints that they have to deal with, customers and competitors.
- *Development strategy.* The overall approach to project development.
- *Development process.* Process by which the software is developed (activities, dependencies, coordination mechanisms), tools and technology used for software development, as well as to submit and handle bugs, patches and feature requests, decision-making processes.
- *Team organization.* Team structure and specific team roles.

- *Socialization conversation and recapitulation.* Actions related to socialization, conversation and recapitulation as perceived by developers.

As to the latter aspects, in the interviews we will identify specific actions that can help building shared mental models. Therefore, the interview protocol will assess how and if socialization, conversation and recapitulation occur within the teams.

4. Analysis: Cognitive mapping techniques

Interview transcriptions will be analyzed using cognitive mapping techniques [24]. Cognitive maps are graphic tools used to represent concepts and ideas a person associates to a given issue (i.e., the topic of the map). Cognitive maps can be used with an explicative, a predictive, and/or a reflective purpose [25]. In this project, cognitive maps will be adopted for an explicative purpose, i.e., finding evidence of the existence of shared mental models, the way models shape team work practices and arise within FLOSS development teams.

Different methodologies have been proposed in the literature to develop cognitive maps. For data collection, the main approach consists of the administration of semi-structured interviews ([26], [27]). Some scholars have also developed more structured schemes [28] or models to make people self-interview, e.g. the self-Q technique by Bougon [29]. To develop maps, documents can also be used rather than interviews.

Based on the interview text, maps will be created by using a technique called Documentary Coding Method [30], which involves identifying the main concepts cited by the respondents and the relationships among them. A cognitive map is characterized by two ontologies, namely concepts and causal links among them [24]. Concepts represent ideas, opinions and key issues associated to the topic of the map. Concepts are linked by causal relationships, which can be mainly distinguished in cause/effect (which do not imply intentionality) or means/end relationships. Concepts are graphically represented by nodes and relationships by arrows. Concepts that represent the cause or the means to achieve a given goal are situated at the arrow's tail, concepts that represent the effect or the end at the arrow's head.

Different methodologies to analyze and compare maps also exist. In most studies quali-quantitative metrics, e.g. number of heads, tails, domain and centrality, are used [31]. Ad hoc metrics have also been defined to compare maps. The most well-known have been developed by [32]. In our study, maps will be analyzed by measuring/examining at least the following quali-quantitative metrics:

- *Map complexity.* It is given by the number of concepts on the map and the link/concept ratio.
- *Heads and Tails* Map heads are concepts represented by nodes that only have arrows going inside. They represent developers' final end/goal and/or the effects of their perception. Tails are concepts represented by nodes that only have arrows going outside. They explain/describe the causes of some perceptions and/or means to be adopted to achieve goals.

- *Domain and Centrality.* Domain and centrality provide information about the importance of concepts. In particular, a concept domain is given by the number of direct links. On the contrary, by the centrality analysis both direct or indirect links are used to assess the importance of concepts, so providing information on those concepts that are often unconsciously considered as the most relevant.
- *Sets.* Sets are groups of concepts that deal with a specific issue or topic. By counting the number of concepts mentioned in the maps for each set it is possible to assess the importance/complexity associated to the object of the set. We also will investigate the characteristics of concepts within sets (i.e. the number of heads, goals, and domain and centrality).

Through cognitive maps analysis we will be able to represent and compare the mental models of the developers about the project and project team so as to gauge the degree of common knowledge and the development of a collective mind as well as to better understand the reasons that underlie team members actions and the dynamics based on which common mental models, if any, arise ([24]; [33]; [34]). We can also examine the distribution of these models, e.g., which parts of the model are shared by most team members and which are common only among the core developers.

The main benefit that derives from the adoption of the maps is the ease of the analysis of different perspectives. The graphical representation facilitates identification of the key issues and the differences among different positions. Moreover, the adopted metrics facilitate the understanding of concepts or relationships not perfectly clear or conscious to individuals. These relationships can be more easily stressed than is the case when other qualitative tools (such as case studies or simple interviews) are used.

Of course, cognitive maps also present some drawbacks. In particular, the stage of the knowledge elicitation (interviews and codification of collected data) is the most critical. This observation is based on the difficulties we encountered in other projects during map development [e.g. 35]. Such consideration is also broadly discussed in the literature. As most of the qualitative research methodologies, the knowledge schemes of the interviewer (i.e., the researcher) can strongly influence the findings. By knowledge scheme we mean the culture, interests and experiences of the interviewer. The researcher's knowledge scheme can influence the way questions are asked (so influencing the answers) and, above all, the way data are analyzed. As already mentioned, there exist some techniques that try to reduce the subjectivity, but they introduce other sources of error [32]. For example, by providing an ex-ante defined list of possible constructs and concepts (though in some cases they can be extended by respondents) the answer possibility of the respondents is limited and can be biased. Based on our previous experience, we have decided to adopt semi-structured interviews so trying to minimize the effects of biases. Despite the drawbacks, we argue that cognitive maps can be effectively used to identify the mental models of the FLOSS team members and to assess if they are shared and how they affect work practices.

5. Expected results

The proposed study will have conceptual, methodological as well as practical contributions. The study fills a gap in the literature with an in-depth investigation of the mental models of FLOSS teams. Furthermore, we will use cognitive maps, which have never been used to investigate mental models within FLOSS development teams. The project will advance knowledge and understanding of FLOSS development and distributed work more generally by understanding the role and the extent of shared mental models within the teams. Understanding the dynamics of action in the teams is important to improve the effectiveness of FLOSS teams, software development teams, and distributed teams in general. As distributed teams are increasingly adopted by firms for a wide range of knowledge work, the study results can indeed be useful for managers willing to adopt distributed teams in their own organization.

References

[1] Bélanger, F. (1998). Telecommuters and Work Groups: A Communication Network Analysis. In Proceedings of the International Conference on Information Systems (ICIS) (pp. 365–369). Helsinki, Finland.

[2] Carmel, E., & Agarwal, R. (2001). Tactical approaches for alleviating distance in global software development. IEEE Software(March/April), 22–29.

[3] Finholt, T., Sproull, L., & Kiesler, S. (1990). Communication and Performance in Ad Hoc Task Groups. In J. Galegher, R. F. Kraut & C. Egido (Eds.), Intellectual Teamwork. Hillsdale, NJ: Lawrence Erlbaum and Associates.

[4] Robey, D., Khoo, H. M., & Powers, C. (2000). Situated-learning in cross-functional virtual teams. IEEE Transactions on Professional Communication(Feb/Mar), 51–66.

[5] . D. Herbsleb, A. Mockus, T. A. Finholt, and R. E. Grinter, "An Empirical Study of Global Software Development: Distance and Speed," in Proceedings of the International Conference on Software Engineering (ICSE 2001). Toronto, Canada, 2001, pp. 81–90.

[6] Massey, A. P., Hung, Y.-T. C., Montoya-Weiss, M., & Ramesh, V. (2001). When Culture and Style Aren't About Clothes: Perceptions of Task-Technology "Fit" in Global Virtual Teams. In Proceedings of GROUP '01. Boulder, CO, USA.

[7] Curtis, B., Walz, D., & Elam, J. J. (1990). Studying the process of software design teams. In Proceedings of the 5th International Software Process Workshop On Experience With Software Process Models (pp. 52–53). Kennebunkport, Maine, United States.

[8] Alho, K., & Sulonen, R. (1998). Supporting virtual software projects on the Web. 7th International Workshop on Enabling Technologies: Infrastructure for Collaborative Enterprises (Wetice 98).

[9] Cannon-Bowers, J. A., & Salas, E. (1993). Shared mental models in expert decision making. In N. J. Castellan (Ed.), Individual and Group Decision Making (pp. 221-246). Hillsdale, NJ: Lawrence Erlbaum Associates.

[10] Rentsch, J. R., & Klimonski, R. J. (2001). Why do 'great minds' think alike?: Antecedents of team member schema agreement. Journal of Organizational Behavior, 22(2), 107–120.

[11] Sutanto, J., Kankanhalli, A., & Tan, B. C. Y. (2004). Task coordination in global virtual teams. Paper presented at the Twenty-Fifth International Conference on Information Systems, Washington, DC.

[12] Crowston, K., & Kammerer, E. (1998). Coordination and collective mind in software requirements development. IBM Systems Journal, 37(2), 227–245.

[13] Espinosa, J. A., Kraut, R. E., Lerch, J. F., Slaughter, S. A., Herbsleb, J. D., & Mockus, A. (2001). Shared mental models and coordination in large-scale, distributed software development. Paper presented at the Twenty-Second International Conference on Information Systems, New Orleans, LA.

[14] Dougherty, D. (1992). Interpretive barriers to successful product innovation in large firms. Organization Science, 3(2), 179–202.

[15] Levesque, L. L., Wilson, J. M., & Wholey, D. R. (2001). Cognitive divergence and shared mental models in software development project teams. Journal of Organization Behavior, 22, 135–144.

[16] Sagers, G. W., Wasko, M. M., & Dickey, M. H. (2004). Coordinating Efforts in Virtual Communities: Examining Network Governance in Open Source. Paper presented at the Tenth Americas Conference on Information Systems, New York, NY.

[17] Edwards, K. (2001, June 11–12). Epistemic communities, situated learning and Open Source Software development. Paper presented at the Epistemic Cultures and the Practice of Interdisciplinarity Workshop, NTNU, Trondheim.

[18] Gasser, L., & Ripoche, G. (2003). Distributed Collective Practices and F/OSS Problem Management: Perspective and Methods. Conference on Cooperation, Innovation & Technologie (CITE2003), University de Technologie de Troyes, France.

[19] Brown, J. S., & Duguid, P. (1991). Organizational learning and communities-of-practice: Toward a unified view of working, learning, and innovation. Organization Science, 2(1), 40–57.

[20] von Krogh, G., Spaeth, S., & Lakhani, K. R. (2003). Community, Joining, and Specialization in Open Source Software Innovation: A Case Study. Research Policy, 32(7), 1217–1241.

[21] Barley, S. R., & Tolbert, P. S. (1997). Institutionalization and structuration: Studying the links between action and institution. Organization Studies, 18(1), 93–117.

[22] Lanzara, G. F., & Morner, M. (2003). The Knowledge Ecology of Open-Source Software Projects. Paper presented at the 19th EGOS Colloquium, Copenhagen.

[23] Hemetsberger, A., & Reinhardt, C. (2004). Sharing and Creating Knowledge in Open-Source Communities: The case of KDE. Paper presented at the The Fifth European Conference on Organizational Knowledge, Learning, and Capabilities, Innsbruck, AU.

[24] Pidd, M. (1996). Tools for thinking modeling management science. Chichester: John Wiley and Sons.

[25] Codara, L. (1998). Le mappe cognitive, uno strumento di analisi per la ricerca sociale e per l'intervento organizzativo. Rome. Carocci Editore.

[26] Eden, C. (1988). Cognitive mapping. European Journal of Operational Research, 36, 1–13.

[27] Laukkanen, M. (1998). Conducting causal mapping research: Opportunities and challenges. In C. Eden & J.-C. Spender (Eds.), Managerial and organizational cognition: Theory, methods and research (pp. 168–191). Thousand Oaks, CA: Sage.

[28] Cossette, P. (1994). Cartes cognitives et organizations. Paris: Eska.

[29] Bougon, M. G. (1983). Uncovering cognitive maps: the Self-Q technique. In G. Morgan (Ed.), Beyond method: Strategies for social research. Beverly Hills, CA: Sage.

[30] Wrightson M.T., (1976). The documentary coding method, in Axelrod R. (ed.), Structure of Decision. The cognitive maps of political elites, Princeton (NJ), Princeton University Press.

[31] Cossette P., Audet M., 1992, Mapping of an idiosyncratic schema, Journal of Management Studies, vol.29, n.3, pp. 325-347.

[32] Markoczy L., Goldberg J., 1995, A method of eliciting and comparing causal maps, Journal of management, vol.21 n.2, pp. 305-333.

[33] Carley, K. M. (1997). Extracting team mental models through textual analysis. Journal of Organizational Behaviour, 18, 533–558.

[34] Carley, K. M., & Palmquist, M. (1992). Extracting, representing and analyzing mental models. Social Forces, 70(3), 601–636.

[35] Albino V., Kuhtz S., Scozzi B. (2004). Cognitive maps on sustainable development in industrial districts: a pilot study, in Johansson B., Karlsson C., Stough, R.R. (eds.), Industrial Clusters and Inter-Firm Networks, Elgar Publ., 149-170, ISBN: 1-84542-010-1.

A Robust Open Source Exchange for Open Source Software Development

Amit Basu

Cox School of Business, SMU
Dallas, TX 75275-0333, USA
abasu@smu.edu

Abstract. This paper addresses the development of mechanisms for the creation of OSSD exchanges that could be used by developers across any geographical range, as long as all the developers can interact via some open network infrastructure such as the Internet. The structure of these exchanges can range from public repositories such as Sourceforge.net to intra-organizational forums for software development within an enterprise. We examine in particular the structure of an exchange model based on protocols for a robust online marketplace.

1 Introduction

Open source software development (OSSD) thrives upon the ability to collaborate with other developers, and to reuse existing code developed by others. Thus, mechanisms for knowledge sharing and search are key resources for such development processes. Effective search requires mechanisms to learn about the availability of code segments that can be useful components in system development, and to obtain those segments when relevant. Effective knowledge sharing requires mechanisms that are sensitive to identities, roles and needs of each participant in the collaborative processes in OSSD.

This paper addresses the development of mechanisms for the creation of OSSD exchanges that could be used by developers across any geographical range, as long as all the developers can interact via some open network infrastructure such as the Internet. The structure of these exchanges can range from public repositories such as Sourceforge.net to intra-organizational forums for software development within an enterprise.

The different types of exchange or repository vary in terms of their support for key processes, and the paper surveys some of the key differences. It then examines one specific type of exchange in particular. The key feature of this exchange, which we call a robust open source exchange (ROSE), is that it enables individuals in specific roles (and groups) to interact in a way that provides them full control over disclosure of information, including identity information. At the same time, it provides robust mechanisms for accountability, so that anyone attempting fraud and/or deception can be reliably disclosed.

While the ability to withhold identity and information may seem counter to the open exchange philosophy underlying OSSD, it has some significant merits when

Please use the following format when citing this chapter:

Basu, A., 2006, in IFIP International Federation for Information Processing, Volume 203, Open Source Systems, eds. Damiani, E., Fitzgerald, B., Scacchi, W., Scotto, M., Succi, G., (Boston: Springer), pp. 99-108

implemented appropriately. The key consideration is that each participating individual controls their information and its disclosure, rather than the exchange itself, its owner, or any third party. Also, such an exchange provides a vital qualification procedure that can promote greater confidence in knowledge sharing and accountability.

2   Key ideas underlying OSSD

Perhaps the best characterization of open source software is in terms of the Open Source Definition [Perens, 1999], which lays out the following features that a program must have to qualify as an open source program:

- Free distribution
- Availability of source code
- Creation and distribution of derived works
- Integrity of each author's source code
- No discrimination against persons or groups
- No discrimination against fields of endeavor
- Distribution of license to all parties who obtain the program

On the other hand, in the enterprise context, while the merits of OSSD are desirable [Persson et al, 2005] the following considerations are important determinants of application development strategy:

- The ability to maintain control over intellectual property as well as applications that are strategic.
- The ability to ensure that developers are trustworthy and have no malicious intent.
- The ability to acquire necessary software development resources without disclosing identities and purposes to the general public (or to competitors).
- The ability to hold developers accountable for their work.
- The ability to set up development projects with schedule, quality and functionality stipulations that can be monitored and controlled.

These two sets of features are completely consistent with an approach that factors in reliability and security as requisites of the software development environment. In the setting of enterprise applications, and particularly with specialized applications having limited applicability across a broad population, an interesting approach to consider is an exchange, which allows providers and users of open-source software to find each other. Note that users may themselves be developers, and also note that the exchange may involve payment or not. Furthermore, the exchange may also be used to assemble the relevant distributed development team, in which specific individuals or groups are assigned roles such as coder, maintainer, GUI Designer, documenter, etc.

Related Work

The idea of using market mechanisms as a basis for either the development or execution of computer programs is not new. In the realm of program control and execution, one of the most interesting approaches is based on the notion of agoric systems (from the Greek work "agora", which refers to a meeting place or market) [Miller and Drexler, 1988]. Computer-based systems and programs can be organized as agoric systems both in the small and in the large. The basis for the former is that software objects encapsulated with rational decision-making methods, can achieve meaningful execution of computer-based systems, when allowed to interact within the structure of a decentralized control mechanism that functions according to the rules of a well-structured marketplace. These rules respond to varying priorities of the autonomous objects, orderly contention for scarce resources such as processors, memory, storage and channels. This conceptualization is not directly related to software development. However, agoric systems can also be modeled in the large, namely at the level of the collection of resources that together construct a program or system. In other words, a collection of developers cooperating with each other in a democratic fashion can also be organized to interact according to the rules of a marketplace. In traditional software development, some of the insights derived from such approaches can be applied to the organization of third-party software development, or "contract programming" and outsourcing. Examples of economic models of such contexts include [Whang, 1992], [Whang, 1995], [Gopal, 2003]

There have also been a number of papers on market-based models for OSSD, on the notion that OSSD inherently relies upon a highly distributed and decentralized organizational model. One of the most interesting perspectives on this issue is presented in [Raymond, 2001], in which the hierarchical control structure of proprietary software development is contrasted with the more "bazaar"-like market-oriented model of OSSD.

Types of Exchanges for OSSD

Perhaps the earliest form of online exchange for OSSD was the online bulletin board and list-servers. These are largely un-moderated sites that allow relatively free access and participation, with relatively few controls and/or rules. While these are useful and inclusive, they don't scale well, and can easily be corrupted with irrelevant and/or unqualified contributions and even disruptive content. Also, the primary focus of these sites is on email-type interaction, and theus they do not have cataloged repositories for code, tolls, etc.

A popular approach to collaborative software development is the use of community-based software exchanges such as GNUenterprise.org [Scacchi, 2005]. In these community sites, there is little or no central control, although there are roles and protocols for interaction and participation. These have largely evolved from online bulletin boards and list-servers, and are largely directed at individual developers.

Another, related type of exchange is a community-oriented exchange that is developed by an OSS vendor. Strictly speaking, many of the exchanges that position themselves as community sites fall into this category. These include SourceForge.net, Eclipse and NetBeans.org [Jensen and Scacchi, 2005b]. The problem with such exchanges is that while the sponsorship of a major stakeholder (the vendor sponsor) promotes participation by individuals, the existence of competitive threats discourages institutional participation, by the sponsor's competitors for instance.

In all these approaches, the primary focus is on the individual developer/coder, rather than institutional participation. Therein lies a major challenge for moving OSSD from the fringes of mainstream software development to a forum and approach for enterprise-level and strategic software tools and applications. It is this challenge that we attempt to address with the proposal in this paper, namely the idea of a Robust Open Source Exchange.

3   A Robust Open Source Exchange (ROSE) Model

In this section, we describe a model for a robust open source exchange (ROSE) based on a set of protocols developed for robust online marketplaces, in [Kalvenes and Basu, 2005]. The protocols were designed to support the following features:

1. Participants in the marketplace have to qualify, through an authentication process conducted by a trustee. The qualification process can also include multiple levels (akin to credit ratings), so that traders can participate in a particular transaction (say at a given value ($) level) only if they are qualified to do so.
2. Buyers and sellers can transact through the marketplace without disclosing their identities or the details of their trades to anyone else, including the operator of the marketplace.
3. Since the marketplace operator has no competitive advantage over other traders, both the operator as well as its competitors can participate in transactions without fear of disclosure of transactions or strategies.
4. Although transactions can be anonymous to everyone other than its participants, any trader who commits fraud can be held accountable and identified by the marketplace operator and trustee.
5. Trader performance in the marketplace can be rewarded, so that trader qualifications can be modified over time.

The OSSD context is different from the transactional marketplace context described above. However, there are important similarities as well. Each of the above features can be reexamined in the OSSD context as follows:

1. Participants in a ROSE have to establish their credentials and be authenticated. This authentication process can also be used to qualify the participant for specific role. For instance, a relatively inexperienced programmer may be qualified to be a coder/contributor, but not a project lead or a tester/SQA (software quality analyst). Note that this in no way violates the spirit of the open software development "bazaar" [Raymond, 2001]. It merely ensures that users of code can trust that the providers are competent.

2. Users can post projects/requirements without disclosing who they are, and providers can bid for the contracts anonymously. At the same time, the qualification system ensures that only qualified bidders can post bids. The bids can be not only for code contribution, but also for other roles (e.g., project lead, tester, maintainer, etc). This is an important consideration if OSSD is to effectively penetrate the corporate software development market. While companies may be open to sharing code and related resources with the software development community, they are unlikely to want to share information about their software development needs and efforts with competitors. By keeping its identity secret during the negotiation phase of engaging external developers, a company can avoid prematurely revealing strategic intents to their competitors. On the other hand, this feature may also be very important for developers. For instance, many OSS developers are professionals who are employed by firms that are not supporters of OSSD, or are committed to proprietary platforms and systems. Such individuals may not be able to participate and contribute to OSSD if their companies knew of this. Protecting their identities while at the same time supporting authentication of their technical capabilities and credentials may be a necessary condition for their participation.

3. The privacy mechanisms and prevention of information asymmetry enables anyone to set up a ROSE, including an entity/firm that is itself a software developer. This is also important, since it has traditionally been difficult for enterprises to achieve the dual goals of having both broad participation in an exchange (which is easier when potential participants know that the exchange will give them access to large and important entities) and prevention of competitive exploitation (the threat of which is greater when a potential participant's competitor is the owner/operator of the exchange).

4. Users can be assured that any provider who bids on a job and wins a contract cannot refute on the commitment even if their identity is not disclosed to the ROSE authority at transaction time. The authority can identify the errant participant through a robust protocol. At the same time, the same protocol cannot be used improperly by the authority itself, without disclosure to the community. Once again, this is an important capability. If companies and individuals are to trust the exchange as a reliable means of connecting with qualified partners, there has to be adequate accountability. At the very least, anyone who violates the

codes of conduct must be identifiable, and held accountable. A common assumption in OSSD is that the openness of the community facilitates poor quality to be detected and problems to be resolved very efficiently due to the viral nature of the development process. While this may be acceptable for certain types of applications and projects, it is inadequate for enterprise-level projects. Therefore a positive feature of the ROSE approach is that it provides support for accountability and substantial recourse for dispute resolution.

5. As providers gain experience and credentials, they can be qualified at higher levels based on their track record at the ROSE. This is particularly important in a setting where individual participants want to offer their services through the exchange. The qualification level at which an individual enters the exchange may be different from their capabilities and credentials after gaining experience on one or more projects. The ability to re-qualify developers at higher levels thus is highly desirable. At the same time, if the identities of developers cannot always be revealed, the rewarding process has to work within those constraints. A positive feature of the ROSE approach is that this is supported as well.

We next describe how the following key processes can be implemented in a ROSE model:

- Registration and qualification of new participants
- Posting of a project RFP (request for proposal) by a prospective consumer
- Posting of bids by prospective providers in response to a project RFP
- Completion of a contract on a project
- Protection of intellectual property

In terms of the degree and scope of anonymity in the ROSE, any or all of the following modalities are possible:

1. Provider (P) and user (U) both disclose their identities throughout the process to everyone.
2. P discloses identity to everyone along with his offer, and U remains private.
3. Both P and U remain anonymous to the rest of the system throughout
4. Both P and U remain anonymous to both the system and to each other throughout.

While any and all of the above modalities may be desirable to support in a ROSE, in this paper we focus on the last case, where the highest level of privacy is desired. Each of the other cases can be supported by methods that are relaxations of the method proposed here.

Protocols for Anonymous Contracting

To start with, a new participant has to register at the ROSE, and be qualified at a certain level. This is done by the applicant obtaining a reliable digital certificate from a credible authority (e.g., a certificate authority firm such as Verisign or AT&T), and proof of qualifications in the form of a resume, transcripts, and endorsements from employers and/or customers. These are provided electronically to a trustee entity. The trustee is a firm or entity that works with the exchange operator, but may be totally independent. The trustee examines the application and supporting materials, and then provides the applicant with a software module (or client-side applet) called a certificate management system (CMS). This module resides and runs on the participant's computer, and enables them to participate in the exchange. Note that while we assume that the CMS is resident on a specific client machine, in principle it could be a mobile module that the participant could keep with them and attach to any machine that they use to access the exchange.

The CMS then generates a number of digital certificates for the participant for use in online transactions on the exchange. These certificates identify the participant, and include their credentials. The CMS blinds these certificates [Schneier, 1996], and then transmits them to the trustee, who then selects an arbitrary but substantial number of the certificates for examination. The trustee requests the blinding key for these certificates from the participant's CMS, and then un-blinds and examines the certificates (opening the certificates with the public key from the participant's original digital certificate). If satisfied that the certificates are all authentic and valid, the trustee then signs the remaining blinded certificates, and returns them to the participant. The participant's CMS then un-blinds the signed certificates, which can then be used as validated certificates for transacting on the exchange. Note that this process ensures that only authenticated entities can participate in the exchange, but neither the trustee, nor the exchange operator can track the participant's behavior on the exchange, since the trustee does not know which specific certificates are being used in each transaction (or who they belong to), and the exchange operator cannot open the transaction certificates, since it does not have the relevant public key.

During the transaction process, each participant (whether a developer bidding on a project or a company offering a project) provides a valid transaction certificate with each message sent to the exchange. These interactions between the different parties can be in the "public domain", in the sense that they are all posted on the exchange and are visible to all participants accessing the exchange and participating in that transaction's negotiation. When at some point there is a convergence between the relevant parties to a commitment to a contract, the parties can exchange signed messages that allow them to continue further communications in a fully attributed manner (i.e., they can identify themselves to each other).

A key feature of this process is that each of the parties has full control of how much information they divulge about themselves, and to whom, as well as when. This is an important consideration in an exchange where control of privacy may be a key constraint.

In the event of any conflict or misconduct, the other party can ask the exchange operator to identify and confront (and/or prosecute) the responsible party. Clearly, this is difficult to do in a setting where neither the trustee nor the operator knows the identities of the parties in any individual transaction. However, we have developed a robust method for this, in [Kalvenes and Basu, 2005]. It is robust, but expensive, since it involves a possibly large number of participants. In the commercial marketplace context, this can be addressed effectively by requiring each participant to put up a substantial escrow deposit held by the marketplace operator. However, this may be impractical in the OSSD setting. In this case, an alternative "penalty" may be blacklisting by the community and expulsion from the exchange.

Another consideration is the revision of developer qualifications based on performance. Again, using techniques developed in [Kalvenes and Basu, 2005], each developer can be given tokens by the exchange and/or the customer for each successful project, and can redeem these tokens with the trustee to revise their credentials.

Additional Considerations for OSSD

The above approach provides an innovative way to build and operate an online exchange for OSSD. However, there are some additional considerations in a ROSE setting that are worth examining. For instance, a big component of the value proposition of any software exchange is the repository of OSS code that is developed by participants, and which can be revised and further developed by other participants. As it turns out, support for this is completely consistent with the ROSE model. Note that the privacy concerns that motivate the ROSE model are driven by the strategic implications of tying applications to the companies that commission them, and the possible conflicts of interest that might constrain developers. The code itself can be easily maintained in an open repository, and issues of copyright can be supported by tagging the code with the certificate of the developer.

Another consideration in the OSSD environment is that projects involve multiple roles, and thus the relevant interactions are not always bilateral, between developer and customer, but possibly multilateral. Furthermore, this multilateral communication may have to be maintained throughout the development process. An interesting question is the extent to which such communication and collaboration would be possible without the different developers, testers, GUI designers, porters, etc. [Yeates, 2005] knowing each other.

Conclusion

In this paper, we propose a model for an online exchange that could be used to support OSSD within a large and distributed community of both developers and user entities. It attempts to address some key concerns about OSSD as it moves from the fringes to the mainstream of software development at the enterprise level. It is intriguing to consider the use of such a model for an open source exchange. While many of the features of the ROSE model suggest a "closed" environment without the community benefits of more typical OSSD environments, it is actually possible for both a ROSE and a public repository (such as sourceforge.net) to coexist within the same context. In other words, the ROSE can be used to facilitate search, authentication, valuation and contracting, all of which are key to having a robust and reliable enterprise development environment. At the same time, once the development team is assembled through the ROSE, the development process itself can be facilitated by a public repository.

References

1. Anandasivam Gopal, Konduru Sivaramakrishnan, M. S. Krishnan, Tridas Mukhopadhyay, "Contracts in Offshore Software Development: An Empirical Analysis", *Management Science*, vol: 49, no. 12, 2003, 1671-1683.
2. Justin R. Erenkrantz and Richard N. Taylor, "Supporting Distributed and Decentralized Projects: Drawing Lessons from the Open Source Community", *Proc. 1st Workshop on Open Source in an Industrial Context*, Anaheim, California, October, 2003.
3. Chris Jensen and Walt Scacchi, "Collaboration, Leadership, Control, and Conflict Negotiation in the NetBeans.org Software Development Community", *Proc. 38th Hawaii Intern, Conf. Systems Science*, Waikola Village, HI, 2005.
4. Chris Jensen and Walt Scacchi, "Experiences in Discovering, Modeling, and Reenacting Open Source Software Development Processes", *Proc. Software Process Workshop*, Beijing, China, May 2005.
5. Joakim Kalvenes and Amit Basu, "Design of Robust Business-to-Business Electronic Marketplaces with Guaranteed Privacy", working paper, Cox School of Business, SMU, 2005.
6. Martin Michlmayr, Francis Hunt and David Probert, "Quality Practices and Problems in Free Software Projects", *Proceedings of the First International Conference on Open Source Systems*, Genova, 2005.
7. Mark S. Miller and K. Eric Drexler, "Markets and Computation: Agoric Open Systems", in Bernardo Huberman (Ed), **The Ecology of Computation**, Elsevier Science, 1988.
8. Bruce Perens, **Open Sources: Voices from the Open Source Revolution**, O'Reilly Media, Inc., 1999.
9. Anna Persson, Brian Lings, Bjorn Lundell, Anders Attsson and Ulf Arlig, "Communication, coordination and control in distributed development: an OSS study", *Proceedings of the First International Conference on Open Source Systems*, Genova, 2005.
10. Eric S. Raymond, **The Cathedral & the Bazaar : Musings on Linux and Open Source by an Accidental Revolutionary**, O'Reilly Media, Inc. (2001).

11. Robert J. Sandusky, "Software Problem Management as Information Management in a F/OSS Development Community", *Proceedings of the First International Conference on Open Source Systems*, Genova, 2005.
12. Walt Scacchi, "Open EC/B: Electronic Commerce and Free/Open Source Software Development", *Proc. 5th Workshop on Open Source Software Engineering,* St. Louis, MO, May 2005.
13. B. Schneier, **Applied Cryptography**, John Wiley, NY, 1996.
14. Whang, S., "Contracting for Software Development", *Management Science*, vol. 38, no. 3, 1992, 307-325.
15. Whang, S., "Market Provision of Custom Software: Learning Effects and Low Balling", *Management Science*, vol. 41, no. 8, 1343-1357.
16. Stuart Yeates, "Roles in Open Source Software Development", OSS Watch, University of Oxford, 2005.

Part IV

Introduction of OSS in Companies and PAs

The Organizational Adoption of Open Source Server Software by Belgian Organizations

Kris Ven and Jan Verelst

University of Antwerp, Department of Management Information Systems,
Faculty of Applied Economics
Prinstraat 13, B-2000 Antwerp, Belgium
{kris.ven, jan.verelst}@ua.ac.be

Abstract. This study reports on five case studies in Belgian organizations that currently use open source server software. Respondents were asked about their motivation to use open source server software. Our results indicate that the lower cost, high reliability and availability of external support are the prime reasons why organizations use open source software. The often claimed advantage of open source software of having access to the source code was found relevant only for those organizations who perform development based on open source software. Some factors that were found relevant in previous studies (such as the support of standards) were however deemed less important by the organizations in our sample.

Key words: open source, organizational adoption, innovation, Linux

1 Introduction

The Linux operating system has evolved considerably since its introduction in 1991. Especially in the last 2–3 years, Linux – and open source software in general – has become a viable solution for commercial organizations. Several factors may account for this. First, open source businesses such as RedHat and SuSe (recently acquired by Novell) have gained momentum and are able to provide the necessary resources to support the enterprise versions of their Linux distributions. Second, large software vendors such as IBM and HP have officially declared their commitment to the Linux operating system. These evolutions have enabled other software vendors such as Oracle and SAP to certify their products for the Linux operating system. Third, open source software has received a lot of attention in the media in the past few years. Moreover, many advantages of open source software are claimed by academic as well as professional literature and by open source advocates. Despite this increased attention and the availability of support for open source software, many organizations are still uncertain whether adopting open source software would be beneficial.

Despite the fact that much research has been devoted to open source software, most studies have focused on the software engineering or social aspects of open source software development. Relatively little effort has been devoted

Please use the following format when citing this chapter:

Ven, K., and Verelst, J., 2006, in IFIP International Federation for Information Processing, Volume 203, Open Source Systems, eds. Damiani, E., Fitzgerald, B., Scacchi, W., Scotto, M., Succi, G., (Boston: Springer), pp. 111-122

to studying the adoption decision of organizations concerning the use of open source software. Although some research has been performed on this topic, additional research is still necessary to increase our understanding of the adoption decision. We will therefore build upon the available literature on this topic, and investigate the reasons why Belgian organizations adopt open source server software.

The rest of the paper is structured as follows. We will start in Sect. 2 by describing the research design of our current study. In Sect. 3, we will discuss our findings and contrast them with previous studies. Finally, in Sect. 4, we will summarize our most important findings and describe their theoretical and practical implications.

2 Research Design

2.1 Scope

The field of open source software is very diverse and complex. It is therefore difficult to reach conclusions that are valid for *all* open source projects. Consequently, in order to reach an acceptable level of internal validity, we must narrow the scope of our study to a specific type of open source software and hence make a certain sacrifice with respect to the external validity.

We decided to focus exclusively on the adoption of open source *server* software. We use the term open source server software to refer to both open source operating systems (such as Linux and FreeBSD), as other open source software for server use (for example the Apache web server or the Bind name server).

This choice is motivated by the fact that Linux is generally considered a stable, mature product that is already in use by a significant number of organizations. Furthermore, many important open source Internet server applications such as Bind, Apache and Sendmail are also considered to be mature and have a dominant market share. Consequently, we expect that the reasons to adopt Linux are similar to the reasons to adopt other open source server software. This hypothesis is supported by the FLOSS study that showed that organizations perceived the benefits of open source operating systems, databases and website applications as rather equivalent [1]. A similar research approach has been undertaken by other researchers [2].

2.2 Methodology

We used the exploratory case study approach to study the organizational adoption decision on open source server software. The case study approach is well-suited to study a contemporary phenomenon in its natural setting, especially when the boundaries of the phenomenon are not clearly defined at the start of the study [3, 4]. We conducted a series of in-depth face-to-face interviews with respondents from five Belgian organizations to identify the factors that influence the decision to use open source server software. Organizations were sampled on the basis of two criteria: the size of the organization measured by the number of employees and the sector in which the organization operated (based on the NACE-BEL classification scheme). Respondents within each organization were selected using the *key informant method*. Since the use of a single respondent has been shown to give inconsistent results [5], we tried to speak to both a senior manager (e.g. the IT manager), and a technical person (e.g. the system administrator) whenever possible.

The interviews took place between July and September 2005. An overview of the cases in our study is shown in Table 1. The interviews were semi-structured, and the format was revised after each interview to incorporate new findings [4]. Each interview lasted 45–60 minutes, was recorded and was transcribed verbatim. In order to increase the validity of the findings, respondents were sent a summary of the interview and were requested to suggest any improvements if necessary. Follow-up questions were asked by telephone or via e-mail. The transcripts were coded by using techniques from grounded theory [6], and were then further analyzed using procedures to generate theory from qualitative data, as described in the literature [4, 7, 8]. Various data displays were used to visualize and further analyze the qualitative data [7, 9].

Table 1. Overview of the organizations in our study

Name	Sector	Employees	Informants	Extent of adoption
OrganizationA	Audio, video and telecommunications	11	2	moderate
OrganizationB	Machinery and equipment	749	2	extensive
OrganizationC	Telecommunications	1346	1	limited
OrganizationD	Publishing and printing	31	1	extensive
OrganizationE	Food and beverages	204	2	moderate

3 Results

Although these case studies are part of an ongoing study, we can already report some interesting results concerning the adoption of open source software. Previous studies have shown that even a limited number of cases can provide a better insight into the adoption decision of organizations [10, 11]. In this section, we will present the most important adoption factors that were encountered during the cross-case analysis, and contrast our findings to previous studies in this field.

3.1 Cost

While the Free and Open Source movement tries to downplay the (*free beer*) cost advantage, lower cost is one of the most important reasons why organizations consider using open source software. We can distinguish between two cost aspects: software and hardware.

The lower or non-existent license costs associated with open source software was cited by all organizations as an important driver towards the use of open source software. None of the organizations made a formal Total Cost of Ownership (TCO) calculation to estimate the long-term costs of open source software. A respondent in OrganizationA was aware that there were many hidden costs in using open source software and was therefore not sure whether the resulting TCO would be positive. This is consistent with other case studies [11].

Many respondents pointed out that the lower cost of open source software is not a sufficient condition for adoption. In most cases, the lower cost combined with the high reliability of open source server software (see Sect. 3.2) was cited as an important way to reduce the costs of the IT infrastructure. Hence, we found support for the *commoditization of IT* that is predicted by some authors [12]. Consistent with this idea, organizations try to lower costs for systems with a low strategic value, such as operating systems and server software [13, 14].

The use of the Linux operating system is also a way for some organizations to lower their hardware costs. All organizations that used Unix mentioned the fact that using Linux could result in a significant reduction in hardware costs. This can be explained by the fact that Linux can operate on Intel hardware, while Unix hardware from Sun or HP is much more expensive. Moreover, the reliability of Intel hardware is considered to be comparable to that of Unix hardware. Organizations that currently use the Windows operating system however, cannot realize any hardware savings since Windows runs on the same hardware as Linux.

Both hardware and software cost were found to be important factors in the decision making process in previous studies [1, 2, 11, 15, 16, 17]. Although some studies hypothesize that lower license costs are a lesser issue for large organizations who have sufficient financial resources, we found no support for this claim. This might suggest that cost savings are an important reason for small as well large organizations in a time in which IT budgets are increasingly under pressure.

3.2 Reliability

Four out of five organizations in our sample indicated that the high reliability of open source server software such as Linux and Apache is one of the main advantages of open source software. A perception present in two organizations was that *"[Open source software] just works, and can run years without any problems."*. The high reliability is however not inherent to open source software. OrganizationB clearly indicated that they consider only those open source projects that have already proven their reliability.

The reliability of Linux was also found to be a major factor contributing to the adoption of Linux in previous studies [1, 2, 15, 16]. In comparison with [2], we notice considerable less variability in the perceptions towards the reliability of open source server software. Two factors can account for this. First, our case studies were conducted 1–3 years after those of [2]. In the meanwhile, Linux has matured further, received a lot of attention in the media and received the backing of large vendors such as IBM. Therefore, organizations may perceive Linux to be more mature and reliable compared to two years ago. Some respondents in our sample indeed indicated that they consider Linux to be more mature compared to some years ago, and that the support of companies such as IBM further increases the trust in open source software. Second, given our limited sample it is likely that we did not capture the whole range of opinions regarding the reliability of open source software.

3.3 Trialability

Trialability is one of the factors in the classic Diffusion of Innovations (DOI) theory and refers to the ability to try out a new innovation on a limited basis before making a decision on whether to adopt the innovation or not. Trailability of an innovation is hypothesized to be positively related to the adoption of that innovation [18]. With respect to open source software, it can be argued that open source software is easier to try out than commercial software, because a full version of the software can be freely downloaded from the Internet.

All organizations in our sample emphasize the importance of being able to try software before using it in a production environment. Although the trialability of open source software is not questioned, a wide range of opinions exists on whether open source software is easier to try out than commercial software. OrganizationA, OrganizationD and OrganizationE consider open source software easier to try out, because it can simply be downloaded from the Internet, without cost and without any administration. OrganizationB and OrganizationC however do not distinguish between the trialability of commercial and open source software, because it is possible to obtain demo or trial versions of commercial software. They admit however that using these trial versions may be a bit more cumbersome since most vendors require prior registration. These two latter companies consider the trialability of open source software a less important advantage. This is in contrast to previous studies on the adoption of open source software, where the trialability of open source software was found to be an important advantage [15, 16].

3.4 Access to Source Code

Having access to the source code of open source software and therefore being able to modify or customize the software is one of the main advantages claimed by open source advocates. However, given the technical nature of applications such as Linux and Apache, it is doubtful whether many users will actually examine and/or modify the source code. The term *Berkeley Conundrum* has been introduced to question the value of the availability of the source code when users do not download, examine and/or modify the source code [19].

Of the five organizations in our sample, three of them (OrganizationC, OrganizationD and OrganizationE) have never made use of the source code to improve or customize the open source software they use. These organizations primarily used stable software such as Linux and Sendmail, and respondents indicated that there was no need to make any modifications to these packages. Consequently, the availability of the source code was not a factor during the adoption decision in these organizations and was not considered to be an advantage (or disadvantage).

OrganizationA and OrganizationB did make use of the source code of some open source packages. These organizations developed organization-specific customizations or incorporated open source components in the IT infrastructure. In these cases, having the source code of the open source components was an advantage during integration and debugging. Consequently, it is not the possibility to make modifications that is valued but rather the insight into the inner workings of a component that can be gained by examining the source code that is greatly appreciated.

These findings are consistent with previous studies which also reported that most users found little need for modifying the source code of stable open source server software, or tried to limit their modifications to customizations [2, 11, 17].

3.5 Switching Costs

All organizations except OrganizationD mentioned that the experience of current employees is important when migrating to other platforms. A possible migration from Unix to Linux is perceived to be much easier than the switch from Windows to Linux. This can be explained by the fact that Linux is basically a Unix clone and many tools (e.g. sed and grep) are shared between both platforms. Except for OrganizationE, all organizations in our sample did have some prior experience with the Unix platform. This means that the current installed base will have a great impact on the ability of an organization to switch to Linux. This is consistent with previous studies on the adoption of Linux [15, 16, 20, 21]. This leads us to conclude that the current experience of employees will have a great impact on the migration costs, since training of personnel is an expensive activity.

3.6 Boundary Spanners

Boundary spanners are individuals within an organization who connect their organization with external information and can bring the organization in contact with new innovations [22, 23]. In the case of open source software, it is possible that the introduction of open source software is mainly a bottom-up initiative in which employees are using open source software at home, and introduce it in their work place when an opportunity arrives.

We have found some support for this hypothesis in our sample. In OrganizationA, OrganizationD and OrganizationE, the introduction of open source software was primarily a bottom-up initiative where a number of employees possessed some knowledge on open source software and introduced it in the organization when appropriate. This was most pronounced in OrganizationA. A respondent there indicated that at the time of the organization's foundation, there were many employees (including the organization's founders) that had a "*firm conviction*" in open source software. As a consequence, most software that was used was open source software. During the next few years, several people holding that "*firm conviction*" left the company. As a result, the choice for open source software became more pragmatic. The role of boundary spanners during the introduction of open source software has also been described in previous research [16].

3.7 External Support

The availability of external support for open source software was cited by almost all organizations as being important. Traditional literature as well suggests that the availability of external knowledge and skills may influence organizations to start using innovations [23]. For open source software, the nature of these external skills can however take different forms.

First, certain Linux vendors such as RedHat and SuSe offer enterprise versions of their Linux distributions, including support services such as automatic updates and access to a helpdesk. In our sample, only OrganizationB deliberately uses a Linux enterprise version including a support contract from SuSe. Having support for an operating system was considered to be very important for this organization, although the support contract was seldom used. OrganizationA also uses a SuSe Linux Enterprise edition, but this was requested by the external company that hosts part of the IT infrastructure. OrganizationE initially installed a boxed version of RedHat Application Server, which came with a one-year support contract. This support was however not extended after this period, since there was little need for it.

Apart from Linux vendors, open source consultancy firms also offer support with respect to the installation and maintenance of open source systems. In our sample, only OrganizationD made use of an external service provider to install the hardware and software infrastructure and to provide technical support when requested. The main reason for outsourcing these tasks is that only one person in this organization is responsible for the IT infrastructure. OrganizationE also relies on an external consultant for resolving technical issues with the open source systems they use.

Hence, having support for Linux is considered by several organizations to be important, especially at the start of the adoption. These results are consistent with the observation that the support for Linux from major companies is an enabler for the adoption of Linux [11, 15, 16, 17, 24]. Moreover, OrganizationC perceives the support for open source software currently as insufficient, which is an important reason for not using Linux. A perceived lack of external support was also found to be an important barrier in other studies [11, 20, 21].

3.8 Vendor Lock-in

It has been argued that one reason why organizations choose Linux and open source software is to be more independent from software vendors and therefore to reduce vendor lock-in [1, 24]. OrganizationA and OrganizationB in our sample indeed mentioned the desire to be independent of a single vendor, and that open source is a way to realize this.

OrganizationC and OrganizationE however minimized the importance of vendor lock-in during software selection. OrganizationC tries to avoid vendor lock-in but opted for the Unix platform where vendor lock-in is considered to be less of an issue, compared to the Windows platform. OrganizationE (the Belgian office of a large multinational firm) does not consider vendor lock-in an issue, since the organization is large enough to negotiate with software vendors.

Although there is mixed support for this factor, we expect that organizations which are trying to reduce vendor lock-in will rather resort to the Unix world, in which Linux is one of the alternatives. Open source software is therefore not the only option to reduce vendor lock-in.

3.9 Open Standards

It has been argued that the adoption of open source software is tightly interconnected with the choice for open standards [11, 13, 24, 25, 26, 27]. The importance of compliance to standards was also found to be a significant factor in a study on the adoption of open systems [28]. We have however found little support for this hypothesis.

OrganizationA expressed no preference for open standards on server level. The other organizations expressed to be in favor of open standards because they ensure data accessability, facilitate integration and result in more enduring platforms. OrganizationB however mentioned that Unix also supports open standards. OrganizationC did not consider the support of open standards an advantage of open source software, although they considered the support of open standards very important during the selection process.

Given the information obtained from this sample, we can deduct that organizations tend to separate the use of open standards from the use of open source software. In general, open source software does support open standards, but organizations do not seem to consider this a reason for choosing open source software.

4 Discussion

4.1 The Adoption of Open Source Software

By analyzing the data obtained from these case studies, we were able to identify several factors that are important during the adoption decision with respect to the use of open source server software.

The lower license costs, combined with a high reliability of mature open source packages such as Linux were found to be the two most important reasons for adopting open source server software. Organizations will therefore not jeopardize their operations by adopting less reliable open source software, just in order to realize cost savings. The fact that organizations tend to primarily appreciate the "free beer" rather that the "free speech" aspect of open source software has been identified as one of the challenges for the open source community [29]. On the other hand, open source software may be an important driver towards the commoditization of IT, replacing commercial platform software by inexpensive alternatives.

Organizations with a Unix installed base may realize additional savings in hardware costs and may experience lower switching costs. These switching costs will be an important barrier for organizations who have a Windows installed base, requiring retraining of personnel. The availability of external support for open source software was also cited as being an important condition for adopting Linux. The often claimed advantage of having access to the source code of open source software was found to be a much less important factor in the adoption decision.

These previous findings are quite consistent with previous literature in this field. On the other hand, some of the factors that were found to be relevant in other studies, such as the support of open standards, the avoidance of vendor lock-in and the trialability of open source software were perceived as less important advantages of open source software. We are currently conducting additional case studies to verify our findings. This initial set of case studies however already provided us with rich information on the adoption decision of organizations.

4.2 Implications

Our study contributes to both theory as practice. Since the open source software landscape has changed considerably in the last 2–3 years, it is useful to reassess the reasons why organizations choose open source software. We contributed to the existing body of knowledge on the adoption of open source software by contrasting the findings of our study, conducted in Belgian organizations, to previous studies. Similarities and differences between these results help to further triangulate the data on the adoption of open source software. This leads to a better understanding of the open source adoption decision by organizations. We also contributed to the general adoption theory by examining the adoption of a specific technology, namely open source server software.

The practical relevance of this study is two-fold. First, organizations will be given more insight in why and when adopting open source software may be beneficial, since it has been argued that organizations should know the real benefits and pitfalls of open source software [30]. Hence, a better understanding of these adoption factors may lead to better planning and more informed decision making. Second, the open source community may benefit as well from the results of this study. Insight into the real reasons why organizations use open source software may help the community to emphasize other advantages of open source software that help increase its adoption. This is important since it has recently been noted that open source communities tend to have limited insight into the opinion of its customers [29].

References

1. Wichmann T (2002) Use of open source software in firms and public institutions – Evidence from Germany, Sweden and UK. FLOSS Final Report – part 1, International Institute of Infonomics, Berlecon Research
2. West J, Dedrick J (2005) The effect of computerization movements upon organizational adoption of open source. In: Social Informatics Workshop: Extending the Contributions of Professor Rob Kling to the Analysis of Computerization Movements. Irvine, California
3. Yin RK (2003) Case study research: design and methods. Sage Publications, Newbury Park, California, 3rd edition
4. Benbasat I, Goldstein DK, Mead M (1987) The case research strategy in studies of information systems. MIS Quarterly 11(3):368–386
5. Phillips LW (1981) Assessing measurement error in key informant reports: A methodological note on organizational analysis in marketing. Journal of Marketing Research 18(4):395–415
6. Strauss A, Corbin J (1990) Basics of qualitative research: grounded theory procedures and techniques. Sage Publications, Newbury Park, California
7. Eisenhardt KM (1989) Building theories from case study research. Academy of Management Review 14(4):532–550
8. Dubé L, Paré G (2003) Rigor in information systems positivist case research: Current practices, trends, and recommendations. MIS Quarterly 27(4):597–635
9. Miles MB, Huberman AM (1994) Qualitative data analysis: An expanded sourcebook. Sage Publications, Thousand Oaks, California, 2nd edition
10. Holck J, Pedersen MK, Larsen MH (2005) Open source software acquisition: Beyond the business case. In: Proceedings of the Thirteenth European Conference on Information Systems. Regensburg, Germany

11. Larsen MH, Mogens JH, Pedersen K (2004) The challenges of open source software in IT adoption: Enterprise architecture versus total cost of ownership. In: Proceedings of IRIS'27 – the 27th Information Systems Research Seminar in Scandinavia

12. Carr NG (2003) IT doesn't matter. Harvard Business Review 81(5):41–49

13. Kwan SK, West J (2005) A conceptual model for enterprise adoption of open source software. In: Bolin S (ed) The standards edge: Open season. Sheridan Books, Ann Arbor, Michigan, pp. 274–301

14. O'Reilly T (2005) The open source paradigm shift. In: Feller J, Fitzgerald B, Hissam S, Lakhani K (eds) Perspectives on free and open source software. MIT Press, Cambridge, MA, pp. 461–481

15. Dedrick J, West J (2004) An exploratory study into open source platform adoption. In: Proceedings of the 37th Hawaii International Conference on System Sciences. IEEE Computer Society, Washington, DC

16. Dedrick J, West J (2003) Why firms adopt open source platforms: a grounded theory of innovation and standards adoption. In: King JL, Lyytinen K (eds) Proceedings of the Workshop on Standard Making: A Critical Research Frontier for Information Systems. Seattle, Washington, pp. 236–257

17. Fitzgerald B, Kenny T (2003) Open source software in the trenches: Lessons from a large scale implementation. In: Proceedings of 24th International Conference on Information Systems (ICIS). ACM Press, New York, NY, pp. 316–326

18. Rogers EM (1983) Diffusion of innovations. The Free Press, New York, 3rd edition

19. Feller J, Fitzgerald B (2002) Understanding open source software development. Addison-Wesley, London, UK

20. Ghosh R, Glott R (2005) Results and policy paper from survey of government authorities. Free/Libre and Open Source Software: Policy Support (FLOSSPOLS) Deliverable D3, MERIT, University of Maastricht

21. Goode S (2005) Something for nothing: Management rejection of open source software in Australia's top firms. Information & Management 42(5):669–681

22. Tushman ML, Scanlan TJ (1981) Characteristics and external orientations of boundary spanning individuals. Academy of Management Journal 24(1):83–98

23. Depietro R, Wiarda E, Fleischer M (1990) The context for change: Organization, technology and environment. In: Tornatzky LG, Fleischer M (eds) The processes of technological innovation. Lexington Books, Lexington, Massachussets, pp. 151–175

24. Varian HR, Shapiro C (2003) Linux adoption in the public sector: An economic analysis. Working paper, University of California, Berkeley

25. West J (2003a) How open is open enough? Melding proprietary and open source platform strategies. Research Policy 32(7):1259–1285

26. Simon KD (2005) The value of open standards and open-source software in government environments. IBM Systems Journal 44(2):227–238

27. West J (2003b) The role of standards in the creation and use of information systems. In: King JL, Lyytinen K (eds) Proceedings of the Workshop on Standard Making: A Critical Research Frontier for Information Systems. Seattle, Washington, pp. 314–326

28. Chau PYK, Tam KY (1997) Factors affecting the adoption of open systems: An exploratory study. MIS Quarterly 21(1):1–24

29. Fitzgerald B (2005) Has open source software a future? In: Feller J, Fitzgerald B, Hissam S, Lakhani K (eds) Perspectives on free and open source software. MIT Press, Cambridge, MA, pp. 93–106

30. Weinstock CB, Hissam SA (2005) Making lightning strike twice. In: Feller J, Fitzgerald B, Hissam S, Lakhani K (eds) Perspectives on free and open source software. MIT Press, Cambridge, MA, pp. 143–159

The Introduction of OpenOffice.org in the Brussels Public Administration

Kris Ven, Dieter Van Nuffel, and Jan Verelst

University of Antwerp, Department of Management Information Systems,
Faculty of Applied Economics
Prinstraat 13, B-2000 Antwerp, Belgium
{kris.ven,dieter.vannuffel,jan.verelst}@ua.ac.be

Abstract. Open source software is increasingly used by public administrations as an alternative to commercial software. In this paper we present a case study of the transition of the ministerial cabinets of the Brussels-Capital Region towards OpenOffice.org. In this case, the decision to use open source software was taken by the Government of the Brussels-Capital Region. The goal of the paper is to outline the implementation trajectory followed and to compare our findings to previous studies in this field as well as other Information Systems literature. Additionally, we discuss how OpenOffice.org was received by end users as well as the IT department that was responsible for the migration. Our findings indicate that although a migration towards OpenOffice.org is feasible, a number of difficulties still remain. For example, end user perceptions of OpenOffice.org are not always favorable and migration costs (document conversion and training) can be significant.

Key words: open source, adoption, public administration, OpenOffice.org

1 Introduction

Open standards and open source software are increasingly used by public administrations (PA) in Europe. A recent survey in 13 European countries has shown that 49% of PAs intentionally use open source software, while another 29% make unaware use of open source software. Moreover, half of the respondents would find an increase in open source software usage useful [1]. This increased use of open source software has received the attention of a number of European research projects, such as the Open Source Observatory[1] of the IDABC (Interoperable Delivery of European eGovernment Services to public Administrations, Businesses and Citizens) and more recently the COSPA (Consortium for Open Source in the Public Administration) project[2].

Although open source software is mainly used on servers, it can be argued that the use of open source software on the desktop could result in considerable

---

[1] http://europa.eu.int/idabc/en/chapter/452
[2] http://www.cospa-project.org

Please use the following format when citing this chapter:

Ven, K., Van Nuffel, D., and Verelst, J., 2006, in IFIP International Federation for Information Processing, Volume 203, Open Source Systems, eds. Damiani, E., Fitzgerald, B., Scacchi, W., Scotto, M., Succi, G., (Boston: Springer), pp. 123-134

higher savings in license costs; since the number of desktop licenses is much larger than that of server licenses. On the other hand, migrating towards open source software on the desktop is far more disruptive for end users and will result in higher migration costs than a migration on server level (e.g. when migrating from MS Internet Information Services to Apache). These factors could explain why the use of open source desktop software is quite limited. Nevertheless, about 20% of PAs included in the FLOSSPOLS study indicated that they make use of OpenOffice.org [1].

Hence, we feel that additional research is required to assess if and how migrations towards open source software could take place. In this paper, we will report on the transition to open source software by the Brussels-Capital Region. The transition primarily concerned the use of OpenOffice.org by the ministerial cabinets of the Government of the Brussels-Capital Region. The rest of the paper is structured as follows. We will start in Sect. 2 by describing the background of the transition. In Sect. 3, the methodology of our present research is discussed. Section 4 describes the implementation trajectory that was followed during the transition. In Sect. 5, experiences from end users and the IT department responsible for the implementation are presented. Finally, conclusions are drawn for future migrations.

2 Background

According to the revision of the Belgian Constitution in 1970, Belgium was officially divided into three regions: the Flemish Region, the Walloon Region and the Brussels-Capital Region. The Brussels-Capital Region consists of the 19 communes of Brussels and is administered by two authorities: the Parliament and the Government of the Brussels-Capital Region. The latter consists of eight Ministries, each having its own cabinet. The Brussels-Capital Region has two official languages: Dutch and French. This requires for example that official documents are composed in these two languages. In 1987, a law was passed that created the *Brussels Regional Informatics Center (BRIC)*. The responsibilities of BRIC include the promotion and assistance of Information Technology (IT) in the local public administrations of the Brussels-Capital Region.

The move towards open standards and open source software by the Brussels-Capital Region was initiated by two decisions. First, a resolution was voted in which the use of open standards and open source software was encouraged in the Brussels-Capital Region in order to facilitate the communication with the citizens of the region. As a result, BRIC was required to consider at least one open source alternative in each project. Second, based on this resolution, the use of open standards and open source software was included in the coalition agreement of the Brussels-Capital Region in 2004. It was decided by the Government of the Brussels-Capital Region that open source office software would be used for the ministerial cabinets of the Brussels-Capital Region. OpenOffice.org was however not mentioned by name.

Within BRIC, OpenOffice.org was introduced in April 2004. In a second phase, from mid-January until mid-February 2005, the ministerial cabinets were migrated to OpenOffice.org. The transition concerned a total of 400 workstations running Windows XP on which OpenOffice.org 1.1 was installed. Apart from the desktops, 4 out of 8 servers of the cabinets were migrated from MS Windows to Linux.

3 Methodology

In order to describe the introduction of OpenOffice.org in the Brussels Public Administration, we opted for a descriptive case study approach. This approach enabled us to describe the phenomenon in its real-life context [2, 3]. The case study used an embedded design, since the use of OpenOffice.org was investigated at BRIC as well as the ministerial cabinets of the Brussels-Capital Region.

Since BRIC was responsible for the IT services both within BRIC and within the ministerial cabinets, we selected two respondents within BRIC using the *key informant method*, namely the director of the IT department and the project leader who was assigned to the OpenOffice.org project. This allowed us to gather more information, since it has been shown that the use of a single respondent leads to unreliable results [3, 4]. Both respondents where closely involved in the migration towards OpenOffice.org. They were responsible for tasks such as planning and coordinating the migration, developing documentation, designing the training sessions and conducting user evaluations.

A first interview took place to gather important background information on the case study. Based on this information, a case study protocol was crafted, including a detailed set of questions, the data collection procedures and the outline of the case study report. The primary mode of data collection was a face-to-face interview which was recorded for future reference. This interview was conducted by a two person team: one researcher was responsible for posing the interview questions, while the other was responsible for taking notes and supplement the interview with additional questions. This also allowed for viewing the case from two perspectives and compare the impressions of both researchers afterwards [2, 5]. Additional sources of evidence were internal documents of BRIC, legislative texts and secondary information such as press releases. Follow-up questions were asked via e-mail. A draft copy of the case study report was reviewed by the respondents in our interview to increase the validity of our findings. The findings of this case study were further compared to findings of previous studies on the adoption of OpenOffice.org and other Information Systems (IS) literature to further ground our conclusions.

4 Implementation

In this section, we will discuss the different phases in which the implementation of OpenOffice.org took place. We will discuss successively the analysis, the training offered to end users, the actual migration and the conversion of document templates. We will finish by discussing the current developments of the project.

4.1 Analysis

The IDA Open Source Migration Guidelines [6] prescribe making a detailed business case for a possible migration towards open source software. The business case should include making a Total Cost of Ownership (TCO) analysis of the various alternatives (proprietary vs. open source solutions) over a certain time period. Migration costs should be included in this analysis.

Although no formal TCO analysis was performed in this case, the main driver of the adoption of OpenOffice.org was cost reduction. The reduction in license costs amounts to a total of 185,000 euro in the first year and 15,000 euro in the following years (a number of remaining workstations will be migrated in the following years, resulting in additional savings). Some authors have warned against a focus on cost savings alone during the adoption of open source software [7].

On the other hand, in compliance with the IDA recommendations, a pilot project was initiated at BRIC in March 2004 to study the feasibility of a transition from MS Office to OpenOffice.org. The result of the pilot project confirmed the feasibility of migrating the ministerial cabinets to OpenOffice.org.

4.2 Training

The importance of training when starting to use a new software package has been described in previous case studies on OpenOffice.org, as well as in traditional IS literature [8, 9, 10, 11]. Training increases the proficiency of end users with the software which in turn increases user acceptance.

The training of end users included a training course in the offices of BRIC and a CD-ROM with additional information. The training course consisted of a voluntary one-day session in which the basic functionality of both Open-Office.org Writer and Calc was explained. For the first sessions, key users of each cabinet (the cabinet clerk and an IT responsible) were invited in order to be able to offer first-line support for users in their cabinet. Two out of eight ministerial cabinets considered the training to be too basic. Since participation in the training was voluntary, these two cabinets decided not to encourage staff members of their cabinet to attend the training sessions. It could be observed in a survey among end users (see Sect. 4.5) that users who reported not having attended the training session also reported more problems in using OpenOffice.org.

As some authors note [7, 12], users should be able to start practice with OpenOffice.org immediately after training, in order to maximize the effectiveness of the training session. Given the narrow time frame of one month that was allocated to the migration (see Sect. 4.3 for the exact time frame), this was impossible to achieve. However, all staff workers received their training within one week before or after their workstation was migrated to OpenOffice.org.

At the end of the training session, a CD-ROM containing a manual, a FAQ list and the installation files of OpenOffice.org was handed out to the participants. The manual and FAQ were mainly adopted from the OpenOffice.org communities on the Internet. It should be noted however that significant differences between the OpenOffice.org localization communities can be established. While the French community is very active and provides much documentation, the Dutch counterpart does not achieve the same quality. A possible explanation could be that the number of native French speakers is much higher than the number of native Dutch speakers. However, this caused no significant problems since the majority of staff members at the ministerial cabinets was native French speaking, and the majority of Dutch speaking staff members experienced little problems in studying the French material.

4.3 Migration

As previously noted, the migration was mandatory for staff members of the ministerial cabinets following the coalition agreement of 2004. Computer equipment of the ministerial cabinets is updated every five years, coinciding with the terms of the Government of the Brussels-Capital Region. For reasons of efficiency and to minimize discomfort for end users, it was decided to migrate to OpenOffice.org 1.1 at the same time the user's workstation was replaced. Hence, the phasing out of MS Office and the installation of OpenOffice.org were performed simultaneously. This means that MS Office was no longer available when OpenOffice.org was installed on the user's workstation, except in a limited number of cases in which the user required advanced functionality of MS Excel or MS Access (e.g. in the finance department). Concurrently, the default data format for internal communication changed from MS Office to OpenOffice.org format. When corresponding with external parties, the export filters of OpenOffice.org were used to save the document in MS Office format. Thanks to these import/export filters, it was decided not to convert existing MS Office documents to the OpenOffice.org format.

Some authors have cautioned against this "big bang" approach since this would increase user resistance towards adopting the software [6, 7, 12]. In this case, it was judged that it was more convenient to immediately switch to OpenOffice.org, without temporarily installing MS Office. It was further expected that users with an initial negative attitude towards OpenOffice.org would continue using MS Office until it was deleted from their workstation. Additionally, changing the default document format to OpenOffice.org format further increased the social norm for staff members to use OpenOffice.org. On the other hand, it will be interesting to analyze the feedback of staff members (see Sect. 4.5) with respect to the migration to check whether this strategy did have an impact on the acceptance of OpenOffice.org.

4.4 Document Templates

A problem that occurred during the migration to OpenOffice.org concerned the use of document templates. The Brussels PA has issued a very rigorous style guide to which all documents within the PA must adhere. BRIC tried to migrate the existing MS Office templates into an equivalent OpenOffice.org template. However several differences between MS Office and OpenOffice.org exist which led to incompatibilities, like for instance incorrect margins. Currently, BRIC is finalizing the OpenOffice.org templates that comply with the style guide of the Brussels PA.

A related difficulty consisted of editing legislative texts because of the very specific format that has to be used. Since Brussels is bilingual, the text must be published in two columns (one for each language) and each paragraph must start on the same level as the corresponding paragraph in the other language (see Fig. 1). Since French paragraphs are in general somewhat lengthier than the Dutch, some adjustments in vertical spacing between paragraphs must be made. In MS Word, a table with two columns and one row was used to realize this layout. However, OpenOffice.org does not support table cells to be spread over more than one page. Therefore, end users had to change the layout and store each paragraph in a different cell. When a cell (i.e. paragraph) does not fit on the bottom of the page, the cell is moved to the following page.

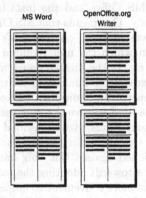

Fig. 1. Formatting of legislative texts in MS Office vs. OpenOffice.org

4.5 Current Developments

With the aim of enhancing end user support in future projects, BRIC recently carried out a survey within the ministerial cabinets in order to gather feedback on the migration. In the survey, staff members are asked about their use of

OpenOffice.org, the training that was received and the experiences with Open-Office.org so far. Although analysis of the results is still being performed, we can already report on preliminary experiences of end users in Sect. 5.

Following the availability of OpenOffice.org 2.0, BRIC internally migrated to this new version in the beginning of December 2005. The OpenDocument format is currently used as the default data format for communication within BRIC, while the OpenOffice.org 1.1 format is still used when communicating with the ministerial cabinets. This upgrade was also performed to prepare a possible migration of the ministerial cabinets towards this new version. Partly based on these experiences, the ministerial cabinets have decided at the end of December 2005 to upgrade to OpenOffice.org 2.0.

5 Experiences

In this section, we will report on the experiences of end users of the ministerial cabinets and BRIC. We will focus on a number of issues that were encountered during the migration, and which lessons were drawn from these experiences.

5.1 User Experiences

As reported in previous studies, the initial attitude of end users towards using OpenOffice.org is an important factor in the success of the transition [7, 12, 13]. While technical problems can generally be solved, user resistance is much harder to overcome. In this case, it can indeed be observed that users who were not convinced before or at the time of training are still opposed to using OpenOffice.org. This confirms the importance of training and information dissemination towards users before the migration takes place.

Traditional literature on individual adoption also emphasized the importance of *perceived ease of use* and *perceived usefulness* of a technology in order to increase end user acceptance [14, 15, 16]. With respect to usability, the perception of staff members at the ministerial cabinets is mixed. In general, users find the usability of OpenOffice.org 1.1 to be lacking compared to MS Office. The most often heard critique is that the look and feel of OpenOffice.org feels outdated. A second difficulty for end users is that some tasks in OpenOffice.org should be performed slightly differently than in MS Office. It was observed that many users tried to work in the same manner they were used to in MS Office, which sometimes caused problems, for example when working with formatting styles. In those cases, BRIC used a procedural training approach [17] in which the preferred procedure was shown during a short personal demonstration. This was sufficient in most cases to alter the end users' old habits.

Another critique of some end users is that OpenOffice.org still lacks functionality that is present in MS Office. These users do not consider OpenOffice.org a fully fledged alternative for MS Office. More analysis of the survey results needs to be performed to establish whether the features reported missing by users are

important in their daily tasks, since a previous study on the adoption of Open-
Office.org by PAs in Italy [7, 12] has shown that the features of OpenOffice.org
are more than adequate for daily use. This mixed perception by end users is
consistent with the observations from a previous experiment in a PA [8]. It is
further hoped that the upgrade from OpenOffice.org version 1.1 to version 2.0
will improve its perception.

It has also been suggested in literature that users may resist working with
open source desktop software, because they fear becoming *deskilled* by moving
away from the industry standard [6, 18, 19]. According to our respondents
at BRIC, this fear was not articulated by end users. In addition, while some
authors note that the switch from proprietary systems to open source software
may result in a decreased productivity shortly after the introduction [8, 19], no
noticeable differences were observed. It must however be noted that no formal
measurement of the productivity was performed.

5.2 Evaluation

The transition to OpenOffice.org has resulted in a number of benefits, but
also involved a number of problems. A first advantage is that OpenOffice.org
uses open standards to save documents [20]. As mentioned in Sect. 2, the support of open standards was an important factor in the decision towards using
OpenOffice.org. On the other hand, despite the fact that the OpenOffice.org
format is an open standard, it is yet only supported by OpenOffice.org. Hence,
when communicating with external parties, documents must be converted to
the MS Office format. Although the conversion performed by OpenOffice.org
works adequately in most cases, some problems may arise when MS Office documents are poorly formatted, or when documents are converted multiple times
back and forth between MS Office and OpenOffice.org format. These issues are
also reported in previous studies [13]. Within the ministerial cabinets, most
documents requiring input from multiple parties mainly involve revisions in the
document text. Therefore, it was agreed upon that documents would be exchanged without formatting between parties, and only when the document was
finalized, formatting was applied either in MS Office or OpenOffice.org. The
use of the Portable Document Format (PDF) was also promoted for documents
requiring no further modifications.

A second advantage of OpenOffice.org was its use of data sources to allow
users to communicate with external databases. Especially the fact that a document can access more than one data source is very valuable. On the other
hand, the implementation of these data sources in OpenOffice.org caused some
difficulties at first. The reference to the data source is not included in the document as it is done by MS Office, but is stored in the user profile at the user's
workstation. Therefore, when the document is exchanged between users, the
data source is lost. This required custom scripting to ensure that each user has
access to the data sources. Another related problem that was reported by end
users was the Mail Merge feature. When using the Mail Merge feature to create

a mailing based on an address list in a database, OpenOffice.org creates a new document for each addressee. Therefore, a script was developed to merge these documents back into one file. In OpenOffice.org 2.0 however, this script has become obsolete, since the user is given the choice between generating a separate file for each addressee, or to generate one large file.

As mentioned in Sect. 4.5, BRIC is already using OpenOffice.org version 2.0 since December 2005. In their experience, it appears that most of the difficulties mentioned above are solved in this new version. In general, OpenOffice.org 2.0 is considered to be an important improvement compared to version 1.1. Apart from the improved functionality, the look and feel more closely resembles that of MS Office which will make it easier to use than the previous version. The key users of each ministerial cabinet have already been migrated to OpenOffice.org 2.0 to provide feedback on this new version. First impressions of these key users confirm that OpenOffice.org 2.0 indeed solves a number of issues that were present in OpenOffice.org 1.1. On the other hand, it is noted by BRIC that OpenOffice.org 2.0 still contains a number of important defects. Although workarounds are possible for most of these problems, they could still have a negative impact on the general perception of OpenOffice.org.

Finally, several authors have noted that migration costs for training, document conversion and building up expertise can be an important barrier to the adoption of open source software [19, 21, 22]. In the past 18 months, BRIC needed to invest a lot of time in building up expertise in OpenOffice.org, developing training material and rewriting several templates that are in use by the ministerial cabinets. However, as mentioned in Sect. 4.1, a TCO analysis was not performed, neither before nor after the implementation. Hence, it is not possible at this time to assess whether the migration has resulted in a lower TCO. Nevertheless, these migration costs only occur once and could be compensated by additional savings in license costs in the following years. Moreover, the time that BRIC has invested in OpenOffice.org has paid off. Thanks to the experience with the prior installation of OpenOffice.org, BRIC was able to reduce the time required for installation considerably. While the initial installation of OpenOffice.org 1.1 at BRIC required 4 days, the upgrade to version 2.0 was completed in 1 day.

6 Conclusion

In this paper we reported on the migration of BRIC and the ministerial cabinets of the Government of the Brussels-Capital Region to OpenOffice.org. Our study has a number of contributions. First, we provided insight into how the migration to OpenOffice.org was undertaken by BRIC. Second, the main contribution of this paper is that it further builds upon previous studies on the adoption of OpenOffice.org as well as traditional IS literature. Hence, the findings of our case study were contrasted with the findings of previous studies. This allowed us to further validate these findings and provided the necessary grounding of our findings in literature. Third, we discussed which successes and shortcomings were encountered during the transition towards OpenOffice.org. It was established that while it is possible to migrate from MS Office to OpenOffice.org for most daily use of an office productivity suite, a number of issues required special attention which are of interest for potential adopters of OpenOffice.org.

We have seen that there were a number of technical issues that arose during the migration towards OpenOffice.org. Much effort was spent on the conversion of organization-specific templates. Additionally, some of the issues we discussed were specific to the environment under study, and were for example due to the bilingualism of Brussels. As a result of these issues, users had to alter their way of working when formatting a document. The import and export filters of OpenOffice.org were deemed sufficient in most cases, although some incompatibilities arose when repeatedly saving a file back and forth in OpenOffice.org and MS Office format. A work-around for this problem has however been devised. User feedback also indicated that OpenOffice.org was not considered a fully fledged alternative for MS Office by most users. For example, some advanced features of MS Office were not supported, and the look and feel of OpenOffice.org was considered outdated by end users. It is however expected by BRIC that the upgrade to OpenOffice.org 2.0 could alleviate a number of important nuisances which will improve its perception by end users. This is supported by the feedback received from the key users who have already been migrated to OpenOffice.org 2.0. This new version however still contains a number of issues which may negatively influence the end user experience.

The migration performed by BRIC also confirmed the importance of proper training for end users. Although the training that was provided by BRIC concerned basic office tasks, it was noted that users who attended the training session reported less problems in their daily tasks. Furthermore, the training sessions also proved to be important in creating an initial positive attitude towards OpenOffice.org, since it was observed that attitudes of end users are difficult to alter after the implementation. Although training material and documentation was available from the OpenOffice.org community, it was observed that there were considerable differences in quantity and quality between the Dutch and French community material. Hence, potential adopters should take differences between language communities into account when using documentation produced by the OpenOffice.org community.

While most of our findings are consistent with previous studies on the migration towards OpenOffice.org, we have found a number of contradictions with previous studies. Based upon the information we obtained from our respondents, users within BRIC and the ministerial cabinets did not articulate a fear for becoming deskilled or did not suffer from any noticeable lapses in productivity shortly after the upgrade. Additionally, the "big bang" approach that was taken did not seem to have a negative impact on the user's perceptions. However, detailed analysis of the user evaluations is required in order to further verify these results.

Thanks to the migration towards OpenOffice.org, BRIC was able to realize a significant reduction in license costs. It remains however unclear whether the resulting TCO of OpenOffice.org in this case was indeed lower, since there were considerable migration costs including training, conversion of templates and building up expertise with OpenOffice.org. The result of these efforts will however be useful in the following years, so these initial costs could be compensated by additional savings in license costs in the future. Organizations and public administrations that are willing to adopt OpenOffice.org should however be aware that the transition will require significant investments in training and data migration, yet the long-term effects of the transition should also be taken into account.

References

1. Ghosh R, Glott R (2005) Results and policy paper from survey of government authorities. Technical report, MERIT, University of Maastricht, Maastricht. Free/Libre and Open Source Software: Policy Support (FLOSSPOLS) Deliverable D3
2. Yin RK (2003) Case study research: Design and methods. Sage Publications, Newbury Park, California, 3rd edition
3. Benbasat I, Goldstein DK, Mead M (1987) The case research strategy in studies of information systems. MIS Quarterly 11(3):368–386
4. Phillips LW (1981) Assessing measurement error in key informant reports: A methodological note on organizational analysis in marketing. Journal of Marketing Research (JMR) 18(4):395–415
5. Eisenhardt KM (1989) Building theories from case study research. Academy of Management Review 14(4):532–550
6. European Communities (2003) The IDA open source migration guidelines. http://europa.eu.int/idabc/servlets/Doc?id=1983
7. Zuliani P, Succi G (2004a) Migrating public administrations to open source software. In: Proceedings of e-Society 2004 IADIS International Conference. Avila, Spain
8. Rossi B, Scotto M, Sillitti A, Succi G (2005) Criteria for the non invasive transition to openoffice. In: Scotto M, Succi G (eds) Proceedings of the First International Conference on Open Source Systems. Genova, Italy, pp. 250–253
9. Kovács GL, Drozdik S, Zuliani P, Succi G (2004a) Open source software for the public administration. In: Proceedings of the 6th Computer Science and Information Technologies (CSIT). Budapest, Hungary
10. Nelson RR, Cheney PH (1987) Training end users: An exploratory study. MIS Quarterly 11(4):546–559
11. Thompson RL, Higgins CA (1991) Personal computing: Toward a conceptual model of utilization. MIS Quarterly 15(1):125–143
12. Zuliani P, Succi G (2004b) An experience of transition to open source software in local authorities. In: Proceedings of e-Challenges on Software Engineering. Vienna, Austria
13. Drozdik S, Kovács GL, Kochis PZ (2005) Risk assessment of an open source migration project. In: Scotto M, Succi G (eds) Proceedings of the First International Conference on Open Source Systems. Genova, Italy, pp. 246–249

14. Davis FD (1989) Perceived usefulness, perceived ease of use, and user acceptance of information technology. MIS Quarterly 13(3):319–340
15. Venkatesh V, Davis FD (2000) A theoretical extension of the technology acceptance model: Four longitudinal field studies. Management Science 46(2):186–204
16. Venkatesh V, Morris MG, Davis GB, Davis FD (2003) User acceptance of information technology: Toward a unified view. MIS Quarterly 27(3):425–478
17. Olfman L, Mandviwalla M (1994) Conceptual versus procedural software training for graphical user interfaces: A longitudinal field experiment. MIS Quarterly 18(4):405–426
18. Fitzgerald B, Kenny T (2003) Open source software in the trenches: Lessons from a large scale implementation. In: Proceedings of 24th International Conference on Information Systems (ICIS). Seattle, Washington
19. Fitzgerald B (2005) Has open source software a future? In: Feller J, Fitzgerald B, Hissam S, Lakhani K (eds) Perspectives on free and open source software. MIT Press, Cambridge, MA, pp. 93–106
20. Kovács GL, Drozdik S, Zuliani P, Succi G (2004b) Open source software and open data standards in public administration. In: Proceedings of the IEEE International Conference on Computational Cybernetics. Vienna, Austria
21. Goode S (2005) Something for nothing: Management rejection of open source software in Australia's top firms. Information & Management 42(5):669–681
22. Dedrick J, West J (2004) An exploratory study into open source platform adoption. In: Proceedings of the 37th Hawaii International Conference on System Sciences. IEEE Computer Society, Washington, DC

Networks of Open Source Health Care Action

Knut Staring[1] and Ola Titlestad[1]

1 University of Oslo, Department of Informatics, Gaustadalleén 23,

N-0316 Oslo, Norway

{knutst, olati}@ifi.uio.no

WWW home page: http://folk.uio.no/knutst

Abstract. This paper reports on an effort to create a network of both developers and users of a public health information system. Through an analysis of capacity, recruitment, and power in the network, issues related to choice of technologies, global-local tensions, and parameters of institutional collaboration, we illustrate a number of challenges. Comparing OSS principles to a "Networks of Action" approach, conditions for learning in organizing training and development of software with participants from Africa, Asia, and Europe, as well as the involvement of advanced students in such efforts are discussed.

Keywords: capacity building, networks, action research, open source software

1 Introduction

Several authors underscore the significance of open source software (OSS) to countries in the South. In contrast to much outsourcing work, it enables skill development in the full software stack (Weerawarana and Weeratunga 2004), and OSS solutions are starting to appear in vertical domains such as health care (Fitzgerald and Kenny 2003). This paper explores how this has played out in practice in one such effort, the Health Information Systems Programme (HISP). HISP is a research-driven network of universities and public health care organisations in Norway and several developing countries in Africa and Asia, targeted at improving development and implementation of computerised health information systems in the south. HISP is developing and providing implementation support of an open source software application (DHIS), a system supporting local level information use and analysis in the primary health care sector.

Braa et al. (2004) put forward an action research approach called "networks of action" that addresses sustainability of information systems in poor countries through establishing a network of sites mutually supporting local learning processes, and aligning interventions with existing institutions. The basic tenets of the open source development model, as spelled out in the classic essay by Raymond (2000) would seem a near perfect fit for such an effort. However, Heeks (2005) is skeptical, and questions whether this isn't a blind alley for developing countries, pointing out that

Please use the following format when citing this chapter:

Staring, K., and Titlestad, O., 2006, in IFIP International Federation for Information Processing, Volume 203, Open Source Systems, eds. Damiani, E., Fitzgerald, B., Scacchi, W., Scotto, M., Succi, G., (Boston: Springer), pp. 135-141

extensive piracy, lack of awareness of OSS, and poor links to global developer communities limit its potential.

Monteiro et al (2005) point out that the dominant accounts of OSS tend to emphasize high quality code and the elite character of hackers. However, just releasing source code (to Sourceforge for example) is not likely to attract enough capable developers, and many projects struggle with labor shortage. In line with the recommendations by Watson et. al. (2004), the project described here has so far relied on advanced students, as well as on hiring fresh local graduates. The strengthening of local knowledge, skills, and institutional capacity in a global network is a central goal to the project addressing sustainability of local implementations.

An important research question is how this "networks of action"-influenced approach affects issues of quality, openness, and participation is a globally distributed OSS development process.

Krishna et al. (2004) point out how differing conceptions of "politeness"can be a source of tension in cross cultural software teams, whereas OSS relies on the initiative of individuals with "itches to scratch" (Raymond 2000) and vigorous discussion. The HISP network represents an interesting case for cross cultural collaboration and the authors will explore how cultural differences have influenced participation around the network.

2 Method

HISP is organized as a long term action research network of researchers and organizations, where researchers must participate in the specific context(s) to obtain insights that can not be understood by studying it "from a distance" (Greenwood and Levin 1998). The empirical evidence was collected partly through interviews and the reading of documents, but mainly through participant observation. Like Duchenaut (2005), we take an interest in the trajectories of the various developers over time, as they e. g. grow into core roles or leave. The authors have been involved with the project for over three years and are coordinating the development process. Additionally, the authors have created and conducted a master level course around HISP development, with student reports and feedback providing additional material.

3 The development network

HISP was initiated in South Africa after the fall of apartheid, and is based on collaboration between academic institutions, health authorities, and private organizations. Funding has been secured through various local and global donors, though mainly by the Norwegian Agency for Development Co-operation (NORAD) and the European Commission (EC). The District Health Information System (DHIS) software was developed in South Africa, and is presently rolled out on a national level there. It has also been introduced in several African and Asian countries. The versions up to and including the current 1.4 are built on the MS Access platform, and the software is provided gratis and with the source code available. A DHIS2 effort was initiated in 2004 aiming to make the DHIS platform and database independent and web enabled (while still serving users without internet connection). There was also need for a more layered and modular architecture supporting distributed development, to allow for the creation of developer teams in several nodes in the global HISP network. Local involvement and capacity building around the network are seen as central to the viability of the project.

3.1 The Oslo node

The HISP project is coordinated from this node, where the authors are based, and several Norwegian master students fill key roles in the development process as part of their master thesis research. These core developers have also been deeply involved as teaching assistants for a project oriented master level course designed around DHIS2 technologies, with a total of 80 students in the course of two semesters. The course projects have prototyped functionality, explored alternative technologies and project extensions. Furthermore, the course has served as a recruiting base for the project. The core developers have done field work in Vietnam and India, while conducting extensive training of the local teams in the technologies used.

3.2 The Saigon node

Initial collaboration was set up with a large local outsourcing company in Saigon where a total of six Vietnamese intern students participated in the DHIS2 development over a period of nine months. The project thus had a local base where both Norwegian researchers and master students could work for shorter or longer periods, and also hold courses in OSS Java technologies for the firm's employees. This collaboration was terminated in July 2005, which prompted the project to seek collaboration with a local university. A research group of students and faculty focusing on DHIS2 technologies was set up in September 2005, and three of the best undergraduate students from this group were subsequently hired to work full time on DHIS2, guided by Norwegian master students doing their fieldwork, who have also conducted seminars on the technologies at the university.

3.3 The Kerala node

The development process for DHIS2 was tried with a number of DHIS 1.3 implementation facilitators, who all had degrees in computer science. However, they turned out to have very little real programming experience, and were quite unfamiliar with both Java and web programming, far less the modern frameworks suggested by the Oslo team. Close to nothing came of this initial foray into creating an Indian development hub. A subsequent effort in the spring of 2005 was similarly ill-fated, and three out of four developers were gone from the project within only a few months.

A third round was initiated in late 2005, when two developers recreated the basic parts of the DHIS 1.4 in a month's time, but using plain JSP without any of the DHIS2 layered architecture or frameworks, and in isolation from the efforts ongoing in Oslo and Vietnam. Their relative success and commitment led to their hiring, and they are now being trained in the DHIS2 technologies.

4 Technology and Process

The initial stage of the DHIS2 involved a time-consuming process of selecting the technological platform and tools to meet the new demands of platform independence, web-enabling, modular architecture and distributed development. The field of web technologies has evolved considerably over the last decade, and the pace of innovation has shown no sign of abating over the two years since the inception of the DHIS2 effort, but remains a complex undertaking.

The so called LAMP[1] stack has become widely popular, helped by a thriving market in inexpensive web hosting solutions and a large range of discussion forum, content management, and blogging software becoming available to anyone with modest technical skills. Thus LAMP were perceived to have a simpler learning curve for less well trained developers.

However, such suggestions were met with strong resistance both from developers in India who had barely heard about them (and similarly were skeptical to the web frameworks and tools introduced by the Oslo developers), as well as from the Norwegian students who regarded the other tools as "toys" (one of them being a committer to a well known open source Java project). While all saw the need to shift away from MS Access towards the web, the decision to use an "object-relational mapping" framework became more palatable to the Indian developers after one ex-employee reported being asked about this in an outside job interview. Similarly, contacts in leading consultancy companies providing views from industry served as an important legitimation strategy for the frameworks chosen. The Oslo students have all had formal exposure to Java, and its position as an established, "enterprise" language backed by huge companies, and therefore palatable to government standard bodies (see e.g. The Uttaranchal guidelines). On the other hand, sorting out the most suitable choices from the plethora of available web frameworks created stress on leaders of the effort. After much search, the project ended up with a stack of advanced modern Java frameworks .

5 Discussion

5. 1 Challenges of building a global network

As we have seen, the HISP effort to cultivate local teams around the global network has proved challenging and time-consuming. Leading forces in the project pursued the latest OSS frameworks and mechanisms, both because of a desire to work with the best tools and concern for the long term viability of the project, as well as for "marketing" within the OSS community, where high quality and general code is highly valued. Difficulties in mastering these tools and technologies has hampered the participation in India and Vietnam, and the substantial amount of time spent on training and supervision of local recruits have taken away valuable coding time from the core developers. Despite the time and efforts spent at building local teams in India and Vietnam, 80-90% of the code in the first milestone release in February 2006 had been committed by the Oslo team. Almost all the code so far produced by the Asian teams have proved to be of limited value, and has not become part of the release. Though all developers have source code commit access, the power of deciding what gets released and what gets factored out or should remain in the "incubator" rests with the coordinators and core developer in Oslo.

In India HISP pay is low, conditions can not compete with big companies, and career prospects uncertain, making it hard to attract highly skilled developers who are much sought after by outsourcing companies. In addition, the Indian project leaders were also too busy with implementation (of a previous DHIS version) to muster the energy needed to learn new technologies.

Open participation is a lot more difficult in practice than most accounts make it, probably because of a bias towards high profile projects and elite developers. The experienced Indian team lost confidence and were bewildered by the new technologies and tools introduced in the DHIS 2 process, and similarly in Vietnam HISP has struggled to establish an independent developer team able to contribute to the project.

5. 2 Distributed OSS development across cultures and contexts

The Norwegian developers had a hard time understanding the lack of internet use on the part of the other developers, both in terms of using mailing lists actively and in more independently seeking out information on technical issues. This is partly due to the fact that ready broadband access is a very recent phenomenon in these nodes. While the culture of always being online and constantly using search engines is second nature to the Oslo team, even people with IT degrees seem to use the web mainly for email. It has been frustrating for the coordinators and core developers in Oslo how difficult it has been to engage Indian and Vietnamese developers in discussions on the mailing list or to get them to document their work on the wiki website. Lack of fluency in English is probably a contributing factor, if you don't master the language you don't have a voice. But it is even more a case of not speaking the "language" of open source and distributed development. In the early stages of the project, project staff in India were very hesitant to enter into discussions on technologies as choice of framework is more than a technological decision; it is a display of power/position. When collaborating on the same modules, the Norwegian students had difficulties of communicating directly with the Vietnamese students as almost all communication on the list from the Vietnamese side was done by the faculty coordinating the group there. To the Vietnamese students it was natural that the leader of the group took care of the communication with Oslo, while the Norwegian students were used to participating more openly in discussions and felt that this hampered effective communication.

6 Conclusion

Building networks of actions (Braa et al 2004) or distributed nodes of locally skilled software developers in a network of developing countries has proved challenging and time-consuming. The differences in programming skills and OSS experiences between the Norwegian core developers and the developer teams in India and Vietnam show that there is a need to adapt the distributed process to fit the whole network. The use of familiar tools and technologies might have changed the situation in the south, but would again have made the project unattractive to the developers in Oslo and other potential contributors. Still, a greater involvement in the technology selection from all the nodes, and especially the Indian, could have given a more unified situation. One important lesson learned here is that coordination of such a distributed process across different contexts and cultures demands much traveling and face to face communication in order to align interests of the network, and to overcome the apparent difficulties of online communication.

The fact that there is a lack of skilled developers and generally poor infrastructure for distributed development in many developing countries is nothing new, and is the very reason for the strong focus on capacity-building and university collaborations (Braa et al 2004) in HISP, and also the main reason to continue this long-term work. However, when it comes to software development and producing quality software on time to demanding customers, the distributed HISP approach seem to need adjustments. This context of software production also clashes with the OSS ethos of "It's done when it's done", and unwillingness to compromise on quality. As a short term goal it seems difficult to establish effective OSS development nodes in India and Vietnam that can deliver quality software, given the resources in HISP. However, as a long-term goal, and part of a long-term strategy on local capacity-building, such a distributed north-south-south development process will have greater chances of success.

References

Braa, J., Monteiro, E., and Sahay, S. (2004) "Networks Of Action: Sustainable Health Information Systems Across Developing Countries," MIS Quarterly (28:3), pp 337-362

Department of Information Technology (2004), "Standards for eGovernment Applications Uttaranchal Portal", http://www.itdaua.org/itda/Attachments/IT_Standards.pdf

Duchenaut, N. (2005), "Socialization in an Open Source Software Community: A Socio-Technical Analysis", Computer Supported Cooperative Work 14:323–368

Fitzgerald, B. & Kenny, T. (2003) Open Source Software the Trenches: Lessons from a Large-Scale OSS Implementation", in ICIS 2003, pp. 316-326.

Heeks, R. (2005) "Free and Open Source Software: A Blind Alley for Developing Countries?", eDevelopment Briefing No. 1 2005, Development Informatics Group, University of Manchester

Krishna, S., Sahay, S., and Walsham, G. (2004), "Managing Cross-Cultural Issues in Global Software Outsourcing", Communicatoins of the ACM, (47:4) pp 62 - 66

Raymond, Eric (2000) "The Cathedral and the Bazaar", http://www.catb.org/~esr/writings/cathedral-bazaar/cathedral-bazaar/ar01s04.html

Weerawarana, Sanjiva and Weeratunga, Jivaka (2004), "Open Source in developing countries", SIDA report

---

[1] Linux, Apache, MySql, and either PHP, Python, or Perl. Recently, Ruby has also received much publicity through the "Ruby on Rails" framework.

[2] The selected technologies are Hibernate, Spring, and Webwork

Licensing Services: An "Open" Perspective

Vincenzo D'Andrea and G.R.Gangadharan

Department of Information and Communication Technology,
University of Trento,
Via Sommarive, 14, Trento, 38050 Italy
{dandrea,gr}@dit.unitn.it

Abstract. Though service orientation is an incipient technology, the inherently infinite potentiality of services makes them to proliferate seamlessly, serving in myriad domains. Licensing of services enables to regulate the commercial use and modifications of service, retaining the copyright with owner of the service. With the growing influence of open source initiatives today, it becomes a significant topic to analyze 'open'ing services. In this paper, we present a concept of 'open service' and analyze the implications of open source approach on service licenses.

1 Introduction

Service oriented computing (SOC) is an emerging distributed systems paradigm, addressing the aspects of real world applications, crossing organizational and technical boundaries. With a vision of dynamically composing service oriented and non-service oriented applications, SOC continues to proliferate as a technology for connecting applications in a loosely coupled manner. Today, web services are being used as a component or utility and offer programmatic interfaces to applications. However, many available web services are not even considered as providing relevant business value. The majority of attention on SOC has been contemplated on its related technical standards and technology integration. Managerial issues and business strategy for implementing SOC have not been studied intensively.

One of the relevant issues from this perspective is the role of licensing for services. In the case of software, licensing is generally considered the way for extending property rights into software. Thus, software licensing [1] is considered to include all transactions between the licensor and the licensee in which the licensor agrees to grant the licensee the right to use some specific software or contents of information for a specific tenure under predefined terms and contracts.

In [2], the author describes a distributed software licensing framework using web services and SOAP. However, [2] addresses a framework using web services but does not address licensing of web services itself. The technical contracts of web services are described in [3], but business and legal contents of contracts are not considered. In [4], we had elaborated the dimensions of web services

Please use the following format when citing this chapter:

D'Andrea, V., and Gangadharan, G.R., 2006, in IFIP International Federation for Information Processing, Volume 203, Open Source Systems, eds. Damiani, E., Fitzgerald, B., Scacchi, W., Scotto, M., Succi, G., (Boston: Springer), pp. 143-154

differing from software and proposed an anatomy of a service license with a set of key negotiation issues.

As the foundations of open source regime rely on licenses, an approach inspired by open source could be considered during the process of conceptualizing licenses for services. The Free / Open Source Software (FOSS) approach protects the unconditional rights of modification and redistribution by the collaborating developers, making the source code freely available [5]. Freedom of distribution and freedom of modification are the core principles of open source licensing. To the best of our knowledge, the idea of making services 'open' is completely new and no previous work exists in this field. In this paper, we present a novel concept of licensing services, inspired by open source movement.

The rest of the paper is organized as follows. Section 2 introduces the concept of service oriented computing. Section 3 presents the distinguishing characteristics of services which preclude the direct adoption of software licenses for licensing services. Section 4 elaborates licensing of services, describing the issues of composition. A comprehensive description of what we mean by 'open' services is elucidated in Section 5. Section 6 describes the consequences of adoption of open principles in services paradigm, drawing some conclusions.

2 Service Orientation of Software

Most of the products fall in a continuum having pure service on a terminal point and pure commodity good on the other one [6]. Software, traditionally, has been perceived as a product, requiring possession and ownership, in order to receive the desired performance. Software-as-a-service [7] is a mechanism of renting software where users are subscribed to the software they use. SOC allows the software-as-a-service concept to expand to include the delivery of complex business process and transactions as a service, allowing applications to be constructed on the fly and services to be' reused everywhere [8].

The idea of software composition and refinement instead of software development from scratch nowadays is elaborated to the platform-independent, distributed and standardized services paradigm [9]. In such paradigm, services reflect self-contained processes that can be described, published, discovered and invoked in a distributed environment, connecting people, processes, and applications. Services are intended to represent meaningful business functionality that can be federated with other services, to enhance more value to the business functionality.

The application of SOC model (see Figure 1) to web resources is manifested by web services to provide a loosely coupled model for distributed processing. Web services are the enabling technology, standardized to construct and integrate applications and organizational interfaces as services, using the Internet as the communication medium and open Internet-based standards [10]. A service is represented by an interface part defining the functionality visible to the external world as a means to access the functionality and an implementation

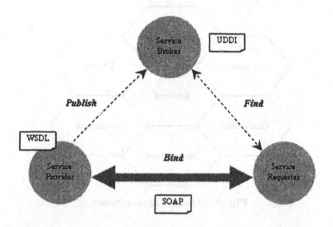

Fig. 1. Service Oriented Computing (Instances with Web Service)

part realizing the interface. The Web Services Definition Language (WSDL) is an XML based interface definition language, describing services as a collection of messages (abstract descriptions of the data being exchanged) and port types (abstract collections of operations), separated from their concrete network deployment or data format bindings. Directories of services are necessary in order to find services usable for a specific application. Universal Description, Discovery, and Integration (UDDI) enables publishing and accessing WSDL specifications in directories. Simple Object Access Protocol (SOAP) is a platform and language independent protocol, providing a way of communication between applications.

3 Dimensional Analysis of Software and Services

Software is an intangible asset, protected by copyright. Being a digital work, it can be vulnerable for perfect copying, and unlimited copies identical to the original can be made. Software is an experience good, whose value is not quantifiable without consumption. Thus, the socio-economic analysis of software signifies distribution strategies. While services (see Figure 2) present several similarities with software, we claim that it is not possible to adopt the software [11] and/or component [12] licensing models directly for licensing services. The reproduction of services could vary in the levels of interface, implementation, and execution (see Section 5 for details). Further, composition of services [13] is significant in reproduction of value added services. The following characteristics of services associated by functional and non-functional properties differing appreciably from software become the cornerstones for licensing of services:

Configurability: Generally software serves as a standalone application licensed by shrink-wrap or click-wrap licenses. In contrast, web services are not

Fig. 2. Service Characteristics

targeted as standalone applications. The rationale behind web services is making network-accessible operations available anywhere and anytime. The counterpart of a software application in terms of services is a reconfigurable composition of distributed services. Service implementation may involve many steps, executed in distributed manner, supporting interoperability and location transparency [14]. In contrast to software components, consumers are not required to download them for local use.

Discreteness: Software ranges from small fragments to sophisticated applications. The separation of a software package will not be meaningful as it was originally intended to function. Similarly, services can also vary in complexity of functions. A service, as a self-contained software module, semantically encapsulates discrete functionality [8].

Autonomy: Unlike general software and components, services are connected to other services and clients using message based methods. They do not require knowledge of any internal structures or context at the client or service side. Thus, loose coupling allows service providers to modify the service interfaces, without impacting consumers.

Interconnectedness: Software programs run on infrastructures and consumers are responsible for maintaining the infrastructure on which the software executes. In case of services, functionality and reliability can be affected by problems in the network between consumers and services. The availability and performance of a service could not be directly guaranteed.

4 Towards Licensing Services

All the characteristics of SOC lead to composability, to form composite services by combining elementary and/or composite services. Service composition [15] is related to the implementation of a web service whose internal logic involves the invocation of operations offered by other web services. Services can be composed (see Figure 3a) as a part of composite service, encapsulating individual services and exposing a different set of operations. Another perspective on composition (see Figure 3b) is by defining the invocation order of individual services [16]. Service composition allows a recursive process of composition of services i.e. a composed service can be composed with an other elementary and/or composite service. Thus, individual services can be composed up to any levels of hierarchies.

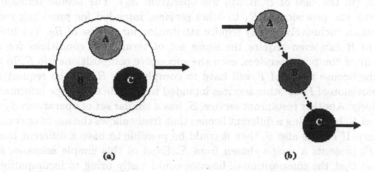

Fig. 3. Service Composition (a) by Encapsulation and (b) by Sequencing

Besides the functional operations, from the point of view of a service consumer, it is important to consider also other, non-functional, aspects of service provisioning, such as the cost or the reliability of a service. These aspects are collectively referred to as Quality of Service (QoS) or non functional properties of a service. The QoS of a composite service is derived from the aggregation of QoS of each individual services, where the aggregation could be a simple combination such as adding the cost of individual services, or taking the maximum among the performances of the individual services to estimate the response time of a composite service. For other aspects, the combination requires the definition of a specific model, such as combining security aspects or reliability, availability, scalability and so on.

Analyzing the characteristics of services as discussed in Section 3, depicts the nature of services differing from software and/or components and rises a requirement for licensing services. Questions of ownership and distribution could impede composition, thereby impacting the reuse of services. Thus, the license of a service [4] is defined as not only the description of the terms and conditions for the use of service as in the case of software, but also a detailed description of clauses regarding reuse.

Though the concept of arbitrarily mixing and matching the services from different providers seems interesting, the basic clauses of service licenses would enforce certain terms and conditions on composition. To illustrate the issues that could arise in the context of licensing web services, we consider a simple scenario where R is a restaurant service providing the following operations: R_0, information on location and opening hours; R_1, the facility for reserving table; R_2, a catalogue of specialty cuisines; R_3, a daily recipe for one of the specialty cuisine. Another service, F, a restaurant finder service uses R, for the following operations: F_1, a restaurant locator giving a list of restaurants close to a given location and using R_0 (as well as similar operations for other restaurants); F_2, for intermediating table reservation, using R_1; F_3, a daily recipe randomly selected among the recipes provided by the restaurants listed using F (in the case of R, it will use operation R_3). The license terms of R may deny the provision of R_3 to other services intended for providing recipe information exclusively or may require attribution for the use of R_3. The license terms of R can even require the same set of terms and conditions for any hierarchy of composed services, even the successive compositions use F. In this case, the license terms of F will have to comply with R, for the request and deny provision of F_3 to other services intended to provide the recipe information exclusively. Another restaurant service, S, has a similar set of operations S_0, S_1, S_2, S_3 as R, but having a different license that freely allows the use of operations anywhere. If F uses also S, then it could be possible to have a different license when F_3 presents a recipe chosen from S. Even in this simple scenario, it is apparent that the composition of licenses could easily bring to incompatibility between the composed services.

The license compatibility is a complex issue, requiring careful attention before attempting to merge licenses. The licensing of a composed service would be based on the licenses used in different service and the way they are combined together. As composition of services is established dynamically ('just-in-time') and composed service is created on-the-fly, the license of composed service would be program generated and needed to be validated by analyzing the licenses of composing services.

5 'Open'ing Services

Free software is a matter of the users' freedom to run, copy, distribute, study, change and improve the software. According to [17], it refers to four kinds of freedom, for the users of the software:

1. The freedom to run the program, for any purpose (freedom 0).
2. The freedom to study how the program works, and adapting to the needs (freedom 1).
3. The freedom to redistribute copies (freedom 2).
4. The freedom to improve the program, and release improvements to the public, so that the whole community benefits (freedom 3).

Open source software, as a superset of free software, exists in a plethora of initiatives today, representing a variety of technology innovations and approaches [18]. Some of the key conditions of Open Source Definition (for authoritative definition, see [19]) are as follows:

1. The software should be freely redistributable.
2. The software must include source code, and must allow distribution in source code as well as compiled form.
3. The software must permit modifications and derived works, and must allow them to be distributed under the same terms as the license of the original software.
4. The rights attached to the software must apply to all to whom the software is redistributed without the need for execution of an additional license.
5. The license must not discriminate against any person or group of persons or any field of endeavor.

Following FOSS definitions [17, 19], we define an 'Open Service' as follows:

1. An 'Open Service' should be free for use.
2. The source code of the interface (WSDL descriptions) as well as the implementation of an 'Open Service' should be available.
3. The service implemented by creating a new service using the source code and interface of an 'Open Service' should be freely distributable as an independent service. The modification of interface and implementation should be permitted.
4. The service using an 'Open Service' as part of a composite service should be freely distributable as an independent service, even when using a separate interface. The modification of interface and implementation should be permitted.
5. Derived services and modified services must be allowed and be capable of distribution.
6. The license must not discriminate against any person or group of persons or any field of endeavor.
7. The license agreement must provide an 'Open Service' "as is" with no warranties either to functional and/or non-functional properties or non-infringement of third party rights.
8. The license must not place restrictions on composition with other services and on distribution of composed services.

Open service perspective enhances the quality properties of a service, leveraging the availability of the source code and the right to modify it. Beyond composition, the 'open'ness of service makes the class of derivative service, a service being modified and re-distributed with more value addition.

Now, we exemplify the freedom and openness exclusively associated with 'open'ing of services, varying in the levels of interface and implementation and in the levels of composition and execution.

1. *Service Usage*

   Service usage describes the freedom to execute a service by other applications, for any purpose. The basics of 'open'ing service allows the use (execution) of service by any other service oriented and/or non-service oriented applications, adhering the given open service license.

2. *Service Implementation*

With the opening of service, we are provided with the freedom to know how the service works and could be adapted to our needs, making the source code of service interface as well as service implementation freely available.

a) A service is described by WSDL. Service orientation obligates WSDL code to be available publicly for service discovery, and composition.

b) In addition, an 'open' service allows the availability of the source code of implementation (the real functionality of a service).

c) The source code of a service wrapping the functionality of another proprietary software partially or fully, can be available publicly with service interface and implementation, except the source code of proprietary software being wrapped in the given service. Consider a spell checker service wrapping PWP[1] spell check API. As PWP is proprietary, its source code can not be available. However, a service can use the PWP spell checker API for spell checking operation. Thus, an 'open' service wrapping the PWP spell checker API allows users to read the source code of interface and implementation of the service except the source code of the wrapped system.

3. *Service Redistribution*

Service redistribution describes the freedom to distribute a service as a separate service. Further, any entity can create a new service which would use the interface of an 'open' service, without the need to implementing the service realization.

a) **Separate and independent service: replica of an 'open' service:** Opening of service allows to create independent services, attributing to the 'open' service. Let S_A be an 'open' service providing a spell checking operation for words, say, $Spell(word)$. Consider S_A provides this service by wrapping PWP spell checker API. Let S_B be an another independent service, providing the same $Spell(word)$, created by replicating the source code of implementation and WSDL of the 'open' S_A. Albeit S_A and S_B are performing the same operations, S_A and S_B are two different services, executed separately.

b) **Separate but dependent service with same interface:** This is a common scenario in SOC; our perspective stresses the attention on licensing aspects. 'Open'ing service adds value to a service by distributing the service, not requiring to implement the service again. Let S_B be a service providing a spell checking operation $Spell(word)$ for words, using (copying) the WSDL interface $Spell(word)$ of 'open' S_A. S_B is designed in such a way that $Spell(word)$ of S_B directly invokes the operation of S_A, executing on the host of S_A.

From a service consumer perspective, in both cases, S_A and S_B are providing exactly the same $Spell(word)$ interface, thus they are interchangeable in an application on the consumer side. The two implementations of S_B are

---

[1] PWP is a fictitious name for a Proprietary Word Processor.

not distinguishable. Theoretically, there will not be any differences in performances of both the services, apart from possible network latency between S_A and S_B.

4. **Service Derivation & Distribution**

   Service derivation and distribution offer the freedom to improve the service, and release improvements to the public, so that the whole community benefits. Opening of services allows to perform modifications on the WSDL interface and implementation of the service and thus, derived services are created. Derived services could be executed independently (together with separate interface and implementation) or could use the implementation of the parent service.

   a) **Separate and independent service: replica of an 'open' service with modified interface and implementation:** Now, consider the case similar to 3(a) with interface of the open service S_A be modified in S_B. The modified interface of S_B provides $Spell(sentence)$ which composes a $parser()$ and repeated invocation of the code derived from S_A, to access PWP API. Now, S_A and S_B are the different services, executing independently. $Spell(sentence)$ of S_B is derived and improved version (having an own additional functionality $parser()$) of $Spell(word)$ of S_A.

   b) **Separate but dependent service with modified interface and implementation:** Consider a service S_B similar to the case of 3(b), but with modified WSDL interface as well as implementation of the open service S_A. $Spell(sentence)$ of S_B comprises a $parser()$ and repeated invocation of the spell checking operation provided by S_A via the interface $Spell(word)$. Thus, the word spell checking operation of S_B is executed in the host of S_A (invoking repetitively the service of $Spell(word)$ of S_A) for spell checking of a given prose $Spell(sentence)$.

The cases presented above are only a partial view of all the possible combinations of derivation (or not) from the source code, modification (or not) of the service interface, and relationship between services (compositional properties). Due to space constraints, the most common and significant cases of SOC have been illustrated and summarized in Table 1.

Table 1. Partial view of 'open'ing of services

Interface	Implementation	Composition	Case
Unmodified	Unchanged	No	3(a)
Modified	Derived	No	4(a)
Unmodified	Unchanged/Derived	Yes	3(b)
Modified	Unchanged/Derived	Yes	4(b)

6 Consequences and Conclusions

The 'open'ing of services significantly contributes to the development of new services from existing services by adding new operations. Consider S_X be an open service. S_Y could be developed by extending S_X in any of the ways discussed in Section 5, keeping S_Y as 'open'. A new service S_Z could be developed by incorporating S_Y, which in turn provides access to S_X operations. S_Z could even enhance S_X, with additional operations.

Free services inspired by FOSS licenses could make value addition by composition, resulting composed services as 'free'. Thus, free services (with free licenses) could create a chain effect on composition of services to be free, even if one of the composing service may be not 'free'.

Let S_P and S_Q be the two individual services of a composite service S. S_P and S_Q may be licensed by free or proprietary licenses not imposing restrictions on the use in a composition. The composition of S_P and S_Q inspired by FOSS scheme, is illustrated in Table 2. Making services free will be highly beneficial

Table 2. Service composition enriching 'Free Culture'

S_P	S_Q	$S = \{S_P, S_Q\}$
Free	Free	Free
Free	Proprietary	Free
Proprietary	Proprietary	Free

for government sectors, education, and non-profitable organizations to explore and enjoy the benefits of services.

'Open'ing services may raise an emergent question of how a service provider could profit by providing services. Many OSS business models are in practice of the community [20]. Some of these business models could be adaptable to the 'open' service context.

1. **Support Seller:** 'Open' services could adopt this scheme where revenue comes from media distribution, branding, training, consulting, and custom development.
2. **Service Enabler:** An 'open' service could be created and distributed primarily to support access to revenue-generating on-line services.
3. **Sell It, Free It:** Like traditional commercial softwares, services would begin their product life cycle as closed and then are converted as 'open' service when appropriate.
4. **Brand Licensing:** An 'open' service provider can charge other service providers/ aggregators/ consumers for the right to use its brand names and trademarks in creating derivative services.

Further, a copyright holder can release his/her works under any license, including multiple licenses and users of that work are allowed use under one of the licenses they choose [21]. Dual licensing is a business model for open source software exploitation based on the idea of simultaneous use of both open source and proprietary licenses [22]. Several open source projects, including MySQL, Perl, and Qt use dual licensing for their business model. Following the dual licensing strategy, a service can be licensed under open source inspired license as well as a proprietary license.

According to GPL [23], the distribution of GPL'd software must include source code. A GPL'd application delivered as a web service is not actually distributed to the end user. Hence, in this case, the application license does not require to disclose the source code. The nature of web services allows users to interact with the application via an interface, without downloading the software. This can result against the 'freedom' of GPL, i.e. users consuming services without having access to the source code as delivered by the providers, retaining the rights to modify and distribute. More precisely, GPL acts on the source code, but not on the use of source code by a service. Consider a service wrapping FWP[2] instead of PWP (a Proprietary Word Processor). As FWP is a GPL'd software, a wrapper for FWP is also GPL'd code. However, GPL does not restrict the use of this FWP wrapper provided by a web service. Since, the service is using only the execution of FWP (not the source code of FWP), GPL does not effect the licensing of composite services based on 'FWP wrapper' service. Even the draft version of GPL3 [24] is silent about this issue.

Nowadays, standards are 'open' in SOC. But, the services developed using these standards are unfortunately 'closed'. If services are 'open', service consumers can add value beyond the concept of composition. Hence, we introduced the concept of open services in this paper and analyze the impacts of open source inspired licenses on SOC. The wedding of services with open source would be beneficial for both communities, spreading services 'open'ly. In our future work, we aim to embed formal licenses in services and make legally enforceable service composition.

References

1. Classen, W.: Fundamentals of Software Licensing. IDEA: The Journal of Law and Technology **37**(1) (1996)
2. Clarke, N.: Distributed Software Licensing Framework based on Web Services and SOAP. http://www.dsg.cs.tcd.ie/~dowlingj/students/clarken/clarken_02.pdf (May 2002)
3. Tosic, V., Pagurek, B.: On Comprehensive Contractual Descriptions of Web Services. In: Proceedings of the IEEE e-Technology, e-Commerce, and e-Service (EEE). (2005) 444–449
4. D'Andrea, V., Gangadharan, G.R.: Licensing Services: The Rising. In: Proceedings of the IEEE Web Services Based Systems and Applications (ICIW'06), Guadeloupe, French Caribbean. (2006)

---

[2] FWP is a fictitious name for a free word processor.

5. Feller, J., Fitzgerald, B.: A Framework Analysis of the Open Source Software Development Paradigm. In: Proc. of the 21st Annual International Conference on Information Systems. (2000) 58–69
6. Wikipedia: Service. http://en.wikipedia.org/wiki/Services (Accessed on 27.12.2005)
7. Bennett, K., Layzel, P., Budgen, D., Brereton, P., Macaulay, L., Munro, M.: Service-Based Software: The Future for Flexible Software. In: Proceedings of the Asia-Pacific Software Engineering Conference (APSEC). (2000) 214–221
8. Papazoglou, M., Georgakopoulos, D.: Service Oriented Computing. Communications of the ACM **46**(10) (2003) 25–28
9. D'Andrea, V., Marchese, M., Gangadharan, G.R., Ivanyukovich, A.: Towards a Service Oriented Development Methodology. In: Proceedings of the Eighth World Conference on Integrated Design and Process Technology, Beijing, China. (2005)
10. Weerawarana, S., Curbera, F., Leymann, F., Storey, T., Ferguson, D.: Web Services Platform Architecture : SOAP, WSDL, WS-Policy, WS-Addressing, WS-BPEL, WS-Reliable Messaging, and More. Prentice Hall PTR (2005)
11. Kendra, G.: The Anatomy of a Technology License. Michigan's Lawyer's Weekly **16**(34) (2002)
12. Chavez, A., Tornabene, C., Wiederhold, G.: Software Component Licensing: A Primer. IEEE Software **15**(5) (1998) 47–53
13. Alonso, G., Casati, F., Kuno, H., Machiraju, V.: Web Services Concepts, Architectures, and Applications. Springer Verlag (2004)
14. Colan, M.: Service Oriented Architecture expands the vision of Web services. http://www-128.ibm.com/developerworks/webservices/library/ws-soaintro.html (2004)
15. Alvarez, P.A., Baares, J.A., Ezpeleta, M.J.: Approaching Web Service Coordination and Composition by means of Petri Nets. In: Proceedings of the 3rd International Conference on Service Oriented Computing. (2005) 185–197
16. Dustdar, S., Schreiner, W.: A Survey on Web Services Composition. International Journal of Web and Grid Services **1**(1) (2005) 1–30
17. Free Software Foundation: The Free Software Definition. http://www.fsf.org/licensing/essays/free-sw.html (Accessed on Jan. 2006)
18. Brown, A., Booch, G.: Reusing Open Source Software and Practices: The Impact of Open Source on Commercial Vendors. In: Proc. of 7th International Conference on Software Reuse. (2002) 123–136
19. Open Source Initiative: The Open Source Definition. http://opensource.org/docs/definition.php (Accessed on Jan. 2006)
20. Raymond, E.: The Magic Cauldron. http://www.catb.org/ esr/writings/magic-cauldron/magic-cauldron.html (1999)
21. Wikipedia: Dual license. http://en.wikipedia.org/wiki/Dual_license (Accessed on 29.12.2005)
22. Valimaki, M.: Dual Licensing in Open Source Software Industry. Systemes d' Information et Management (2003)
23. Free Software Foundation: GNU General Public License. http://www.gnu.org/copyleft/gpl.html (Accessed on Jan. 2006)
24. Free Software Foundation: GNU General Public License Version 3. http://gplv3.fsf.org (Accessed on Jan. 2006)

Perceptions and Uptake of Open Source in Swedish Organisations

Björn Lundell, Brian Lings, and Edvin Lindqvist

University of Skövde, P.O. Box 408, SE-541 28 Skövde, Sweden

{bjorn.lundell | brian.lings | edvin.lindqvist}@his.se,

WWW home page: http://www.his.se/lunb

Abstract. There are many different ways in which Open Source ideas can be adopted by business, and influence the way in which companies do business. A number of different surveys have been conducted in different countries with the purpose of understanding the state of practice with respect to Open Source in companies. A number of different business models have been observed, ranging from the use of Open Source infrastructure products to basing a company's entire business model on Open Source. In this paper we report on a study of the perceptions of Open Source and the uptake of open source products and development models in Swedish companies. We investigate this from the standpoint of stakeholders in those companies which have an expressed interest in Open Source, allowing a more in-depth analysis of the extent to which Open Source has influenced business thinking. From our analysis we find that uptake is much higher than reported in earlier studies, but is still concentrated in SMEs, consistent with the findings of previous studies. There is increased evidence of interest beyond the simple use of OS components at the (LAMP) infrastructure level. In particular, a significant proportion of the companies are in a symbiotic relationship with the OS community, supporting both through participation in existing projects and the release of new software under OS licences.

Keywords: Open Source in Swedish Companies, Qualitative Survey, Open Source Adoption, Perceptions of Open Source.

1 Introduction

Open Source (OS) is an issue of increasing significance for organisations today [1], all the more so given current perceptions that it can offer effective business solutions and new business opportunities. Most companies will be aware at least of elements of the LAMP suite [2], even if they are not yet using them. However, as well as involvement in conventional OS component adoption many companies are getting involved in open source software (OSS) development projects, considering that in itself this can bring competitive advantages. There is in particular a strong European interest in Open Source (or Libre), with an ITEA report [3] suggesting that 70% of

Please use the following format when citing this chapter:

Lundell, B., Lings, B., and Lindqvist, E., 2006, in IFIP International Federation for Information Processing, Volume 203, Open Source Systems, eds. Damiani, E., Fitzgerald, B., Scacchi, W., Scotto, M., Succi, G., (Boston: Springer), pp. 155-163

OSS developers live within the EU, and several EU funded projects investigating the phenomenon (e.g. FLOSS, COSPA, Calibre, OSIRIS, COSI).

A number of surveys have considered the OS phenomenon from a variety of perspectives [4-8]. There have been few previous studies of the OSS phenomenon in a Swedish context. One notable recent exception is the study by Dahlander and Magnusson [9]. Case studies were undertaken in three Swedish companies, investigating the relationship between companies and the OS community. This led to a characterisation of three types of relationship: parasitic (in which the commercial interest is indifferent to its effect on OSS) – of great concern to the OSS community[1] as over-exploitation can threaten the "OSS ecosystem"; symbiotic (in which each gains advantage); and commensalistic (referring to a commercial interest not harming the OSS project). Apart from benefiting by improving an OSS product on which a company relies, a symbiotic relationship may result from less obvious benefits. For example, Lussier [10] details an instance of process enhancement in a company brought about through the experience of its developers in an OSS development project. Within our study we found evidence of symbiotic and commensalistic relationships.

The FLOSS project [11] included a telephone survey of companies and public organisations in Germany, Sweden and the UK with at least 100 employees. Those identified as using OSS (in total 395 for the three countries) were further surveyed, using a quantitative questionnaire. The lowest represented sector in this survey was found to be large Swedish companies (at least 500 employees).

The goal of the research reported here was to investigate the state of practice with respect to Open Source in Swedish companies across the SME and large company sectors which have adopted OSS. In particular, it was designed to get an insight into the views of key individuals influencing OS practice and policy within the companies.

2   Research Method

In this paper, we report on a telephone survey of companies selected via purposeful sampling. The survey is a qualitative study of Swedish practitioners within companies known to be active users of OSS. Company size was not a selection factor. The qualitative techniques used are designed to lead to richer information on the phenomenon studied, but do not allow any claim that the results are representative of organisations generally. However, the FLOSS project suggests that Swedish companies lag somewhat behind those in the UK and Germany in their uptake of OS, so the level of OS perceptions reported here may somewhat under-represent those held more generally within the EU.

Sampling was conducted starting from an initial shortlist of practitioners known by the researchers to be interested in OS. Prior knowledge of OS-related activities

---

[1] A recurring concern raised by practitioners during the EU FP6 Calibre series of industrial conferences/workshops.

informed further searches in IT magazines and on the WWW for company involvement in OS, and for practitioner involvement in OS-related seminars and conferences within Sweden. The appropriateness of a qualitative approach with such sampling is in line with the conclusions of Nikula and Jantunen [8], who observe that "companies basing their business on OSS are likely to be better suited for qualitative methods".

The purposeful sampling led to 45 telephone interviews, conducted in Swedish (the native language of all interviewees and the interviewer) and transcribed. Of these, 5 interviews resulted in conversations with practitioners whose companies had no current involvement with OS. Any quotes from these 5 non-adopters are clearly noted in the text. All quotations used in the analysis phase and reported in the paper are translations into English.

The interviews were conducted over a two month period, and based on a number of open questions – a sub-set of which had one or more follow-up questions depending on the initial response. Specifically, questions for the analysis reported in this paper related to:

1. The concept of Open Source
2. Company use of OS products
3. Company participation in OS projects

3   Results

3.1   Perceptions of OS

Question: What is your immediate reaction when I say "Open Source"?

Firstly, it should be noted that the question deliberately probes immediate connections with the term, and that on several occasions this caused respondents to hesitate before replying. As put by one consultant: "is this a context where I must explain from the start what is meant by Open Source code, or can I take for granted that these people know what the term means? I ask myself whether I need to explain or not".

There is a great variation in perceptions of the OS phenomenon, which correlates reasonably well with the level of involvement with OS. In particular, we see four categories of involvement, the top level having two variants:

0:    no OS
1:    use of OS infrastructure internally
2:    use of OS infrastructure and applications
3:    involvement in code generation
        variant 1: commensalistic

variant 2: symbiotic

The main discriminator of the category 3 companies is that OS is immediately associated with the business or process levels, or an ideological view. Respondents typically stressed one or other of these views, although some hesitated to give a short answer - in particular those heavily involved in OS projects ("that is a good question ..."; "I don't know, but ..."). However, their deep knowledge of the concept became evident during the course of the interview.

Those emphasising a process view associate the concept with, for example: "a development model", "collaboration and an ability to influence" or "that you develop the software together with the users". Some were more elaborate in their responses, for example "Freely available source code to tools or software where you try to use a large community over the whole world ... with Linux as the prime example" and "... Eclipse and such things ... a way of working in which you are contributing and use code in different ways."

Those taking a business view tend to associate the concept with their own business: "We build our entire business on it, so [the company] is my first thought."

The ideological view primarily stressed the OS community concept, placing it above the idea of OS products, for example "I think of community, and as a second thought of tools", in particular implying a "free-basis community" with "non-ownership". Only one respondent in the study used the term "libre", which is common in the South of Europe.

A smaller group primarily associated OS with free access to the source code – a rather pragmatic view. Several respondents stressed the ability to modify source code: "literally that you get access to the source code and are allowed to modify the source code"; "I am allowed to play with it myself, if I want". This can be contrasted with the view from a non-OS user whose immediate association in this regard was rather different: "you are expected to modify [the code]".

The main discriminator of the category 0, 1 and 2 companies was an emphasis on OS products, sometimes specific products, and properties of OS products - including quality and cost.

On the product side, the major association was with the LAMP suite - for example "My first thought is Linux". However, some were non-specific "application servers and testing tools, and similar things" and others went beyond LAMP in including desktop products also: "Linux, MySQL, Apache, OpenOffice etc.".

On the properties side, although many placed "no cost" uppermost in their minds, several referred to the quality of OS products: "I really think about very competent software" or even both: "software at no cost that often is just as good as commercial".

3.2   Company use of OS products

Question: Does your company use any Open Source products

After this confirming question, the interviewer asked about the most important OS products for the company, and their general experience in using these products.

Overall, in citing the most important OS products for their company: 75% cited elements of the LAMP stack; 50% cited other infrastructure products; 12% cited Open Office; and 10% cited OS tools for application development. Perhaps not surprisingly, with one exception all companies mentioning Open Office also mentioned Linux. In terms of quality, no negative comments were made about any OS product actually adopted. Some of the larger companies not heavily into OS development show higher scepticism, but more involved respondents did not share this scepticism. For example, "our experience is that [OS products] are very secure, and have become more stable over time; if you follow the distributions, you can see that it has improved over time".

The attitude of the respondents towards OS usage depended largely on the level of company involvement in OS. For example, a developer from a large company which ships products with OS components commented: "we have really tried to explore and asses the quality, so we typically don't read about them - instead we want to dig into the source code and assess the quality". Others differentiate between products which they ship, and those they use internally. For example, for one SME "as a consultancy company, we have adopted some OS products which we deploy at customer sites ... but Open Office is a product we use on a daily basis ourselves".

There is a perception that it takes longer to become productive using the LAMP stack, with developers able to more quickly use proprietary development tools "out of the box". However, the view of experienced LAMP developers is that this is not an ongoing problem.

An experienced OS developer, commenting on the quality of OSS, states that, in his view, it is "always good". Further, "functionality has increased significantly but above all the number of areas in which you can use OS". The Office package, for example, "wasn't available in a usable form five years ago but this is not at all a problem today." Another advantage seen with OS is that using OS products there is a better response to development questions. In the words of one developer: "Open Source is interesting because there is a potential for quickly developing code and quickly getting responses to questions in a way which you do not get in a commercial environment."

Alongside this, astute developers are aware of the broader costs of adopting software: "It is absolutely not for free, because you have to invest time in order to understand the software, and there is no possibility of writing formal complaints if it doesn't perform adequately. There is a certain risk associated with it". However, in his experience "the support in itself is easily as good as for commercial products".

Some company experience is with OS products not so commonly adopted amongst Swedish companies: "We use ObjectWeb, from a European OS consortium, which I would call a hidden pearl. We have used this in a large project at a customer site, and it runs on like a Swiss clock."

Finally, many companies are aware of the licensing advantages of OS: "What I like most with OS is the licence model. It gives a freedom and control over your IT investment, and that I think is a very important factor."

3.3   Company participation in OS projects

Question: Does your company participate in any Open Source projects

After a positive response to this question, the interviewer clarified which ones and in what way the company was involved. Those not participating were asked whether there was a specific reason.

Of the companies actually using OSS within a development environment, 75% actively contribute to OS projects in one way or another. That is, 75% can be classified as having a symbiotic relationship with the OS community, the remaining 25% having a commensalistic relationship. Over 50% of all the companies in the survey were in one of these categories.

A number of companies proved to be highly active in the OS community. In the view of one developer: "life is too short not to get involved in OS development". Others are so heavily involved in OS within their business model, that they take it as a firm responsibility to be aware of, and actively encourage successful projects: "If you look on SourceForge there are 1,000,000 projects 950,000 of which consist of a piece of code which is going nowhere. There are a number which win in the longer term, and it is part of our job to identify those, and become active in them."

The level of activity varied widely. Some companies started OS projects by releasing source code under an OS licence. Others were strategically involved in OS projects as "committers" and other leading roles, including responsibility for publicity. In other cases there was a lower level of interaction, including bug reports and submitting bug fixes for consideration.

4   Discussion and Conclusions

Open Source In this paper we have illuminated perceptions amongst stakeholders in Swedish companies adopting OS. These perceptions seem to graduate from OS perceived as specific tools and products to something which can revolutionise business models and development processes. One important factor seems to be the level of company commitment to OS, in that practitioners in companies contributing to OS projects or modifying OS code seem much more aware of the broader issues related to OS. Developer involvement with OS projects is apparent in half of the companies approached, and in the majority of these the relationship can be said to be symbiotic.

The observation about the very small percentage of OS projects which are likely to be successful may partly relate to the fact that most OS projects are developed by a tiny number of developers [12, 13]. Within the projects adopted in Swedish companies, the vast majority are large, well known projects with significant diffusion. They can therefore be considered low risk.

It is also worthy of note that large companies (over 250 employees) within the sample are more conservative in there uptake than SMEs, being primarily involved only at the level of adopting products from the LAMP suite. However there are exceptions, including both a large IT and a non-IT company, the latter with very specific requirements. Further, we found only one example of inner source development; that is, development of software within a company using Open Source processes and principles [14].

One question is why profit-oriented companies enter the OS field [15]. A number of Swedish companies now see a business in repackaging OS components and offering added value. Many adopt OS products and components within their own development activities, for competitive advantage. Some go further, releasing the products they have developed under OS licences. A strong motivation for both company and individual involvement in OS projects is seen as personal skills development. A major motivation for releasing code as OS is to gain benefit from a larger user and developer community. Of course, a prerequisite for obtaining such benefit is that the community can be built and sustained - something which has been shown to be complex [16].

Overall, the survey suggests that organisational involvement in OS development is a promoter of change: of perceptions, development processes and ultimately business models. This is a phenomenon worthy not only of monitoring but of studying, to understand the key tools, techniques, architectures, development methods and licensing for promoting symbiotic relationships. Such alignment is a challenge both for the OS communities and commercial software development organisations.

It is perhaps worth conjecturing how such alignment might be supported. OS champions within larger organisations might help this process by promoting inner source projects within their organisation. By doing this, the OS development model will be taken in-house, and organisational learning follow. OS communities could make it easier for organisations to assess the maturity and quality of products, thereby benefiting from wider uptake and increased interest and subsequent contributions. Responsiveness to contributions from commercial organisations is an issue which has been raised; it is sometimes difficult for organisations with substantive contributions to find an OS developer with upload rights who is willing to accept.

In conclusion, this study complements the findings of the FLOSS quantitative survey of Swedish companies, concentrating on qualitative issues in order to understand the underlying dynamics behind the OS phenomenon in companies adopting OS. In essence, though, some see the growth of OS usage in stark terms, as expressed by one interviewee: "Our company wouldn't be where it is today if not for Open Source".

162   Björn Lundell, Brian Lings, and Edvin Lindqvist

4 Acknowledgements

This research has been financially supported by the European Commission via FP6 Co-ordinated Action Project 004337 in priority IST-2002-2.3.2.3 'Calibre' (http://www.calibre.ie), and also by Sparbanksstiftelsen Alfa.

5 References

1. P. J. Ågerfalk, A. Deverell, B. Fitzgerald, and L. Morgan. Assessing the Role of Open Source Software in the European Secondary Software Sector: A Voice from Industry, In Proceedings of the 1st International Conference on Open Source Systems (Scotto, M. and Succi, G. Eds.), p. 82-87, Genoa, Italy (2005).

2. G. Lawton. LAMP Lights Enterprise Development Efforts, IEEE Computer, September, p. 18-20 (2005).

3. ITEA. ITEA Report on Open Source Software, ITEA: Information Technology for European Advancement. ITEA Office Association, January 2004, www.itea-office.org (2004).

4. P. Gustafson and W. Koff. Open Source for Business. Computer Science Corporation, California, <www.csc.com/features/2004/uploads/LEF_OPENSOURCE.pdf>, September, (2004).

5. M. Schütz, N. Khan, and A. Chand. A Baseline Survey on Free and Open Source Software (FOSS) in the South Pacific: Knowledge, Awareness, and Usage, ICT Capacity Building at USP Project, The University of South Pacific, ISBN 982-01-0640-0 (2005).

6. e-Cology. Open Source Software – OSS – In Canada: A Collaborative Fact Finding Study, e-Cology Corporation, <www.e-cology.ca/canfloss/report/CANfloss_Report.pdf>, September (2003).

7. J. Giera. The Costs And Risks Of Open Source, April 12, Forrester Research Inc., Cambridge, US (2004).

8. U. Nikula, and S. Jantunen. Quantifying the Interest in Open Source Systems: Case South-East Finland. In Proceedings of the 1st International Conference on Open Source Systems (Scotto, M. and Succi, G. Eds.), p. 192-95, Genoa, Italy (2005).

9. L. Dahlander and M. G. Magnusson. Relationships between open source software companies and communities: Observations from Nordic firms. Research Policy, 34(4), 481-493 (2005).

10. S. Lussier. New Tricks: How Open Source Changed The Way My Team Works, IEEE Software, 21(1), 68-72 (2004).

11. FLOSS. FLOSS Final Report – Part 1: Free/Libre Open Source Software: Survey and Study, University of Maastricht, The Netherlands www.infonomics.nl/FLOSS/report (2002).

12. S. Krishnamurthy. Cave or Community? An Empirical Examination of 100 Mature Open Source Projects, First Monday, **7**(6), www.firstmonday.org/issues/issue7_6/krishnamurthy/> (2002).

13. L. Zhao and S. Elbaum. Quality assurance under the open source development model. Journal of Systems and Software, **66**(1), 65-75 (2003).

14. V. K. Gurbani, A. Garvert and J. D. Herbsleb. A Case Study of Open Source Tools and Practices in a Commercial Setting. In Proceedings of the 5th Workshop on Open Source Software Engineering, p. 24-29, ACM (2005).

15. C. Rossi and A. Bonaccorsi. Why profit-oriented companies enter the OS field? Intrinsic vs. extrinsic incentives, In Open Source Applications Spaces: Fifth Workshop on Open Source Software Engineering (5-WOOSE) May 17, ACM (2005).

16. J. West and S. O'Mahony. Contrasting Community Building in Sponsored and Community Founded Open Source Projects, In Proceedings of the 38th Annual Hawaii International Conference on System Sciences (HICSS'05) - Track 7, January 03-06, 2005, IEEE Computer Society, Los Alamitos, 10p (2005).

A study on the introduction of Open Source Software in the Public Administration

Bruno Rossi[1], Barbara Russo[1], and Giancarlo Succi[1]

1 Free University of Bolzano-Bozen, Faculty of Computer Science,
Domenikanerplatz 3, 39100 Bolzano-Bozen, Italy
{bruno.rossi,barbara.russo,giancarlo.succi}@unibz.it
WWW home page: http://www.case.unibz.it

Abstract. This paper reports about a study on the introduction of Open Source Software (OSS) in a Public Administration located in Europe. The Public Administration examined has introduced OSS as a means to save on the license costs and to have a larger space for customisation purposes. The adoption of new software may have an impact on the employees' productivity that need to be addressed. In this article, we compare the usage of OpenOffice.org and Microsoft Office. Data about the usual office activities performed by the users participating to the experimentation have been collected by means of an automated non-invasive data collection tool. The result of this study reports a similar usage pattern of both suites in terms of workload, but a different approach in using functionalities provided by each software. A further analysis on the life cycles of documents elaborated with the office suites seems to validate the similarities among the software solutions examined.

1 Introduction

The introduction of Open Source Software (OSS) in substitution or in parallel with Closed Source Software (CSS) is an argument that acquired recently great relevance. The proposed savings in terms of license costs and the broader opportunities for software customisation are arguments that interest particularly private and public companies. There are many studies and market researches on the convenience of the migration that privilege one of the two solutions, depending mainly of the factor of cost considered [1]. A complete migration is not an easy step, especially in working environments where the interdependencies and the vertical integration is a key issue [2]. Supporters of OSS also stress the importance to avoid the realisation of phenomena of lock-ins, situations in which a company commits itself to a single supplier or single data format [2, 3]. There are cases of successful migrations, like the city of Calgary in Canada [4] or the region of Extremadura in Spain [5]. But there are also cases of unsuccessful deployment, like the city of Nürnmberg [6] or delays and over expenditures like the case of the city of Munich [7], both cases in Germany. The case study discussed in this paper concerns an European Public Administration. For two months a successful migration to OSS on the desktop side has been monitored. The analysis reported has focused on the software for office automation. The contribution to the field of this study is an evaluation of the similarities and

Please use the following format when citing this chapter:

Rossi, B., Russo, B., and Succi, G., 2006, in IFIP International Federation for Information Processing, Volume 203, Open Source Systems, eds. Damiani, E., Fitzgerald, B., Scacchi, W., Scotto, M., Succi, G., (Boston: Springer), pp. 165-171

differences in usage patterns of OpenOffice.org and Microsoft Office. This can shed some light on the effect of a transition on the routine of the office work in a PA.

2 The Study

2.1 Study description

The study has been based on the data collected from a Public Administration in Europe during a migration to the OpenOffice.org suite. This office automation suite offers similar functionalities as the ones offered by Microsoft Office. It is composed by a word-processor, spreadsheet software, presentation software and a drawing tool. The Public Administration (PA) examined has been adopting OSS for some time; the analysis we report refers to a situation, where the proprietary and open solution coexisted in the working environment. To monitor the time spent on different solutions, data have been collected with the aid of the PROM software [8]. With a non-invasive impact, the software gives the opportunity to register for every document the time spent, the name of the document and the functions used. This last feature is at the moment still limited, but can give useful insights of the different patterns of usage between the two solutions. The monitoring of users as we report in this paper has been performed during 2 months with both solutions installed in parallel. 100 users have been involved in the experimentation.

2.2 Dataset distribution

To have an idea of the evolving situation during the first two months of the experimentation, we can see in figure 1 the comparison between Microsoft Office and OpenOffice.org usage. The figure refers to the average number of documents worked by all users on a specific day. As these numbers seem to report the daily averages are very.

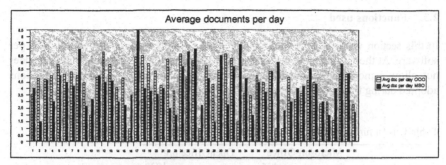

Fig. 1. Average number of OpenOffice.org documents per day (outlined) and MS Office documents per day (in black).

In Figure 2 the total daily number of documents per solution is reported. This is the global sum of all the documents handled daily by all users participating to the experimentation.

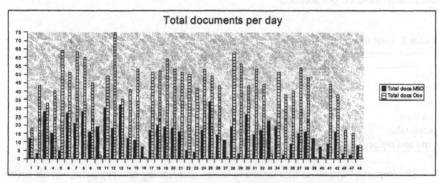

Fig. 2. Total OpenOffice.org documents per day (outlined) and MS Office documents per day (in black).

From this table can be derived that more users are in fact adopting the open solution. At the end of the period considered, the documents handled with OpenOffice.org have been 4.032 against 1.206 opened with Microsoft Office. This to justify that the migration examined is already in a mature state, in which the new technology introduced is taking over the old one.

The purpose of these figures is to give an idea of the existing situation in the PA that is the focus of our study.

2.3   Functions used

In this section we report the functionalities used on the different suites, divided per software. At the moment, the version of the software used for the data collection does not allow a more fine-grained analysis. In table 1 the total numbers of functions adopted during the study. These were selected being the most representative one.

Table 1. Total functions used according to application type

	Microsoft Office	OpenOffice.org
Open	145	1038
Save As	205	1321
Print	170	1109
Spelling	178	578
Insert table	2	43
Find and replace	7	39

In table 2, the same functions are reported, this time normalised with the number of documents handled per solution.

Table 2. Total functions weighted per document handled

	Microsoft Office	OpenOffice.org
Open	0.15	0.24
Save As	0.21	0.31
Print	0.18	0.26
Spelling	0.18	0.13
Insert table	0.00	0.01
Find and replace	0.01	0.01

The impact of activities like inserting tables and finding and replacing words seem very low in both solutions. We could not trace keyboard shortcuts, so the analysis in this sense is limited. In general the usage pattern of OpenOffice.org seems different, with more actions performed, like opening documents, saving and printing. Spelling instead had a higher impact in Microsoft Office than in OpenOffice.org.

2.4   Documents life cycle

To deepen the analysis of the differences between the two solutions, we derived a concept similar to the one of Product Life Cycle (PLC), in our case applied to documents. The concept of Product Life Cycle was first introduced by Theodore Levitt in 1965 [9]. Typical stages in a product life cycle are: Introduction, Growth, Maturity and Decline. There are many different variations of the Product Life Cycle model that differ mainly in the names used to describe the different stages and the purpose of the underlying analysis. A similar model has been used to study the diffusion of new technology [10]. In figure 3 a typical product life cycle is depicted, together with the different phases of maturity.

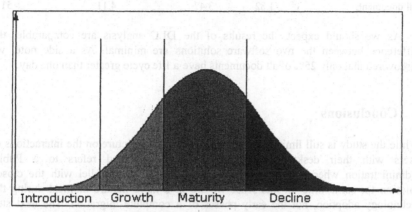

Fig. 3. A typical product life cycle, with four phases of maturity (Introduction, Growth, Maturity, Decline).

- The Introduction phase is where the product is introduced on the market, in this phase marketing has the strongest importance than in other phases.
- The Growth phase is where the increase in sales supported by marketing becomes considerable.
- In the Maturity phase the sales are stabilised and the speed of increase of sales is slowly reduced until it begins to become negative.
- In the Decline phase, the product is no more attractive to possible customers that may prefer a more technological concurrent product.
In the Product Life Cycle, the duration of each phase may be different between different products, as the adoption curve may have a different aspect.
We decided to model the DLC as a measure of software usage to further discover existing analogies between CSS and OSS. Following an analogy with PLC, we considered the life of a single document, as composed from different phases: its creation phase that starts with the generation of the underlying file, the growth phase where the document usage increases, the maturity where the usage reaches maximum levels and the decline phase, when the document's usage begins to decrement to the complete halt. To perform this task we analysed all 5.238 documents and divided them in two groups, the ones handled with OpenOffice.org and the ones handled with Microsoft Office. Subsequently, we reported the life of each document into the PLC model framework. The last step was to analyse the distribution of the derived DLCs. In table 3 we report the results obtained. The average length of the documents is very similar in a comparison between both solutions.

Table 3. Comparison of DLC of all documents, the scale is in days. Averages marked with a * have been obtained by excluding documents with a life cycle of one day

Application	Avg DLC length	St. Dev.	Avg DLC length*	Max DLC length
Microsoft Office	1.83	3.45	4.64	51
OpenOffice.org	1.78	3.74	4.06	46
All documents	1.82	3.47	4.11	51

As we should expect, the results of the DLC analysis are comparable, the difference between the two software solutions are minimal. As a side note, we discovered that only 25% of all documents have a life cycle greater than one day.

3 Conclusions

While the study is still limited, we are getting a clearer picture on the interactions of users with their desktop software. The study reported refers to a Public Administration where OSS has already been adopted in parallel with the closed solution for some time. In this sense we are in a more mature moment during the technology adoption, not the early phases of a complete migration. The next step would be the complete adoption of OSS for office automation, if the feasibility study performed show favourable. The results of our analysis show that proprietary and open solution can coexist on the working environment on the desktop side. Also the average number of documents per day seems comparable. Focusing on the functions used, some activities seem to be more adopted by users with the open solution than the closed one. During our study, some function we thought at first important were rarely used. A more fine-grained analysis will be possible with more accurate software for data collection, collecting more measures necessary to evaluate fully all the functions used. The analysis and evolution of the documents' life cycle, a concept borrowed from economics, seem also to justify the strong similarities between the two solutions offered.

References

1. The Yankee Group (2005) *North American Linux TCO Survey*;
www.yankeegroup.com, June 2005

2. C. Shapiro, and H. R. Varian *Information Rules: A Strategic Guide to the Network Economy* (Harvard Business School Press, 1999).

3. S. Liebowitz, S. Margolis, *Winners, losers & Microsoft, Competition and Antitrust in High Technology* (Oakland, Calif. : The Independent Inst. , 1999)

4. Real World Linux 2004 Conference and Expo Reports, (May 2004); http://www.realworldlinuxbiz.com/artman/publish/printer_rwl04rp.shtml

5. Extremadura Linux Migration Case Study (2005); http://insight.zdnet.co.uk/software/linuxunix/0,39020472,39197928,00.htm

6. Stadt Nürnberg (2004). *Strategische Ausrichtung im Hinblick auf Systemunabhängigkeit und Open Source Software*; http://online-service.nuernberg.de/eris/agendaItem.do?id=49681

7. Landeshauptstadt München (2003). Clientstudie *der Landeshauptstadt München*; http://www.muenchen.de/aktuell/clientstudie_kurz.pdf

8. A. Sillitti, A. Janes, G. Succi, T. Vernazza,*Collecting, Integrating and Analyzing Software Metrics and Personal Software Process Data*, EUROMICRO 2003, Belek-Antalya, Turkey, 1 – 6 September 2003.

9. T. Levitt, *Exploit the Product Life Cycle* (Harvard Business Review, Vol 43, November-Dicember 1965, pp 81-94)

10. M. Bass Frank, "A New Product Growth Model for Consumer Durables, 1969, Management Science, 15, pp215-227)

Exploring the potential of OSS
in Air Traffic Management

Jean-Luc Hardy and Marc Bourgois
EUROCONTROL Experimental Center
Innovative Research Department
91222 Brétigny-Sur-Orge CEDEX France
{jl.hardy,marc.bourgois}@eurocontrol.int,
WWW home page: http://www.eurocontrol.int/eec/

Abstract. This paper introduces a project that aims at defining an Open Source
Software (OSS) policy in the field of Air Traffic Management (ATM). In order
to develop such a policy, we chose to investigate first a set of predictive hypotheses. Our four initial hypotheses were presented, refined and discussed in
bi-lateral meetings with experts in the ATM field and in several conferences
and workshops with OSS experts. At a roundtable, jointly organized by
CALIBRE and EUROCONTROL, we confronted early open source experiences and insights in the ATM domain with experiences and knowledge from
a panel of OSS experts and practitioners from academia and industry. The
revised initial hypotheses are presented using a fixed format that should
facilitate further evolution of these hypotheses.

1 Introduction

EUROCONTROL is the European Organisation for the safety of Air Navigation. It
has as its primary objective the design and development of a safe and seamless pan-
European Air Traffic Management (ATM) system in Europe. Founded in 1960 as a
civil/military intergovernmental organisation, it is now a world leader, pioneering
advances in ATM technology, operational procedures and system interoperability.
The number of Member States has grown from the original 6 to 36.

Many ATM projects are implemented partially or totally through software
developments. Proprietary software is the usual practice in the ATM industry. Most
software produced by the EUROCONTROL Agency is outsourced. Presently, OSS
principles and licenses are not included in the official Intellectual Property Right
(IPR) policy of EUROCONTROL.

The next section presents the structure of the study in five parts: a project
(OSIFE), a network (CALIBRE), an event (roundtable), a formalism, and a
knowledge base.

2 The OSIFE project

By the middle of 2004 we started a study project to get a better understanding of the
potential impact of the OSS movement on ATM. The OSIFE acronym was coined:
"Open Source Implications For EUROCONTROL". We started by reviewing the

Please use the following format when citing this chapter:

Hardy, J.-L., and Bourgois, M., 2006, in IFIP International Federation for Information
Processing, Volume 203, Open Source Systems, eds. Damiani, E., Fitzgerald, B., Scacchi,
W., Scotto, M., Succi, G., (Boston: Springer), pp. 173-179

basic literature concerning Open Source and Free Software. The outcome was a definition of the scope, the objective and the method of the project.

In terms of scope, we decided to limit our investigation to the impact of OSS on the core business of EUROCONTROL, i.e. ATM. In terms of objective, we want to understand if, when and how OSS could impact the business in ATM. In terms of method, we chose to describe our insights as a set of predictive hypotheses. To launch the debate, four broad hypotheses about the potential of OSS for ATM were introduced [1]. They can be summarized as follows: the OSS paradigm will

1. facilitate the harmonization of ATM,
2. maintain or improve the quality of ATM software,
3. affect the ATM industry in a positive way,
4. help EUROCONTROL to better meet its public service obligation.

3   The CALIBRE network

Through this first presentation, it became clear that the ATM community was interested about OSS, that further investigations were needed, and that networking was necessary to gather facts and arguments about the 4 hypotheses. During 2005, networking proceeded twofold: within the ATM world and within the OSS world.

To explore the ATM world, we made numerous contacts inside EUROCON-TROL. It transpired that many experts involved in the improvement of ATM systems are unaware or unclear about the OSS paradigm. For example, OSS is often wrongly considered as equal to freeware. However, we also had the nice surprise to discover a few projects and experiences where the OSS concepts were used or considered helpful.

To explore the OSS world, the CALIBRE consortium [2] quickly appeared as the appropriate network. It is supported by the European Sixth Framework Programme. As part of its commitments to promote the OSS paradigm in Europe, CALIBRE facilitates an industry forum called CALIBRATION, which provides contacts with representatives of other industries.

The CALIBRE conference at Limerick in September 2005 was a first opportunity to present the 4 initial hypotheses of OSIFE to the OSS community and to collect feedback. The second opportunity was a CALIBRE workshop at Krakow, about quality, safety and security in OSS initiatives. In preparation for the Krakow workshop we were stimulated to deepen our comprehension of these issues: following discussions with EUROCONTROL colleagues at the EUROCONTROL Maastricht ATC centre we introduced two new hypotheses, one about safety and the other about security.

4   The OSS-in-ATM roundtable

Assuming that the stimulating spirit of the CALIBRE network could help to increase the OSS awareness among ATM circles, we dreamed about a meeting between both worlds: the OSS world and the ATM world. Aside the OSS2005 conference in June 2005 at Genova, the idea of such a meeting was proposed to B. Fitzgerald, CALIBRE project leader and immediately endorsed. The format chosen for this meeting was a roundtable on the subject: "Potential of OSS in ATM" [3]. It was co-organised with CALIBRE and took place in December 2005 at the EUROCONTROL Experimental Center (South of Paris). It drew a participation of 28 persons from the CALIBRE expert circle, the EUROCONTROL staff, and the ATM industry. Several outcomes were expected from such a confrontation: (i) increased awareness of the OSS paradigm in the ATM circles; (ii) better appreciation of the relevance of early open source experiences in the ATM domain; and (iii) modification or confirmation of the validity of the hypotheses.

5   The formalism used to describe hypotheses

The discussion about our hypotheses and the difficulty to extract knowledge from the abundant OSS literature calls for the adoption of some kind of formalism to describe pros and cons. The CALIBRE team has used SWOT analysis in previous cases to help clarify the potential of OSS [4].

In this paper, we use the SWOT analysis to articulate a model that should facilitate the identification of the critical semantic elements of each hypothesis and should help to trace the evolution of the hypotheses.

The SWOT analysis of a system classifies facts intrinsic to the system in terms of strengths or weaknesses and facts intrinsic to its environment in terms of opportunities and threats. For the purposes of our research, we try to predict how strengths and weaknesses of a system in the environment − the OSS paradigm − translate to opportunities and threats for the system in focus − the ATM system.

Systematic matching of threats with strengths and opportunities with weaknesses leads to the identification of positive (win-win) and negative (loose-loose) synergies between a system and its environment:

a)   (How) could OSS strengths become an opportunity to compensate or correct some of the weaknesses of the ATM systems?

b)   (How) could OSS weaknesses become a threat for the ATM systems?

6   The knowledge base of hypotheses

The preliminary hypotheses of the OSIFE project have been revisited using insights that were collected through the networking process, including lessons learned from the roundtable. To respect the 6 pages limitation of the proceedings, only 3 critical hypotheses are presented in this paper, about quality, safety, and security. Quality, and more specifically safety, is the bread and butter of the ATM domain.

6.1   On the quality of ATM software

In our research we take an external perspective on quality. We interpret wide adoption of software and complexity of systems constructed with that software as indications of high quality software.

It is a fact that ATM systems are complex, essentially   because of the highly sophisticated user interfaces and the stringent performance requirements put onto the ATM systems. The complexity of ATM systems is continually increasing with their ever-increasing interconnectivity.

> 6.1a   Fact (ATM weakness):
> *Most ATM software applications are complex.*

There is ample evidence of the wide adoption of OSS for tools like operating systems, databases etc. which are undoubtedly complex. Such achievements are only possible if OSS indeed has high intrinsic quality.

> 6.1b   Fact (OSS strength):
> *OSS can result in complex applications with high quality.*

Several authors are sceptical about generalisations of quality statements on OSS, for two reasons: either because in the absence of a hierarchical development team where one person is in charge of the product, "modifications can be made to an individual module that could have a deleterious effect on the maintainability of the open-source software product as a whole" [5], or because "in the absence of firm design and documentation standards, and the ability to enforce those standards, the quality of the code is likely to suffer" [7] .

> 6.1c   Fact (OSS weaknesses):
> *Quality of OSS cannot be guaranteed in the absence of a hierarchical development team and firm standards for design and documentation.*

Taking all these arguments together we logically come to:

> 6.1d   Hypothesis:
> *OSS can result in complex ATM applications with high quality, provided that a hierarchical development team and firm standards for design and documentation are enforced.*

6.2   On safety in ATM

The first objection raised when considering a change to the ways ATM systems are developed or operated is that the change will not be compatible with the stringent safety-critical constraints of the field. Not surprisingly, this objection was prominent in the feedback from attendees at presentations on the potential introduction of OSS, both from an ATM audience [1] and from an OSS audience [8, 9].

During our research we noted the lack of OSS penetration for safety-critical applications. No examples could be found in the literature, neither could any be recalled by the OSS expert panel at the roundtable.

6.2a   Fact (OSS weakness):
OSS does not propose specific solutions for safety-critical systems.

6.2b   Fact (OSS strength):
By facilitating the peer review process,
an OSS approach can eliminate some safety-critical problems.

Does this mean that the ATM domain cannot benefit from the potential of OSS? No, it merely means that the safety-critical applications in ATM should not be the first to be explored. But then again, there are very many non safety-critical components in the overall ATM system, so plenty of opportunities to build experience with OSS exist. In fact, one ATM expert at the roundtable ably, but provokingly argued that ATM applications are not safety-critical at all, because by definition the traffic is constantly kept conflict free, offering several minutes of reaction time for the humans in the system to deal with outages of automated components. The argument continues to identify the avionics components as the truly safety-critical parts. Nonetheless we can conclude:

6.2c   Hypothesis:
The safety of ATM systems will be improved through OSS practices, provided
that the peer review process is actively engaged in.

6.3   On security of ATM systems

The second objection that comes to mind when considering the introduction of OSS in ATM is that OSS could create security problems. The security issue has gained prominence because of 9/11. This event has demonstrated that security attacks beyond the worst scenario ever imagined for aviation can happen and that a creative paranoia to guard against such attacks is justified.

6.3a   Fact (ATM weakness):
Security flaws in ATM can have catastrophic consequences.

In the OSS literature, the concept of security symmetry is discussed [10]. As summarized by Brian Fitzgerald [private communication]: «'Security Symmetry' is a reference to Ross Andersen's conjecture (discussed in [11]) which proposes that open systems may be more prone to security attacks (because 'evil' crackers can see the code) but this is balanced by more opportunity to identify and fix potential security flaws in the first place (because 'good' hackers can also see the code). »

6.3b   Fact (OSS weakness):
'Evil' crackers can exploit security risks.

6.3c   Fact (OSS strength):
'Good' hackers can detect and eliminate security risks.

In addition, the OSS paradigm allows software users to check any code incorporated:

6.3d   Fact (OSS strength):
Users can perform a security screening of any code incorporated.

Considering ATM, the security of the operational system (i.e. the run-time system) is normally guaranteed by strict physical isolation. For example, operational ATM systems are completely isolated from the internet, and regular audits to ensure this are common practice.

6.3e Fact (ATM strength):
Non-ATM systems (including people) cannot
access the ATM operational system.

When taken all together, 6.3e cancels out 6.3b:

6.3f Hypothesis:
The security of the ATM system will be improved through OSS practices,
particularly if the software is subject to a security screening.

B. Fitzgerald concluded: «Breaking the security symmetry would be trying to shift the balance more towards realising the benefits, at the expense of incurring the risks.» For ATM, leveraging the security symmetry would require a security screening in the acceptance protocol.

7 Conclusions

This article exploits a formalism for systematically accumulating knowledge about the potential of the OSS in ATM. Starting from a preliminary set of predictive hypotheses, a networking process, engaging both the OSS and the ATM worlds, has been efficient in producing novel insights. The analysis of the outcome from the roundtable is still going on and further refinement of our hypotheses is expected.

8 References

1. J-L. Hardy and M. Bourgois, Open Source Implications for EUROCONTROL (OSIFE), in: Proceedings of the 3rd EUROCONTROL Innovative Research Workshop, edited by Eurocontrol (December 2004).
2. CALIBRE, Limerick (March 6, 2006); http://www.calibre.ie.
3. M. Bourgois, J-L. Hardy, J. O'Flaherty, and J. Seifarth (Eds), Proceedings of the roundtable "Potential of OSS in ATM" (Brétigny, France, December 2005); http://www.oss-in-atm.info.
4. P.J. Ågerfalk, A. Deverell, A. Fitzgerald, and L. Morgan, Assessing the Role of Open Source Software in the European Secondary Software Sector: A Voice from Industry, in: Proceedings of the First International Conference on Open Source Systems (OSS2005), edited by M. Scotto and G. Succi (Genova, Italy, July 2005), pp. 82-87; http://oss2005.case.unibz.it/download.php.
5. S. Schach, B. Jin and D. Wright, Maintainability of the Linux kernel, in: Proceedings of 2nd Workshop on Open Source Software Engineering, ICSE2002, edited by J. Feller, B. Fitzgerald, F. Hecker, S.C. Hissam, K.R. Lakhani, and A. van der Hoek (Orlando, Florida, 2002);   http://opensource.ucc.ie/icse2002.

6. J. Feller, B. Fitzgerald, S. Hissam, and K. Lakhani (Eds.), Perspectives on Free and Open Source Software (The MIT Press, Cambridge, USA, June 2005).
7. S. Rusovan, M. Lawford and D. Parnas, Open Source Software Development: Future or Fad? In: [7], pp. 107-121.
8. CALIBRE, 2nd International Conference: The Next Generation of Software Engineering Integrating Open Source, Agile Methods and Global Software Development (Limerick, Ireland, September 9, 2005), http://www.calibre.ie/events/conferences.php.
9. CALIBRE, Quality and Security Workshop (Krakow, Poland, October 18, 2005); www.calibre.ie/events/workshops.php.
10. J. Feller, B. Fitzgerald, S. Hissam, and K. Lakhani, F/OSS Project Leaders and Developers, in: [6], page XXIX.
11. R. Anderson, Open and Closed Systems Are Equivalent, in: [6], pp. 127-142.

Part V

Empirical Analysis of OSS

Institutional Entrepreneurs and the Bricolage of Intellectual Property Discourses

Ann Westenholz

Department of Organization and Industrial Sociology, Copenhagen
Business School, Kilevej 14, 2000 Frederiksberg, Denmark.
(aw.ioa@cbs.dk)

Abstract. Commercial software firms are increasingly becoming involved
with open source communities. In this research-in-progress paper I briefly
analysed a single firm case that demonstrates how an institutional entrepreneur
mixes in an innovative way different discourses in an attempt to legitimise a
new mode for developing software applying both open and closed source codes.
The institutional entrepreneur does this by creating new distinctions in his daily
software developing work. I am not arguing that the institutional entrepreneur is
creating these new distinctions in an instrumental rational process, but that the
distinctions emerge in sensemaking processes along his 'doing' something in
the firm.

1 Introduction

In the paper I focus on how intellectual property rights develop within software
development that involves both business firms and open-source communities, and on
the role of institutional entrepreneurs in this development. The basic assumption is
that the parties involved are embedded in different institutional logics concerning the
understanding of the nature of intellectual property right, implying their different
perceptions of and practices for knowledge sharing and organizing product
development. What are the stories about intellectual property rights emerging from
this interface? And what role does the institutional entrepreneur play in this
development?

The issue is attempted elucidated from the perspective of New Institutional
Organization theory (DiMaggio and Powel, 1983 ; Meyer and Rowen, 1983; Scott,
1995) and concerns how institutions change – in casu 'intellectual property right'. In
the 1970s and 1980s New Institutional theory represented a novel perspective within
organization theory compared to the rational one by singling out institutions as
independent variables that could explain organizational behaviour. However, by
understanding institutions as independent variables New Institutional theory became
unable to explain organizational change. A number of researchers have since
attempted to develop a New Institutional theory capable of explaining organizational
change as the outcome of the role that institutional entrepreneurs play in the
development (Borum and Westenholz, 1995; Boxenbaum and Battilana, 2004; Brint
and Karabel, 1991; Christensen and Westenholz, 1997; DiMaggio, 1988; Fligstein,
1997; Friedland and Alford, 1991; Greenwood and Hinings, 2002,; Oliver, 1991;

Please use the following format when citing this chapter:

Westenholz, A., 2006, in IFIP International Federation for Information Processing,
Volume 203, Open Source Systems, eds. Damiani, E., Fitzgerald, B., Scacchi, W., Scotto,
M., Succi, G., (Boston: Springer), pp. 183-193

Scott, 1995; Seo and Creed, 2002; Tolbert and Zucker, 1983). In the paper, I elaborate these ideas by combining the theory of institutional entrepreneurs with discourse theory. (Collinson, 1988 1992; Gabriel, Handy and Phillips, 2004; Graesser, Gernsbacher and Goldman, 2003; Grant, Hardy, Oswick and Putnam, 2004ba and b; Jørgensen and Phillips, 2002; Wetherell, Taylor and Yates, 2001).

In the paper I draw on a project-in-progress[1], and the paper is thus a first step toward elucidating the issue. Section 2 of the paper describes a single case in which a business firm uses open-source. Section 3 describes the historical-social context of the case, and section 4 accounts for the theories underlying the analysis. In section 5 I analyze the case and conclude in section 6.

2   The case

John is about forty years old, and worked in the media world in the past. In the mid-1990s he started a Danish IT firm. In 2000, he wanted to publish a product he had developed as an open-source programme, in order to disseminate it and encourage others to elaborate on it. John had learned about open source from a programmer with whom he had collaborated. He was attracted by the idea because, as he says: 'It makes knowledge sharing possible. I think that what we are doing is universal, and should be accessible for all applications involving our product. Therefore it made sense to involve people working with similar problems in the development of the basic functions. Based on these functions, tailor-made solutions could be developed for various customers.'

During 2000, John became increasingly burdened with debts that required him to find venture capital. Although he succeeded in attracting capital, the venture capitalists would not accept open source as part of their business recipe. John was sacked, and in early 2001 found himself without a firm.

John mortgaged his flat and hired three employees who have developed a new model from scratch. As their point of departure, they downloaded an open programme from the Internet, further developed it, and subsequently uploaded the elaborated version, making it available for others. In further developing the programme, they collaborated with IT programmers who formally worked in other places, while simultaneously working openly on the Internet. As John says: 'To resolve problems at the same speed as was possible via the Internet would require several hundred employees. Many of the problems concern very specific issues, and when we inquire on the Internet it is rarely more than 24 hours before we have one or several responses. '

But even as John's employees draw their knowledge from the Internet, others have started to ask them questions via the Internet. If the questions concern issues that do not interest them but are easily resolved, they respond. As one of John's employees

---

[1] The name of the project is Institutional Entrepreneurs and it is financed by the Danish Social Research Council 2005-2009. Homepage: www.IICO.dk

says, 'It's cool being able to produce something that others can use and to help some of the guys in the USA that you admire: Just do so and so.' Being able to respond to questions gives people status in the open-source community. But as John says: 'We don't spend a week correcting errors for somebody in the USA if it isn't something that we can use.'

John's firm makes money by adapting the product to the specific needs of specific customers. If Microsoft had developed the product, similar adaptations to customer needs would be required. The difference is that had Microsoft developed the product, the customer would have to pay a start fee, which is not the case when the product is available as an open-source programme. The advantage for John's firm is, however, that having developed the product, it occupies the cutting edge. It will take some time before others become equally adept at adapting it to customer specific needs. But it also means that the firm must compete for producing the best quality rather than dominating the market, leaving customers with few other options.

John says that his firm rests on 'a reverse line of thought in relation to traditional economy and business strategy: 'It has taken a long time and we have been subject to great ridicule, but it has been fun to see that the customers now realise the great advantage of our approach. They have started to demand open-source products. The concept suddenly starts to spread - and quickly now.'

Sometimes the firm is also involved in the development of closed-systems products, as when the firm collaborates with hardware producers who are working with closed codes. But the closure is immaterial, according to John, because the product cannot be used in other contexts. 'It's fine. There are situations in which it is better to produce your own things and keep them as a business secrets, particularly if it concerns an area.' Nevertheless he admits that other programmers may be able to transfer the codes to other situations, but the company with which John collaborate will not concede to openness for the product. He has accepted this condition, because 'It's worth more to us to produce this for 'CLOSED-SYS' under the conditions which they stipulate. Then we can work for others in the way we prefer. So in the case of 'CLOSED-SYS', we work with a closed system.' John estimates that about 10% of the firm's jobs involve working with closed codes, and he does not expect this share to change to any appreciable extent.

(The data for this case description was gathered in 2002)

3   The historical social context of the case

The case about John and his firm is the story about how different institutional logics governing open and closed codes respectively meet and mix – an issue of different understandings of 'property rights to intellectual work'. The story is far from an isolated occurrence, and today we observe many different ways of mixing the two logics in the production of software. In Denmark, for instance, various interest organisations/groups have emerged over the last two years that work for the dissemination of open source commercial suppliers and producers. And the phenomenon is far from local, but a global one.

In order to understand this development it might be fruitful to look into what has happened with the concept of 'property' over the last decades. Traditionally the concept of property embraces a number of rights that in various ways are allocated to individuals, groups or society. In the capitalist production the concept of property is tied to firms and embedded in a conception of the right of private owners to manage the firm, yield profit, and wind up/transfer/sell the firm to others. In western societies the prevailing assumption has been that combined these three rights were related to the efficiency of the firm (Lindkvist and Westenholz, 1987). Concurrently with production being transformed from material production to the production of intellectual work (innovations, ideas, knowledge, information, symbols, expressive manifestations, images, music, etc., detached from specific physical objects) the intellectual property right has attracted growing attention in society, and some researchers argue that intellectual property rights require a specific justification. The reason is, among other things, that non-physical phenomena like intellectual work are not immediately reduced from being shared with and used by many people such as physical phenomena are reduced by being shared with or used by others besides the owner. (Barlow, 2002; Coleman and Hill, 2005; Cornish, 2004; Davis, 2004a; Rivette and Kline, 2000; Stahl, 2005; Thierer and Crews, 2002; Wright, 1979).

One of the most characteristic sectors in society that has placed the discussion of intellectual property rights on the agenda in recent years is that of *software development within the hacker-culture*[2] related to the communities 'Free Software' and 'Open Source' and the concept of 'copyleft'. (Davis, 2004 b; DiBona, Ockman and Stone, 1999; Kaisla, 2001; Laurent, 2004; Moody, 2002; Pavlicek, 2000; Raymond, 1999; Rosen, 2005; Stahl, 2005; Torvads, 2001; Wark, 2004; Weber, 2004; Williams, 2002). Within private software firms many saw the hackers as a kind of communist movement, but the boundary between private business and the hacker community was surprisingly transgressed by the end of the 1990s. Among other things the privately owned Netscape announced that it would publish its source codes on the Internet and thus make the codes accessible to the public. This triggered a process through which managers and hackers developed a marketing strategy aiming at making private firms interested in the working methods of hackers. Previous ethical imperatives were shelved in exchange for a more instrumental concept that would be easier to understand for private business firms. Among other things the concept introduced the possibility of privatising software modifications and demand payment for their applications. The concept 'free software' was exchanged for 'open source', and a growing number of private firms have started using Open Source over the last five-six years. (DiBona, Ockman and Stone, 1999; Fink, 2003; Hippel and Krogh,

---

[2] The term 'hacker' is applied here in the same way as the hacker-community does: a hacker is an enthusiastic, often highly intelligent person who develops IT software in collaboration with other hackers across universities and firms. Thus, a hacker is not someone involved in criminal acts and hacking into others' computers.

2003; Holck, Larsen and Pedersen, 2004; Jørgensen, 1999; Kaisla,2001; Koch, 2005; Larsen, Holck and Pedersen, 2004; Pavlicek; 2000, Raymond, 2001; Weber, 2004).

4   Theoretical background

In recent years different perspectives have been applied to studying the right to intellectual work, such as an issue of moral/philosophy, of economic theory, of law and of organisational sociology. The present research –in-progress paper will apply the latter approach, with a focus on the theory of *new-institutional organisational sociology* that investigates how the social construction of intellectual property unfolds in the meeting between business firms and voluntary communities.

New-institutional theory focuses in particular on cognitive institutions – that is internalised symbolic images of reality – and less on regulative and normative institutions. (DiMaggio and Powell, 1983; Friedland and Alford 1991, Meyer and Rowen, 1983; Scott, 1991; Scott, 1995). The theory, which was developed in the late 1970s and 1980s, understands cognitive institutions as independent variables, which implies "a turn toward cognition and cultural explanations and an interest in properties of supra-individual units of analysis that cannot be reduced to aggregations or direct consequences of individuals' attributes or motives" (DiMaggio and Powell, 1991). This understanding of cognitive institutions as independent variables has subsequently been subject to severe criticism as it made it unsuitable for explaining institutional *changes*. A number of researchers have attempted resolving this problem by introducing an 'actor' as independent variable. They have thus gone back to where the new-institutional theory started its criticism: that individuals have motives and attitudes that, under certain circumstances, contribute to explain institutional changes. (Brint and Karabel, 1991; DiMaggio, 1988; Oliver, 1991; Scott, 1995; Tolbert and Zucker, 1983). Other researchers have attempted solving the problem – not by going back to individual motives and attitudes as the explanatory power of institutional changes – but by further developing new-institutional theory by adding to it a phenomenon called *institutional entrepreneurs*. Institutional entrepreneurs are socially constructed actors of social capabilities to motivate others to collaborate by bringing about in social practices characterised by multiple institutional logics a shared sense making and identity. These logics constitute the organising principles and they are accessible to organisations and individuals interested in further developing micro processes through which the parties make sense of what has happened, what is happening, and what is going to happen. (Borum and Westenholz, 1995; Boxenbaum and Battilana, 2004; Christensen and Westenholz, 1997; Fligstein, 1997; Friedland and Alford, 1991; Greenwood and Hinings, 2002; Seo and Creed, 2002). The theory of institutional entrepreneurs is currently in the process of being developed, and the project wishes to contribute to further develop this phenomenon focusing on the explanatory power of institutional entrepreneurs in relation to the emergence of intellectual property.

In further developing the phenomenon 'institutional entrepreneurs' I shall argue for the fertility of combining new-institutional organisational theory and organisational discourse theory. (Graesser, Gernsbacher and Goldman, 2003; Grant, Hardy, Oswick and Putnam, 2004ba; Jørgensen and Phillips, 2002; Wetherell, Taylor and Yates, 2001). Organisational discourse theory refers to the structural collection of texts embedded in practice when talking and writing (in casu about intellectual property). The assumption is that discursive practice not only describes things, but also 'do' them in that the discourse brings life to the phenomena by categorising and combining them in ways that make sense in an otherwise meaningless reality. Within the realm of discursive theory it is methodologically relevant to distinguish between 'discourses-in-use' and 'discourses-in-context'. (Grant, Hardy, Oswick and Putnam, 2004 b). The latter concept 'discourses-in-context' is not alien to new-institutional concepts such as cognitive institutions/institutional logics as institutional contexts are used for understanding the formation of language. (Grant, Hardy, Oswick and Putnam, 2004 b). By supplementing new-institutional organisational theory with 'discourses-in-context' analyses it becomes possible to elucidate the way in which institutions prevail in everyday discourses. This will balance and concretise new-institutional organisational theory, but it will not bring the theory further in the analyses of institutional changes. For this purpose the approach of 'discourses-in-use' is applicable in that it focuses on interaction in micro processes through which discourses are attempted authorised through, and counter-discourses are produced to escape authorisations. (Collinson, 1988 1992, Gabriel, Handy and Phillips, 2004).

5   And back to the case and the social context

Looking at the historical development in which John's firm is embedded, several discourses-in-context' concerning the right to intellectual work are emerging within software development. Each of these discourses points towards heroes and villains in the development. This has been analyzed by, among others, Szczepanska, Bergquist & Ljungberg (2005) who identifies a 'hacker discourse' developed within various software developing movements and communities. In the discourse a 'hacker' appears who in most cases is characterized as the creative and genuinely interested troubleshooter developer – a character or an identity that marks a difference between 'us' and 'the others'. In the 1990s the hacker-discourse split into two as a result of arguments over how to approach and to organize software development. One of the discourses, the 'free-software-discourse', strongly emphasizes the ideological aspects of the freedom to hack and to get and use information, whereas the other one, the 'open-source-discourse' attaches less importance to the ideological aspects of freedom and more to the concrete product developed by using open codes. Both discourses share the ambition to produce free software of high quality, but the differences between the discourses are sufficient to identify two stories about 'hackers' each of which is closed around an 'us' and sees the others as – 'the others'. Nevertheless both stories share a mutual enemy represented by Microsoft which is characterized as the 'evil empire' as opposed to hackers, who like to see themselves as romantic rebels. Microsoft has responded by developing its own *'proprietarian-discourse'* that tells a story about not only the necessity of firms protecting their codes, but also about the importance of firms possessing the property right to intellectual work in order to secure society innovation. In this story the hackers are identified as the villains comparable to communists and anti-American behavior. As Szezepanska and others stress it is interesting that all three discourses claim to support 'the American way' in their attempts to legitimize their own discourse in the societal arena.

Turning to John and his firm we can now see that John operates as an institutional entrepreneur. John operates at the firm level, and in his local context he draws on the open-source-discourse and the proprietarian-discourses. The nature of his entrepreneurship is not to (further) develop *one* of the two discourses as e.g. Stallman, Raymond and Gates have done, but to *mix* them in his daily practice in the firm. Mixing the discourses requires that John renders them legitimate, enabling him to live with himself and persuade his employees and other partners of collaboration to accept the mix. For this purpose he applies two techniques: First of all he develops a distinction between 'universal themes' and 'specific themes' in software development. When developing 'universal themes' one should keep one's hacker identity whereas it is fine to work in closed codes if the theme is specific and cannot be used by others anyhow – according to John's arguments. Second, he develops a pragmatic/instrumental attitude toward working with closed codes for CLOSE-SYS arguing that it creates the financial possibility for working with open codes, which is what he prefers – his substantive values. In the terminology of March and Olsen (1989:23) John applies a logic of consequentiality working together with CLOSE-SYS and logic of appropriateness when he is working with open codes. Both logics seem to have functioned in his daily practice.

6 Conclusion

I have briefly analysed a single firm case that demonstrates how an entrepreneur brings into an organizational IT field an open-source-discourse-in-use, a field in which the nature of the dominant discourse-in-context and discourse-in-use are properietarian. This causes *problems of legitimacy* for the entrepreneur, and he fails in his attempt to procure from the organizational field the necessary resources for developing and continuing the company; he is unable to render the open-source concept legitimate. Financially he only survives by selling his apartment for contributing to the assets of the company. At this point in the process the entrepreneur sticks to his open-source and does not assume the character of an *institutional* entrepreneur. Only late in the process does he 'assume character' as an institutional entrepreneur by mixing in an innovative way different discourses in an attempt to legitimise a new mode for developing software applying both open and closed source codes. He does this by *creating new distinctions* in the discourse–in-use applied in his daily software developing work (universal versus specific themes; and instrumental versus substantive values). I am not arguing that the institutional entrepreneur is creating these new distinctions in an instrumental rational process, but that the distinctions emerge in sensemaking processes along his 'doing' something in this firm.

In the further study it would be interesting to:

- identify other discourses-in-context and discourses-in-use within software development,
- identify other ways of mixing (other) discourses in the daily software development and analyse how these are established as discourses-in-use,
- analyse whether and how new/mixed discourses are disseminated in the field of software development. Here it would be relevant to incorporate different analytical units as institutional entrepreneurs (e.g. individuals, firms, communities), and different analytical levels (global level, nationally level, organizational level, and the level of concrete projects).

References

Barlow, John P. (2002) Intellectual Property , Informational Age. In: Thierer, Adam and Clyde Wayne Crews Jr. (eds.) *Copy Flights – The future of intellectual property in the information age*. Washington, D.C.: CATO Institute

Borum, Finn and Ann Westenholz (1995) The incorporation of Multiple Institutional Models – Organizational Field Multiplicity and the Role of the Actor. In: W. Richard Scott and Søren Christensen (eds.) *The Institutional Construction of Organizations – International and Longitudinal Studies*. Thousand Oaks: Sage Publ.

Boxenbaum, Eva, and Julie Battilana (2004) *The Innovative Capacity of Institutional Entrepreneurs – A Reconstruction of Corporate Social Responsibility*. Academy of Management Annual Conference. New Orleans, August 6-11, 2004

Brint, S. and Karabel, J. (1991) Institutional Origins and Transformations: The Case of American Community Colleges. In Powell, W.W. and P. J. DiMaggio (Eds.) *The New Institutionalism in Organizational Analysis*. Pp. 337-360 Chicago:University of Chicago Press.

Christensen, Søren and Ann Westenholz (1997) The social/behavioural construction of employee as strategic actors on company boards of directors. *American Behavioral Scientist*: 40:4

Coleman, and Hill (2005) The Social Production of Ethics in Debian and Free Software Communities: Anthropological Lessons for Vocational Ethics.In: Koch, Stefan ed. *Free/open Source Software Development*. Hershey: IDEA group Publishing

Collinson, D. (1988) 'Engineering humor': Masculinity, joking and conflict in shop-floor relations. *Organization Studies*, 9: 181-99

Collinson, D. (1992) *Managing the shop floor: Subjectivity, masculinity, and workplace culture*. New York: De Gruyter

Cornish, William (2004) *Intellectual Property – Omnipresent, Distracting, Irrelevant?* Oxford: Oxford University Press

Davis, Lee (2004 a)Intellectual property rights, strategy and policy. *Economics of Innovation and New Thechnology*, 13(5):399-415

Davis, Lee (2004 b) Levaranging copyrights to appropriate profits in the nes 'information' industries. *Paper presented at the AHRB Copyright Research Network Conference, London*

DiBona, Chris, Sam Ockman and Mark Stone (eds.) (1999) *Open Sources – Voices from the Open Source Revolution.* Beijing: O'Reilly

DiMaggio, P.J. (1988) Interest and Agency in Institutional Theory. in Zucker, L.G. (ed.) *Institutional Patterns and Organizations: Culture and Environment.* Pp. 3-21. Cambridge, MA: Ballinger.

DiMaggio, P.J. and Powell, W.W. (1983) The Iron Cage Revisited: Institutional Isomorphism and Collective Rationality in Organizational Fields. *American Sociological Review*, 48:147-160.

DiMaggio, P.J. and Powell, W.W. (1991) Introduction. In Walter W. Powell and P.J. DiMaggio (Eds.) *The New Institutionalism in Organizational Theory.* Chicago: University of Chicago Press.

Fink, Martin (2003) *The Business and Economics of Linux and Open Source.*Uppersaddle River, NJ: Prentice Hall PTR

Fligstein, Neil (1997) Social Skill and Institutional Theory. *The American Behavioral Scientist* (40:4)

Friedland, R. and Alford, R.R. (1991) Bringing Society Back In: Symbols, Practices, and Institutional Contradictions. In W.W. Powell and P.J. DiMaggio (Eds.) *The New Institutionalism in Organizational Analysis.* Pp. 232-263. Chicago: University of Chicago Press.

Gabriel, Yiannis (2004) Narratives, Stories and Text. In: Grant, David, Cynthia Hardy, Cliff Oswick and Linda Putnam (eds.): *The SAGE Handbook of Organizational Discourse*, London: Sage Publications

Graesser, Arthur C., Morton Ann Gernsbacher and Susan R. Goldman (2003) *Handbook of discourse processes.* Mahwah: Lawrence Erlbaum Associates

Grant, David, Cynthia Hardy, Cliff Oswick and Linda Putnam (eds.) (2004a): *The SAGE Handbook of Organizational Discourse*, London: Sage Publications

Grant, David, Cynthia Hardy, Cliff Oswick and Linda Putnam (2004b): Introduction: Organizational Discourse: Exploring the Field. In: Grant, David, Cynthia Hardy, Cliff Oswick and Linda Putnam (eds.) (2004): *The SAGE Handbook of Organizational Discourse*, London: Sage Publications

Greenwood, Royston, Suddaby, Roy and C.R. Hinings (2002) Theorizing Change: The role of professional associations in the transformation of institutionalised fields. *Academy of Management Journal*:45,1

Hippel, Eric von and Georg von Krogh (2003) Open Source Software and the 'Private-Collective' Innovation Model: Issues for Organization Science. Organizational Science vo. 14, no. 2: 209-223

Holck, Jesper, Michael Holm Larsen and Mogens Kühn Pedersen (2004) *Identifying Business Barriers and enablers for the adoption of open source software.* ISD

192   Ann Westenholz

2004, Thirteenth International Conference on Information System Development – Advances in Theory, Practice and Education. Vilnius, Lithuania, 9-11 September

Jørgensen, Marianne and Louise Phillips (2002) *Discource analysis – as theory and method.* London: Sage Publ.

Jørgensen, Niels (1999) *Giv det hele væk!* Handelshøjskolen i København

Kaisla, Jukka (2001) *Constitutional Dynamics of the Open Source Software Development.* Department of Industrial Economics and Strategy, CBS

Koch, Stefan ed. (2005) *Free/open Source Software Development.* Hershey: IDEA group Publishing

Larsen, Michael Holm, Jesper Holck and Mogens Kühn Pedersen (2004) *The Challenges of Open Source Software in IT Adoption: Enterprise Architecture versus Total Cost of Ownership.* IRIS 2004, Information System Research in Scandinavia, Falkenberg, Sverige, 14-17 August

Laurent, Andrew M. St. (2004) *Open Source and Free Software Licensing.* Beijing: O'Reilly

Lindkvist, Lars och Ann Westenholz (red.) (1987) *Medarbetarägde företag I Norden – Historisk Parentes eller framtida möjlighet?* Nordisk Ministerråd, NU:1

March, James G. and Johan P. Olsen (1996) Institutional Perspectives on Political Institutions. *Governance: An International Journal of Policy and Administration,* Vol 9, No. 3: 247-264

Meyer, John W. and Brian Rowan (1983) Institutionalized Organizations: Formal Structure as Myth and Ceremony. *American Journal of Sociology* (2)

Moody, Glun (2002) *Rebel Code – Linux and the open source revolution.* London: Penguin Books

Oliver, Christine (1991) Strategic responses to institutional processes. *Academy of Management Review* (18:1)

Pavlicek, Russell C. (2000) *Embracing insanity – open source software development.* Indianapolis: Sams Publ.

Raymond, Eric, S. (1999) *The Cathedral and the Bazaar – Musings on Linux and Open Source by an accidental revolutionary.*Beijing: O'Reilly

Rivette, Kevin G. and D. Kline (2000) Discovering new value in intellectual property.*Harvard Business Review*: 54-66

Rosen, Lawrence (2005) *Open Source Licensing – Software Freedom and Intellectual Property Law*, New Jersey: Pearson Professional Education

Scott, W. Richard (1991) Unpacking Institutional Arguments. In: Walter W. Powell and Paul J. DiMaggio (eds.) *The New Institutionalism in Organizational Analysis.* Chicago: the University of Chicago Press

Scott, W. Richard (1995) *Institutions and Organizations.* Thousand Oaks: Sage Publ.

Seo, Myeong-Gu and W.E. Douglas Creed (2002) Institutional Contradictions, Praxis, and Institutional Change: A Dialectical Perspective. *Academy of Management Review*: 27,2

Stahl (2005) 'The Impact of Open Source Development on the Social Construction of Intellectual Property'. In: Koch, Stefan ed. *Free/open Source Software Development.* Hershey: IDEA group Publishing

Szczepanska, A. M., Bergquist, M., & Ljungberg, J. (2005). High Noon at OS Corral: Duels and Shoot-Outs in Open Source Discours. In: J. Feller, B. Fitzgerald., S. A. Hissam, and K. R. Lakhani, eds. *Perspectives on Free and Open Source Software*. Cambridge, Mass.: MIT Press.

Thierer, Adam and Clyde Wayne Crews Jr. (eds.) (2002) *Copy Flights – The future of intellectual property in the information age*. Washington, D.C.: CATO Institute

Tolbert, Pamela S. and Lynne G. Zucker (1983) Institutional Sources of Change in the Formal Structure of Organizations: the Diffusion of Civil Service Reform, 1880-1935. *Administrative Science Quarterly* (28)

Torvalds, Linus (2001)*Just for Fun – The story of an accidental revolutionary*. New York: Texere

Wark, McKenzie (2004) *A Hacker Manifesto*. Cambridge, Mass.: Harvard University Press

Weber, Steven (2004) *The Succes of Open Source*. Cambridge, Mass.: Harvard University Press

Wetherell, Margaret, Stephanie Taylor and Simeon J. Yates (2001) *Discource theory and practice – A reader*. Sage Publ.

Williams, Sam (2002) *Free as in Freedom – Richard Stallman's crusade for Free Software*. Beijing: O'Reilly

Life cycle of Defects in Open Source Software Projects

Timo Koponen

1 Department of Computer Science, University of Kuopio
P.O.B 1627, FIN-70211 Kuopio, Finland
timo.koponen@uku.fi

Abstract. We studied the maintenance process from the viewpoint of defect management and the defect life cycle. First, we outline a model for the defect life cycle based on ISO/IEC standards, the Framework for Open Source maintenance process, and the Bugzilla defect management system. Thereafter, we analyze defects from two Open Source software projects. The aim of the study was support the maintenance reliability. However, we found that most of the defects did not follow the life-cycle model. Defects were usually directly resolved from initial state without being assigned.

1   Introduction

Most Open Source software users are not software developers or programmers and they are rarely able to modify or repair software. So it is hard to imagine that software will be adopted if users do not have confidence in the software itself and in the maintenance provided Open Source users are often encouraged to report defects and request enhancements, and for this they need a channel to communicate with developers. Many projects use dedicated systems such as Bugzilla [1] for defect reporting and management. These systems provide a communication channel and a system for maintenance process management.

Nowadays, the reliability of the maintenance process is based on a well-described process. A standard model of the maintenance process is presented in the Software Engineering Body of Knowledge (SWEBOK), ISO/IEC 12207 and ISO/IEC 14764 standards [2], [5]. These ISO/IEC Maintenance standards describe the activities required and their inputs and outputs [2], [5], but it is not known if the standard model is applicable for Open Source maintenance. In our earlier studies, we described a framework for the Open Source maintenance process [4] and found it similar to the ISO/IEC Maintenance standard.

However, a well-defined process does not provide reliability if it is not followed. In fact, it is not known if the defects in Open Source projects follow the described process. This study explored defect management and the life cycle of defects in Open Source projects. Our first objective was to define a model for the life cycle of the defect. The second objective was to find the most common life cycles from the case studies and compare them with the life-cycle model. The third objective was to evaluate reliability of the maintenance process by analyzing life cycles. The rest of the article is organized in the following way. Section 2 presents background of the study. Section 3 introduces the case studies and data. Section 4 explains and analyzes

Please use the following format when citing this chapter:

Koponen, T., 2006, in IFIP International Federation for Information Processing, Volume 203, Open Source Systems, eds. Damiani, E., Fitzgerald, B., Scacchi, W., Scotto, M., Succi, G., (Boston: Springer), pp. 195-200

the results of the case studies. Section 5 presents related work and Section provides a brief conclusion.

2 Background

Defect management systems (DMS) allow users to report problems, bugs or enhancement requests as a defect. They also provide flexible possibilities to track, control, and assign defects. These features allow the maintenance process to be managed. Defect management systems present defects as defect reports.

A defect report contains many attributes but we focused on analyzing the attributes *state* and *resolution of the defect*. The *state* describes the defect's condition, such as new or resolved. In the Bugzilla defect management system defects can be in the seven states presented in Table 1. It is not allowed to transit between all states directly: for example, it is not allowed to transit from *closed* to *new*. To illustrate the allowed state changes we drew a state transition diagram (Figure 2), which presents the allowed state transitions in the Bugzilla defect management system.

Table 1. States of the defect in the Bugzilla defect management system

State	Explanation
Unconfirmed	Defect has been recently added and it is not confirmed yet.
New	Defect has been recently added and others have confirmed it.
Assigned	Defect has been assigned to proper person.
Resolved	Defect has been resolved but it is in quality assurance.
Verified	Defect has been resolved and accepted by quality assurance.
Closed	Defect has been resolved, verified and closed
Reopened	Defect was resolved but now it has been reopened for some reason.

A defect should be resolved even it does not lead to changes or modification of software. *State* does not describe the outcome of the defect so *resolution* is needed to express this . Earlier studies have shown that many of the resolved defects do not cause changes to software [3]. Table 2 shows the *resolutions* that are possible in the Bugzilla system. Figure 2 and Framework for Open Source Maintenance process [4] show that the most common defect life-cycles should be similar to those presented in Table 3. Some of the defects can be classified as duplicate or invalid immediately and they can be resolved without assignment. On the other hand, a defect that leads to changes in the source code should always be assigned.

Table 2. Resolutions of defects in the Bugzilla defect management system

Resolution	Explanation
empty	Defect does not have resolution yet
Fixed	Defect is fixed and changes have been made
Works for me	Defect does not occur in other users' systems
Won't fix	Defect is not a fault or real problem; or it is a feature
Invalid	Defect is invalidly reported or information is missing
Duplicate	Defect is a duplicate

Table 3. Expected defect life-cycles

Resolution	Life-cycle
Fixed	Unconfirmed→New→Assigned→Resolved→Verified→Closed
Other	Unconfirmed→Resolved→(Verified)→Closed

3 Case studies

To study the life cycles of defects in the real world, we collected and analyzed defects of the Apache HTTP Server and Mozilla Firefox. These are widely used and their quality is highly appreciated so they are representative case studies. We selected a two-year time-period for analysis, and all the defects reported between September 2003 and September 2005 were analyzed. This sampling produced 1266 defects from Apache and 27681 from Mozilla. The resolutions of the analyzed defects are presented in Table 4.

Table 4. Resolution of the defect in Apache and Mozilla

Resolution	Duplicate	Fixed	Invalid	Won't fix	Works for me	Later	Remind	Not resolved
Apache	162	288	370	84	33	5	1	323
Mozilla	10038	2414	3404	714	3730	0	0	7381

Table 4 shows that Apache had 943 resolved defects and Mozilla had 20 300 resolved defects. However, not all of the resolved defects led to a change or modification of software. In the case of Apache, 288 defects (less than 31 percent of all resolved defects) ended up *fixed,* and in the case of Mozilla 2414 defects (less than 12 per cent of resolved defects) ended up *fixed.* Furthermore, there were also two additional resolutions, Remind and Later, in the Apache. Those states were rarely used.

However, the final state and resolution does not explain defect processing and the defect management process so we analyzed the life cycles of the defects in both case studies. Table 5 presents the most common defect life-cycles in the Apache and Mozilla projects.

Table 5. Two most common defect life-cycles in the Apache and Mozilla projects

Apache		Mozilla	
247	New→Resolved	3764	Unconfirmed→Resolved→Verified
511	New→Resolved→Closed	11133	Unconfirmed→Resolved

A direct transition from the state *new* to the state *resolved* is the most common life-cycle of defects in the Apache project. There was no significant use of the state *unconfirmed*. However, according to Bugzilla [1] *unconfirmed* should be the initial state of the defect. Furthermore, there was also a new state, *needinfo,* meaning that the defect report did not contain all the necessary information.

A direct transition to the state *resolved* is also very common in Mozilla. However, in this case, it was usually from *unconfirmed* to *resolved*. In addition, it seems to be very uncommon to close a defect, so most defects end up *resolved*. Furthermore, we found state transitions that were not allowed, such as a transition from *verified* or *resolved* to *unconfirmed*. However, all state transitions were allowed in the Apache project.

4 Results

As the cases in the previous section show, the defect life cycles do not correlate with the life-cycle model and the state of the defect transits almost directly to the state *resolved*. Furthermore, Table 4 also shows that most of the defects did not lead to a change or modification of software. In case of the Apache, over 800 of 943 defects transited directly from the state *new* to the state *resolved*. The most common life cycle in the Apache project is presented with bold black line in Figure 2.

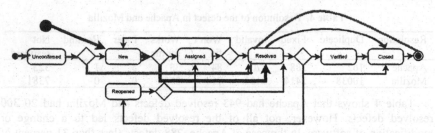

Figure 2. The most common defect life cycle in the Apache (Black bold line) and in the Mozilla (Gray bold line)

According to the life cycle model it means that those defects did not lead to changes in the source code. The resolutions of the defects in the Apache project are presented in Table 7. It shows that there were also defects that led to change or modification.

Table 7. Resolution of defects with most common life cycle

Project	Duplicate	Fixed	Invalid	Later	Won't fix	Works for me
Apache	65	142	236	2	47	0
Mozilla	5409	246	2443	0	326	2709

As we see in Table 4, only about 290 defects, which is about 30 per cent, lead to fixes. However, these defects should have followed the life cycle model. Surprisingly, 142 of 288 defects that led to source code changes were changes directly from the state *new* to *resolved*. Furthermore, there were other almost direct jumps to the state *resolved*, which together covered 237 of 288 fixed defects (82 per cent). Thus, only 51 of 288 defects (18 per cent) that were fixed followed the life cycle model and went through the states *new, unconfirmed, assigned* and *resolved*. If we then look at Mozilla, we can see in Table 6 that over 16 000 of 20 300 defects jumped directly from the state *unconfirmed* or *new* to *resolved*. The most common life cycle in the Mozilla project is presented with bold gray line in Figure 2.

According to the life cycle model, those defects did not cause changes in the source code. The resolutions of the analyzed defects from the Mozilla project are presented in Table 4: only about 2400 defects were fixed, which is less than 12 per cent. However, these defects should have followed the expected life cycle and others should have jumped more or less directly to *resolved*. Surprisingly only 246 of 11 133 defects that jumped directly from *unconfirmed* to *resolved* were fixed. However, there were other almost direct jumps to *resolved*, such as from *unconfirmed* to *resolved* via *new*, which together covered 1652 of 2414 fixed defects (68 per cent). Thus, 748 of 2414 defects (31 per cent) that led to fixing followed the expected life cycle or went through at least the states *new* or *unconfirmed*, *assigned* and *resolved*. There were also 14 defects that could not be classified into either group because they had so many state changes.

Despite the number of defects, both cases have similar characteristics. The proportion of defects that led to changes (fix) was relatively small. Most of the defects transited directly to the state *resolved* and it was possible to have a *resolution*. It seems that developers just pick up a defect and resolve it without assigning, and they did not update the state of the defect before it was resolved. However, the state of the defect does not tell the whole truth since defect management systems allow users to leave comments without changing the status of the defect. There were also discussions in the mailing lists, which we did not analyze in this study.

5 Related Work

To our knowledge, this is the first work that studies a defect life cycle in Open Source projects. However, the defects and defect management systems have been previously studied from other viewpoints. Mockus et al. [6] has studied defects and changes of the source code in the Apache and Mozilla projects. They compare the numbers of changes and defects per developer in commercial projects. Furthermore, they measure defect density in the projects and compare it with the size of the source code. Huntley [7] has studied the defects of the Apache and Mozilla projects from the viewpoint of Organizational learning. Fisher et al. have combined version control and defect information in their studies [8] creating a release history from the version control system and bug tracking system. They describe the changes of the source code and defects from the release history viewpoint.

5 Conclusion

We studied maintenance process and expected that the life cycle of defects would be similar to the maintenance process, with several states during the process. However, the study shows that the defect life cycle in two well-known Open Source Software projects was much more straightforward. The state of the defect was set to *resolved* directly after the initial state. More surprisingly, the outcome of the defect did not seem to have any relation with its life cycle: even the defects led to changes they were not assigned. The states of the defect could be simplified to *open* and *closed*. These two states are enough to cover 84 per cent of all defects in the Apache project and 79 per cent in the Mozilla project. So, the usage of a defect management system does not seem to be efficient in the Open Source projects studied. It is generally claimed that defect management is a crucial part of maintenance, leading to the assumption that users cannot rely on the maintenance of Open Source Software.

To improve maintenance reliability from the user's viewpoint, these software projects should use defect management more intensively or publish a document explaining the procedures in use. At least, developers should assign a defect when they start working with it so that users and other developers could see that the defect is being dealt with. Unfortunately, similar data have not been published concerning a proprietary project. In our experience, proprietary projects have a similar type of defect life cycle.

7 References

1. Bugzilla.org, 2005. http://www.bugzilla.org
2. ISO/IEC. ISO/IEC 12207:1995/Amd 2002: Software Engineering: Software life cycle processes. ISO/IEC, 2002.
3. T. Koponen and V. Hotti. Defects in open source software maintenance - two case studies - apache and mozilla. In *Proceedings of The 2005 International MultiConference in Computer Science and Computer Engineering*, Las Vegas, NV, USA, 2005. CSREA Press.
4. T. Koponen and V. Hotti. Open source software maintenance process framework. In *5-WOSSE: Proceedings of the fifth workshop on Open source software engineering*, pp. 1-5, New York, NY, USA, 2005. ACM Press.
5. IEEE Computer society. *Guide to the Software Engineering Body of Knowledge (SWEBOK)*. IEEE Computer society, Los Alamitos, California, USA, 2001.
6. A. Mockus, R. Fielding, and J. Herbsleb. Two case studies of open source software development: Apache and mozilla. *ACM Trans. Softw. Eng. Methodol.*, 11(3):309-346, 2002
7. C. Huntley. Organizational learning in open source software projects: An analysis of debugging data. *IEEE Transactions on Engineering Management*, 50(4), 2004.
8. M. Fischer, M. Pinzger, and H. Gall. Populating a release history database from version control and bug tracking systems. In *ICSM '03: Proceedings of the Inter- national Conference on Software Maintenance*, pp. 23, Washington, DC, USA, 2003. IEEE Computer Society.

Insiders and outsiders: paid contributors and the dynamics of cooperation in community led F/OS projects

Evangelia Berdou

Media and Communications Department, London School of Economics and Political Science, Houghton Street, London W2A 2AE, UK

e.berdou@lse.ac.uk

Abstract. This paper examines the role of paid developers in mature free/open source (F/OS) communities. In particular it provides a typology for their involvement based on their employment and sponsorship arrangements and elaborates a framework for understanding the dynamics of cooperation developing between them and the volunteers based on their community ties. The evidence presented is drawn from individual interviews conducted with volunteer and paid contributors from the GNOME and KDE projects within the context of a PhD research focusing on commercialization and peripheral participation in F/OS communities. The paper highlights the various interdependencies that form between communities and companies and adds to our understanding of the dynamics of commercialization in F/OS projects.

1 Introduction

Companies contribute to F/OS projects in many ways. They support promotional activities and community conferences, including providing venues, travel costs and hardware. The website and the CVS tree of the GNOME project, for example, is hosted by Redhat and KDE's is hosted by Trolltech. However, arguably the most important and, many would say, the most potent form of involvement of companies in projects, since it has a direct impact on the development process, is through their contributing labour by committing employees to the development process.

This issue has been largely overlooked in the F/OS literature. This paper addresses this gap by providing a typology for the involvement of paid contributors in community led projects and contributes to our understanding of their involvement in terms of their community ties. The aim of the paper is to highlight certain aspects of commercialization in community led projects. The study is based on PhD research into the dynamics of cooperation in F/OS projects, which investigates commercialization and peripheral participation (integration of new coders and participation of non-coders).

Please use the following format when citing this chapter:

Berdou, E., 2006, in IFIP International Federation for Information Processing, Volume 203, Open Source Systems, eds. Damiani, E., Fitzgerald, B., Scacchi, W., Scotto, M., Succi, G., (Boston: Springer), pp. 201-208

2 Background to the study

This section situates the argument within the context of existing contributions related to commercialization of F/OS communities and outlines the theoretical and methodological framework for the study.

2.1 F/OS communities in/and the economy

The considerations of commercialization issues needs to be positioned within the corpus of contributions related to commercialization of F/OS communities. F/OS communities have often been considered to occupy a space between the organized supply of products and services offered by firms and the wider, emergent, market dynamics of software production, supply and demand. O'Mahony [1], for example, talks of community managed open source projects as a new type of commercial actor and von Hippel [2] considers open source development as the template for an innovation process which is primarily driven by software users.

At the same time it has often been argued, by both practitioners and academics, that the motivations of developers contributing to F/OS projects differ significantly from those underlying proprietary software development [3-5]. This view has been interpreted as suggesting a contrast between two kinds of economic rationality; the gift economy and the exchange economy. Whereas the first is based on the principle of reciprocity, upholds the idea of software as a public good and is often associated with abundance, the second relies predominantly on monetary flows, market transactions and is organised around a scarcity of resources.

This interpretation has been challenged on several fronts by researchers who draw attention to the interconnections between the two spheres of economic activity. David Lancashire [6], for example, employs a political economy perspective to explain the distribution of F/OS development worldwide. At the same time large scale surveys of F/OS communities indicate that approximately half of F/OS developers have earned money through their work in F/OS [7].

Although there has been considerable progress in understanding the links between the exchange economy and the gift economy at the level of developer motives, few studies have examined in detail how commercialization affects cooperation within projects. O'Mahony [1] approached the issue by focusing on the organizational structures that projects develop in order to interface with companies and West and O'Mahony [8] contrasted the dynamics of cooperation between community led and sponsored projects. Freeman and Siltala [9] have highlighted the hybrid practices developing in GNOME and Open Office due to corporate involvement. Adopting a different perspective Lin [10] examined developers' practices in firms that participate in F/OS development and the forms and tensions that arise from this collaboration. In addition, Dahlander and Magnusson [11] have examined the types of relationships companies develop with communities. Lastly, Krishnamurti and Tripathi's [12] study of bounty programs that offer developers monetary incentives for addressing specific software issues, highlights an alternative used by companies to participate in the development process rather than directly hiring developers.

This paper complements these contributions by developing a framework for understanding the dynamics of cooperation between corporate actors and volunteers through the involvement of paid developers. The theoretical and methodological framework for the research reported here is outlined in the next section together with highlights of the empirical data and the method of analysis.

2.2 Theoretical framework, empirical data and method of analysis

The study draws on the communities of practice perspective [13] and mobilizes Foucault's idea of relational power [14] in order to study relations between the volunteer community and commercial actors with stakes in the development.

The communities of practice perspective argues that society's knowledge is organized in different communities of practice, which are essential groups formed around the pursuit of a shared enterprise[15]. The approach offers an intuitive way of understanding F/OS development (since F/OS communities are essentially built around the practice of developing software) and has been adopted within the context of other investigations of F/OS [16-18]. In the context of this paper it is argued that F/OS communities do not constitute a homogenous community of practice consisting only of experienced and new (peripheral) developers, but form *constellations of practices* [13].

Foucault argued that power is neither a zero-sum game where different actors compete for resources nor something that is given or exchanged, but rather is something that is exercised; a force that creates complex dependencies and invites a diversity of initiations and reactions on the part of the people involved in them. The idea of relational power does not imply that the relations to be examined are symmetrical, but is meant to acknowledge and map the multiple interdependencies and structures that are developed within the context of this study.

Both these approaches have methodological implications. The idea of F/OS communities as constellations of practice draws attention to the different groups of contributors operating within projects, groups with distinctive characteristics and modes of engagement (volunteers, paid developers external to the community, community integrated developers). At the same time, the idea of relational power guides an investigation that aims to highlight the interdependencies forming between the different groups of contributors at different levels of interaction.

The data presented in this paper are drawn from 40 individual, semi-structured interviews conducted with volunteer and paid contributors from the GNOME and KDE projects between 2004-2005. Their analysis involved a two-step process. First the materials were organized thematically and then were analysed in more depth using a form of discourse analysis. This involved the identification of the particular domains of reference, types of calculation and forms of statement connected with specific knowledge domains, and the examination of the associations made between them [19] (F/OS, traditional working environments, volunteerism, professionalism, etc).

3 Research findings

Based on the analysis of the empirical data, a typology for understanding sponsorship and employment in community led F/OS projects is developed (section 3.1) followed by a consideration of the dynamics of cooperation developing between volunteer and paid developers based on the latters' community ties.

3.1 Types of employment and sponsorship

From the analysis of the interview data it seems that, depending on the kind of mandate they are given, paid developers can be divided in the following categories:

a. Those that have a **free sponsorship**. This group receives no clear instruction from their employers about what they should be working on. They are usually former volunteers who are expected more or less to work on the same things that they were contributing to before they were hired.

b. Those that have **a clear mandate** from their employers as to what they should be doing. For example, some developers working at Linux distribution companies, are expected to help integrate different aspects of the project into company products or build on top of their projects' platforms to create commercial applications.

c. Those that are have **KDE or GNOME "friendly" jobs**. These are people who are hired by companies or departments of companies with a strong F/OS orientation. They are usually hackers who are expected to work on developing proprietary company products, but who are also allowed to spend part of their time working on community projects. Their working terms, can be formal or informal, and resemble part-time free sponsorship.

d. Those that are being hired or compensated in order to solve a particular problem or develop a specific application. This type of involvement is akin to **sub-contracting**. For example, Sun Microsystems, a company involved in Gnome development has hired developers from Wipro, a large Indian software house, to help them on certain aspects that their own team did not have the time to deal with. This category could also include development conducted within the context of bounty programs, and self-employed developers.

3.2   Working from the outside and the inside: external and community

integrated contributors and community development

In addition to the above categorization, there is an important distinction to be made between contributors that formerly worked for the project on a volunteer basis and those external programmers who are commissioned to work on it without having any previous ties with the community. Proprietary developers that are brought to work on community projects have to learn the ways of the community and adjust to the rhythms and the demands of F/OS development. Most interviewees tended to think that this group has significant difficulties in adjusting to the often unstructured work flows of the community.

Some of these problems have been resolved. The regularization of release cycles for GNOME and KDE, for example, allows companies to better time the release of their own products. Although they stressed the frequent incommensurability of community and corporate agendas and processes (which was often seen as a divide between the F/OS way and proprietary development) almost all the interviewees believed that these days communities are doing more to accommodate companies' needs. Despite the progress being made, however, there appear to be more gaps than areas of contact in the more formal aspects of community-corporate cooperation, such as the incommensurability between companies' Quality Assurance processes and those of the community (such as its bug-tracking systems).

On the community's part companies' contributions to the code base can be too specialized for the overall aims of the project and, consequently, the issue of "pushing the patches upstream" (i.e. integrating them into the main development tree) does not make any sense, or they may be relevant. In the latter case companies usually pursue integration because it saves on the time and effort required to maintain the changes made to the code base. An underlying assumption in the acceptance of code submitted by paid contributors is that it is done on the same kind of *meritocratic basis* that applies to the rest of the community.

Some of the issues are aptly illustrated by the case of Wipro. Wipro, an Indian Software House, was subcontracted by Sun Microsystems to work on the GNOME project. Although they were expected to work with the community, Wipro developers were not expected to become members. Their success was measured according to specific metrics (bugs fixed, bugs logged). Due, however, to their lack of prior knowledge about the code base and to the inadequacy of available documentation they had to resort to asking for information on community mailing lists and chat channels. The presence of some 10 new developers all asking questions stretched the learning resources of the community and created a stir among volunteer developers.

Developers that worked as volunteers or paid developers who became accepted as community members based on their longstanding contributions, carry with them a network of connections and an extensive know-how of community processes that both facilitates their work in terms of its acceptance by the community and helps connect corporate and community teams.

In companies such as Sun Microsystems that have large teams of developers working on F/OS projects, these people sometimes assume the role of intermediary between the rest of the corporate team and the community.

A company's strategy to recruit volunteers who are already on a "critical path"[1] in the project, who are heavily involved in central aspects of development, means that very often employed contributors are maintainers of key parts of the project. It is a

---

[1] I would like to thank Luis Villa for suggesting this term.

plausible hypothesis that the combination of their potential as volunteer contributors with the opportunity to work full-time in the project enhances their position as core developers. These central actors not only have the ability to control key aspects of the project, but also have an interest in keeping an eye on its overall development.

At the same time employed community members demonstrate an increased sensitivity to community issues, which makes them cautious with regard to balancing community and company interests. Employers' links with projects and with the F/OS source community in general affects developers' relations with their employer and influences their everyday working life. Where companies have strong ties with the F/OS world the confluence between community and corporate interests appears relatively uncomplicated. The fact that they do not need to explain community processes and policies makes the developers' relationship with the management easier. More importantly, in contrast to working in a company with a less developed F/OS culture, upholding community values and ideals seems to be conducted not in opposition (we and the rest of the company) but collectively (we with the rest of the company in F/OS).

4 Conclusions

This paper elaborated an initial framework for understanding the role of paid developers in community led F/OS projects. After developing a typology of their employment/sponsorship arrangements (free sponsorship, clear mandate, F/OS-friendly jobs, subcontracting) the differing community ties of employed developers were examined.

The role of developers with weak community ties, those external to the community, is consistent with the view of companies as external actors in the development process, whose involvement in the project is regulated through community values and mediated through appropriately developed institutional interfaces. The case of community-integrated employees, however, suggests that the boundaries between corporate and community actors are often permeable. More specifically, it appears that in most cases the connections between companies and projects develop at different levels of involvement and hinge upon complex interpersonal dynamics. Many of the elected members on the Foundation and the KDE e.V. Boards for example, are either hired or self-employed contributors.

It should be noted that despite their involvement in projects, companies generally avoid exercising direct pressures on the community, since it is in their interests that projects retain their largely volunteer basis. It appears that the preservation of the balance in favour of the gift economy is as much to the benefit of companies as is that of communities.

The analysis in this paper is a first attempt to untangle some of the complex issues underlying community-corporate cooperation in F/OS projects. One of the most important emerging questions is whether paid developers constitute a distinctive group, not just at the level of engagement with the community, but at the level of their contributions. The interview data suggest that the group of community integrated employed developers includes members of the group of core developers, programmers who contribute to the programs' most critical parts. This question is addressed through examining the findings of a social network analysis of the Gnome's Foundation and KDE e.V. members (see [20]). The question of how employment/sponsorship arrangements affect cooperation between paid and volunteer developers and how community and corporate boundaries are managed within the context of development is not addressed in this paper.

Despite its limitations the paper proposes a framework for understanding the complex interdependencies that frequently develop between companies and communities not only at the institutional level, but within the context of mundane development. In addition it offers a view of F/OS projects not as uniform communities organized around a homogenous practice, but as complex spaces incorporating different types of contributors. In doing so it invites an examination not just of the differences and barriers existing between the exchange and the gift economy, but of the ways they are embedded in each other.

The research was funded by the Greek State Scholarships Foundation (IKY). In its later stages the study was supported by the EU Digital Business Ecosystem (DBE) project (contract no 507953) http://www.digital-ecosystem.org/ . The views expressed in this paper are those of the author.

References

1. C. S. O'Mahony, 'The emergence of a new commercial actor: community managed software projects.' Doctoral Dissertation, Stanford University, Department of Management Science and Engineering Management, (2002).
2. E. von Hippel, Open Source Projects as Horizontal Innovation Networks-by and for users. MIT Sloan School of Management, Working Paper No. 4366-02, Boston, MA 2002 (accessed 23/07/2003).
3. M. S. Elliot and W. Scacchi, Free Software: a Case Study of Sofware Development in a Virtual Organization Culture. Working Paper, Institute for Software Research, UC Irvine, April 2003, available at: http://www.ics.uci.edu/%7Ewscacchi/Papers/New/Elliott-Scacchi-GNUe-Study-Report.pdf 2003 (accessed 6/06/04).
4. K. Lakhami and R. G. Wolf, Why hackers do what they do: Understanding Motivation Effort in Free/Open Source Software Projects. MIT Sloan School of Management Working Paper No. 4425-03, 2003 (accessed 01/03/04).
5. E. S. Raymond, The Cathedral and the Bazaar. The Cathedral and the Bazaar: Musings on Linux and Open Source by an Accidental Revolutionary, ed. E. S. Raymond (O'Reilly, Sebastopol, CA, 2001MC).
6. D. Lancashire, Code, Culture and Cash: The Fading Altruism of Open Source Development, *First Monday, peer-reviewed journal on the Internet* 6(12) (2001).

7. P. David, A. Waterman and S. Arora, FLOSS-US/ The Free/Libre/Open Source Developer   Software   Survey   for   2003:   A   First   Report. http://www.stanford.edu/group/floss-us/report/FLOSS-US-Report.pdf,   2003 (accessed 5/5/04).

8. J. West and C. S. O'Mahony, Contrasting Community Building in Sponsored and Community   Founded   Open   Source   Projects. http://opensource.mit.edu/papers/westomahony.pdf, 2004 (accessed 25/07/04).

9. S. Freeman and J. Siltala, Freedom and Profit: how suits and hackers are working it out on the desktop. Working paper presented in 4/EASST Joint Meeting, Paris 26/08/04 http://personal.inet.fi/koti/jsiltala/juha/floss/freedom-profit-paper.pdf, 2004 (accessed 19/01/06).

10. Y. Lin, Hybrid Innovation: How Does the Collaboration Between the FLOSS Community and Corporations Happen? , *Forthcoming in Knowledge, Technology and Policy* XVIV (1) (2005).

11. L. Dahlander and G. M. Magnusson, Relationships between open source software companies and communities: Observations from Nordic Firms, *Research Policy*,(34): p. 481-493 (2005).

12. S. Krishmamurti and A. Tripathi, Bounty Programs in Free/Libre/Open source Software (FLOSS): An Economic Analysis", in The Economics of Open Source Software Development (Forthcoming), J. Bitzer and P. Schroeder, Editors (Elsevier Publications, 2005).

13. E. Wenger, Communities of Practice: Learning, Meaning and Identity (Cambridge University Press, Cambridge, 1998).

14. M. Foucault, The Subject and Power, in Michel Foucault: Power/ Essential works of Foucault 1954-1984. Vol. 3, J. D. Faubion, Editor (Penguin Books, London; New York, 1982) p. 326-348.

15. E. Wenger and J. Lave, Situated learning: Legitimate Peripheral Participation (Cambridge University Press, Cambridge, 1991).

16. K. Edwards, Epistemic Communities, Situated Learning and Open Source Software Development. http//opensource.mit.edu/papers/kasperedwards-ec.pdf, 2001 (accessed 1/03/05).

17. S. Sharma, V. Suguraman and B. Rajagopalani, A framework for creating hybrid open source communities, *Information Systems Journal.* 12: p. 7-25 (2002).

18. M. S. Elliot and W. Scacchi, Free Software Developers as an Occupational Community: Resolving Conflicts and Fostering Collaboration. In revised version in ACM Group'03 Conference. 2003. Sanibel Island, FL 9-12.

19. G. Kendall and G. Wickham, Using Foucault's methods (Sage, London, 1998).

20. E. Berdou, 'Commercialization and Peripheral Participation in Community led Free/Open Source Projects: Evolving Forms of Work and Power at the Intersection of Online and Offline Worlds.' Doctoral Dissertation, London School of Economics and Political Science, Media and Communications Department, (Forthcoming 2006).

Adopting Open Source for Mission-Critical Applications: A Case Study on Single Sign-On

Claudio Agostino Ardagna[1], Ernesto Damiani[1], Fulvio Frati[1], and Salvatore Reale[2]

[1] University of Milan - via Bramante 65, Crema (CR), Italy
ardagna,damiani,frati@dti.unimi.it
[2] Siemens S.p.A.
Carrier Research & Development Radio Access - Network Management, Via Monfalcone 1, 20092, Cinisello Balsamo (MI), Italy salvatore.reale@siemens.com

Abstract. In this paper, we describe a specific selection process for security-related open source code, based on a methodology aimed at evaluating open source security frameworks in general and Single-Sign-On (SSO) systems in particular. Our evaluation criteria for open source security-related software include the community's timeliness of reaction against newly discovered vulnerabilities or incidents.

Keywords: Open Source, Security, Single Sign-On, Authentication, Federation, Trust Model.

1 Introduction

Accessing information on the global Net has become a fundamental requirement of the modern economy. Recently, focus has shifted from access to data stored in WWW sites to invoking *e-services* such as e-Government (e-Gov) services, remote banking, or airline reservation systems [4]. In the above scenario, the problem of securing access to network resources is of paramount importance. More specifically, security requirements include: *i) confidentiality,* data should be released to authorized users only; *ii) integrity,* unauthorized data insertion, modification or deletion must be prevented; *iii) availability* users must always be able to access data whereby they are authorized for, preventing, for instance, attacks such as *Denial of Service* (DoS). In order to satisfy these requirements, some basic security mechanisms are available:

- *identification and authentication* supporting users identification and verification of their identity;
- *access control* evaluating access requests submitted by users against predefined access control rules in order to grant or deny the access;
- *audit* monitoring access requests post-evaluation, to find out security infringements;

Please use the following format when citing this chapter:

Ardagna, C.A., Damiani, E., Frati, F., and Reale, S., 2006, in IFIP International Federation for Information Processing, Volume 203, Open Source Systems, eds. Damiani, E., Fitzgerald, B., Scacchi, W., Scotto, M., Succi, G., (Boston: Springer), pp. 209-220

- *cryptography* protecting data integrity and confidentiality by ensuring that data stored or transmitted are kept secret and only authorized users can decrypt them.

Security issues represent a critical aspect for most software applications. Due to the criticality of this requirement, proprietary solutions are widespread, because many companies consider them more secure and reliable. Adoption of open source solutions, especially at the middleware level, is slowed down by the fact that most companies do not completely trust the open source community and consider open source middleware a potential "backdoor" for attackers, affecting overall system security. However, proprietary security solutions have their own drawbacks such as vendor lock-in, interoperability limitations, and lack of flexibility. Recent research suggests that the open source approach can overcome these limitations [3, 18]. It is also widely acknowledged that open source solutions may in the end improve security, as they give both attackers and defenders greater visibility of software vulnerabilities [9]. In this paper, we discuss the idea of adopting open source for some key security-related functionalities, including access control and authentication systems, and discuss the requirements that open source security solutions must follow to be suitable for large scale deployment. In particular, our work focuses on open source Single Sign-On (SSO) solutions [2]. SSO gives a mechanism to manage authentication process and allows users to enter a single username and password to access systems and resources, to be used in the framework of an open source e-service scenario.

2 Basic Concepts

The huge amount of services available on the Net has caused unchecked proliferation of user accounts. Typically, users have to log-on to multiple systems, each of which may require different usernames and authentication information. All these account may be managed independently by local administrators within each individual system [12, 11]. SSO [8] systems are security frameworks aimed at simplifying log-on process, managing users multiple identities and presenting users credentials to network applications for authentication. SSO approach provides reduction of time spent by the users during log-on operations to individual domains, failed log-on transactions, time used to log-on to secondary domains, and costs and time used for users profiles administrations. SSO also increases services usability and provides simple administration thanks to a single, centralized administration point. Additional motivations that suggest SSO adoption are provided by *Sarvanes Oxley* (SOX) directive and the *Health Insurance Portability and Accountability Act* (HIPAA) that mandate provisions for maintaining the integrity of user profile data as an essential component of an effective security policy. HIPAA, for example, explicitly states that companies are required to assign a unique profile for tracking user identities. Also, it mandates procedures for creating, changing, and safeguarding profiles. Traditional authentication policies infrastructures do not even come close to fulfilling these requirements.

2.1 Requirements of a Single Sign-on solution

We are now ready to list the requirements that a Single Sign-On solution should satisfy [2]. Our analysis brought us to formulating the following seven functional requirements: *i) Basic Authentication*: SSO systems must provide an authentication mechanism. Usually, authentication is performed through the classic username/password log-in, whereby a user can be unambiguously identified; *ii) Strong Authentication*: for highly secure environments, the traditional username/password authentication mechanism must be integrated with strong authentication mechanisms based on biometric properties of the user (fingerprints, retina scan, and so on); *iii) Authorization*: after the authentication process, the system must determine the level of information/services the requestor can see/use. *iv) Secure Exchange of Client Status Information*: the SSO system architecture implies the exchange of user information in secure manner between SSO server and remote services during authentication and authorization processes *v) Multi-domain Management*: the SSO system could provide support for managing authorizations (e.g. role acquisitions and revocations) that apply to multiple domains; *vi) Provisioning*: a provision is a pre-condition that must be met before an action can be executed. It is responsibility of the user to ensure that requests are sent only to environments satisfying all pre-conditions; *vii) Federation*: a user should be able to select the services she wants to federate and de-federate to protect her privacy and to select the services to which she will disclose her own authorization assertions.

Several non-functional requirements can also be identified, namely:

i) Autonomy a SSO server should be a stand alone module in order to clearly separate the authorization point from business implementations, avoiding the replication and the ad-hoc implementation of authorization mechanisms for each domain; *ii) Standard Compliance*: it is important for a SSO to support standard communication protocols fostering integration in different environments; *iii) Centralized Management*: centralization of authentication and authorization mechanisms and, more in general, centralization of identity management implies a simplification of the user profile management task; *iv) Cross-Language availability*: SSO solutions should permit the integration of services implementation based on different languages, without substantial changes on services code; *v) Password Proliferation Prevention*: the system should support parsimonious creation of costly resources such as passwords and public-private key pairs.

3 Open source Single Sign-on systems

Now, we shall briefly introduce some Open Source Single Sign-on systems. Our description will be made with reference to the above requirements and some other evaluation parameters. For more architectural details about these Single Sign-on systems see [2].

Central Authentication Service. Central Authentication Service (CAS) [5, 20] is an open source framework developed at Yale University. It implements a SSO mechanism aimed at providing a *Centralized Authentication* to a single server and *HTTP redirections*. When an unauthenticated user sends a service request, this request is redirected from the application to the authentication server (CAS Server), and then back to the application after the user has been authenticated. The CAS Server is therefore the only entity that manages passwords to authenticate users and transmits and certifies their identities. The information is forwarded by the authentication server to the application during redirections by using session cookies. CAS is composed of modular Java servlets that can run over any servlet engine and provides a web-based authentication service.

SourceID. SourceID [19], first released in 2001 by Ping Identity Corporation Company, is an open source multi-protocol project for enabling identity federation and cross-boundary security. SourceID focuses on simple integration and deployment within existing Web applications and provides high-level developer functionalities and customization. SourceID also implements Liberty Alliance Single Sign-On specifications [16] and it is a framework that integrates SSO features into new and existing Web portals. The lower level implementation of Liberty specifications, as for instance SOAP, SAML, Liberty features, protocols and metadata schemas, are transparent for Web developers. From the architectural point of view, SourceID system is composed by three modules plugged into the middle of Web applications to provide SSO facilities: *i) Profile* implements the Liberty Single Sign-On features, as for instance Federation, Single Sign-On and Log-Out, *ii) Message* provides features to create specific XML messages (for instance Liberty protocol and authentication), and *iii) Utility* provides functionality as Exception Handling, Data Format encoding and decoding.

Shibboleth. Shibboleth [17] is an open source implementation of Internet2/MACE, aimed at developing architectures, policy structures, practical technologies, to support sharing of Web resources subject to access control. Shibboleth is not only a SSO implementation, but it is a more general architecture that tries to protect privacy and more in general to manage user credentials. However, in this paper, we focus on the Shibboleth SSO implementation that is very close to Liberty Single Sign-on specifications [16]. The lower level implementation relies on different standards as HTTP, XML, XML Schema, XML Signature, SOAP and SAML. As in Liberty Alliance approach, Shibboleth uses Federation concept, named *Shibboleth Club*, between identity and service providers.

Java Open Single Sign-On (JOSSO). T Java Open Single Sign-On (JOSSO) is an open source J2EE-based SSO infrastructure aimed at providing a solution for centralized platform-neutral user authentication[14]. In the JOSSO architecture we can identify three main actors: *i) Partner application*, a web application that uses SSO Gateway services to authenticate users; *ii) SSO Gateway*, represents the SSO server and provides authentication services to users who need authentication with partner applications; *iii) SSO Agent*, is a SSO Gateway client installed on managed services. More specifically, JOSSO supplies: *i) components-based framework*, since it provides a component-oriented infrastructure to support multiple authentication scheme, credential, and session stores, *ii) support for integration with Tomcat web container*, without requiring code customization, *iii) cross platform*, allowing integration with Java and non-Java applications, using standard solutions such as JAAS, SOAP, EJB, servlet/JSP and Struts, and *iv) support for strong authentication*, through the use of X.509 standard certificates.

Open Web SSO. The Open Web SSO [15] project provides core identity services for implementing transparent Single Sign-On as an infrastructure security component. In this paper, we will do not discuss Open Web SSO in detail because it is still in a very early stage of development.

4 Evaluation of OSS Single Sign On Systems

Generally speaking, few organizations rely on internal guidelines for the selection of open source products. In most cases, users select an open source solution which is readily available and fulfills their functional requirements. Several researchers [6, 10] have proposed more complex methodologies dealing with the evaluation of open source products from different perspectives, such as code quality, development flow and community composition and participation. In this paper, we put forward the idea of a specific selection process for security-related open source code. A major challenge is to establish a security-specific evaluation methodology capable of reducing users mistrust. e.g. due to the feeling that security open source applications are an "intrinsic backdoor" for attackers. Our main evaluation criteria highlight the promptness of reacting against newly discovered vulnerabilities or incidents. Applications success depend on the above principle because a low reaction rate to new vulnerabilities or incidents implies higher risk for users that adopt the software, potentially causing loss of information and money.

4.1 Evaluation principles

To select and find out the metrics that have to be evaluated in order to compare different security-related OSS implementations, let us first spell out the principles our analysis will be based on. We consider six partially overlapping macro-areas:

Generic Aspects (GA). An open source application must be categorized in terms of its generic aspects, i.e. ones not related to its purpose or scope, including all the quantitative attributes proposed in the literature [6] that effectively describe a generic open source implementation. Such aspects include: the duration and size of the project, the programming language, the number of downloads and accesses.

Developers Community (DC). A critical success factor for any open source project is the composition and diversity of the developers community. A high number of developers allows sharing of diverse backgrounds and skills, giving vitality and freshness to the community and helping in solving problems, including bugs definition and fixing. Examples of DC properties are the number of developers and their roles, the existence of a core group and its stability over time.

Users Community (UC). The success of an open source application can be measured in terms of number and profile of the users that adopt it and rely on it. Obviously, measuring and evaluating the users community is less simple than doing so for developers because users interacting with an open source project are often anonymous. The overall quality of the users community, however, can be estimated by means of the number of downloads, the number of requests, the number of posts inside the forum, and the number of users subscribed to the mailing list. A qualitative measure of this macro-area could be the profile of the users adopting the project: if users belong to well-known companies or organizations and report positive results, their importance arises.

Software Quality (SQ). This area include metrics of quality built into the software by the requirements, design, code and verification processes to ensure that reliability, maintainability, and other quality factors are met. A subset of this macro area is the evaluation of code quality via coarse-grained factors such as operating system support, language support, level of modularity, compliance with the standards and so forth.[1]

Documentation and Interaction support (DIS). This macro area is composed of two major sub-areas: traditional documentation that explains the characteristics, functionalities and peculiarities of the software and support in terms of time allotted by developers to give feedback about the project and documentation, through forums, mailing lists, whitepapers, and presentations.

Integration and Adaptability with new and existing technologies (IA). A fundamental tenet of open source projects is full integration with existing technologies at project startup and a high level of adaptability to new technologies presented during project life. Another aspect that arise is the ability of the developers community to solve and fix bugs and react to new vulnerabilities.

---

[1] As far as evaluating code quality is concerned, we remark that open source SSO systems lend themselves to quality assurance and evaluation based on shared testing and code walkthrough as outlined in [1]. However, comparing reference implementations based on code walkthrough is outside the scope of this paper.

4.2 Evaluation parameters

In this section we provide a description of the metrics (see Table 1 and 2) we used to evaluate critical open source security applications. This set of metrics will be later used for comparing open source SSO architectures (see Section 5).

Within the above areas, we can now define quantitative metrics. They can be orthogonally divided in two categories: *i) Core Metrics (CM)*, including all metrics that can be readily computed from current technologies, statistics, and information on the projects; *ii) Advanced Metrics (AM)*, including all parameters that require additional information and some privileged access to the development group. Advanced metrics may be available only as rough estimates or not available entirely. A brief definition of the parameters semantics is shown in Table 1 and 2. For a detailed explanation of advanced metrics, we refer to Section 4.3.

4.3 Advanced Metrics

Advanced Metrics represent the evaluation parameters that would require privileged access to the developers community. Otherwise, they can be estimated based on raw data. In particular, we propose three major metrics: *i) Reaction Rate*, estimating the average time the developers community took to find solutions to newly discovered vulnerabilities. This parameter measures the community vitality in reacting against vulnerabilities that represent the main problem in security applications; *ii) Incident Frequency*, which measures the robustness of the application with respect to discovered vulnerabilities; *iii) Group/Developers Stability*, which measures the degree of stability of developers group. Regarding the first two parameters, we remarks that various security-related Web portal provides databases that contain information about vulnerabilities and related incidents summaries. In particular, three main portals stand out: *Secunia* (http://secunia.com/) that offers monitoring of vulnerabilities in more than 6000 products, *Open Source Vulnerability Database* (OSVDB) (http://www.osvdb.org/) an independent database that provides technical information about vulnerabilities and, finally, CERT that provides a database containing information about vulnerabilities, incidents and fixes. Further, we describe how to use the CERT database, the more complete and well supported repository of security concerns, in order to describe problems related to vulnerabilities and incidents prevention. The last metrics, *Groups/Developers Stability*, is not easy to estimate from outside the developers community, due to the fact that does not exist a formal categorization of the information related to the users and developers that belong to a particular project. It may be however available to insiders, e.g. to companies that adopted an open source product and openly contribute to its community.

CERT The Computer Emergency Response Team (CERT) [7] is an organization focused on ensuring that appropriate technologies and systems management practices are used to resist to attacks on networked systems, to

Core Metrics			
Name	Definition	Values	Area
Age	Age of the project	Days	GA
Project Core Group	Evaluate the existence of a group of core developers. Further analysis could evaluate the composition of the group	Boolean	GA,DC
Number of Core Developers	Number of core developers contributing the project. Core developers are defined as the persons that contributes both to the project management and code implementation	Integer	DC
Number of Releases	Number of releases since project start up	Integer	SQ,IA
Bug Fixing Rate	Measures the rate of bug fixed. This rate is computed as: $\frac{\#ofbugsfixed}{\#ofbugsdetected}$	[0..100]	SQ,IA
Update Average Time	Measures the vitality of developers group and in other word the mean number of days to wait for a new update (releases or patches). This metrics is computed as: $\frac{age}{\#ofpatches+\#ofreleases}$	days	SQ,IA
Forum and Mailing List Support	Check forum and mailing list availability	boolean	GA,DIS
Number of Users	Number of users that adopt the application. When not available, this parameter is approximated as: $\frac{\#ofdownloads}{\#ofreleases}$	Integer	UC
Documentation Level	Level of documentation of a project, in terms of API, user manuals, whitepapers	Mbyte	DIS
Code Quality	Qualitative measure of code quality. Several standard source code metrics could be adopted.		SQ,IA
Community Vitality	Represents the vitality of the community in terms of number of forum threads and replies: $\frac{\#offorumreplies}{\#offorumthreads}$	Real	DC,UC

Table 1. Evaluation Metrics Definition: Core Metrics

limit damages and ensure continuity of critical services despite successful attacks, accidents, or failures. The CERT is located at the Software Engineering Institute (SEI), a Federally Funded Research and Development Center (FFRDC) operated by Carnegie Mellon University. The CERT Coordination Center (CERT/CC), a major center for internet security problems, component of the larger CERT Program, was established in November 1988 after that the "Morris Worm" brought down much of the internet and demonstrated the growing network susceptibility to attack. For the purposes of the present paper, we take into consideration CERT information about vulnerabilities, incidents and vulnerabilities fixing, which provides the raw data over which our advanced metrics are computed.

Advanced Metrics			
Name	**Definition**	**Values**	**Area**
Reaction Rate	Average time needed by the developers community to find solutions for newly discovered vulnerabilities. More specifically, it represents the project developers ability in reacting to the set V of vulnerabilities. It is defined as follows: $\dfrac{UpdateAverageTime}{\sum_{i=1}^{n} \dfrac{(Fixing\_Date(V_i) - Discovering\_Date(V_i))}{n}}$ where $V_i \in V$ and $n = |V|$		IA
Incident Frequency	Measures the number of incidents due to vulnerabilities. This parameter is computed as: $\dfrac{\#of incidents}{|V|}$		IA
Group/ Developers Stability	Measures the degree of stability of a developers group. Each developer is classified as *stable* or *transient* where stable is a developer that continuously contributes code. The exact number of contributions to make a developer stable are project-dependent. This value is computed as: $\dfrac{\#of stable developers}{\#of developers} * 100$	[0..100%]	DC

Table 2. Evaluation Metrics Definition: Advanced Metrics

US-CERT Vulnerability Notes Database A vulnerability [13] is defined as a set of conditions that leads or may lead to an implicit or explicit failure of the confidentiality, integrity, or availability of an information system. Examples of the unauthorized or unexpected effects of a vulnerability may include executing commands as another user, accessing data in excess of specified or expected permission, posing as another user or service within a system, causing an abnormal denial of service, inadvertently or intentionally destroying data without permission and exploiting an encryption implementation weakness that significantly reduces the time or computation required to recover the plain text from an encrypted message. Common causes of vulnerabilities are design flaws in software and hardware, patched administrative processes, lack of awareness and education in information security, and advancements in the state of the art or improvements to current practices, any of which may result in real threats to mission-critical information systems. The accidental introduction of defects into software is expected to comprise a significant portion of the vulnerabilities addressed by this framework. CERT alerts users to potential vulnerabilities to the security of their systems and provide information about how to avoid, minimize, or recover from the damage. A vulnerabilities database is maintained by US-CERT [21] and contains descriptions of vulnerabilities, their impacts, and solutions. US-CERT publishes information on a wide variety of vulnerabilities. Descriptions of these vulnerabilities are available from this web page in a searchable database format, and are published as "US-CERT Vulnerability Notes".

The notes are very similar to alerts, but they may have less complete information. In particular, solutions may not be available for all the vulnerabilities in this database. The US-CERT Vulnerability Notes database is cross-referenced with the Common Vulnerabilities and Exposures (CVE) catalog.

CERT/CC Incident Notes CERT Incident Notes have become a core component of US-CERT's Technical Cyber Security Alerts and Current Activity; this bulletin provides information about the exploiting of the vulnerabilities to convey an attack to the affected systems. In particular, incident notes provide information such as the overview and description of the incident and optionally the solution to the vulnerability that causes the incident.

Vulnerability Fixing US-CERT Vulnerability Notes Database and CERT/CC Incident Notes provides additional information about the solution applied to fix the discovered vulnerabilities. It is widely acknowledged that most of the incident reports of computer break-ins received at the CERT/CC could have been prevented if system administrators and users kept their computers up-to-date with patches and security fixes. US-CERT provides only the link to the available patches and security fixes that are usually hosted on the vendor sites. In summary, most information necessary to calculate the provided advanced metrics set is already available on the Net. Unfortunately, this information is in raw format and then is difficult to automatize the calculation of the metrics. Substantial pre-processing is needed to compute these metrics, that are of paramount importance in evaluating the risk of open source security applications adoption. We are currently working on a tool for security metrics (Sect. 6)

5 Open Source Comparison

Table 3 gives a comparison of open source Single Sign-On implementations. Before discussing it, we remark that while CAS, SourceID and JOSSO are fully dedicated SSO systems, Shibboleth is a more comprehensive framework which contains, among other things, a SSO implementation. Focusing on the comparison, we remark that as shown by the table, all the analyzed systems are quite stable due to the fact that their startup happens more than a year ago. The CAS implementation stands out; it has a long time history because it started about five years ago. A common characteristic of the projects is that they are managed by a consolidated core group that gives stability to the project and coordination to open source community. Also the level of documentation is similar and is included between 6.80 MB of JOSSO and 10.05 MB of CAS. Although CAS seems the more lively project due to the great number of releases, we argue that the more active and viable implementation is JOSSO, because it provides a new release every 21 days, while CAS implementation only provided a release every 79 days. This gap could give to adopters of the JOSSO

Metrics	CAS	SourceID	Shibboleth	JOSSO
Age (GA)	1500 days	812 days	926 days	489 days
Project Core Group (GA,DC)	Yes	Yes	Yes	Yes
Number of Core Developers (DC)	5	N/A	5	2
Number of Releases (SQ,IA)	19	7	10	7
Bug Fixing Rate (SQ,IA)	N/A	N/A	0%	67%
Update Average Time (SQ,IA)	79 days	116 days	92,6 days	21 days
Forum and Mailing List Support (GA,DIS)	Mailing List Only	Mailing List Only	Mailing List Only	Yes
Number of Users (UC)	45	N/A	N/A	3161 approx.
Documentation Level (DIS)	10.05 MB	8.96 MB	7.04 MB	6.80 MB
Community Vitality (DC,UC)	N/A	N/A	N/A	3,12

Table 3. Comparison of proposed implementations at 31 December 2005

framework an higher assurance of the project's reliability, because continuous releases keep the implementation up to date and resistant to new technologies and vulnerabilities. However, JOSSO very short update time is also influenced by the fact that the project is the youngest; probably, in the next year, the update average time will rise although it will probably maintain the lowest update average time. Regarding other metrics, for the sake of conciseness we avoid a complete discussion. It is easy to see that JOSSO is the only implementation that furnishes all the information allowing a complete metrics measurement. To conclude this overview, our analysis showed that JOSSO is the most suitable and flexible open source SSO solution if analyzed from security point of view.

6 Conclusions

In this paper, we presented a quantitative approach to the comparative evaluation of security-related software. Then as a case-study, we compared five major implementations of Single-Sign-On systems. Our evaluation methodology relates on a structured set of metrics specifically designed for security-related open source systems. Some of these metrics are based on event logs of some well-known security portals (e.g., the CERT one) and their computation would be made much easier should CERT support some level of data warehousing. We are now working on a tool for creating a warehouse of quantitative data about security events to be used in the framework of our evaluation.

Acknowledgments

This work was supported in part by the European Union within the PRIME Project in the FP6/IST Programme under contract IST-2002-507591 and by the Italian MIUR within the KIWI and MAPS projects.

References

1. S. Abiteboul, X. Leroy, B. Vrdoljak, R. Di Cosmo, S. Fermigier, S. Lauriere, F. Lepied, R. Pop, F. Villard, J.P. Smets, C. Bryce, K.R. Dittrich, T. Milo, A. Sagi, Y. Shtossel, and E. Panto. Edos: Environment for the development and distribution of open source software. In *The First International Conference on Open Source Systems*, pages 66–70, Genova (Italy), July 2005.
2. C.A. Ardagna, E. Damiani, S. De Capitani di Vimercati, F. Frati, and P. Samarati. CAS++: an open source single sign-on solution for secure e-services. *Submitted to 21st IFIP International Information Security Conference "Security and Privacy in Dynamic Environments"*, May 2006.
3. C.A. Ardagna, E. Damiani, F. Frati, and M. Madravio. Open source solution to secure e-government services. *Encyclopedia of Digital Government*, 2006.
4. C.A. Ardagna, E. Damiani, F. Frati, and M. Montel. Using open source middleware for securing e-gov applications. In *The First International Conference on Open Source Systems*, pages 172–178, Genova (Italy), July 2005.
5. P. Aubry, V. Mathieu, and J. Marchal. Esup-portal: open source single sign-on with cas (central authentication service). In *Proceedings of EUNIS04 - IT Innovation in a Changing World*, pages 172–178, Bled (Slovenia), 2005.
6. A. Capiluppi, P. Lago, and M. Morisio. Characteristics of open source projects. In *CSMR*, page 317, 2003.
7. CERT-CC. Cert coordination center. http://www.cert.org/.
8. Jan De Clercq. Single sign-on architectures. In *International Conference on Infrastructure Security, InfraSec, LNCS*, 2002.
9. C. Cowan. Software security for open-source systems. *IEEE-SEC-PRIV*, 1(1):38–45, January/February 2003.
10. J. Feller and B. Fitzgerald. A framework analysis of the open source software development paradigm. In *ICIS*, pages 58–69, 2000.
11. B. Galbraith and et al. *Professional Web Services Security*. Wrox Press, 2002.
12. The Open Group. Single sign-on. http://www.opengroup.org/security/sso/.
13. John T. Chambers and John W. Thompson. Vulnerability disclosure framework. Final report and recommendations by the council, National Infrastructure Advisory Council, January 2004.
14. JOSSO. Java open single sign-on. http://sourceforge.net/projects/josso/.
15. OpenSSO. Open web sso. https://opensso.dev.java.net/.
16. Liberty Alliance Project. http://www.projectliberty.org/.
17. Shibboleth Project. http://shibboleth.internet2.edu/.
18. E.S. Raymond. The cathedral and the bazaar. http://www.openresources.com/documents/cathedral-bazaar/, August 1998.
19. SourceID. Open source federated identity management. http://www.sourceid.org/.
20. Yale University. Central authentication service. http://tp.its.yale.edu/tiki/tiki-index.php?page=CentralAuthenticationService.
21. US-CERT. Vulnerability notes database. http://www.kb.cert.org/vuls/.

Participation in Free and Open Source Communities: An Empirical Study of Community Members' Perceptions.

Andrew Schofield[1] and Professor Grahame S. Cooper[2]

1 Information Systems Institute, University of Salford, Salford, M5 4WT,
UK, a.j.schofield@pgt.salford.ac.uk,
WWW Home page: http://www.postgrad.isipartnership.net/~aschofield/
2 School of Computing, Science, and Engineering, University of Salford,
Salford, M5 4WT, UK, g.s.cooper@salford.ac.uk,
WWW Home page:
http://www.cse.salford.ac.uk/profiles/profile.php?profile=G.S.Cooper

Abstract. Although the defining factors of Free and Open Source Software (FOSS) are generally seen as the availability and accessibility of the source code, it is what these facilitate that is perhaps of more significance. Source code availability allows the sharing of code, skills, knowledge, and effort, focused on a particular piece of software under development. The result of this is the FOSS community, which although often perceived as a single group, is actually many small groups, each bound by a common interest in a particular piece of software and using the Internet as a communication medium. Although there have been studies focusing on the motivation of FOSS developers to contribute to software, there has been little investigation into the motives, attitudes, and the culture within the communities as a whole. There is much more to most of these communities than software development. Many also have extensive support networks for the use of software, portals for research, and social facilities. This paper describes the results of an investigation into how FOSS community members perceive the communities that they belong to, their reasons for joining in the community, and the manner in which they participate.

1 Introduction

Free and Open Source Software communities remain elusive and intangible despite the significant amount of research that has been done on the subject. The significance of these communities is also something that has been under much debate. Some authors (Raymond, 2000; Lanzara & Morner, 2003; Oh & Jeon, 2004) describe FOSS communities as entirely virtual systems that operate almost exclusively over the Internet on a global scale. Other authors (Krishnamurthy, 2002; O'Mahony & Ferraro, 2004) maintain that in many cases, a significant amount of FOSS communities often operates off-line in the 'real world', and that a considerable quantity of FOSS development is actually performed by individuals. It is probable that in actual fact, FOSS development is a mixture of both these theories. While some projects will have large numbers of people working on them, other projects may have few or a single developer. Furthermore, although some projects will exist entirely online, others may involve off-line meetings between people, especially between the core development team and in projects originating from within organisations (Schofield & Mitra 2005).

The community members themselves are not easily put into categories. The work by Zhang & Storck (2001) illustrates this issue by putting forward the definition of "peripheral members". These are members of the FOSS community that may not directly participate within the community. To take this idea further, the only visible members of a FOSS community are those who participate in discussion forums, bulletin boards, named code development, or those who make themselves known in other ways. Members who visit the on-line communities, perhaps reading from forums, but not posting anything, may still be considered to be part of the community but will remain unknown to other members. In contrast to this, it is the belief of many authors (Sagers, 2004; O'Mahony, 2004) that social interaction is the foundation to FOSS community existence, which suggests that without a critical mass of participating members, a community cannot exist.

How members interact with their community is ultimately defined by the available interaction mechanisms and the particular needs of the member. There are several reasons why people may choose to become part of a FOSS community. The bulk of the literature on this subject has focused on the motivation of developers (Hann et al 2004; Hertel et al 2003; Lakhani & Wolf 2003; Scacchi et al 2005; Schofield & Mitra 2004). Suggested reasons include; pragmatic reasons for needing specific software functionality, enjoyment of software development as a hobby, educational benefits, feelings of belonging to a community and/or to a large scale movement, the need for recognition, self-gratification from a sense of achievement, and career advancement though skill acquisition. Although the above work gives some insight into the reasons members have for being involved in community-based FOSS development, it does not provide a whole picture of motivation in FOSS communities beyond software development, nor how members' perception of the community defines their participation

2   Research Method

The data collected for this research used a predominantly quantitative on-line survey method. Reaching members of FOSS communities for data collection is inherently difficult, for the reasons of intangibility and levels of participation explained above. The sample set of this research consisted of a particular type of Open Source group within the UK, the Linux User Groups (LUGs). The term is slightly deceptive as most of these groups do not only concentrate on the Linux Operating System but on a wide variety of other Open Source operating systems, application and programs. The research findings presented in this paper are based on the 145 survey submissions received

Although the survey was directed at the UK LUGs, it was open for others to participate. Analysis revealed that of the total number of submissions, approximately 12% came from people who were not part of a FOSS society, club, or user group. Many of the LUGs are involved in software development in some way, and members may also be involved in other software development communities. The survey used dealt with individuals' experiences of on-line FOSS communities in general, not specifically the LUGs, and although for some members, experience of a FOSS community will only be the LUG, others will certainly have a broader experience including other communities. The survey results demonstrate this, as many members have referred to other communities in their submissions.

The survey itself dealt with several aspects of FOSS communities and the attitudes and participation of community members. This paper covers the areas of the survey that collected data about the specific reasons a member may have for participating, in terms of the actual activities involved, and how and for what purpose a member makes use of communities.

3 Research Findings

The basic motivation for anyone making use of an on-line FOSS community is to perform some function, i.e. to use an on-line tool to achieve a desired action. It is which functions a member uses and why they use them that the initial phase of the research attempted to discover. This section of the survey collected community members' perceptions of what they actually do within FOSS communities and the pragmatic reasons for participating. Research subjects were presented with several possible reasons for making use of on-line FOSS communities;

- To find out how to perform a task in a software application (Problem solving).
- To help other people to use software applications (Providing support).
- To suggest alterations or improvements to software programs (Peer review).
- To contribute bug fixes or code improvements (Software development).
- To meet people or talk to people with similar interests (Social exchange).

The survey question was designed to allow members to select more than one reason or to specify one or more of their own. Expressed as the actual number of choices, figure 1 shows how many members chose the above reasons i.e. 127 members chose (not exclusively) problem solving to be a reason for participating in a FOSS community. Figure 2 shows this data presented in percentage form (i.e. 25% of all the choices submitted by all members were for providing support).

As not all members of FOSS communities are developers, it was expected that the peer review, and software development factors would be less popular than those relating to support. In addition to these choices, members also posted other reasons including: being the leader/manager of a community, lurking (Members may have many reasons to lurk perhaps born out of a simple interest in observing discussion), to encourage the advocacy of FOSS, to build business relations, to learn industry standards and trends, and finally, just for fun!

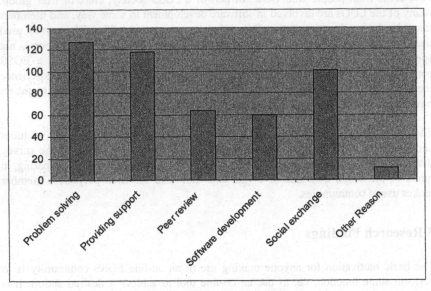

Figure 1: Reasons for Participation

The first phase of the research identified the reasons why community members participate in FOSS communities, in terms of what activities they are involved in. The next phase of the research was to investigate how these community activities are used,

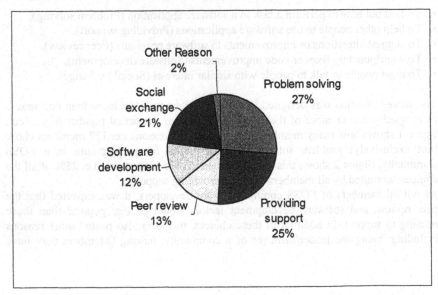

Figure 2: Reasons for Participation as a Percentage

and to collect self-reflective perceptions of why they are used in the manner to which

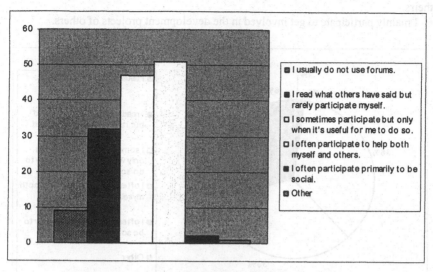

Figure 3: Use of Support Forums

the member refers. This phase of the research was split into two sections; the first looking exclusively at the community aspects which provide support for the use of software, and the second at the aspects revolving around software development.

The members were presented with the following alternative ways of interacting with FOSS support community forums:

- I usually do not use forums.
- I read what others have said but rarely participate myself.
- I sometimes participate but only when it's useful for me to do so.
- I often participate to help both myself and others.
- I often participate primarily to be social.

Many members chose to leave additional comments for this question, almost all of which stating that they preferred mailing lists to discussion boards. There was some suggestion that discussion boards were more for beginners, and that they are more focussed on specific issues as oppose to mailing lists which have more general coverage. The interface of the majority of discussion boards was also criticised and listed as another reason for members preferring mailing lists.

Finally, those members with software development experience were asked how they use FOSS community functions for software development. The following possibilities were given and, as before, members could specify their own alternatives.

- I mainly participate just to get help with my own development work.

- I participate both to receive help myself with my own work and to help others with theirs.
- I mainly participate to get involved in the development projects of others.

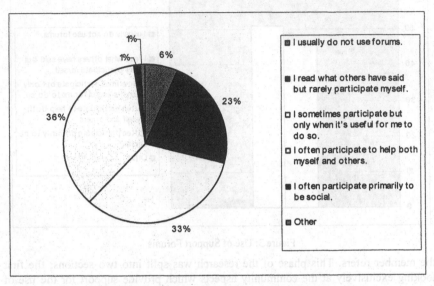

Figure 4: Reasons for Participation as a Percentage

- I mainly participate to be sociable.

The order of the questions in the survey and the request that the completion of this question is by developers only, is based on the assumption that all developers are also users of FOSS software. More specifically this means that both users and developers will make use of the support forums, but that only developers will make use of the software development forums. It is acknowledged that in some cases these may be the

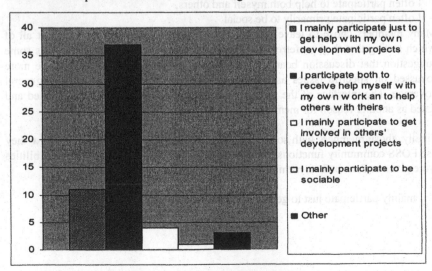

Figure 5: Use of Development Forums

same forums but it is still possible to separate the two activities.

Again the members were also given the opportunity to provide their own answer to the question in case none of these options were appropriate. For this question members were asked to choose only one option from the list. Figure 3 shows the choices made by the members and Figure 4 the results as a percentage.

Figure 5 shows the results of this question being put to the developers and Figure 6 shows the same data in a percentage format.

Other uses specified by the developers were: to use the development forums as a source of research material, to disseminate software to others, to use FOSS development activities for personal professional development, and again, just for the fun of it.

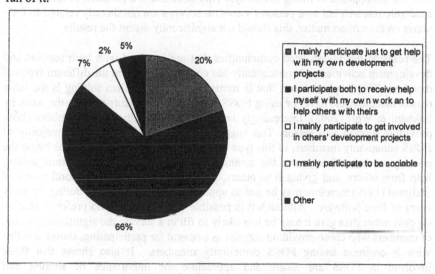

Figure 6: Use of Development Forums as a Percentage

4 Research Analysis

By their very nature, FOSS development and the communities performing it are open to anyone who wants to get involved at any level. The fact that they are also facilitated by the Internet means that a community is not usually confined by any geographical constraints, but rather exists on an international or global scale. It is this fact that justifies the use of the UK Linux/Open Source User groups as the sample set for this research. The groups may have members from all over the world and each member is likely to be involved with a myriad of other diverse communities. The collection of the data for this research itself is a good example. The request for participation was sent to specific UK groups and resulted in submissions arriving from many other countries which were not specifically targeted. An acknowledged potential limitation of the research is that LUGs are perhaps more likely to focus on support than other kinds of FOSS community. There are some communities that are almost entirely focused on software development and much less on support. Although many LUG members are involved in other communities there is no way of proving that the members reached by this survey are entirely representative of FOSS community members in general. It may be that communities are far more focused on software development than has been demonstrated by this research. Furthermore, it is acknowledged that the data has only been collected from FOSS community members who are not opposed to filling in surveys. This of course is a potential problem for all academic research but as a person's views on surveys are not directly related to their views on the subject matter, this should not significantly distort the results.

The research has investigated communities that are involved with both support and development activities and consequently has collected data from the different types of members. The data has shown that in terms of support, problem solving is the main reason that members have for using FOSS communities, concurring with the work by Lakhani & Wolf (2003). Interestingly however, only slightly fewer members chose providing support as a reason. This suggests two things; firstly that the majority of FOSS community members, in this type of community, perceive support as being the primary reason or function of the community. Secondly that members rank getting help from others, and giving it to others, as equally important. The moral views of Stallman (1999) therefore may be just as applicable now as they were during the early years of Free Software . Although it is possible that members who prefer to receive support rather than give it may be less likely to fill in a survey, the significant number of members who chose providing support as a reason for participating, shows that this view is common among FOSS community members. It also shows that those involved in FOSS are aware and appreciate the importance of sharing and collaboration in community systems as well as software development.

Members also saw peer review and actual software development as being of equal importance. Since peer review can be performed by member who may have little or no knowledge of software development, in the programming sense, this highlights the importance of the user in the FOSS development process and the close user-developer relationship that exists (Scacchi 2005). It also demonstrates that FOSS communities are highly involved in the development of software, even when many of the participating members are not contributing code and may not even be programmers. These contributions would instead be in the form of software testing, bug reporting and general suggestions on function and operation (Pavlicek 2000; Moody 2001; Raymond 1999). If these results are to be considered representative of FOSS communities in general, the results would suggest that only approximately 50% of member activities within the community are for reasons of software development. This supposition is however dependent on the factors of survey participation and sample set community types.

An extremely interesting result was the apparent importance of social exchange within the communities. 70% of the surveyed members, stated that meeting and talking to people with similar interests was one of their main reasons for their participation. This made up 21% of the reasons for member participation (See Figure 2). Sagers' (2004) and O'Mahony's (2004) work would seem to fit in with these findings. However, in specific terms of support and development (See figure 4 through 6), only around 1% of members felt that social factors drove them to use support or development forums. This suggests that the social activities within the communities are not confined either to support or development activities but instead extend to broader social interest.

The second phase of the research, investigating how members use the communities, has also produced some interesting results and helped to define the different types of members that make up a community. From this sample set, the majority of members (36%) use communities for getting support with their software and giving support to others. Logically this means that many members will login to a FOSS community website only to help others with their problems, quite possibly with no tangible benefit to themselves. This correlates with the results of the first phase, in which 25% of members listed providing support as a reason for participation (See Figure 2). A slightly smaller number of members stated that they would participate only if it was useful for them to do so, suggesting that, in terms of support, the two types of community members are those who perceive giving and taking as being equally important, and those who require some incentive or personal benefit for them to participate. Additionally, Zhang & Storck's (2001) research into "peripheral members", supports the research's finding that approximately 23% of members will observe the community but rarely participate themselves. This too could be a matter of incentive but is a very difficult subject to research given the apparent unwillingness of the members to participate. It is quite possible that there are a great deal more members that very rarely participate in the sample communities and consequently were not reached by this survey.

The members of the community involved in development provided a much more clear-cut set of results. The majority of them (66%) stated that they were involved in FOSS development communities both to get help with their work, and help others with theirs, again demonstrating the attitude of collaboration and team work that exists within FOSS. Only 20% of members said that they participated only to get help with their own work. This mirrors the findings from the support communities but indicates that the bi-direction collaborative aspects are more important in actual software development. Only a very small number of members participated to get involved in others projects. It is likely that these will be new members, attempting to get involved with projects for educational purposes.

5 Conclusions

The presented research has extracted information about FOSS communities from the very members that they consist of. It is this unique viewpoint that has revealed the very interesting inferences that have been taken from the research findings. It has looked at the ways in which members of a FOSS community perceive the group that they are in, and has revealed some of the very specific motivational aspects involved.

Although FOSS communities are still often seen as ad-hoc and chaotic, the research has shown that it is common interest and community relations that bind these communities together, and allows them to produce both knowledge and software in such an effective fashion. The research has demonstrated that there is strong sense of sharing and collaboration within communities that support FOSS development and use. This manifests itself in two main ways, firstly in the areas of software development where code, ideas and suggestions are shared and secondly in the software support area, where information about software use is the object of transfer. It is this code and knowledge generation and transference between community members with diverse sets of expertise and backgrounds that allows FOSS communities to function so well.

6 References

Dibona, C., Ockham, S., Stone, M. (1999), Open Sources: Voices from the Open Source Revolution, O'Reilly & Associates, Inc., CA, USA

Hann, I. H., (2004) "Why Developers Participate in Open Source Software Projects: And Empirical Study", Twenty-Fifth International Conference on Information Systems.

Hertel, G., Niedner, S., Herrmann, S. (2003), "Motivation of Software Developers in Open Source Projects: An Internet-based Survey of Contributors to the Linux Kernel", Research Policy, Special Issue on Open Source Software Development, Available at: http://opensource.mit.edu/papers/hertel.pdf, Accessed (February 2004)

Krishnamurthy, S., (2002) "Cave or Community? An Empirical Examination of 100 Mature Open Source Projects", Available at http://opensource.mit.edu/, Accessed (Feb 2005)

Lakhani, K. R., Wolf, R.G. (2003), "Why Hackers Do What They Do: Understanding Motivation Effort in Free Open Source Software Projects", MIT Sloan School of Management   Working   paper,   Available   at: http://freesoftware.mit.edu/papers/lakhaniwolf.pdf, Accessed (February 2004)

Lanzara, G.F., Morner, M. (2003), 'The knowledge ecology of Open-Source Software Projects', paper presented at seminar on 'ICTs in the contemporary world' at LSE Department of Information Systems on 2nd October

Moody, G. (2001), "Rebel Code: How Linus Torvalds, Linux and the Open Source Movement Are Outmastering Microsoft", The Penguin Press, England

O'Mahony, S., Ferraro, F., (2004) "Hacking Alome? The Effects of Online and Offline Participation on Open Source Community Leadership", Available at http://opensource.mit.edu/, Accessed (Dec 2004)

Oh, W., Jeon, S., (2004) "Membership Dynamics and Network Stability in the Open-Source Community: The Ising Perspective" Twenty-Fifth International Conference on Information Systems.

Pavlicek, R. C. (2000), "Embracing Insanity: Open Source Software Development", Sams Publishing, USA

Raymond, E. S, (1999), "The Magic Cauldron",
Available at: http http://www.catb.org/~esr/writings/cathedral-bazaar/magic-cauldron/ (Accessed December 2003)

Raymond, E. S, (2000), "The Cathedral and the Bazaar",
Available at: http://www.catb.org/~esr/writings/cathedral-bazaar/cathedral-bazaar/ (Accessed November 2003) and in Dibona et al (1999)

Sagers, G.W., (2004) "The Influence of Network Governance Factors on Success in Open Source Software Development Projects", Twenty-Fifth International Conference on Information Systems.

Scacchi, W., Feller, J., Fitzgerald, B., Hissam, S., Lakhani, K., (2005) "Understanding Free/Open Source Software Development Processes", Available at: (http://www.ics.uci.edu/~wscacchi/Papers/New/SPIP-FOSS-Intro-Dec2005.pdf) (Accessed December 2005)

Schofield, A., Mitra, A. (2004), "Complexities of Classifying Open Source: Developing a Framework for Categorising Open Software Development", UK Academy of Information Systems conference 2004, Glasgow, UK.

Schofield, A., Mitra, A. (2005), "Free and Open Source Software Communities as a Support Mechanism", UK Academy of Information Systems conference 2005, Newcastle, UK

Stallman, R. (1999), "The GNU Operating System and the Free Software Movement", in Dibona et al (1999).

Zhang, W. & Storck, J, (2001) "Peripheral Members in Online Communities", Americas Conference on Information Systems, Boston, USA.

Collaborative Maintenance in Large Open-Source Projects

Matthijs den Besten[1,2], Jean-Michel Dalle[1,2] and Fabrice Galia[3]
[1] Université Pierre et Marie Curie, Paris, France
<jean-michel.dalle@upmc.fr>
[2] Université Paris-Dauphine, Paris, France
<matthijs.denbesten@lamsade.dauphine.fr>
[3] Université Panthéon-Assas Paris II, Paris, France
<galia@u-paris2.fr>

Abstract. The paper investigates collaborative work among maintainers of open source software by analyzing the logs of a set of 10 large projects. We inquire whether teamwork can be influenced by several characteristics of code. Preliminary results suggest that collaboration among maintainers in most large open-source projects seems to be positively influenced by file vintage and by Halstead volume of files, and negatively by McCabe complexity and size measured in SLOCs. These results could be consistent with an increased attractivity of files created early in the history of a project, and with maintainers being less attracted by more verbose code and by more complex code, although in this last case it might also reflect the fact that more complex files would be de facto more exclusive in terms of maintenance.

1 Introduction

Teams in general, and virtual teams in particular, enjoy an increasing interest from scholars in organizational science.[1,2] In the absence of a strong managerial hand, it is not obvious indeed how team members collaborate – especially when the members are located in various parts of the world. Nonetheless, in many circumstances virtual teams appear to be remarkably successful and until now, no real and clear understanding exists of the conditions of their success and efficiency.

In this context, the work of virtual teams is at least partly traceable in the activity logs that those teams leave behind in their virtual environments. Open source software projects are natural candidates in this respect, i.e. for quantitative empirical studies of virtual teams, given their increasing economic success and the free and easy access they typically provide to such data.[4] Several steps in this direction have already been made by others[3]. This conviction that the by-products of collaboration provide a wealth of data that could be harnessed is also behind the study of collaborative maintenance activity in open source project logs that we present here..

Section 2 introduces open source software and reviews some of the research done in that area. In section 3, we describe the database we studied and how we created it, and we introduce a few important methodological caveats. It is followed, in section 4,

Please use the following format when citing this chapter:

den Besten, M., Dalle, J.-M., and Galia, F., 2006, in IFIP International Federation for Information Processing, Volume 203, Open Source Systems, eds. Damiani, E., Fitzgerald, B., Scacchi, W., Scotto, M., Succi, G., (Boston: Springer), pp. 233-244

by an analysis of the results of our investigations. We conclude by briefly pointing out several avenues for further research.

2   Open Source Software

Open source software (OSS) is a type of software that has become increasingly prevalent over recent years. In contrast to closed source software, in OSS the human readable source code of the software program is distributed along with the program itself. With this source code it becomes then possible for users of the program to scrutinize the inner workings of the program and to adapt the program to their needs. The most famous example of OSS is Linux, an operating system developed based on Unix that is developed by Linus Torvalds and many other developers.[5] Microsoft, a dominant player in the market for operating systems, acknowledged the strength of Linux very early on, in what is now known as the "Halloween document"[6], and since then, the software industry has looked for ways to adapt features of the open source development model in more traditional closed environments.[7,8]

Yet, there is still something particular, and largely puzzling, about the OSS development model. In general, what is understood as the OSS development model is that it corresponds to the community-based voluntary self-organizing effort of various virtual teams of physically dispersed computer programmers to develop software – that is itself open to inspection to everyone who is interested. Eric Raymond famously likened the OSS development model to the interactions that are going on in a "bazaar".[9] However, since then, several case studies of open source software projects showed that in many projects hierarchies tend to persist and that there is larger diversity in organizational forms from one project to the other than would have been expected.[10] Indeed, in so far as there is a OSS development model, recent research seems to point towards an "onion model" of organization in which a core team of just a few developers is aided by a larger group of co-developers who are in turn aided by an even larger group of bug-submitters and feature-requesters, etc.[11] That is, open source development typically involves the participation of a large number of users who report bugs and request features, to be compared to a more limited number of co-developers who suggest software code that addresses those bugs and features; and to yet a smaller set of core developers who review the suggested code contributions and incorporate them in the existing code base.

What makes open source software projects particularly attractive as a topic for research is that virtually the whole development process is recorded and that the archives of these recordings are freely available for investigation. More in particular, open source software projects typically feature mailing lists where developers discuss their work and non-developers submit requests or ask for help. In addition, there may be discussion forums and bug tracking tools. Last, but not least, the source code is available and, when, as is often the case, a version control system is employed, in fact all old versions of the source code so that the development process can be traced back to the start. Researchers of software engineering have started to make use of this wealth of data to inform their investigations. Notable examples are the work of Walt

Scacchi[12], who performed an in-depth ethnographical analysis of the implicit ways in which requirements are gathered in open source projects, and that of Mockus and Herbsleb[13], who studied the pace with which bugs were resolved based on information in mailing lists and software logs. Hashler and Koch[14] propose a larger scale mining of the available information and discuss what kind of questions could be explored on the basis of that information.

The data that we looked at for our particular investigation of the allocation of tasks in open source software project teams was extracted from logs of development activity that are maintained by software version control systems. Version control systems are used by development teams in order to keep track of what was contributed, when and by whom. If conflicts arise due to a change in the code, a version control system makes it possible to undo that change and revert to the source code as it was before the change was made. Note, however, that in most OSS projects, a possible change has already been thoroughly reviewed before it is applied to the source code. Also, the people who commit the change are not necessarily the ones who wrote the code incorporated in that change. Rather, they are likely to be the *maintainers* of a part of the source code, who after a review of a change suggested by others, decide it is a good change and apply it to their part of the source code. In some cases, each change has to be approved of by a committee of core developers. In other cases, the review of suggested changes is completely up to the digression of the maintainer of the part of the source code to which the change is applied.

3   Database & Caveats

To create a database adapted to our investigations, we selected a set of open-source projects, attempting to obtain a set that was diverse in terms of product complexity, task uncertainty, and target audience. In addition, the projects needed to have a minimum amount of code, contributors and development history: in the list below, the logs typically span a period of five to ten years. Obviously, only those projects that provided easy access to their code repositories could qualify. In the end we settled for ten projects: An operating system – *NetBSD*, a data base – *PostgreSQL*, a web server – *Apache*, a web browser – *Mozilla*, an instant messaging application – *Gaim*, a secure networking protocol – *OpenSSH*, a programming language – *Python*, a compiler – *GCC*, an interpreter for the PostScript language and for PDF – *Ghostcript*, and a version control system – *CVS*. Several of these projects, most notably Mozilla and Apache, have already received a lot of attention from researchers. Others, like Gaim, stand out because of the amount of activity or because of the sheer length of activity. Finally, and although we only selected "large" projects, we selected projects whose sizes belong to different orders of magnitude (in terms #contributors, #files, #years of history), which could have an impact on their characteristics, and we would precisely like to discriminate between characteristics of projects and features more generally associated with the open-source mode of software development. There are also strong and potentially relevant differences among these projects in terms of organization and in terms of maintenance policies.

We extracted CVS logs for all these projects. CVS is the most widely used version control system for open source software development and its logs are relatively easy to parse.[15] The log lists for each file each revision of that file and for each revision when the revision was made, who was responsible for the revision and how many lines of code were added to and deleted from the file as a result of the revision (example given in Annex). At this level of analysis, we have restrained our sample to all the files that contain source code written in C or C++ i.e. to files with .c, .C, .cc, or .cpp suffixes. However, in some projects, e.g. *Python*, most code is obviously written in another language (e.g. *python*, precisely). In others, specially in *gcc*, there is a large portion of test files.

For each of the 10 projects, we computed descriptive data similar to what is available for various open-source projects[18], reported partially in Table 1. Then, more specifically for the purpose of studying collaborative maintenance, for each file that was studied and for each month we computed how many distinct maintainers had committed a change to that file during that period, and how many commits the file had received during the same period.

Before we proceed to presenting our investigations and their results, a few caveats have to be mentioned, which appeared as we progressed in the series of experiments that we conducted with our database.

1. About the constitution of the database and its suitability for econometric inquiries, it is not fully clear where the boundaries of a given project are. For instance, Apache and Mozilla have their own repositories but both host multiple applications. Lacking a clear rule for now about where to draw these limits, we decided that in the case of Apache, we would restrict ourselves to the logs concerning Apache HTTP Server 2.0. In the case of Mozilla, we considered the whole suite. In the case of NetBSD, we only looked at the kernel of the operating system, while in the case of OpenSSH, which is part of OpenBSD, we focused at the subdirectory within OpenBSD where OpenSSH resides.

2. The first date recorded in the repository does not necessarily coincide with the creation date of the project. However, the earliest record in the log does not necessarily coincide with the start of the project itself as the decision to adopt CVS could have been made well into the development of the project: A case in point is GCC, which started well before the first recorded commit in 1997.

3. For now, we only consider the main branch and ignore activity in other development branches. More generally, it is not completely clear when a file is really part of the project's code base. That is, some files are explicitly deleted when they are no longer needed, but we cannot be sure that this policy is always enforced. Some files are "born dead" (which happens when a file is created in a branch other than the main branch). Sometimes files that are registered as dead are "revived". All of this is mainly *CVS*-specific.

4.   Finally, it might be necessary to investigate at some point whether CVS accounts could be used by more than one maintainer, which could create another potential source of bias.

4 Empirical Investigations

To study collaborative maintenance activity, the econometric tests presented in this paper address two different measures for each file, the average number of maintainers per month ("maint's"), and the average number of revisions per month ("revisions"). The first measure can be considered as an indicator of collaborative maintenance while the second addresses activity more specifically.

However, previous investigations[20] have attracted our attention to the time variability of collaborative maintenance and activity on a given file. We had typically found that in 80 to 90% of the cases, only one maintainer had committed a change to a given file during a given month. As a consequence, we investigate also two other variables: the maximum number of maintainers per month over the period ("max maint's") and the maximum number of revisions of files per month over the period ("max revisions") in order to address this issue. These last two variables focus on intensive periods of maintenance and activity to deal with the fact that there are large periods of low activity, which is rather intuitive once said, but which we fear might create a significant bias: in doing so, they allow us to focus specially on periods of *teamwork*.

We run several specifications for all 10 projects, trying to explain four dependant variables (maint's, max maint's, revisions and max revisions) by the size of the file defined as its number of single lines of code ("SLOCs"), the maximum McCabe complexity index for all functions in the file ("McCabe"), Halstead volume ("Halstead") of the file, and the date of creation of the file ("Relative creation date").

Taking *Apache* as an example (Table 2), we find that:

a. maint's is explained positively by the relative creation date of the files: even controlling by their age, younger files attract on average more maintainers than older ones. A similar, but opposite, dependence characterizes max maint's: in that case, the older the file the higher the maximum number of maintainers during one month. Similar dependencies (positive for revisions and negative for max revisions), and therefore similar tentative explanations, characterize activity: still controlling by their age, younger files attract more activity on average, but a lower maximal activity per month. Generally, younger files tend to attract a higher average number of maintainers per month, and a higher average number of revisions per month, but lower maxima in both cases.

→ This could be explained by a larger global audience of the project, meaning that more recent files could attract more numerous maintainers just because the population of developers would be larger, because the growth of the total number of maintainers for the project over time, meaning that the files could therefore be "touched" by more maintainers simply because there are more maintainers in the project. At the same time, older files have more intense (collaborative) maintenance & activity peaks: this could maybe be related to older files – files with an older *vintage* – being more attractive to development and maintenance activity because of their importance in the project, or to the fact that early development activity was more collaborative in itself, due for instance to the role of initial core teams.

b. File size, measured in SLOCs, does not explain the average number of maintainers per month on a file, nor the average number of revisions per month, except when associated with Halstead, but has always some explanatory power for the related maxima. McCabe is not significant for maint's, whereas it is for the 3 other dependent variables. Halstead is significant for the estimations of all 4 dependent variables, and renders SLOCs insignificant: indeed, Halstead is more strongly correlated to SLOCs (though both complexity variables actually are). Adjusted R2 are considerably higher for both maxima with Halstead.

→ This could be consistent with the idea suggested above that there are limited periods of intense activity for files, outside of which "normal" activity is less relevant for this kind of analysis. In all circumstances, Halstead has a strong explanatory power, which is relatively intuitive is we analyse it as a combination of size and complexity of code.

c. Results with Halstead are therefore presented in synthetic form for all 10 others projects in Table 3. There are only few differences such as the absence of explicative power of the relative creation date for *gaim*, except for maint's, which would notably deserve further and more specific investigations. The significance of SLOCs, and the sign of the dependence when it exist, appear more subject to variations than for Halstead, but might point more to a measurement issue more than to actual differences among projects, save at least for Python where it is probably in relation with the number of files written in python, precisely, and which have therefore been excluded for now from our analysis.

→ These results confirm the robustness of the findings and interpretations presented above, and suggest that these characteristics could generally characterize the open-source mode of development in large projects. Together with results obtained for Apache, they might also suggest more subtle dependencies associated with other measures of code size (SLOCs) or complexity (McCabe).

d. In this last respect, and turning back to Apache, Table 4 presents an additional estimation of max maint's using Halstead, SLOCs, McCabe, and Functions (which gives the number of functions in a file). Interestingly, all these variables are significant: a higher number of functions tends to significantly increase the maximum number of maintainers in a file; on the contrary, higher McCabe and SLOCs significantly decreases the number of maintainers.

→ This finding could be consistent with an enhanced division of labour between maintainers inside a given file when more modular, i.e. allowing for more maintainers when there are more functions; and with more complex and longer files being more difficult to maintain and less attractive for maintainers respectively.

e. Finally, Table 5 also presents a more complete estimation of max revisions using Halstead, SLOCs, McCabe, Functions and now Max maint's, as it appears reasonable indeed to suggest that the maximal activity on a file could be explained by the maximum number of maintainers. It is indeed so, and the relative creation date, SLOCs and Functions lose all statistical significance, which Halstead and McCabe retain.

→ This validates the idea that vintage explains the maximum number of maintainers on a file and thus indirectly its maximum activity, and also that the division of a file into functions is consistent with organizing maintainer collaboration more than with explaining activity per se. Halstead and McCabe have a strong positive and negative explanatory power vis a vis activity, respectively, controlling by the number of maintainers: therefore, they could also provide explanations for the attractivity of a file per se (in terms of contributions).

Generally speaking, and awaiting further confirmation of these results on a larger collection of open-source projects, our investigations suggest that a metrics of code size and complexity such as Halstead volume and file vintage are major determinants of teamwork on files. In this respect, the significance of vintage could be consistent with the idea that core teams play a specially significant role when projects are recent. In this general framework, more modular code – here, more functions in files – is associated with more maintainers, which is consistent with insights from modularity theory and with a more efficient division of labour. Still in this context, more complex files attract a lower number of collaborative maintainers, maybe because they induce a more exclusive selection of who could maintain a given piece of specially complex code. Finally, more "verbose" code – more lines of code for a given complexity – is less attractive for maintainers, perhaps because it could correspond to less attractive features inside projects. These findings appear consistent with suggestions[18,19] according to which maintainers would respond to technical considerations, either based on use value or on challenge and peer regard, in their motivations and in their choices among modules, and therefore in the global allocation of efforts in large open-source software projects.

5 Further Work

This paper documented investigations of detailed development records to study collaborative maintenance in open-source projects. The success that many of these projects have had in recent years and the voluntary nature of their development process make them extremely interesting to study, especially since abundant documentation of the development history of each project is readily available on the Internet. We came to the conclusion that collaborative maintenance in large open-source projects seems to be generally influenced by Halstead volume and also by the vintage of the files in a given project. Further studies are needed to uncover the role played by various factors which would be candidates to increase the explanatory power of the simple econometric models presented in this paper, including notably more technical characteristics of files. Furthermore, the extent to which maintainers actually coordinate their work is not yet clear, nor are the dynamic interplay of the variables we have studied or the fact that such dynamics can give birth to hot spots. It could be interesting too to study more qualitatively subsets of files, and more deeply the interactions between maintainers within files.

Acknowledgments

Our research has been partly supported by *Calibre*, a EU FP6 Coordination Action. The support of the US National Science Foundation (NSF Grant No. IIS-0326529 from the DTS Program) is also gratefully acknowledged by one of us (JMD).

REFERENCES

1. C. U. Ciborra, *Teams, Markets and Systems* (Cambridge University Press, 1993).
2. J. Olson and K. M. Branch, in: Communication, Management Benchmark Study, edited by E. L. Malone (Office of Science, Department of Energy, Washington D.C., 2002) pp. 133–142.
3. W. van der Aalst, B. van Dongen, J. Herbst, L. Maruster, G. Schimm, and A. Weijters, Workflow Mining: A Survey of Issues and Approaches, *Data & Knowledge Engineering*, 47, 237–267 (2003).
4. S. Koch and G. Schneider, Effort, Cooperation and Coordination in an Open Source Software Project: Gnome, *Information Systems Journal*, 12(1), 27–42, (2002).
5. J. Y. Moon and L. Sproull, Essence of Distributed Work: The Case of the Linux Kernel, *First Monday*, 5, (2000).
6. V. Valloppillil, Open source software: A (new?) development methodology. Microsoft memo, 1998 (unpublished).
7. J. Matusow, S. McGibbon, and D. Rowe, in: Proceedings of the 1st International Conference on Open Source Systems, edited by M. Scotto and G. Succi, (Genoa, 2005), pp. 263–266.
8. G. D. Prato and D. Gagliardi, in: Proceedings of the 1st International Conference on Open Source Systems, edited by M. Scotto and G. Succi, (Genoa, 2005), pp. 237–240.
9. E. S. Raymond, The Cathedral and the Bazaar, *First Monday*, 3 (1998).
10. S. Krishnamurthy, Cave or Community? An Empirical Investigation of 100 Mature Open Source Projects, *First Monday*, 6 (2002).
11. K. Crowston and J. Howison, The Social Structure of Free and Open Source Software Development, *First Monday*, 10 (2005).
12. W. Scacchi, Understanding the Requirements for Developing Open Source Software Systems, *IEE Proceedings – Software*, 149, 24–39 (2002).

13. A. Mockus, R. T. Fielding, and J. D. Herbsleb, Two Case Studies of Open Source Software Development: Apache and Mozilla, *ACM Transactions on Software Engineering and Methodology*, **11**, 309–346 (2002).

14. M. Hahsler and S. Koch, Discussion of a Large-Scale Open Source Data Collection Methodology, *Proc. HICSS* **38**, (2005).

15. G. Robles, S. Koch, and J. M. González Barahona, Remote Analysis and Measurement of Libre Software Systems by Means of the CVSAnalY Tool, *Proc. ICSE* **2**, (2004).

16. J. Howison, M. Conklin, and K. Crowston, in: Proceedings of the 1st International Conference on Open Source Systems, edited by M. Scotto and G. Succi, (Genoa, 2005), pp. 54–60.

17. A. Capiluppi, A. E. Faria, and J. F. Ramil, Exploring the Relationship between Cumulative Change and Complexity in an Open Source System, *Proceedings of the Ninth European Conference on Software Maintenance and Reengineering* (2005).

18. J.-M. Dalle and P. David, Simulating Code Growth in Libre (Open-Source) Mode, in: *The Economics of the Internet*, edited by N. Curien and E. Brousseau, (Cambridge University Press, 2005).

19. J.-M. Dalle and P. David, The Allocation of Software Development Resources in 'Open Source' Production Mode, Discussion Paper 02-27, 2003 (Stanford Institute for Economic Policy Research).

20. M. den Besten and J.-M. Dalle, Assessing the Impact of Product Complexity on Organizational Design in Open Source Software: Findings & Future Work, *Proceedings of the ECCS 2005 Satellite Workshop: Embracing Complexity in Design* (2005).

ANNEX

Table 1: Descriptive elements of the sample in the database. Other statistics available upon request.

	First month of act.	Files (#)	"c" files (#)	maint's (total #)	maint's (av)	max maint's (av)	revisio ns (av)	max revisio ns (av)	McCa be (av)	Halstead (av)	SLOCs (av)
apache	07/96	4133	657	79	7.67	2.60	32.38	5.96	18.24	14483.73	523.85
cvs	12/94	1062	287	30	3.67	1.41	23.74	3.01	19.25	16643.53	1456.00
gaim	03/00	5158	681	39	3.62	1.74	26.91	4.62	17.10	25181.14	3581.71
gcc	08/97	34757	16405	250	2.56	1.19	6.30	1.46	17.62	4526.51	3546.63
gostscript	03/00	2819	932	23	3.68	1.76	9.08	1.76	25.04	21445.66	3197.25
mozilla	03/98	40545	8370	595	7.77	1.90	21.11	3.31	15.39	18064.63	1606.94
NetBSD	03/93	19514	7081	267	6.48	1.66	18.00	2.94	10.03	15846.91	7805.33
openssh	09/99	289	138	50	5.32	2.21	35.56	4.93	19.67	13779.09	9230.17
postgresql	07/96	4102	904	25	4.53	1.92	42.00	4.38	18.75	17190.52	1246.06
python	08/90	4643	419	88	5.94	1.94	31.59	4.78	21.53	33965.03	14453.06

Table 2: Econometric estimations (OLS) for *Apache*. Dependent variables: average number of maintainers per month, maximum number of maintainers per month, average number of revisions per month, and maximum number of revisions per month (parameter estimate, above, and standard error, below). Stars signal confidence levels − 95% = *, 99% = **, and 99.9% = ***.

	maint's	maint's	Max maint's	Max maint's	revisions	revisions	Max revisions	Max revisions
Intercept	0.14039***	0.12214***	3.21049***	2.93030***	0.60443***	0.39800***	6.56893***	4.98504***
	0.02860	0.02683	0.11575	0.09999	0.12597	0.11208	0.58216	0.48336
SLOCs	1.165E-5	4.30E-6	4.090E-5**	-1.189E-4**	1.3514E-4	1.579E-5***	7.047E-4***	-2.0944E-4
	1.227E-5	1.212E-5	5.047E-5	4.553E-5	5.404E-5	5.064E-5	2.5383E-4	2.2009E-4
Mc Cabe	6.8159E-4	------	7.39E-3***	------	8 89E-3**	------	4.469E-2***	------
	6.4246E-4	------	2.56E-3	------	2.83E-3	------	1.288E-2	------
Halstead	------	2.12E-6***	------	3.280E-5***	------	2.786E-***	------	1.855E-4***
	------	7.54826E-7	------	2.83E-6	------	1.5E-6	------	1.370E-5
Relative creation date	9.11E-3***	8.95E-3***	-3.433E-2***	-3.057E-2***	1.824E-2***	1.948E-2***	-7.575E-2***	-5.449E-2***
	1.05E-3	9.9214E-4	4.10E-3	3.58E-3	4.61E-3	4.15E-3	2.060E-2	1.733E-2

Table 3: Summary of econometric tests (OLS) for all 10 projects with variable Halstead. Full results, including results with variable McCabe, available upon request. Stars signal confidence levels – 95% = *, 99% = **, and 99.9% = ***; (-) signals a negative coefficient.

Project	Apache				CVS				Gaim			
	maint's	max maint's	revisions	max revisions	maint's	max maint's	revisions	max revisions	maint's	max maint's	revisions	max revisions
Intercept	***	***	***	***	***	***	***	***	***		***	***
SLOCs			***								***	**
Halstead	***	***	***	***		***	***	***	***	***	***	
Relative creation date	***	(-)***	***	(-)***	***	(-)***	***	(-)***	***			
Adjusted R2	0.1456	0.3272	0.1792	0.3210	0.1668	0.2392	0.2233	0.3601	0.2116	0.0256	0.5750	0.0615

Project	GCC				Ghostcript				Mozilla			
	maint's	max maint's	revisions	max revisions	maint's	max maint's	revisions	max revisions	maint's	max maint's	revisions	max revisions
Intercept	***	***	***	***	***	***	***	***	***	***	***	***
SLOCs	(-)***	***	(-)***	***	(-)**	***	***	***	(-)*	***		**
Halstead	***	***	***	***		***	***	***	***	***	***	***
Relative creation date	***	(-)***	***	(-)***	***	(-)***	***	(-)***	***	(-)***		(-)***
Adjusted R2	0.2259	0.3091	0.2731	0.3334	0.0360	0.4648	0.2028	0.4648	0.0313	0.2623	0.1341	0.2862

Project	NetBSD				OpenSSH				PostgreSQL			
	maint's	max maint's	revisions	max revisions	maint's	max maint's	revisions	max revisions	maint's	max maint's	revisions	max revisions
Intercept	***	***	***	***	***	***	***	***	**	***	***	***
SLOCs		***	***	***	***	***		***		**		
Halstead	***	***	***	***		***	***	***		***	***	***
Relative creation date	***	(-)***	***	(-)***		(-)***	(-)***	(-)***	***	(-)***	***	(-)***
Adjusted R2	0.0780	0.2765	0.1001	0.2496	0.1657	0.5289	0.3576	0.4869	0.1413	0.2593	0.1814	0.3229

Project	Python			
	maint's	max maint's	revisions	max revisions
Intercept		***		***
SLOCs	(-)**	(-)***	(-)**	(-)***
Halstead		***	***	***
Relative creation date	***	(-)***	***	
Adjusted R2	0.0946	0.2830	0.0553	0.1137

Table 4: Further econometric estimations (OLS) for *Apache*. Dependent variables: maximum number of maintainers per month and maximum number of revisions per month (parameter estimate, above, and standard error, below). Stars signal confidence levels – 95% = *, 99% = **, and 99.9% = ***.

	Max maint's	Max maint's	Max maint's	Max revisions	Max revisions	Max revisions
Intercept	3.21049***	2.93030***	3.07637***	6.56893***	4.98504***	-2.61835***
	0.11575	0.09999	0.10384	0.58216	0.48336	0.75211
SLOCs	4.090E-5**	-1.1890E-4**	-5.1764E-4***	7.047E-4***	-2.0944E-4	1.00E-3
	5.047E-5	4.553E-5	1.2736E-4	2.5383E-4	2.2009E-4	5.4907E-4
Mc Cabe	7.39E-3***	------	-9.55E-3**	4.469E-2***	------	-3.457E-2**
	2.56E-3	------	2.97E-3	1.288E-2	------	1.272E-2
Halstead	------	3.280E-5***	4.708E-5***	------	1.855E-4***	1.0795E-4***
	------	2.83E-6	3.96E-6	------	1.370E-5	1.918E-5
Functions	------	------	8.26E-3***	------	------	-1.657E-2
	------	------	2.41E-3	------	------	1.032E-2
Max maint's	------	------	------	------	------	2.64696***
	------	------	------	------	------	0.19833
Relative creation date	-3.433E-2***	-3.057E-2***	-3.053E-2***	-7.575E-2***	-5.449E-2***	-2.358E-2
	4.10E-3	3.58E-3	3.61E-3	2.060E-2	1.733E-2	1.643E-2
Adjusted R2	0.1580	0.3272	0.3669	0.0909	0.3210	0.5243

Case Studies and Experiments

Part VI

Case Studies and Experiments

Comparing macro development for personal productivity tools: an experience in validating accessibility of Talking Books

Gabriella Dodero[1], Katia Lupi[1], and Erika Piffero[1]

1 DISI, Università di Genova, Via Dodecaneso 35, 16146 Genova, Italy
dodero@disi.unige.it, {katia.lupi, erika.piffero}@gmail.com
WWW home page: http://sealab.disi.unige.it/Krakatoa/DisiAbles

Abstract. We describe an experience in developing macros for both Power Point and Impress, to be used in accessibility validation for educational multimedia (Talking Books) designed for visually impaired people. Minor disadvantages in the use of Impress are outlined, which however do not constitute a serious obstacle to adoption of Open Source tools for our purposes.

1 Introduction

There is a number of experiences and studies on how personal productivity tools are being used, and the issues in migrating from one proprietary environment, like MS Office, to an open source one, like OpenOffice.org, have extensively been dealt with (see for example [1]). However the issue of macro development in either environments has not yet received comparable attention, and most of available studies about macros are related to their use in spreadsheets or word processors [2].

This paper describes an experience in validating accessibility of Talking Books, i.e. multimedia training materials, developed with the two most popular personal productivity tools (Impress and PowerPoint) and validated by means of macros. It is the natural follow-up of a previous experience [3, 4], where we described how Cultural Heritage professionals without technical expertise may produce a Talking Book, a computer based teaching aid both for normal and for visually impaired people. The first Talking Book was developed with PowerPoint, following the detailed instructions in the manual [5].

The guidelines to be followed in order to make an accessible Talking Book are partly suggested in such a manual, partly derived from Italian legislation about accessibility [6, 7], as well as from the expertise of therapists employing computer based aids for visually impaired people. Once the content of the Talking Book has been developed, a tedious manual task is started, by enforcing compliance to the accessibility rules, in order to make it truly accessible. Automation of compliance checks to accessibility rules avoids such a task, and it is made possible by a suitable set of macros.

Two implementations of such a validation procedure have been undertaken [8, 9], by developing macros for both PowerPoint and Impress (respectively using Visual

Please use the following format when citing this chapter:

Dodero, G., Lupi, K., Piffero, E., 2006, in IFIP International Federation for Information Processing, Volume 203, Open Source Systems, eds. Damiani, E., Fitzgerald, B., Scacchi, W., Scotto, M., Succi, G., (Boston: Springer), pp. 247-252

Basic for Applications and Basic). Such macros have been used both to test the existing Talking Book for accessibility, and for developing new ones.

This paper describes our experiences and compares the two implementations.

2 Development of a Talking Book

Talking Books are usually created by people with minimal computer literacy, having expertise or interest in cultural or entertainment activities of visually impaired people. So, creators of Talking Books may be schoolteachers, parents of disabled children, CH university students or museum personnel, all of them not being professional software developers.

Talking Books creators are interested in making certain contents accessible, and the availability of open source applications saves them licence costs, both for creation and for redistribution of the Talking Book to other visually impaired people (of course costs due to reproduction of copyrighted contents, if any, cannot be avoided). To this aim, a new manual was prepared [10], which details the various operations to be done, illustrating how to use OpenOffice.org Impress to create a Talking Book, on a PC equipped with Windows XP.

Then, we developed macros, that should be applied by the Talking Book creator when he/she decides to validate his product for accessibility, either during the development, slide by slide, or when the Talking Book is completed. Compliance with accessibility guidelines requires the following checks:

- Font size greater or equal to 20;
- Font must be one out of : Arial, Tahoma, Verdana, Times New Roman;
- Italic modifier not allowed;
- Double spacing between words;
- Check of brightness for text and background with the following formula (Red, Green and Blue are the RGB components of text or background colors): $((Red * 299) + (Green * 587) * (Blue * 114)) / 1000 >= 125$
- Check of contrast between text and background colors with the following formula (considering Color1 the text color and Color2 the background color):
  $[Max (Red1, Red2) - Min (Red1, Red2)] +$
  $[Max (Green1, Green2) - Min (Green1, Green2)] +$
  $[Max (Blue1, Blue2) - Min (Blue1, Blue2)] >= 500.$

When the check is performed, the macro user (Talking Book creator) is prompted with a list of possible incompatibilities. Then he/she may decide whether to manually correct them, or let the macro automatically perform the suggested modifications.

In this way such a macro may be used as a pure validator, or even, it may be used to automatically transform a non accessible file into an accessible one. In fact, as a useful side result, these macros may be applied to presentations for lectures or conferences (PowerPoint or Impress files without audio components), so that visually impaired people in the audience are not discriminated.

3   Validation macros

Macro development within Microsoft PowerPoint and OpenOffice.org Impress can be done by means of two very similar object oriented programming languages, respectively Visual Basic for Applications and Basic. Our macros must access objects, and possibly change their properties in order to implement the above described checks. The two tools use different objects and properties in order to define a presentation, and the example provided in the Appendix (the function removing the Italic modifier) gives a flavour of such differences, most of which are just syntactical ones. The only significant difference in internal object structure and properties is described hereafter.

A Power Point presentation consists on a set of slides, each one containing various shapes. Inside shapes we may find text frames, that is where macros must operate. Shapes describe an area inside the slide, having properties like HasTextFrame (true if there is text inside).

An Impress presentation is composed by a set of draw pages, each one made by a set of typed elements called shapes. Text is contained only inside shapes having certain types, so if we wish to identify where text can be found, we have to check if the current shape has one of the following types: TitleTextShape, SubTitleShape, TextShape, OutlinerShape.

For both tools, it is possible to customize the toolbar by adding a new button in order to activate the accessibility validation macro on a new presentation.

On the other hand, we found a minor but sometimes annoying difference in macros behaviour. OOo does not apply macros to currently selected text elements, while Power Point makes no difference in treatment between selected and non selected texts.

During macro development, we carefully searched websites devoted to macro developers, like for example www.bettersolutions.com, www.ooomacros.org and others. We realized that the Web provides many more details, useful examples, and explanations on how to manipulate Power Point objects with respect to what is available about Impress objects.

Specifically, we were unable to find the object names and properties of background colors, so the check on contrast between background and text colors has not yet been implemented in the Impress macro. The documentation describing such objects and their properties for OOo appears more difficult to be searched than it is for Power Point, and the effort required to find out the names and properties we need, by actually inspecting the source code, is possible in principles, but appears too big. However the frequent updates to OOo related sites make us confident that information about background color properties will soon be available as well.

This would complete our experience, so that our macros will finally be made available to the public.

4. Conclusions

We have described our experience in developing macros for both Power Point and Impress, to be used in accessibility validation for educational multimedia (Talking Books) designed for visually impaired people. We experienced minor disadvantages in the use of Impress macros, which however do not constitute a serious obstacle to adoption of Open Source tools for our purposes.

Use of macros for improving accessibility inside personal productivity applications is a technique which has proven successful for Microsoft Word (see for example [11, 12]), yet it has not received so far a widespread diffusion as one might expect. Furthermore, the application of macros inside validation tools for Talking Books, as those we have developed, is the only one we are aware of.

It should be remarked that there are two types of stakeholders for accessibility validating tools: creators of Talking Books (or just creators of PowerPoint and Impress presentations), and visually impaired people, who in the end shall be the users of such products (or the audience of such a presentation). The first experiences collected with the creators (a group of Cultural Heritage university students, developing Talking Books to illustrate the contents of various Museum rooms to visually impaired visitors) showed the ease of use of the validation tools, especially appreciating the possibility of automatic corrections. Almost no one in the creators group was aware of the existence of the OOo toolset, while most of them had some familiarity with the MS Office suite. They all worked with Impress without difficulties, following the detailed instructions in [10].

The resulting Talking Books are being experienced with a real audience including both normal and visually impaired people, inside the Museum. Meantime, conference presentations with accessible slides have already been given (at a national Computers and Disabilities conference, HandyTED 2005) with both normal and visually impaired attendees.

5 Acknowledgements

The authors are grateful to Silvia Dini from Istituto Chiossone, who gave precious suggestions about accessibility guidelines for visually impaired people, and to the CH students from the Museology Course of Dr.A.Traverso, who developed the Talking Books.

6 References

[1] COSPA Consortium for Open Source in the Public Administration. Website: www.cospa-project.org

[2] I.C. Laurenson, Introduction to OOo macro development, OOCON 2005, Koper, September 2005. Website: http://marketing.openoffice.org/ooocon2005/.

[3] P. Signorini, Multimedia products for visually impaired people in archaeological museums, Graduation Thesis (in Italian), University of Genova, Laurea in Conservazione dei Beni Culturali, July 2005.

[4] G.Dodero, P.Garibaldi, P.Signorini, and A.Traverso, Visually impaired people and archaeology: a Talking book to know the "Principe delle Arene Candide", Proc. HandyTED 2005 (in Italian), ITD-CNR, Genova, November 2005. Website: www.itd.cnr.it/handyted2005.

[5] R. Walter, How to create talking books in Power Point 97 and 2000, ACE Centre 2002. Website www.auxilia.it.

[6] Dispositions to ease access of disabled individuals to computer based systems, Italian Law no. 4/2004, appeared on GU n. 13 on 17 Jan 2004. Website: http://www.innovazione.gov.it/ita/news/2003/cartellastampa/doc_leggestanca.shtml.

[7] Requirements for compliance with Law 4/2004, Act of the Italian Ministry of the Innovation and Technologies, appeared on GU n.183 on 8 July 2005.

[8] K.Lupi, Talking Books for Visually Impaired People: user interfacing features, Final Report (in Italian), University of Genova, Laurea in Informatica, Oct. 2005.

[9] E.Piffero, Access to heritage related information for visually impaired users, Final Report (in Italian) University of Genova, Laurea in Informatica, Oct. 2005.

[10] L.De Lucia, How to create a Talking Book with OpenOffice.org 2.0, Final Report (in Italian), University of Genova, Laurea in Informatica, 2006.

[11] A.Cantor, Enhancing the accessibility and usability of Microsoft Office applications using Visual Basic, Technology and Persons with Disabilities Conference, California State University at Northridge, 2004. Website: http://www.csun.edu/cod/conf/2004/proceedings/csun04.htm .

[12] A.Cantor, Macros FAQ, version2.0.(2005). Website: www.cantoraccess.com/macro-docs/macrosfaq.htm

Appendix: Two functions for removing the Italic font modifier

```
Public Function correctItalic()
    For i = 1 To ActivePresentation.Slides.Count
        With ActivePresentation.Slides(i)
            For k = 1 To .Shapes.Count
                If .Shapes(k).HasTextFrame Then
                    With .Shapes(k).TextFrame.TextRange.font
                        If .Italic = msoTriStateMixed Or .Italic = msoCTrue Or .Italic = msoTrue Then
                            .Italic = False
                        End If
                    End With
                End If
            Next k
        End With
    Next i
End Function
```

```
Function correctItalic (slides)
for i = 0 to slides.getCount()-1
    slide = slides.getByIndex(i)
    if slide.hasElements()then
        for k = 0 to slide.getCount()-1
            shape = slide.getByIndex(k)
            tipo = shape.getShapetype()
            if tipo = "com.sun.star.presentation.TitleTextShape" or
            tipo ="com.sun.star.presentation.TextShape" or
            tipo = "com.sun.star.presentation.SubtitleShape" or
            tipo = "com.sun.star.presentation.OutlinerShape" then
                fPosture = shape.getText().CharPosture
                if fPosture = com.sun.star.awt.FontSlant.ITALIC then
                    testo = shape.Text
                    cursor = shape.createTextCursor
                    cursor.CharPosture = com.sun.star.awt.FontSlant.NONE
                    testo.CharPosture = com.sun.star.awt.FontSlant.NONE
                    testo.InsertString(cursor, "", false)
                End If
            End If
        Next k
    End if
Next i
End Function
```

The function in the top box is written for Power Point, the one in the bottom box is written for Impress.

A tool to support the introduction of GNU/Linux desktop system in a professional environment

Francesco Di Cerbo[1], Daniele Favara[1], Marco Scotto[2],

Alberto Sillitti[2], Giancarlo Succi[2], Tullio Vernazza[1]

1 DIST – Università di Genova
Via Opera Pia, 13I-16145 Genova
{Francesco.DiCerbo, Tullio.Vernazza}@unige.it,
Daniele.Favara@gmail.com
WWW home page: http://www.lips.dist.unige.it

2 Libera Università di Bolzano/Bozen
Piazza Domenicani, 3
I-39100 Bolzano-Bozen,
{Marco.Scotto, Alberto.Sillitti, Giancarlo.Succi@unibz.it
WWW home page: http://www.unibz.it

Abstract. The introduction of a GNU/Linux-based desktop system in a large company is often problematic, in terms of technical issues but especially for employees' training costs. Mainly, these obstacles are represented by different hardware configurations that might require several ad-hoc activities to adapt a standard release to the specific environment, including company's application profile. On the other hand, GNU/Linux live distributions provide to the users' community new and interesting capabilities, as self-configuration and better usability, but loosing compatibility with original distributions, that is unaffordable in professionals scenarios. DSS (Debased Scripts Set) is an answer to both questions. It is a live distribution that includes an unmodified Debian-based Linux release and a modular-designed file system.

Keywords: GNU/Linux, live distributions, meta-distribution, early user-space, usability, scalability, large environments application deployment

1 Introduction

When dealing with massive installation of desktop computers in a professional scenario, usually the choice falls on proprietary solutions for both the operating system and deployment tools. This happens thanks to their capability to lower total costs in many aspects, first of all simplifying overall complexity and time required for deployment operations.

Please use the following format when citing this chapter:

Di Cerbo, F., Favara, D., Scotto, M., Sillitti, A., Succi, G., and Vernazza, T., 2006, in
IFIP International Federation for Information Processing, Volume 203, Open Source
Systems, eds. Damiani, E., Fitzgerald, B., Scacchi, W., Scotto, M., Succi, G., (Boston:
Springer), pp. 253-260

254   Francesco Di Cerbo, Daniele Favara, Marco Scotto,
         Alberto Sillitti, Giancarlo Succi, Tullio Vernazza

The introduction of GNU/Linux[1] desktop systems in large companies is often problematic for both startup and successive maintenance operations. These obstacles are often represented by different hardware configurations that may require several ad-hoc activities to adapt a standard release to the a specific environment. On the other hand, GNU/Linux live distributions provides to the users' community new and interesting capabilities, such as self-configuration and better usability, but the trade-off is represented by some relevant differences with the distributions from which they derive. Such differences make them useless in a professional scenario.

DSS (Debased Scripts Set) is an answer to previous issues. It is a live distribution based on an unmodified Debian[2]-based Linux release (Ubuntu[3]), including a pure "stock" kernel, i. e. a standard distribution-provided precompiled Linux kernel[4]. DSS includes innovative hardware detection and configuration techniques, even if based on sound and largely adopted software (such as hotplug daemon), that is loaded since the very first boot operations. Combining these aspects with a modular software package approach, made it possible by using a   specialunification file system (Unionfs [5]), DSS is also able to deploy, in a single package, a customized company-specific release containing both the operating system and all the desired applications. To summarize, DSS is a framework that allows an easy customization of a 100% Debian-based GNU/Linux live-cd distribution. It provides tools to repackage all the modifications into a derived Linux distribution. Morevover, thanks to its smart file system design, completely constituted by modular parts loaded at runtime, it may be easily repackaged again into a live distribution.

State of the art – Knoppix live distribution

Knoppix[6] may be considered the pioneer of GNU/Linux live distributions, both for diffusion, also demonstrated by a large number of works based on it, and historical reasons.
However, its approach to make a Debian GNU/Linux distribution bootable from a CD / DVD / USB pen-drive, makes its use, in a professional setting, practically impossible, except for data recovery or hardware testing. Its severe modifications to the standard Debian distribution, cross-combining unstable and testing versions, makes new application's distribution and upgrade quite difficult, requiring a great effort to bring to stability a new hypothetical desktop installation based on Knoppix.
Moreover, "exotic" hardware suffers about Knoppix deep-kernel specificity, fit to its hardware detection requirements. Uncommon or not completely supported hardware often comes with drivers usually not contained in standard kernels, which may be provided with commercial license, incompatible with GPL (Generale Public License) statements and so undeliverable inside Debian. In this cases, the adoption of Knoppix can be a great deal. Last but not least, hardware detection and configuration

techniques come with special boot applications (knoppix-autoconfig, hwsetup, kudzu), that require a constant maintenance process to be able to recognize new or uncommon hardware. Moreover, their approach, based on kernel-space routines, forces successive setups (e.g. file systems configuration) to be unfit to use user-space libraries and applications, to give a user flexibility in data and device access, especially in case of plug-and-play USB hardware. Such features use ad-hoc scripts running with maximum privileges, which may lead to security problems, particularly critic in an industrial environment.

DSS main features

DSS adopts a completely new approach to live distributions based on a "early user-space"[7] mode. It is a set of libraries and programs (that are available even without a running Linux kernel) which provide various functionalities required while a Linux kernel is coming up .

The "Early user space" mode allows DSS to use hotplug, a daemon program normally used for hardware discovery and configuration in standard non-live GNU/Linux distributions, since the first boot. This is a great advantage, as the booting kernel relies on already detected hardware, and using its 2.6 series features, may automatically load needed kernel modules to use just discovered hardware, quite like in a common installed GNU/Linux system. Due to this feature, DSS does not require developing and maintaining an ad-hoc kernel, but it may use a stock one, exactly like any other Debian release.

"Early user-space" mode is based on initramfs, a chunk of code that unpacks a compressed file system image (in cpio format) midway through the kernel boot process. It replaces the old initrd file system format, which contained a set of kernel modules stated to be available at boot time, before mounting root file system and so before having all kernel resources available. The main advantage of initramfs is its capability to be used with ramfs, a file system designed to work on physical RAM, scalable in size, instead of usual initrd. This allows DSS, in conjunction with unionfs, to save time in the boot phase: instead of setting up a boot environment for hardware detection/configuration operations, DSS directly sets up a final working environment, and when the kernel finishes its startup operations, the boot process is over, with a simple environment update. This because RAM allocated since boot start for required boot operations does not need to be freed/removed, and running klibc environment is not used anymore except for boot process. Eventually, it is possible to allocate all available RAM on system to improve overall performances, reducing physical medium access delays. Moreover, DSS adopts unionfs, a file system designed to merge different devices, allows to group physical devices with ramfs devices to set up final root filesystem.

In this way, except for a small set of scripts which effectively coordinates boot process, no ad-hoc component is used to bring a Debian GNU/Linux release to be live bootable and completely able to fulfill hardware detection/configuration for Linux's supported peripherals.

DSS is also designed to be a meta-distribution framework, allowing creation of derivative distribution, both live or in standard package, built up upon a pure Debian release, in a very simple way. This feature is provided thanks to a special modular file system design, made possible by adoption of Unionfs[8].

DSS root filesystem is split into modules, which are added together via Unionfs.

All modules in DSS are compressed archives, which can be mounted at runtime, as filesystem. These modules contains programs and libraries, which are merged together into a unique filesystem, thanks to Unionfs; additivity in modules management permits to create a final filesystem layout which may be different from distribution to distribution, allowing different installation profiles, e. g. a server one, without graphical server, or a customized GNU/Linux desktop distribution, containing a specific corporative environment ready-to-use.

Moreover, as compressed modules are merged in an ordered way, a single installation may be multi-purpouse, including or excluding any of them from boot loader parameters. This feature is very important to contain different installation profiles in a single location, and it's extremely useful in a network installation, or in a DVD release, for example.

Module creation process is also very simple, and it may be created in two way: non-interactive, which relies on "debconf" program, just producing a list of desired debian packages to include in outcoming module, and a script would download packages and compress them into a cpio archive, or in an interactive way, booting DSS, using "synaptic" program and then executing another script. Resulting archives may be redistributed inside a standard DSS release without any further modifications to original status.

Key technology: UnionFS

Unionfs is a stackable file system that operates on multiple underlying file systems. It merges the updated contents of multiple directories but keeps their original physical content separated. The Dsslive implementation of UnionFS merges the Dsslive RAMdisk with the read-only file systems on the boot CD so it's possible to modify any read-only file as if it was writeable. UnionFS is part of FiST, File System Translator project. Its goal is to address the problem of file system development, a critical area of operating-system engineering. The FiST lab notes that even small changes to existing file systems require deep understanding of kernel internals, making the barrier to entry for new developers high. Moreover, porting file system code from one operating system to another is almost as difficult as the first port.

FiST, developed by Erez Zadok and Jason Nieh in the computer science department at Columbia University, combines two methods to solve the above problems in an innovative way: a set of stackable file system templates for each operating system, and a high-level language that can describe stackable file systems in a cross-platform portable fashion. The key idea is that with FiST, a stackable file system would need to be described only once. Then FiST's code-generation tool would compile one system description into loadable kernel modules for different operating systems (currently Solaris, Linux and FreeBSD are supported).

DSS inside UnionFS

Dsslive within the "pre-USS" script mount different compressed file systems in different mount points and uses a read-writable directory as last layer, with a outcome to have just one final mount point (the root directory). UnionFS allows DSS to virtually merge- (or unify-) different directories (recursively) in a way that they appear to be one tree; this is done without physically merging the directories content. Such namespace unification has a benefit in allowing the files to remain physically separate, even if they appear as belonging in one unique location. The collection of merged directories is called a union, and each physical directory is called a branch. When creating the union, each branch is assigned a precedence and access permissions (i.e., read-only or read-writable). Unionfs is a namespace-unification file system that addresses all of the known complexities of maintaining Unix semantic without compromising versatility and the features it offers. It supports two file deletion modes that manage even partial failures. It allows efficient insertion and deletion of arbitrary read-only or read-writable directories into the union. Unionfs includes in-kernel handling of files with identical names; a careful design that minimizes data movement across branches; several modes for permission inheritance; and support for snapshots and sandboxing.
Unionfs has an n-way fan-out architecture [5,6]. The benefit of this approach is that Unionfs has direct access to all underlying directories or branches, in any order.
Even if the concept of virtual namespace unification appears simple, there are three key problems that arise when using it as root file system of Dsslive.
The first is that two or more unified directories can contain files with the same name. If such directories are unified, duplicate names must not be returned to user-space for obvious reasons. Unionfs solves this point defining a priority ordering of the individual directories being unified. When several files have the same name, files from the directory with higer priority take precedence.

The second problem relates to file deletion. Files with same name could appear in the directories been merged or files to be deleted reside on a read-only branch. Unionfs handles this sitruation inserting a without, a special high-priority entry that marks the file as deleted.

When file system code finds a without for a file, it simply behaves as the file doesn't exists.

The third problem is relegated to the previous one and it involves mixing read-only and read-write directories in the union. When users want to modify a file that resides in a read-only branch, Unionfs performs a "copyup", the file is copied to the higher priority directory and modified there.

Unionfs and The Upstream Salmon Struct (USS)

The power of Dsslive resides on its design, offering high modularity and allowing the customization as easy as possible. This has been achieved by designing the USS and using Unionfs as background.

The unified root file system is made of the content of different modules, each module is a squashfs compressed file system:

1.base: console mode module, it contains a basic bootstrapped debian system;
2.kernel: it contains the /lib/modules/ directory plus kernel related utilities;
3.xserver: graphical mode modules, (in case of file names clash, the priority in the unified directory is defined by sorting the modules name);
4.deliver: it contains the runlevel scripts needed to reconfigure "debconf" database and the environment reading the user configuration from /proc/cmdline passed to kernel at boot from boot loader (e.g.: locales information, force screen resolution);
5.overall: the read-writable branch, it can reside in ram or even be an external hd;

Base, kernel and xserver use is self-explaining enough, but the packages inside those modules are stored using a "noninteractive" debconf frontend, and so they maintain their own default configurations, that's why Dsslive can be considered a pure debian system booting from a cdrom. Anyway to allow the user to use his own locales settings (i. e. language, keyboard) and video card optimized drivers, some packages need to be reconfigured: and this is made using the runlevel scripts in deliver.

Deliver

The scripts in "yuch-bottom", the directory within the initramfs, write the environment variables in the file /etc/deliver.conf, parsing command line parameters from boot loader, as lang(uage), username, hostname etc. Deliver uses those variables to reconfigure some packages, upgrading at the same time the debconf database.

The scripts in deliver are plain text bash scripts, this allows DSS use not only for a i386 livecd distribution, but even for powerpc or sparc computers, and all the other 11 architectures that debian supports, making DSS fully architecture-independent.
Thanks to its scripts, DSS, to be ported from an architecture to another, just needs a right initramfs and the deliver module, without caring about kernel customization, as it is sufficient a pure debian stock kernel.
Dsslive, differently from knoppix, uses debconf to configure the system, which provides a consistent interface for configuring packages, allowing to choose from several user interface frontends. It supports even a special "pre-configuration" of software packages before they are actually installed, which allows massive installation or upgrade sessions demanding all necessary configuration informations up front, without user interactions (frontend "noninteractive"). It allows to skip over less important questions and informations while installing a package, giving anyway a chance to revise them later.
It is also interesting to remark that debconf itself is completely a Debian supported tool, and its use is not customized at all: another key point into 100% Debian compatibility.

Conclusion

DSS is a 100% Debian live distribution, and may be proficiently used to install a pure Debian system on a desktop pc. Thanks to its features, it's very simple to customize starting base version, in a way to meet, for example, large-scale installations with specific requirements, such as in large companies networks. Its maintenance is not effort-prone, due to adoption of standardized technologies, but their use in a live environment, thanks to DSS innovative design, represents a unicum in current scenario. Moreover, there are no limitations to port DSS into any of Debian supported architectures, of to use it in embedded systems.

References

[1], Stallman, R. et al., Free Software, Free Society: Selected Essays of Richard M. Stallman, , www.gnu.org
[2], Ian Murdock, "Overview of the Debian GNU/Linux System", Linux Journal, Volume 1994 Issue 6es
[3], Ubuntu group, Ubuntu philosophy, , http://www.ubuntu.com/ubuntu/philosophy
[4], D. Rusling, The Linux Kernel, , http://www.tldp.org/LDP/tlk/tlk.html
[5], E. Zadok and J. Nieh, FiST: A Language for Stackable File Systems, 2000
[6], Knopper, K. "Building a self-contained auto-configuring Linux system on an iso9660 filesystem", Usenix 2000 Conference

[7] Petullo, M., "Encrypt your root filesystem", Linux Journal,Volume 2005 , Issue
129 (January 2005) Page: 4, 2005,ISSN:1075-3583
[8], CP Wright, J Dave, P Gupta, H Krishnan, E Zadok, Versatility and Unix
Semantics   in   a   Fan-Out   Unification   File   System,   ,
http://www.fsl.cs.sunysb.edu/docs/unionfs-tr/

A Framework for Teaching Software Testing using F/OSS Methodology

Sulayman K Sowe[1], Ioannis Stamelos[1] and Ignatios Deligiannis[2]

[1] Department of Informatics, Aristotle University of Thessaloniki,
54124 Thessaloniki, Greece. Tel: +30-2310-991927 Fax: +30-2310-998419
sksowe@csd.auth.gr, stamelos@csd.auth.gr
[2] Information Technology Department, Technological Education Institute,
54700 Thessaloniki, Greece. igndel@it.teithe.gr

Abstract. In this paper we discuss a framework for teaching software testing to undergraduate students' volunteers. The framework uses open source software development methodology and was implemented in the "Introduction to Software Engineering" course at the department of Informatics, Aristotle University, Greece. The framework is in three phases, each describing a teaching and learning context in which students get involved in real software projects activities. We report on our teaching experiences, lessons learned and some practical problems we encountered. Results from preliminary evaluation shows that students did well as *bug hunters* in the bazaar and are willing to participate in their projects long after graduation.

1 Introduction

Software engineering (SE) educators are always in search of relevant materials and novel pedagogies that will provide life-long learning experiences and improve the quality of students learning outcomes. However, the teaching and learning situation in SE courses in most universities is acute. Students do not get the chance to participate in long-term projects where they can be exposed to the SE principles and techniques we teach them. In most cases students have to complete their assigned projects in one semester, making it difficult for them to be involved in large and long-term projects. The reality is that SE education does not always expose students to "real-world" projects [3]. Involving students in software projects in local companies is one way of exposing them to real software projects. However, [7] concluded that most companies are not willing to sacrifice their software to students. By utilizing Free and Open Source Software (F/OSS) projects freely available in the Internet, computer science (CS) lecturers may overcome this obstacle. F/OSS projects are *'bazaars of learning'*-they offer a meaningful learning context in which students can be exposed to real-world software development. In this paper we present a framework which provides such a context. The framework was implemented as a pilot program to teach *software testing* in the Introduction to Software Engineering (ISE) course. Fifteen undergraduate students took part in the program. Our evaluation of the

Please use the following format when citing this chapter:

Sowe, S.K., Stamelos, I., and Deligiannis, I., 2006, in IFIP International Federation for Information Processing, Volume 203, Open Source Systems, eds. Damiani, E., Fitzgerald, B., Scacchi, W., Scotto, M., Succi, G., (Boston: Springer), pp. 261-266

framework shows that students did well in software testing in F/OSS projects. Our contribution may also strengthen some areas of the IEEE/ACM CS curriculum guidelines [4], which recommends that a CS curriculum should incorporate *Capstone projects*. Like F/OSS projects, capstone projects are managed by the students and solve a problem of the student's choice.

F/OSS in Software Engineering Education: The Bazaar model [5] of developing F/OSS represents a decentralized software development where volunteers develop software online, relying on extensive peer collaboration through the Internet. In F/OSS projects, the developer-user alliance exposes the source code to a large number of testers and ensures rapid evolution of the code. According to Linus Law ("*Given enough eyeballs all bugs are shallow*"), many people (testers, debuggers, co-developers) looking at the source code will ensure that bugs/defects will be found and fixed quickly. Many studies (e.g. [1, 2, 3, 6]) see F/OSS as a pedagogical tool and a viable methodology which gives students practice in dealing with large quantities of code written by other people. Important as these studies are, a framework for teaching SE courses in general and software testing in particular in the informal context of F/OSS is lacking in the literature. The overlook might be that the F/OSS paradigm has some peculiar characteristics which make teaching in this context harder to integrate into the formal SE curricular structure of most universities.

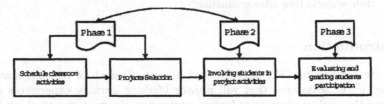

Fig. 1. F/OSS Teaching and Learning Framework.

2 F/OSS Framework for Teaching Software Testing

The Introduction to Software Engineering (ISE) course, in which the framework was implemented, is offered as a 12 weeks course during the 5th semester. The F/OSS framework for teaching software testing is shown in Figure 1.

2.1 *Phase 1*

At the beginning of the semester we discussed with the 150 students enrolled in the course about involving them in software testing in F/OSS projects. Fifteen students volunteered to take part. For the first two weeks the students received 8hrs of lectures on the following topics:

- *F/OSS project* (Activities and Testing in F/OSS).
- *F/OSS communities* (Formation and Roles).
- *Communication* (Etiquettes of forums/mailing lists).
- *Collaborative platforms* (CVS, Bugzilla, Bug Tracking Systems (BTS), etc).

At the end of the session students were guided to browse projects hosted at *sourceforge.net*. In choosing a project, students were asked to pay particular attention to the following *F/OSS projects selection criteria*:

- operating system (Linux, Windows) and programming language used,
- number of developers and how active the forums are,
- development status (Alpha, Beta, Mature).

Having identified their projects, each student was asked to make a class presentation, detailing the history of the project, bug reporting procedures, and testing tools used.

2.2 *Phase 2*

In week 3 students learnt how to register in their projects, use bug tracking systems, and browse and report bugs. They practiced writing fictitious bug reports for their colleagues to criticize. In their projects, students implemented the testing strategy shown in Figure 2.

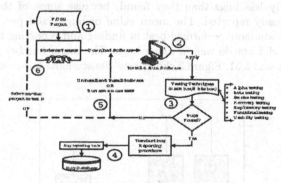

Fig. 2. F/OSS Testing Strategy.

They download and installed the software (1 - 2) and applied various software testing techniques (3). This may result in the discovery of bugs, which are then logged into the project's bug database using standard bug reporting procedure and tools (4). Where a student is not able to find a bug, he/she may run more tests (5) or selected another project to continue testing (6). Every time a student submitted a bug, he/she notifies the lecturer. Students were asked to continuously login to check the status of their submission and engage community members. During the fifth week students who already made progress in their projects by finding and submitting 2-3 bugs were asked to make a class presentation to discuss their experiences (e.g. types of bugs found, how they were found, what they think caused the problem, how they reported them, and what responses, if any, were received).

2.3 *Phase 3*

Based on their presentations and testing activities, the students were graded as follows: Class presentation (10%), Project participation (12%), Concise bug reports (13%), and Testing activity (15%).

3 Results and Discussions

In validating the framework we discuss students' participation in their respective projects and the results of a survey we conducted.

3.1 Students Testing Activates

At the end of *Phase 2*, two students withdrew from the program. The remaining 13 tested in 16 projects[1], found 72 bugs, reported 68, fixed 15, and received 43 replies from the F/OSS community. The mean numbers of bugs found and reported per student were 5.54 and 5.23, respectively. This means that students reported slightly less bugs than they found, because some of the bugs they found were already reported. The mean value of bugs fixed per student was 1.15. Thus, the students performed best in finding and reporting bugs in their projects. They did not do well in fixing bugs. The mean number of responses to a bug report was 3.31. Figure 3 shows how the students fair in each activity.

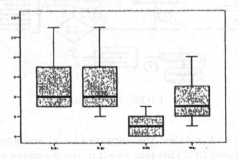

Fig. 3. Distribution of students' testing activities. (*bfn*)=bugs found. (*brp*)=bugs reported. (*bfx*)=bugs fixed. (*rep*)=replies to a submitted bug.

---

[1] Games (8), Mozilla Suite (4), Multimedia (2), Mobiles and Networks (1), Astronomy (1)

3.2 Survey results

In week 6 the students were invited to complete an online questionnaire containing 21 items. The aim of the survey was to validate the framework from students' point of view. Ten students completed the survey. We group the responses into five categories.

1. Students Motivation. According to the survey students enjoyed software testing in F/OSS projects (100%) and would continue testing in their projects after graduating (90%). Furthermore, most students would prefer to have their other CS courses taught using F/OSS methodology (90%).

2. The Teaching Context. 80% of the students reported getting help from the lecturer when selecting their projects, making it easy for 60% of them to find a project to participate in. While students collaborated and discussed their projects amongst themselves (90%), 80% preferred discussing their projects and bug reports (50%) with the lecturer.

3. Using F/OSS Testing Tools. 80% of students prefer the BTS to report bugs because it is easy to use.

4. Testing Activity. On average, students used the software for at least 1-2 days (50%) before they could find any bugs. Since students found the BTS easy to use, the process of reporting bugs was also easy (90%). While it was easy for most students to describe the bugs they found (70%), 20% found this exercise difficult. When asked if finding bugs in their projects was easy, students responses were evenly split (50% - 50%). Students were able to read and understand bugs others reported (80%), but only a few (30%) are able to fix any bugs reported in their projects. Even a smaller percentage (20%) were able to fix their own bugs. So our students could best be described as *bug hunters* than bug fixers. In this role students are able to contribute to their projects 'eyeballs' just looking for and contributing bugs.

5. F/OSS Community Response. At the beginning many students were hesitant that they were not getting prompt feedback, but 70% of them later reported that their projects' communities are very responsive. 60% reported that their projects (or rather the portals which host the project) provided useful information to help them in their bug reporting activity.

4 Conclusion

In this paper we have proposed a framework for teaching software testing using F/OSS methodology. The implementation of the framework in a formal CS course with a sample of fifteen undergraduate volunteers was discussed. Our experience shows that SE education could benefit from such a teaching and learning approach by exposing students to "real-world" software engineering projects. The projects in which the students tested were very responsive and appreciative. While we have already graded and published the students results, we still continue to get emails from them about responses they received from their projects. We enthusiastically continue to respond accordingly. Our presentation resolves two key issues about F/OSS in SE education. Firstly, project-based CS courses need not depend on closed-source projects outside the university in order to give students experience in real-world projects. Second, it is possible for CS lecturers to integrate the informal F/OSS teaching and learning context into their formal curricular structure to teach CS courses (e.g. software testing). It was satisfying to note that most students will continue participating in F/OSS projects after the end of our pilot program. However, we were faced with the hard reality that students must complete their testing activity at the end of the semester.

Validity threats and future work: Our data set consists of a small random sample of student volunteers, about 10% of the students in the ISE course. Thus, there is danger in generalizing the results to other CS courses, classes, and possibly to other universities, where sample size, skills, and backgrounds of the students are probably different. However, because there are few published results in this area, we hope that our findings will act as a base for further research in this area. We plan to repeat the program with a larger sample next semester. Furthermore, we are currently conducting two online surveys (post-students survey and staff survey) to help us further validate the framework.

References

1. D. Carrington, and S. Kim, Teaching Software Engineering Design with Open Source Software.*33rd ASEE/IEEE Frontiers in Education Conference,*(May 16, 2005); http://www.cs.wm.edu/~coppit/csci690-spring2004/papers/1273.pdf
2. M. D. German, Experience teaching a graduate course in Open Source Software Engineering. In *Proceedings of the first International Conference on Open Source Systems*. Genova, 326-328 (2005)
3. C. Liu, Enriching software engineering courses with service-learning projects and the open-source approach. In *Proceedings of the 27th international Conference on Software Engineering*, ICSE '05. ACM Press, 613-614 (2005).
4. Software Engineering 2004 Curriculum Guidelines for Undergraduate Degree Programs in Software Engineering, *IEEE/ACM Joint Task Force on Computing Curricula*, (2004), (December 10, 2005); http://sites.computer.org/ccse/SE2004Volume.pdf
5. S. E. Raymond, *The Cathedral and the Bazaar*. O'Reilly, Sebastopol,(1999).
6. S. K. Sowe, A. Karoulis, and I. Stamelos, A Constructivist View of Knowledge management in Open Source Virtual Communities. In A. D. Figueiredo, A. P. Afonso (Eds), *Managing Learning in Virtual Settings: The Role of Context*. Idea Group Inc., 285-303 (2005).
7. Z. Alzamil, Towards an effective software engineering course project. In *Proceedings of the 27th international Conference on Software Engineering, ICSE '05*. ACM Press, 631-632 (2005).

Organization of Internet Standards

Mehmet Gençer[1], Beyza Oba[2], Bülent Özel[1], and V. Sinan Tunalıoğlu[1]

[1] İstanbul Bilgi University, Department of Computer Science
Kurtuluş Deresi Cad. No:47 34440 Dolapdere, İstanbul, Turkey
{mgencer,bulento,vst}@cs.bilgi.edu.tr
WWW home page http://cs.bilgi.edu.tr/~mgencer
[2] İstanbul Bilgi University, Institute of Social Sciences
İnönü Cad. No:28 34387 Şişli, İstanbul, Turkey boba@bilgi.edu.tr

Abstract. In this study we look at a body of standards documents in RFCs(Request For Comments) of IETF(Internet Engineering Task Force). The cross references between these documents form a network. Approaches from social network analysis are deployed to assess centrality of artifacts in this network and identify cohesive subgroups and levels of cohesion. Our results demonstrate major groups centered around key standard tracks, and application of network metrics reflect different levels of cohesion for these groups. As application of these techniques in such domains is unusual, possible uses in open source projects for strategizing are discussed.

1 Introduction

Open Source Software(OSS) has a good reputation for its compliance with standards. Capability of open source processes for handling such externalities is a major reason of interest on and adoption of this social network analysis methodology[15]. Most such externalities are formalized elsewhere by authoritative bodies of standardization, with close cooperation with the open source software development community.

In this study we analyze several aspects of the body of standards documents in RFCs(Request For Comments) of IETF(Internet Engineering Task Force). IETF is an organization with major influence in development of Internet standards. Formation of IETF standards resembles very much the processes in open source development: influential members first issue RFCs reporting current practices and propose solutions to interoperability problems of Internet technologies, later these proposals are converged into standards. The process is similar to the development and release cycles in software development.

There are some major motivations which makes the organization of IETF standards interesting for us: (1)full history of its development is recorded in RFCs themselves and available for longitudinal analysis, and (2)techniques for assessment of structural interdependency and insights about its evolution which may be gained from such analysis, can be equally applicable to other domains such as structure of software conglomerates, like Debian GNU/Linux packages.

Please use the following format when citing this chapter:

Gençer, M., Oba, B., Özel, B., and Tunalıoğlu, V.S., 2006, in IFIP International Federation for Information Processing, Volume 203, Open Source Systems, eds. Damiani, E., Fitzgerald, B., Scacchi, W., Scotto, M., Succi, G., (Boston: Springer), pp. 267-272

Also as a practical result, such analysis provide hints on importance level of some contemporary standardization efforts.

Our aim in this research is (1)to assess relative importance of Internet standards, and inter-dependencies among them using techniques from social network analysis practice, (2)to identify groups of standards that are related to each other more so than they are to the rest, and levels of cohesion in these groups, and (3)to find stabilization patterns of structural centrality through longitudinal analysis. Development of such approaches can be valuable, for example, in identifying critical segments of similar conglomerates(e.g. software conglomerates like Debian GNU/Linux), in management of processes within them(e.g. release scheduling and team splitting), in partitioning of training programs, and similar strategizing tasks.

An overview of data and the network analysis approach is summarized in section 2. Results for influence and its historical development are presented in section 3, and findings for specialization in section 4. An overview of results and possible other applications of social network analysis methods in OSS processes are discussed in section 5.

2 Standards data and network analysis methods used

Software development processes are studied for the mechanisms of their evolution as a coherent system, and as a community practice of actors[13, 6]. Other research on software call our attention to importance of discursive practices and alignment of software development efforts[10]. Clusters and their formation in similar collaboration systems have been a subject of interest. There exist in social sciences research, valuable frameworks and methodologies for assessment of structural features of networks and their evolution[1, 12, 11, 7, 8, 9]. There is also a group of methods in computer and informatics developed for analyzing different structures(such as for web page rankings) within surprisingly similar terms[5]. However, not only that, to our interest, their application to domains of software processes and standards formation is limited, but also there is much way to go for developing frameworks for sensibly combining these different lenses for a better identification and understanding of structural features common in different contexts[4, 14, 2].

There are over four thousand RFC documents published by the IETF. Most standards start as *informational* class documents. *Best Practices* documents are more influential than *informational* ones. But *standard* class RFC are by far the most important within this collection. In this study we have used only the 1.460 standard class RFCs for analysis. The referral relations between the RFCs is a directed relation. Although there may be several references from one document to another, a dichotomous relation is assumed in the analysis, as the number of references varies greatly.

Our method for analyzing this data consists of several steps:

1. Selection of structurally important standards based on prestige measures. These standards have more influence than others.
2. Identification of subgroups formed around influential standards, key technological questions addressed by them, and their cohesion levels. Subgroups, analysis of their cohesion, and connections between subgroups are important in understanding specialization in growing networks.
3. Sampling of historical patterns of centrality metrics for some key standards and demonstration of stabilization patterns in structural development of Internet standards.

3 Structural importance and influence

Degree prestige(number of references) and relative in-degree prestige[14] are used for assessment of structural importance of a node in a network. Table 1 shows top 15 RFCs according to these centrality measures. Fig.1 is a graphical representation of top 55 nodes, where labels reflect the ranking of RFCs. Density(ratio of existing relations to possible number of relations between nodes) of the RFC network is found to be 0.003716. As best demonstrated by top 7 nodes which have many relations to each other, success of an Internet standard is closely related to its positioning with other standards and success of its siblings.

3.1 Historical development of influence

There are not many established methods available for longitudinal analysis of network formation. One would expect that standards that appear earlier would have higher centrality measures as recent standards are built by referencing the older ones. However results shown in Table 1 only partially confirms this insight.

Table 2a shows changes in density of the network through years. Unlike earlier years of Internet standards, the density decreases as standards becomes more specialized on certain issues, but the rate of decrease is becoming lower.

Table 2b shows changes in relative degree prestige of some key standards through years. This sample is insufficient to suggest a unifying pattern. However it is worth noting that in all of the first three cases, centrality measure first rises to a climax, followed by a decrease as the standard ages and possibly replaced by newer versions at a later stage.

4 Subgroups and specialization

Many standards are related to some others in terms of the technical issues they address. Fig.1 shows how relations concentrated around standards that are influential. Three major groups are identifiable in the network. One group

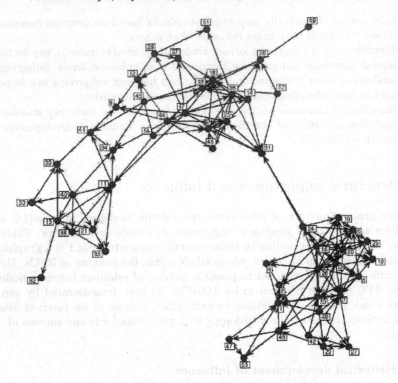

Fig. 1. Groups of standard class RFCs. Top 55 nodes according to degree prestige. Three subgroups are identifiable here: (1) the group on the bottom-right is "network management" related standards, (2) bottom-left group is mostly related to Internet protocol and its security extensions, and (3)top-middle is a mixed group including standards such as www domain names, e-mail content, etc.

which seems quite isolated is related to network management protocols. Another group includes Internet protocol and its security extensions. There is also a third group in Fig.1, however there are many links between the second and third groups.

Further assessment is helpful in understanding the cohesion of these groups. Relative cohesion of a group is defined as the ratio of the number of ties between group members to the number of ties to outside nodes[14]. That ratio can be regarded as relative strength of "centripetal" and "centrifugal" properties of the group. This measure for the first group in Fig.1 is found to be 2.25, whereas it is 0.47 and 0.65 for the second and third group, respectively. A value larger than one should be regarded as an indicator of stronger in-group ties(centripetal). Thus, it is only the first group(network management protocols) which exhibit this level of cohesion. Its only link with other major standards is indirectly

Table 1. Top ranking RFCs according to in-degree and relative in-degree prestige measures.

	Deg.(rel) RFC: Year, Short title
1	141(0.0966) 1213 : 1991, MIB-II for Network Man. of TCP/IP internets
2	129(0.0884) 1212 : 1991, Concise MIB definitions
3	127(0.0870) 2578 : 1999, Structure of Management Information(SMIv2)
4	126(0.0863) 1155 : 1990, Structure and identification of management information for TCP/IP-based internets
5	125(0.0856) 2579 : 1999, Textual Conventions for SMIv2
6	118(0.0808) 2580 : 1999, Conformance Statements for SMIv2
7	111(0.0760) 1905 : 1996, Protocol Operations for SNMPv2
8	108(0.0740) 2234 : 1997, Augmented BNF for Syntax Specifications
9	89(0.0610) 2045 : 1996, MIME Part One: Format of Internet Message Bodies
10	89(0.0610) 1906 : 1996, Transport Mappings for SNMPv2
11	79(0.0541) 2401 : 1998, Security Architecture for the IP
12	76(0.0521) 1035 : 1987, Domain names - implementation and spec.
13	72(0.0493) 1034 : 1987, Domain names - concepts and facilities
14	69(0.0473) 2396 : 1998, URI: Generic Syntax
15	64(0.0438) 2460 : 1998, IPv6 Specification

Table 2. Historical changes in structure: (a)changes in the network density through years, and (b)changes in relative in-degree prestige of some RFCs.

(a)

Year	Density
1992	0.033560
1995	0.017480
1998	0.011691
2001	0.008563
2004	0.007312

(b)

	1992	1995	1998	2001	2004
RFC-1035(1987)	0.0242	0.0495	0.0608	0.0553	0.05584
RFC-1213(1991)	0.3273	0.2473	0.1597	0.1369	0.1269
RFC-1738(1994)	-	0.0177	0.0486	0.0415	0.0393
RFC-2045(1996)	-	-	0.0608	0.0636	0.06980

through node 31(UTF-8 standard), which has an important role in this sense not captured by degree prestige measure.

5 Conclusion

Our results for structural features of the interrelated system of IETF standards demonstrate that methods from social network analysis can be applied to standards or software processes, and to our best knowledge such cross applications of these methods are rare. Structural measures are valuable in determining which artifacts in a system are more influential, can deteriorate the overall quality of a system when they malfunction, or whether introduction of new relations may compromise integrity. As our results suggest, higher levels of subgroup cohesion(i.e. refined specialization) brings success.

Our research was limited as there are many more centrality measures such as betweenness centrality[14, 3]. These were not preferred in this study as their interpretation may be problematic in a first probation, compared to more direct measures we have used. However, note that role of some standards such as UTF-8 which is not captured by prestige centrality can be successfully assessed by incorporation of other measures, such as betweenness centrality. There has been criticisms in the past regarding the meaning of several network analysis instruments[4]. Despite their value in quantitative assessment of structural features of interlinked artifacts, most network metrics has to be combined with due attention to the discourse of application.

Approaches for historical analysis of such networks are limited in the literature[14]. Our results are very limited but nevertheless hints on existence of common patterns. Further research is needed, for example to understand whether subgroup cohesion levels show any such patterns over time, or whether any of these instruments can be consolidated into models for forecasting structural features.

Most parts of our analysis can be applied to similar systems. For example releases of Debian distributions are known to have timing problems. Identification of structural bottlenecks and subgroups in software processes, can improve release schedules and further help in successful management of workforce allocation in such development efforts.

References

1. Borgatti SP (2005) Social Networks 27:
2. Bonacich P, Lloyd P (2001) Social Networks 23/3:191–201
3. Burt RS (1995) Structural holes : the social structure of competition. Harvard University Press, Cambridge, Mass
4. Cook KS, Whitmeyer JM (1992) Annual Review of Sociology 18/1:109–127
5. Kleinberg J (1999) Journal of the ACM 46/5:604–632
6. Lehmann F (2004) First Monday 9/11
7. Oliver AL, Ebers M (1998) Organization Studies 19/4:549–583
8. Oliver AL (2001) Organization Studies 22/3:467–489
9. Powell WW, Koput KW, Smith-Doerr L (1996) Administrative Science Quarterly 41:116–145
10. Raymond ES 2004 The art of Unix programming. Addison-Wesley, Boston
11. Ring PS, van de Ven AH (1994) Academy of Management Review 19/1:90–118
12. Stephenson K, Zelen M (1989) Social Networks 11:1–37
13. Tuomi I (2000) First Monday 6/1
14. Wasserman S, Faust K (1999) Social Network Analysis: Methods and Applications. Cambridge University Press, Cambridge New York
15. West J (2002) Journal of Research Policy 32/7:1259–1285

Contributor Turnover in Libre Software Projects

Gregorio Robles and Jesus M. Gonzalez-Barahona

GSyC/LibreSoft, Universidad Rey Juan Carlos, Spain
{grex,jgb}@gsyc.escet.urjc.es

Abstract. A common problem that management faces in software companies is the high instability of their staff. In libre (free, open source) software projects, the permanence of developers is also an open issue, with the potential of causing problems amplified by the self-organizing nature that most of them exhibit. Hence, human resources in libre software projects are even more difficult to manage: developers are in most cases not bound by a contract and, in addition, there is not a real management structure concerned about this problem. This raises some interesting questions with respect to the composition of development teams in libre software projects, and how they evolve over time. There are projects lead by their original founders (some sort of "code gods"), while others are driven by several different developer groups over time (i.e. the project "regenerates" itself). In this paper, we propose a quantitative methodology, based on the analysis of the activity in the source code management repositories, to study how these processes (developers leaving, developers joining) affect libre software projects. The basis of it is the analysis of the composition of the core group, the group of developers most active in a project, for several time lapses. We will apply this methodology to several large, well-known libre software projects, and show how it can be used to characterize them. In addition, we will discuss the lessons that can be learned, and the validity of our proposal.
Keywords: open source, human resources, turnover, mining software repositories

1 Introduction

Employee turnover (the ratio of the number of workers replaced in a given period to the average number of workers), is known to be high in the (proprietary) software industry [1]. In the libre software world[1], the study of turnover has not been a research target (at least to the knowledge of the authors) profusely. Most of the attention has been focused on the organizational structure of the

---

[1] In this paper we will use the term "libre software" to refer to any software licensed under terms compliant with the FSF definition of "free software", and the OSI definition of "open source software", thus avoiding the controversy between those two terms.

Please use the following format when citing this chapter:

Robles, G., and Gonzalez-Barahona, J.M., 2006, in IFIP International Federation for Information Processing, Volume 203, Open Source Systems, eds. Damiani, E., Fitzgerald, B., Scacchi, W., Scotto, M., Succi, G., (Boston: Springer), pp. 273-286.

projects, and how developers move to a central position in that structure, but not on how they are replaced when leave it.

In this line, probably the best known model about the organizational structure of libre software projects is the *onion model* [2, 3, 4], a visual analogy that represents how developers and users are positioned in communities. In this model, it is possible to differentiate among core developers (those who have a high involvement in the project), co-developers (with punctual, but frequent contributions), active users (that contribute only occasionally) and passive users [8, 7].

But the onion model provides only a static picture of a project, lacking the time dimension that is required for studying joining and leaving processes. Advancing to fill in this shortcoming, it has been complemented by Ye et al. with a more theoretical identification and description of the roles, including also some dynamism [11]. According to this refinement, a core developer is supposed to go through all the outlying roles, starting as a user, until she eventually reaches the core group. An alternative approach is proposed by Jensen and Scacchi [6], who have studied and modelled the processes of role migration for some libre software communities, focusing on end-users who become developers. They have found different paths for this process, concluding that the organizational structure of the studied projects is highly dynamic in comparison to traditional software development organizations.

With respect to abandonment, it is worth mentioning a study [9] which analyzes how many Debian developers leave the project, and how this affects it (i.e. what happens to those software packages that become unmaintained). The authors propose a half-life parameter, defined as the time required for a certain group of contributors to fall to half of its initial population, which is of 7.5 years for the Debian project.

Given these precedents, the research goal for the study presented in this paper is to gain further understanding of the evolution of libre software developers, and especially of the "core group", those most active. Therefore, we will study the evolution over time of this core in some libre software projects. We consider at least two possible scenarios: one in which the first core group is highly stable and does not change over time, and one in which the core group "regenerates". This first case (which will be codenamed the *code gods* scenario) assumes that projects rely heavily on their initiators and that their absence would suppose a great loss for, if not the *death* of, the project. The second scenario assumes that as time passes, the core group changes its composition with some of the initial members leaving the project, but others joining and filling the gap. One of the main goals of this study is to find which of these two approaches is the most common in libre software projects.

This paper is organized as follows. First, the methodology that has been used to extract information from source code management systems is described. The next section contains the results of applying the methodology to 21 large libre software projects. Finally, conclusions are drawn and some hints about further research are given.

2 Methodology

Our methodology is based on mining source code management system repositories, in our case the well-known and widely-used CVS systems. We analyze the log history of the versioning systems using CVSAnalY [10], a tool that retrieves the information related to every commit to the repository, and inserts it to a database where it can be conveniently analyzed.

To identify the "generations" of the core developers, we split the project life-time into ten equally large intervals, which means that intervals will be of different lengths depending on the project, but will have the same relative importance in the context of its history. Selected projects for this study are all at least three years old, and therefore the minimum length of the time interval is more than three months (which is considered to be significative enough, although further research should clarify if this is a correct assumption or not).

For each interval we consider the activity measured in terms of commits to the repository. The most active 20% of all commiters (rounded by excess) for that interval is what we consider the "core group". Therefore, for each project we identify ten different core groups, one per interval. Of course, the composition of the core group in each interval depends on the total number of commiters in that interval. If only 10 commiters participated in the first interval, the core group would be composed of two persons. If in the last interval the number of participants is 19 commiters, the core group would have 4 members. This means that the core group has always the same relative importance, despite the growth in number of developers in the project.

Some other possibilities for selecting the fraction of commiters that form a core groups, or the duration of the intervals could be considered. Using these other approaches would lead to different definitions of "core group" and "generation". However, after experiencing with some of them (we tried with thresholds of 5% and 10%, and with 5 and 20 intervals), we have found that they do not give more insight.

The technique we use is based on visualizing the contribution of the core groups over time. We identify the core group in the first interval, and then plot its contribution not only for the first time interval, but also for all the others. After that, we go on with the core group that corresponds to the second interval, plotting the aggregated contribution of all of its members for all the intervals, and so on, until we have done that for the core groups in all the intervals. In the end, we obtain ten curves (one per core group) which show the evolution of the contributions for all of them since the beginning to the end of the project.

To better understand the visual information that the plots provide, it is important to notice that core groups may have members in common. This is the case if a commiter is part of the most active 20% in several time intervals. This is not easy to identify at first sight, since we plot only the aggregated contribution of all the members of the core group. Though, in some cases, subsequent core groups will be composed by the same persons. In that case, this will be easy to identify visually, as the corresponding curves will have exactly the same shape.

For each project, we will plot the resulting data in three different graphs, which differ in how the contribution of the various core groups (the vertical axis) is represented:

- Absolute graph. Displays the absolute number of commits by each core group (vertical axis) for each interval over time (horizontal axis).
- Aggregated graph. Displays the aggregated number of commits by each core group since the beginning of the project (vertical axis) vs. time (horizontal axis). This graph is the integral of the absolute graph.
- Fractional graph. Displays the fraction of the total commits performed by each core group for each interval (vertical axis) vs. time (horizontal axis). This graph provides the same information than the absolute graph, but normalized by the number of commits performed in each period.

From our experience the fractional plot is usually the better one to perform the generations analysis. Nonetheless, it should be compared to both the absolute and the aggregated graphs since, for instance, periods of little or a lot of activity cannot be identified in the fractional graph.

From the observation of the resulting graphs, it can be inferred whether the same core group rides the project from its beginning to current days or not.

3 Observations on some libre software projects

The 21 case studies shown in the next subsections will help us considering the convenience of this methodology. Among them, we have selected three examples to illustrate the study more in detail. Two of them can be considered as canonical patterns: no generations (The GIMP), and several generations over time (Mozilla). The third one (Evolution) shows results which cannot be assigned to the previous patterns. The rest of case examples, up to 18, will provide us with some evidence about the most frequent pattern found in large libre software projects.

3.1 Observations on The GIMP

The GIMP can be considered as a canonical example of a project with "code gods". Table 1 provides a small summary of the most important facts related to our analysis. The size of the code developed is over half a million lines of code, with an activity of more than 100,000 commits (which means that The GIMP is a very active project).

Although The GIMP started before December 1997 (which is why the date appears in brackets in table 1), it was only then when it was uploaded to the GNOME CVS repository, so we have only data from that moment onwards. The version 1.0 of The GIMP was released in June 1998, so we can consider it a stable project by that time. The length of the intervals in which we have divided the project is slightly over half a year (7.5 months).

Project	The GIMP
Size	557 K
Commits	125,590
Start	(Dec 97)
Ver 1.0	Jun 98
Interval	7.5 months
Generations	Code god

Table 1. Summary of the most important facts for The GIMP project.

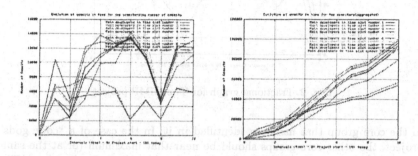

Fig. 1. Right: Absolute graph for The GIMP project. Left: Aggregated graph for The GIMP project.

Figure 1 shows on the left the absolute graph of commits for each core group and for each interval. We can see that there are at least two groups (generations), as it seems that the core group in the beginnings is different from the ones found in the rest of the intervals. In any case, the members of these core groups do not all leave the project as their contribution in subsequent intervals is in the thousands.

A detailed study of the developers forming the core groups yields that one of the most active is present in all of them. The second and third most active developers enter during the third interval (which starts around mid-99) and stay in the project until today.

The plot on the right in figure 1 strengthens this perception. Here the commits performed by each core group are displayed as aggregated. Parallel curves are indicative of core groups for which the most contributing developers are the same. We can easily identify the first two core groups as their curve is below the rest of the curves for later intervals. On the other hand, the shape of the curves from the core group in the third interval onwards shows that they only differ in the number of members of the core group, which as we have seen is variable depending on the total number of contributors for a given interval.

The fractional graph, depicted in figure 2, gives further information. Now the vertical axis has been normalized to 100% of the total commits done in a given interval. By definition the maximum in each interval will correspond

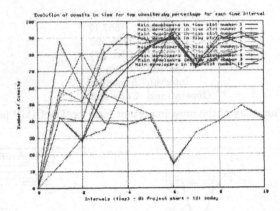

Fig. 2. Fractional graph for The GIMP project.

to the core group that has been identified in it. In the case of a "code gods" project, the other core groups should be near that maximum (or at the same level) as the composition has not changed much over time. In the case of The GIMP this is true, except for the first two intervals, as we have seen in the previous plots. There is a fall of the contribution of the two first core groups, especially in the sixth interval, where it lies under 20%.

Interestingly enough, all core groups show a development share of more than 80% in their corresponding intervals, and even over 90% for those core groups after the third interval. This shows again evidence about the inequality that exist in the contributions of libre software projects. We knew by now that a 20%-80% Pareto distribution is a common work distribution pattern in libre software projects [5]; these graphs shows that, at least for The GIMP (but we will see that this happens in almost all other projects considered in this paper) this is general even for (large enough) time intervals in the project.

3.2 Observations on Mozilla

We have selected the Mozilla Internet suite as the example of libre software project in which several generations can be identified. Mozilla is a well-known libre software project, the follow-up of the Netscape Internet suite. Mozilla is a multi-million project, with more than three million source lines of code. The CVS activity around the project is over 650,000 commits, more than five times larger than that of The GIMP (which is by itself already a large libre software project); Table 2 summarizes the relevant information for our analysis.

The Mozilla project started in 1998. Although its beginnings were not very promising, the project surpassed its early problems, and its version 1.0 was released in June 2002. Following our methodology, we have ten intervals of 6.5 months each, slightly below the 7.5 months used for The GIMP.

Project	Mozilla
Size	3,414 K
Commits	663,454
Start	(Oct 1998)
Ver 1.0	Jun 2002
Interval	6.5 months
Generations	Multiple

Table 2. Summary of the interesting information on Mozilla.

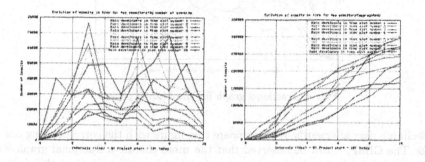

Fig. 3. Right: Absolute graph for the Mozilla project. Left: Aggregated graph for the Mozilla project.

Figure 3 groups the absolute (left) and aggregated (right) plots of the ten core groups for each interval. At first sight, we can already see that there exist many differences between these plots and the corresponding ones of The GIMP. The absolute graph shows interesting information about the overall activity in the repository. It can be seen how in the first two intervals, and for the fifth one, the peak of the core groups is not that high, a fact that is indicative of less activity. Attending to the aggregated graph, we can see how the number of curves which follow their own way (i.e. are not parallel one to each other) is larger. In other words, the composition of core groups varies more frequently than in The GIMP.

Once more, the figure which provides more information is the fractional one (see 4). It shows clearly several generations over time. For all of them, there are peak values of over 75% in their intervals (over 80% in later ones).

Interestingly enough, the core group in the last interval contributed already in the early stages a small amount of commits (around 5%). Its contribution grows then almost continuously (the sequence in the ten intervals is the following: 5%, 11%, 18%, 21%, 21%, 34%, 27%, 55% and finally 78% where it is the leading core group). The core group that achieves its peak contribution in the first interval has an opposite trend with a substantial decline as time passes. In between we find several core groups that have both behaviors found in the first and last core group: an increasing shape until they arrive to the peak and a

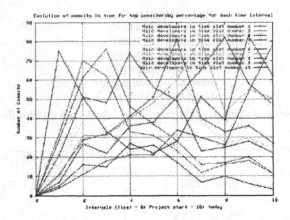

Fig. 4. Fractional graph for the Mozilla project.

declining part afterwards. If we compare this figure with the corresponding one for The GIMP, it can be observed that the more chaotic a fractional graph is (or the less background color we can see in it), the more generations there are. "Code god" projects have a tendency to show parallel curves, while projects with many generations show a lot of curves crossing each other.

3.3 Observations on Evolution

Finally, we have selected a project which shows a mixed behavior between code gods and generations. This is the case of Ximian Evolution (currently renamed to Novell Evolution), a groupware solution for the GNOME project. Table 3 shows the most important information about this software, a medium-sized application with around 200 KSLOC. The amount of commits is in the order of magnitude of The GIMP.

The history of Evolution gives further insight about the results which will be shown below. Evolution started as a community-driven project in December 1998. By the end of the 1999 it was chosen by a small start-up company called Ximian as a strategic application. This meant that hired developers started to work on it, changing its governance to one more typical of a company-driven project. Version 1.0 was delivered in late 2001. The duration of each interval is around 6.4 months, similar to the one for Mozilla and The GIMP.

The absolute graph on the right of figure 5 gives a clear idea of the lower activity that prevailed in Evolution before Ximian developers took over the project in the third interval. Then, an increase in activity can be observed during several years (reaching up to 16,000 commits in each interval), declining in the last year to values close to 9,000 commits per interval. The aggregated graph on the right supports our findings: we can see how the first two core groups (which are identical in their composition) do not contribute after the

Project	Evolution
Size	208 K
Commits	92,333
Start	Dec 1998
Ver 1.0	Dec 2001
Interval	6.4 months
Generations	Composition

Table 3. Summary of the interesting information on Evolution.

initial periods, while the third one shows to be a combination of the first two with some new developers that have prevailed from then. The other core groups show the typical code god behavior with almost parallel curves.

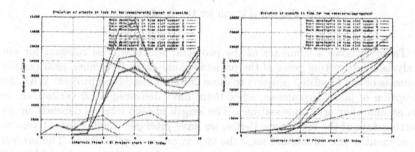

Fig. 5. Right: Absolute graph for the Evolution project. Left: Aggregated graph for the Evolution project.

The fractional graph shown in figure 6 is the best one to observe the mixed behavior. We can see how during the first three (even four) intervals we have a similar pattern to multiple generations. From then on, the code god pattern is clearly identifiable with a small reminiscence from the past in the curve that achieves its peak in the third interval and that does not disappear in the following intervals.

3.4 Observations on other libre software projects

In this subsection we want to infer which of the three described behaviors (code-god, multiple, composition) is the most common pattern in large libre software applications. The selected case studies are part of GNOME (Gnumeric, GTK+, Galeon and Nautilus), KDE (kdelibs, KOffice, kdepim, kdebase, kdenetwork and KDEvelop), Apache (jakarta-commons, xml-xalan and ant), Mono (mono and mcs) and FreeBSD. In the case of FreeBSD, we analyze only the src module of its CVS repository which contains many applications besides the kernel.

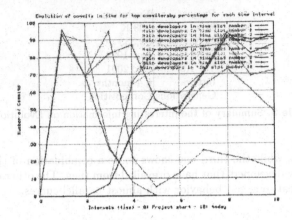

Fig. 6. Fractional graph for the Evolution project

Table 4 shows a summary of the projects, which will be relevant for our analysis. The starting years of the projects range from December 1993 (earlier commits of the FreeBSD project) to June 2001 for the Mono project. With the exception of jakarta-commons, all of them have delivered a 1.0 version, so we can assume they are stable software. The length of each interval depends on the starting date of the repository. Hence, we have intervals ranging from 1 year to three months (for Mono and mcs, the two *younger* applications). The project size, the number of commits and commiters have been added to give additional insight on the applications and to show that they can be considered large in size and in number of contributors.

Fractional graphs for the selected projects are shown in the two 2x4 matrix tables (tables 5 and 6). They have been ordered, putting those that have several generations (multiple) first, then those that have a composite behavior and finally the projects that have a *code god* behavior. After a quick inspection of the fractional graphs, it is easy to classify eight of the projects as having multiple generations, six as showing a composite model, and finally only two projects behaving as having code gods.

4 Conclusions and further research

In this paper we have shown a methodology to answer the question of how the transition (developers joining and leaving) in a libre software project is. We have used the methodology to classify projects in three categories: those based on "code gods", those with generations of core developers, and those which show a mixed model. Most of the projects we have analyzed enter clearly into one of the presented categories.

Project	Start	Ver 1.0	Size	Interval	Commits	Commiters	Type
FreeBSD (src)	Mar 93	Dec 93	1500K	12.1	554,764	352	M
kdelibs	May 97	Jul 98	615K	8.3	217,961	441	M
jakarta-commons	Mar 01	-	429K	3.3	39,370	72	M
mcs	Jun 01	Jun 04	1081K	2.7	32,566	114	M
kdenetwork	Jun 97	Jul 98	293K	8.1	98,282	332	M
kdevelop	Dec 98	Dec 99	386K	6.2	69,890	152	M
koffice	Apr 98	Jan 01	780K	7.1	172,564	247	M
kdepim	Jun 97	Jul 98	512K	8.1	93,632	284	M
gtk+	Dec 97	Apr 98	388K	7.7	68,279	265	C
galeon	Jun 00	Dec 01	90K	4.5	31,153	110	C
xml-xalan	Nov 99	Oct 00	337K	4.9	54,267	32	C
kdebase	Apr 97	Feb 99	362K	8.3	330,009	450	C
ant	Feb 00	(Aug 03)	120K	4.7	43,955	33	C
nautilus	Feb 98	May 01	200K	7.3	63,760	236	C
gnumeric	Jul 98	Jun 02	229K	6.9	81,019	166	G
mono	Jun 01	Jun 04	222K	2.7	11,936	91	G

Table 4. Summary of the findings for a generations analysis applied to the projects listed in the first column. Start is the starting date of the CVS; Ver 1.0 the date of version 1.0 if available, size gives the size of the software in SLOC, interval gives a tenth of the life-time (in months), commits the total number of commits, commiter the total number of commiters and generations their type (G = code gods, M = multiple, C = composition).

The methodology we present is quantitative, based on the data publicly available in the CVS repository of the projects. It uses information about the history of source code management systems (mainly who performed commits and when he did it), and could be therefore influenced by different policies that projects may have regarding the use of versioning systems. However, we have checked that using other parameters, such as number of lines changed (instead of number of commits) yield similar results.

Further research should study how much the selection of the interval length affects the (visual) results. Our experience so far proves that selecting time slots larger than five to six months are sufficient to identify the existence of several generations, but it does not allow to recognize the total number of them.

On the other hand, our sample is composed of large libre software projects. An interesting future research activity could be to investigate the results obtained from applying this methodology to projects with a smaller number of contributors.

The research we make public here is backed by a reasonably large number of projects analyzed, but can of course be improved in the future by analyzing more cases, and by comparing the results to other studies, such as the growth of the code size, or of the change over time of the project structure. Our results show that a majority of projects have multiple core groups over time, so that a natural regeneration process can be inferred. Projects that are still led by founding core groups have been the less frequent, with only 3 cases over 21 applications under consideration.

In any case, the study of the behaviour of human resources in libre software projects, and the relationship between its join/leave patterns and the evolution of the project, is a field to explore. Our study tries to be a first step in this direction, focused on studying its dynamics, and on finding how projects cope with the changes caused by those patterns.

References

1. Barry W. Boehm, editor. *Software risk management*. IEEE Press, Piscataway, NJ, USA, 1989.
2. K. Crowston, B. Scozzi, and S. Buonocore. An explorative study of open source software development structure. In *Proceedings of the ECIS*, Naples, Italy, 2003.
3. Kevin Crowston and James Howison. The social structure of oss development teams. In *Proc Intl Conf on Information Systems*, Seattle, USA, 2003.
4. Kevin Crowston and James Howison. The social structure of free and open source software development. *First Monday*, 10(2), February 2005.
5. Rishab A. Ghosh and Vipul Ved Prakash. The orbiten free software survey. *First Monday*, 5(7), May 2000.
6. Chris Jensen and Walter Scacchi. Modeling recruitment and role migration processes in OSSD projects. In *Proceedings of 6th International Workshop on Software Process Simulation and Modeling*, St. Louis, May 2005.
7. Stefan Koch and Georg Schneider. Effort, cooperation and coordination in an open source software project: GNOME. *Information Systems J*, 12(1):27–42, 2002.
8. Audris Mockus, Roy T. Fielding, and James D. Herbsleb. Two case studies of Open Source software development: Apache and Mozilla. *ACM Transactions on Software Engineering and Methodology*, 11(3):309–346, 2002.
9. Gregorio Robles, Jesus M. Gonzlez-Barahona, and Martin Michlmayr. Evolution of volunteer participation in libre software projects: evidence from Debian. In *Proc 1st Intl Conf Open Source Systems*, pages 100–107, Genoa, Italy, July 2005.
10. Gregorio Robles, Stefan Koch, and Jesus M. Gonzalez-Barahona. Remote analysis and measurement of libre software systems by means of the CVSAnalY tool. In *Proc 2nd Workshop on Remote Analysis and Measurement of Software Systems*, pages 51–56, Edinburg, UK, 2004.
11. Yuwan Ye, Kumiyo Nakakoji, Yasuhiro Yamamoto, and Kouichi Kishida. The co-evolution of systems and communities in Free and Open Source software development. In Stefan Koch, editor, *Free/Open Source Software Development*, pages 59–82. Idea Group Publishing, Hershey, Pennsylvania, USA, 2004.

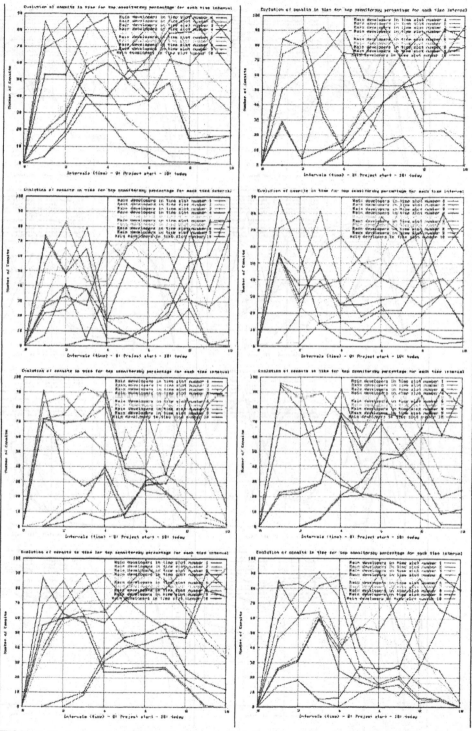

Table 5. 2x4 matrix with fractional generation plots for 8 libre software systems. Projects with heavy generational turn-over have been situated at the top. More information can be found in table 4.

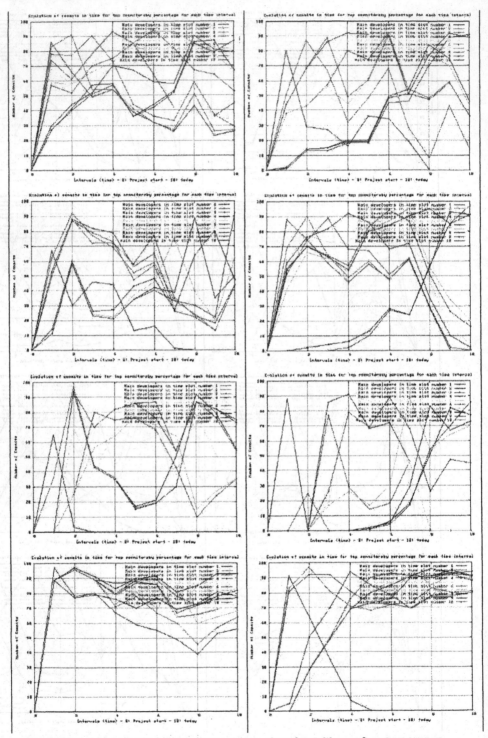

Table 6. 2x4 matrix with fractional generation plots for 8 libre software systems. Projects with heavy generational turn-over have been situated at the top. More information can be found in table 4.

Critical Success Factors for Migrating to OSS-on-the-Desktop: Common Themes across Three South African Case Studies

Daniel Brink, Llewelyn Roos, James Weller and Jean-Paul Van Belle
Department of Information Systems, University of Cape Town
Private Bag, Rondebosch 7701, South Africa
jvbelle@commerce.uct.ac.za
www.uct.ac.za

Abstract. This paper investigates the critical success factors associated with the migration from proprietary desktop software to an open source software (OSS) desktop environment in a South African context. A comparative case study analysis approach was adopted whereby three organisations that have migrated to desktop OSS were analysed. For diversity, one case study each was drawn from government, private industry and the educational sector. Most of the findings agree with those in the available literature though there are notable differences in the relative importance of certain factors.

1. Introduction

The market share of OSS is growing significantly [1]. Some of the factors contributing to the growth include the rising prices of Microsoft products, increased availability of OSS, increased quality and effectiveness of desktop OSS software and the drive for open standards in organisations and governments [1].

Correspondingly, there has been an increased interest and awareness of OSS in South Africa. Whilst OSS has been accepted as a viable alternative to proprietary software (PS) in the network server market for some time, desktop usage of OSS still remains fairly limited [2]. The high PS licensing and computer hardware costs in South Africa relative to the developed countries in combination with the several other perceived advantages of OSS have prompted several OSS on the desktop pilot projects in the education, public and private sectors. However, because no comprehensive follow-up study has been conducted to investigate the long-term outcomes of these projects, little is known about the true benefits and problems associated with the migration to desktop OSS in South Africa, why these migrations were undertaken in the first place, or how to successfully go about migrating to desktop OSS [3]. This lack of knowledge was the inspiration for our research.

This research seeks to uncover the *critical success factors associated with the migration to desktop OSS in a South African context* by means of a multiple case study analysis approach. In this paper, *desktop OSS* comprises those OSS applications that are utilised by every day users to perform daily work tasks. Hopefully future migrations to desktop OSS may be assisted by taking cognisance of the critical success factors found in this research.

Please use the following format when citing this chapter:

Brink, D., Roos, L., Weller, J., and Van Belle, J.-P., 2006, in IFIP International Federation for Information Processing, Volume 203, Open Source Systems, eds. Damiani, E., Fitzgerald, B., Scacchi, W., Scotto, M., Succi, G., (Boston: Springer), pp. 287-293

2. Previous Research

A number of researchers have proposed methodologies or guidelines to implement Desktop OSS. The Lachniet [4] framework focuses on the pre-work which needs to be done before migrating to desktop OSS in a corporate environment. The pre-migration tasks are divided into three sections: administrative tasks, application development tasks and information technology tasks with each grouping sub-divided in a number of tasks.

The methodology suggested by the Wild Open Source Inc consultants [5] consists of three phases: the planning phase, design phase and implementation phase. Here, the users are not involved in the migration process and only receive training at the very end of the migration. Also, their methodology does not specify how the migration should be done, merely stating that it should be planned and documented.

NetProject proposes an OSS Migration Methodology which divides the migration into following five exercises: data gathering and project definition phase, justification for the migration and estimate migration costs, Piloting phase, complete roll-out and implementation monitoring against the project plan [6].

3. Research Methodology

The main research question which is explored in this paper is "What are the critical success factors for migrating to desktop OSS, particularly in a South African context?" Because of the nature of the question, the research is exploratory as opposed to explanatory in nature. A qualitative approach was chosen as appropriate for this research because it enables researchers to make sense of a situation and gain a much richer understanding of a process or experience, via the analysis of people's spoken words and or writings, than a quantitative approach permits. The research methodology adopted was case study research because of its ability to provide subtle yet deep insights into social phenomena surrounding Information Systems [7]. Three case studies were conducted; one in each of the government, private (business) and education sectors. Thematic analysis was utilised to analyse data obtained in the case studies. First, theme analysis was performed for each case study separately. In a second round the common themes relating to the critical success factors across all three case studies were extracted. Two data gathering instruments were used for this research; semi-structured interviews and document analysis. The semi-structured interviews were held with stakeholders from three different organisation levels: management level staff who was involved in the decision to migrate to desktop OSS; IT support staff who was involved in the migration process and/or support of the OSS; and users who experience the desktop OSS on a day-to-day basis. In addition, relevant document were also studied.

4. The Three Case Studies

Three case studies were analysed. For diversity, these were drawn from three different sectors: government, private (business) and education.

4.1   Case Study 1: Novell SA

In 2003, Novell acquired SUSE, the developer of a popular Linux distribution, which would become the new platform for their product range. In 2005, a corporate decision was taken to migrate Novell globally towards OSS. Being a relatively small office with a young management team, Novell SA made the decision to blaze the trail for desktop migration and adopt the Linux desktop across the country and employees were switched directly from Microsoft Windows to Linux overnight. Today there are no Microsoft Windows machines in Novell SA, except for a few software engineers who keep a copy for application compatibility testing. The rapid adoption of Novell Linux Desktop across South Africa did cause some problems as expected, but they were quickly resolved as the software matured.

4.2   Case Study 2: Mossel Bay Municipality.

The Municipality of Mossel Bay, a coastal town located in the Western Cape endeavoured to migrate to desktop OSS after software licensing issues, related to Microsoft products in use, were raised by the Business Software Alliance (BSA). In response to the letters from the BSA and the threat of possible legal issues, the majority of the PCs in the Financial Department were migrated to Linux, as the users use primarily network-based financial systems, email and spreadsheets. Although a number of different productivity suites and Linux versions were tested, the final configuration consisted of OpenOffice running on Novell SUSE Linux. In order to run Linux with a Graphical User Interface (GUI) some of the PCs had to be upgraded. The total duration of the migration to OSS was about 3 months. The IT Manager classifies the migration as a success, but admits that it "*did not solve all the problems; at this point in time* [the Municipality is] *still under-licensed*".

4.3   Case Study 3: Pinelands High School

Pinelands High School (hereafter referred to as "the school" or "Pinelands") is a secondary education school in the Cape Town metropolitan area. Their catalyst for getting OSS software onto more desktops at Pinelands was the failure of the school's intercom and announcements system in January 2004. The amount required to completely replace the existing system was considered exorbitant by school management. At this point, the IT Manager came up with the idea to replace the announcements system with a computer-based one. The new computer-based announcements system, affectionately known as IntraCom, is a web-based application running on the school's intranet. Furthermore, staff can access the internet and email, as well as produce text documents, spreadsheets and presentations, using OpenOffice.org, all from the comfort of their own classroom.

5. Common Emergent Themes across the Case Studies

Each of the cases was first analysed on its own, with a number of emergent themes emanating from each case. The emergent themes exposed in each of the three cases analysed were then synthesised into a group of themes found to be both common and of importance across all three cases. Based upon these derived themes, Critical Success Factors (CSFs) for the migration to desktop OSS are then presented.

5.1   Financial Motivating Factor
In all three cases, the primary reason for migrating to desktop OSS was financially related. For *Novell*, it was a case of moving into an emerging market and gaining competitive advantage, in order to secure better long-term financial performance. For the Mossel Bay Municipality, the move was required in order to avoid a large fine from the *BSA* or the expense of purchasing and maintaining a large number of *Microsoft Windows* licenses.   For Pinelands, desktop OSS provided a cheap alternative to replacing the school's defunct intercom system. Thus, consistent with the literature [8], financial reasons seemed to be one of the key drivers when deciding to migrate to desktop OSS.

5.2   Top Management Support
In all cases, the migration project was strongly supported by top management. In the case of *Novell*, the project was championed globally; in Mossel Bay, the project was endorsed by Council and finally, in the Pinelands case, the school's governing body fully backed the migration. This is essential since a project which introduces such a drastic degree of change into the organisation inevitably meets with fierce resistance from those affected, and migration to desktop OSS is no exception.

5.3   User Awareness and Communication
Although no strong evidence is available from the analysis of the Pinelands High School case study, both the *Novell* and Mossel Bay Municipality cases provide evidence of the value of facilitating good communication between management and users, as well as the creation of user awareness early on the migration process. *Novell* created a large and informative internal website called *OpenZone*, containing information on the why, how and when of the project, including discussion forums where participation was incentivised. Additional, a local advocate/expert was identified in each department. Mossel Bay Municipality also instigated significant user awareness and communication measures.

5.4 Detailed Planning, Analysis and Testing

In all three cases, the importance of thorough planning, as well as the effects of improper planning, was apparent. In the *Novell* case, extensive planning and analysis was conducted before the migration commenced. This included the discovery of affected users and application dependencies, the construction of an application and hardware inventory, a list of new application requirements, as well as the derivation of a detailed time frame and list of objectives. With the Mossel Bay Municipality, the first rollout attempt was a failure due to technical problems, caused by not fully testing the system before handing it over to users, not correctly investigating the hardware requirements of some of the software installed, as well as installing office productivity software that did not meet user requirements. In Pinelands, several unique technical and functional requirements were overlooked due to the "one size fits all" approach of the *tuXlabs* implementation plan.

5.5 Training

All of the organisations studied conducted user training as part of the migration process but their approach, attitude and methods towards training all varied significantly. The best training practices were evident at *Novell*. By acknowledging the fact that individuals possess different styles and paces at which they learn, a flexible training programme was implemented, using web-based interactive tutorials, watching webcasts and training documentation. This fosters an active learning style. In contrast, Mossel Bay Municipality utilised the passive approach initially. Introductory seminars for the Linux desktop and *OpenOffice.org* were held, but some users did not attend. As a result, the trainer spent a lot of time running around in the office assisting users with problems, once the migration was rolled out. The training received at Pinelands High School was found to be of little use and once, again, attempts to conduct passive training sessions were not particularly successful.

5.6 Pilot Project and Partial Migration

[4] argues for implementing a pilot migration project with only a select group of users. Analysis of the three cases revealed a general agreement amongst the IT Managers interviewed with the arguments presented in the literature. Whilst Novell managed to leverage its resources to enable a complete migration, both Mossel Bay Municipality and Pinelands High School found it impossible to migrate fully to desktop OSS. This was due to the presence of "mission critical" legacy applications that no suitable OSS alternative could be found for. In both cases, this meant that *Microsoft Windows* had to be retained on some of the organisational computers.

5.7 Support

In all cases, the importance of post-implementation support was highlighted. In the case of *Novell*, a 24 hours, 7 days per week helpdesk is available, along with numerous online support websites, to assist users in resolving problems. Furthermore, a large base of in-house support is available. Mossel Bay municipality outsources a large part of its desktop OSS support, as only the IT Manager possesses detailed in-house support skills. Furthermore, the majority of interviewees felt that the level of support required at Mossel Bay was not being met. At Pinelands High School, support also remains a problem and forms a large portion of the IT budget.

6. Conclusion and Summary

This research aimed to identify critical success factors for projects dealing with migration towards OSS-on-the-desktop, in a developing world context. This was done by an in-depth analysis of three case studies.

Consistent with the literature, the main driver for deciding to migrate to desktop OSS was the promise of financial benefits, such as decreased license costs and the ability to redistribute funds that would have been spent on software licenses to other areas. No evidence of any of the migrations being motivated by political or social responsibility factors could be found. There was also mention of intangible benefits, such as the freedom from vendor lock-in and the ability to customise the software should one wish to do so. Other supposed benefits identified in the literature, such as improved security, did not appear to be important to the organisations studied.

The problems of legacy applications preventing total migration, user resistance and high support costs were identified in all of the case studies. Problems related to training, specifically the general perception of non-usefulness of training and the lack of a hands-on, practical approach to training, were identified.

Future research should investigate to which extent these findings can be generalised to other contexts. The researchers are currently using the findings as a basis for the development of a more comprehensive migration methodology.

7. References (abbreviated list)

[1] Wheeler, D. Why Open Source Software / Free Software (OSS/FS, FLOSS, or FOSS)? Look at the Numbers! (2 April 2005) http://www.dwheeler.com/oss_fs_why.html.

[2] Prentice, S. & Gammage, B. Enterprise Linux: Will Adolescence Yield to Maturity? Gartner Symposium/ITxpo (2005).

[3] Bruggink, M. Open Source Software: Take It or Leave It? The Status of Open Source Software in Africa, International Institute for Communication and Development, (16 June 2003) http://www.ftpiicd.org/files/research/reports/report16.doc.

[4] Lachniet, M. Desktop Linux Feasibility Study Overview, (20 August 2004), http://lachniet.com.desktoplinux.

[5] Wild Open Source. Steps to Take when Considering a Linux Migration, (25 August 2005), http://www.wildopensource.com/technology_center/steps_linux_migration.php

[6] Netproject. IDA OSS Migration Guidelines, (29 August 2005), http://www.netproject.com/docs/migoss/v1.0/methodology.html.

[7] Walsham, G. 'Interpretive Case Studies in IS Research: Nature and Method', *European Journal of Information Systems*, 4(2), 74-81 (1995).

[8] Gardiner, J.; Healey, P.; Johnston, K. & Prestedge, A. The State of Open Source Software (OSS) in South Africa, Unpublished Technical Report, University of Cape Town, 2003.

Impact of OSS on Social Networks

Part VII

Impact of OSS on Social Networks

Communication Networks in an Open Source Software Project

Jeffrey Roberts[1], Il-Horn Hann[2], Sandra Slaughter[1]

1 Tepper School of Business, Carnegie Mellon University
Pittsburgh, PA {jroberts, sandras}@andrew.cmu.edu

2 Marshall School of Business, University of Southern California
Los Angeles, CA, hann@marshall.usc.edu

Abstract. This study explores the nature of the social network and the patterns of communication that exist in an open source software development project, the Apache HTTP (WEB) server project. Our analysis of archival data on email communications between developers in the Apache HTTP server project suggests an interesting pattern of communication. We find that the core developers self-organize into three sub-groups that communicate intensely in completing the project. Our analysis also reveals that a few prominent developers who are centrally located in the network are driving communications within the project. We identify the implications of our findings and suggest areas for further research.

1 Introduction

Open source software (OSS) development, i.e., public software development projects where participants can read, modify, and redistribute the software source code [1] is arguably one of the most exciting phenomena in the software industry today. Open source has played a fundamental role in the development of the Internet by contributing to such remarkable software as TCP/IP, BIND, Sendmail, Linux, and the Apache WEB server. From a software engineering perspective, the open source community has harnessed the Internet like no other by making it the critical piece of its communication and collaboration infrastructure. This prima facie simple innovation has resulted in a revolutionary organization of software production and has sparked discussion on a wide variety of issues, ranging from project organization, software development methodology, information architecture, and standards to incentives and intellectual property rights. The open source movement has also been of great interest for academics. Researchers with diverse backgrounds such as computer science, psychology, sociology, and economics have started to investigate the topic, making open source development a truly interdisciplinary research field.

The first works in this rapidly developing field were descriptive in nature [e.g., 2] followed by theory driven explanations [e.g., 3] and early empirical research [e.g., 4–7]. Many of the early explorations into the inner workings of the open source development process have sought to explain the mechanisms by which open source projects attract and motivate volunteers to produce such seemingly high quality software [e.g., 2, 8]. One aspect, however, of the OSS phenomenon that has received

Please use the following format when citing this chapter:

Roberts, J., Hann, I.-H., and Slaughter, S., 2006, in IFIP International Federation for Information Processing, Volume 203, Open Source Systems, eds. Damiani, E., Fitzgerald, B., Scacchi, W., Scotto, M., Succi, G., (Boston: Springer), pp. 297-306

relatively little attention is the nature of the project communication in open source projects.

We are specifically interested in advancing the understanding of project communication and its role in managing the process of creating open source software. How open source developers communicate and interact is an interesting and important question given the geographic distribution of the developers and the unstructured process of software development in the open source context (compared to software development in a closed source setting). This study utilizes archival data to explore the nature of the social network and the patterns of communication that exist in one OSS project, the Apache HTTP (WEB) server.

2   Communication and Social Networks in OSS Projects

In his seminal work on embeddedness, Granovetter [9] outlines how the structural properties of social networks can be significant in explicating outcomes. Researchers have linked an individual's position within social networks to advantages such as promotions [10] or to disadvantages such as turnover [11]. From an embeddedness perspective, social interaction plays an essential role in one's ability to access organizational resources and hence impact one's performance [12].   OSS projects exist largely to perform a specific task or goal, like building an operating system (Linux), a WEB server (Apache) or WEB browser (Mozilla Firefox). The success of an individual within an OSS project requires significant project specific knowledge and/or access to others who may possess information required for success. The "knowledgeable" individual may be especially important in an OSS project as many customary artifacts and processes of software engineering, such as design documentation and methodologies, are typically non-existent [2].

To observe or measure this knowledgeable individual within an OSS project we use the network measure of centrality. In the context of an OSS project's communication network, centrality refers the relative prominence of a developer in the project's network structure [13]. In this case, the degree centrality of a developer measures the number of other developers to which that developer is in contact. So, degree centrality can be taken as a measure of a developer's involvement or participation in the project's communication network [14].

Recent advances in communication technologies and the Internet have greatly improved the ability of individuals to collaborate across time and geographical distance. There can be little doubt that these advances are responsible for the explosive growth in OSS projects, both in terms of numbers of projects and participants [15]. One prominent form of communication is email. In a recent on-line article, Bezroukov [16] compares the collaboration among OSS developers to that of academic researchers. One key observation made in this work is crucial role that email plays in OSS project management. In contrast, researchers exploring the role of email in scientific collaborations have found the email alone does not stimulate new relationships; rather, it serves to enhance existing relationships [17, 18]. Thus, an interesting and unresolved question is how email-based communication is conducted in an open source setting and the relationship between project communication characteristics (or patterns) and project processes and/or outcomes. This question is important because the developers in OSS projects are distributed, and email is the primary communication mechanism available for coordinating their work.

3 Research Setting

To evaluate the social and communication network in an open source context, we targeted one project from the Apache Software Foundation (ASF) as the basis for empirical investigations. The Apache HTTP (WEB) server and associated projects are some of the most successful OSS products to date. The Apache server, the original ASF project, and its derivatives, have a dominant 70% share of the WEB server market [19]. Since its inception, the Apache WEB server has had over 7,000 source code contributions from more than 400 different open source developers [20]. The ASF is a not-for-profit corporation that provides the legal, organizational and financial infrastructure for the software projects gathered under the ASF open-source umbrella. Each of the ASF projects operates autonomously controlling all aspects of product development including project management, requirements specification, architecture, design, development, testing, and configuration management. ASF projects are characterized by a "collaborative, consensus based development process, an open and pragmatic software license, and a desire to create high quality software that leads the way in its field" [21]. Membership in the ASF is by invitation only and is based on a strict meritocracy. Those contributors who exhibit a commitment to the ideals of open-source software development and sustained participation may be nominated for membership by another ASF member.

The ASF encompasses a significant number of subprojects related to the development and support of a full-featured WEB server product offering. Although any of the Apache subprojects might provide an interesting vehicle to explore communication patterns, we concentrated on the HTTP server project for the following two reasons. First, for the time period studied, the HTTP server project was one of the largest and most successful ASF projects both in the number of developers and contributions. Second, access to archival data for this project proved to be less problematic than for some of the smaller ASF projects.

4 Data Sources

One basic tenet of OSS is that the development process and resulting products are "open" and freely available. Fundamentally, OSS projects represent large-scale publicly distributed software development processes. As such, and in keeping with free and open access, all OSS work products are placed in the public domain under various "free software" licensing arrangements.

For the purposes of this study, a participant refers to anyone participating in the Apache developer discussion group during the period in question. Apache developers are those individuals who have made a source code contribution to the Apache project during the time period studied. The "Apache Core" includes those Apache developers who make up the nucleus of the Apache HTTP project. There are approximately 22 Core participants. These 22 individuals account for more than 80% of all source code submissions to the Apache HTTP project. To operationalize the communication between Apache developers, two constituent or dyad communication matrices (i.e., adjacency matrices) were constructed from Apache developer email archives to record email communications between each dyad or pair of developers. The Apache projects maintain email list-serves to conduct all project related activities. The software used to maintain the email lists is fully RFC-822 compliant and supports conversation threads. A series of scripts were written to reconstruct conversation threads, identify the participants and produce various "flavors" of matrices suitable for input into UCINET. For the purposes of this research, a person participating in a thread was recorded as having a communication with all other thread participants.

5   Results

In this section we briefly describe some of the characteristics of the Apache communication network for the period we studied. Of interest here is the fact that the structure of the communication network essentially supports or reinforces what we already know about the Apache project from examination of the patch level contributions. That is, imagine the project as a funnel or a set of concentric circles, progressively getting refined or smaller. In other words, as participation increases the number of participants decrease. The full communication adjacency matrix for the focal period contains 453 nodes (individuals) and has a network density of .0218. Given the number of individuals involved in this network, we could have anticipated a relatively sparse network [22]. As a refinement on this network, we reduced the nodes to only those participants who were known to be active contributors to the Apache project during the period in question. This reduced the matrix to 83 nodes having a much greater network density of .25. As a further still refinement, we reduced the nodes to only those participants who were known to be in the Apache Core during the period in question. This reduced the matrix to 22 nodes with an extremely dense structure measured at .72.

To get a visual sense of the proximity, in terms of shared communication, of the Apache Core developers, we conducted a Multidimensional scaling (MDS) metric analysis of the similarity of the Core developers' communication matrix. The goal of our MDS analysis was to detect meaningful underlying dimensions that help to explain observed similarities in patterns of communication frequency among the Apache Core developers. Several measures of similarity were explored including Pearson's product-moment correlation and mean-centered cross products.

Interestingly, this analysis reveals three identifiable sub-groups even within the relatively small Core of the Apache development team.   These sub-groups are

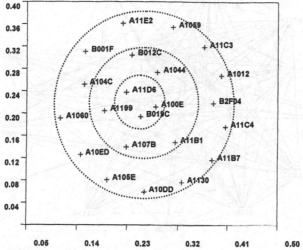

Fig. 1. Apache Core Communication Pattern Similarities – Metric MDS
identified in a series of concentric circles in Figure 1.

We further visually explore the nature of the Apache Core developer's communication network by plotting the dyadic communication relationships between core developers using the MDS coordinates to position the developers in a graph. The resulting graph, or sociogram, represents the communication relationships among Apache Core developers (represented by points or nodes) and a "communicates-with" relationship (represented by connecting lines.) Figure 2 shows the full Apache Core communication network.

Fig. 2. Apache Core Communication Sociogram – Complete

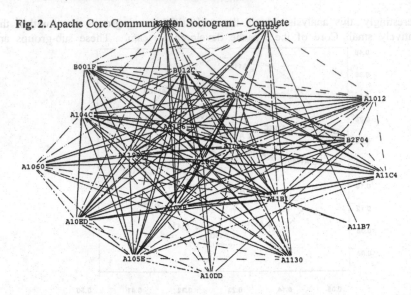

Figure 3 shows the network from the perspective of MDS Group 1. In this graph, members of Groups 2 and 3 each appear as a single collective entry. It is easily discernable from this graph that the MDS Group 1 developers constitute a fully connected communication graph.

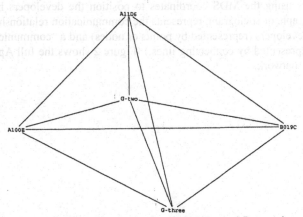

Fig. 3. Apache Core Communication Sociogram – MDS Group 1 Perspective

Similarly, Figures 4 and 5 show the network from the perspective of MDS Groups 2 and Group 3, respectively.

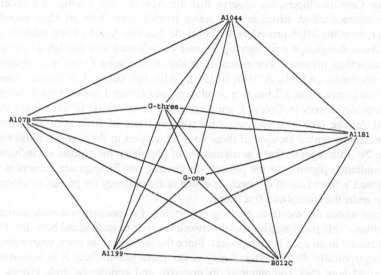

Fig. 4. Apache Core Communication Sociogram – MDS Group 2 Perspective

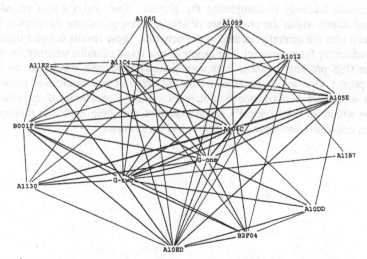

Fig. 5. Apache Core Communication Sociogram – MDS Group 3 Perspective

6 Discussion

From the network density measures, MDS plots of communication pattern similarity, and sociograms displaying the communication network structure of the Apache Core developers, we observe that the Apache Core maintains a relatively dense communication structure with active participation from all Core members. Further, from the MDS procedure we conclude that this Apache Core exhibits three identifiable sub-groups with varying degrees of influence and similarity within the communication network. For example, as shown in Figure 3, Group 1 consists of three developers (A100E, A11D6, B019C). Although Group 1 is smaller than the other two groups (Group 2 has five developers, and Group 3 has thirteen developers) the three developers in Group 1 are among the most central or prominent in the overall Apache core communication network in terms of their network centrality scores (see the central location of these three developers in the network illustrated in Figure 2). This suggests that a small number of prominent individuals are influencing communication patterns for the project. In general, our findings are consistent with Krackhardt's "Iron Law of Oligarchy", which is the tendency for groups to ultimately end up under the control of a few people.

Open source represents an exciting opportunity for research in a wide variety of disciplines. This paper applies social network analysis to understand how developers communicate in an open source project. Since the developers in open source projects are geographically distributed and may never meet face-to-face, it is important to understand how they communicate to organize and coordinate their efforts. Our analysis of the Apache HTTP server project suggests an interesting pattern of communication where the core developers self-organize into sub-groups that communicate intensely in completing the project. Our analysis also reveals that communications within the project are driven by a few prominent developers in one sub-group who are centrally located in the network. These results suggest interesting opportunities for future research. For example, one could examine whether developers in other OSS projects organize their communication patterns similar to the HTTP server project. One could also consider the influence of communication patterns on aspects of project performance or outcomes. Lastly, measures of influence and position within an OSS project's social networks may help explicate relationships between individual developer participation and performance.

7   References

1. OSI, The Open Source Definition, The Open Source Initiative, (Accessed: May 2001); http://opensource.org/docs/definition_plain.html

2. E. Raymond, *The Cathedral and the Bazaar: Musings on Linux and Open Source by an Accidental Revolutionary* (O'Reilly, Cambridge, 1999).

3. J. Lerner and J. Tirole, The Simple Economics of Open Source, The National Bureau of Economic Research, Inc. (Accessed: April 2001); http://papers.nber.org/papers/W7600

4. K. Lakhami, and E. von Hippel (2000). How Open Source Software works: "Free" user-to-user assistance. MIT Sloan Open Source Project, (Accessed: October 2001); http://opensource.mit.edu/papers/lakhanivonhippelusersupport.pdf.

5. A. Mockus, R. Fielding and J. Herbsleb, A Case Study of Open Source Software Development: The Apache Server, *Proceedings of the Proceedings of the 22nd International Conference on on Software Engineering*, Limerick Ireland (2000).

6. S. Koch and G. Schneider, Results for Software Engineering Research into Open Source Development Projects Using Public Data, Open Source Research Community, MIT Sloan Open Source Project, (Accessed: April 2001); http://opensource.mit.edu/papers/koch-ossoftwareengineering.pdf

7. I. Stamelos, L. Angelis, et al., Code Quality Analysis in Open Source Software Development, *Information Systems Journal* 12(1), (2002).

8. B. Fitzgerald and J. Feller, Open Source Software: Investigating the Software Engineering, Psychosocial and Economic Issues, *Information Systems Journal* 11(4), (2001).

9. M. Granovetter, Economic Action and Social Structure: The Problem of Embeddedness, *American Journal of Sociology* 91(3), 481-510 (1985).

10. R.S. Burt, *Structural holes: The social structure of competition* (Harvard University Press, Cambridge, 1992).

11. D. Krackhardt and L.W. Porter, The snowball effect: Turnover embedded in communication networks, *Journal of Applied Psychology*, 71, 50-55 (1986).

12. D. Brass, Being in the Right Place: A Structural Analysis of Individual Influence in an Organization, *Administrative Science Quarterly*, 29, 518-539 (1984).

13. J. Scott, Social Network Analysis (Sage Publications, Thousand Oaks, 2000).

14. L.C. Freeman, *Centrality in Social Networks: Conceptual Clarification, Social Networks* 1, 215-239 (1979).

15. R.A. Ghosh, Interview with Linus Torvalds: What motivates free software developers?, *First Monday* 3(3), (1998).

16. N. Bezroukov, Open Source Software Development as a Special Type of Academic Research, *First Monday* 4(10), (1999).

17. R.E. Kraut, C. Egido, et al., Patterns of Contact and Communication in Scientific Research Collaboration, *Intellectual Teamwork: Social and Technological Foundations of Cooperative Work*. J. Galegher, R. E. Kraut and C. Egido Eds., (L. Erlbaum Associates, Hillsdale), 149-171 (1990).

18. K. Carley and K. Wendt, Electronic Mail and Scientific Communication: A Study of the SOAR Extended Research Group, *Knowledge: Creation, Diffusion, Utilization* **12**(4), 406-440 (1991).

19. Netcraft, The Netcraft WEB-server Survey, (Accessed: August 2005); http://news.netcraft.com/archives/2005/08/01/august_2005_WEB_server_survey.html

20. I. Hann, J. Roberts, S.A. Slaughter and R. Fielding, Economic incentives for participating in open source software projects. *Proceedings of the 22nd International Conference on Information Systems*, Barcelona (2002).

21. Apache Software Foundation, (Accessed: March 2001); http://www.apache.org/foundation/, Apache Software Foundation.

22. S.R. Barley, J. Freeman, et al, Strategic alliances in commercial biotechnology, *Networks and Organizations: Structure, Form, and Action*, N. Nohria and R. G. Eccles Eds., (Harvard Business School Press, Boston), 311-347 (1992).

Impact of Social Ties on Open Source Project Team Formation

Jungpil Hahn[1], Jae Yoon Moon[2], and Chen Zhang[1]

1 Krannert School of Management, Purdue University
West Lafayette, IN 47907, USA
{jphahn, zhang153}@mgmt.purdue.edu

2 Business School, Hong Kong University of Science and Technology
Clear Water Bay, Kowloon, Hong Kong
jmoon@ust.hk

Abstract. In this paper, we empirically examined the role of social ties in OSSD team formation and developer joining behavior. We find that the existence and the amount of prior social relations in the network do increase the probability of an OSS project to attract more developers. Interestingly, for projects without preexisting social ties, developers tend to join the project initiated by people with less OSSD experience. This research fills a gap in the open source literature by conducting an empirical investigation of the role of social relations on project team formation behavior. Furthermore, the adoption of social network analysis, which has received little attention in the OSS literature, can yield some interesting results on the interactions among OSS developers.

1 Background and Motivation

The creation of industrial-strength software code (or software development) has traditionally been regarded as an activity that can only be effectively conducted and managed within a firm setting. Recently however, an alternative model of software development, the open source software development (OSSD) in which programmers in Internet-based communities collaborate to voluntarily contribute programming code, has emerged as a promising approach to developing high-quality software [1]. During the past few years, a number of open source software (OSS) products, ranging from end-user applications (e.g., Emacs and OpenOffice), programming languages (e.g., Perl and PHP) to applications supporting the Internet infrastructure (e.g., sendmail), have been widely adopted. The prominence garnered by well-known OSS projects such as the Apache Web Server and the Linux operating system kernel are testimonies to the attractiveness and viability of OSSD as an alternative to the conventional proprietary model of producing software [1-3].

Despite the impressive success of some OSSD projects, it is a harsh reality that the vast majority of OSS projects fail to take off and become abandoned. One of the main reasons cited for the failure of OSS projects is the lack of developers in the project teams, or the inability of the project to bring together a critical mass of developers [2, 4]. Since it is typically the case that OSSD projects do not provide monetary rewards for developers' contributions, many OSSD projects are under-

Please use the following format when citing this chapter:

Hahn, J., Moon, J.Y., and Zhang, C., 2006, in IFIP International Federation for Information Processing, Volume 203, Open Source Systems, eds. Damiani, E., Fitzgerald, B., Scacchi, W., Scotto, M., Succi, G., (Boston: Springer), pp. 307-317

staffed and consequently are not well-equipped to deal with the complexity in software development. Hence, in order to understand and solve the key problems related to staffing, it is important to understand the dynamics of software team formation – how developers self-organize into project teams.

In this paper, we undertake an empirical examination of the formation of OSS project teams from a social network perspective. The OSSD community is essentially a complex collaborative social network endowed with social capital. Just as the social position of a firm within inter-organizational networks influences its alliance strategies and consequent outcomes [5-6], we argue that social relations forged during past collaborations will have an impact on how OSS project teams take form. However, despite the apparent relevance and importance of social capital in OSSD, only a few studies have examined its impact on developer behavior in team formation from a social network perspective. In this paper, we ask ourselves whether the existence and amount of prior social ties in an OSS project helps it attract additional developers. The remainder of this paper is organized as follows. In section 2, we present our theoretical background and develop our research hypotheses. We outline the empirical research methodology in section 3 and present the results in section 4. We conclude in section 5 by discussing the implications, contributions and directions for future research.

2   Theoretical Background and Research Hypotheses

This study draws from two streams of research – 1) open source software development (OSSD), and 2) social network analysis and network structure. We review and synthesize the relevant literature to develop our research hypotheses.

2.1   Open Source Software Development (OSSD)

Since its emergence, OSSD has posed many interesting questions for researchers in many fields. A number of researchers have addressed the factors that motivate individuals to participate in OSSD despite the lack of monetary compensation. Among the possible explanations for developers' participation in OSS projects are incentives related to career concerns and ego gratification [7]. Hars and Qu [8] identify both intrinsic motivations such as altruism and extrinsic motivations such as direct compensation. Another study surveys the motivations of the contributors to a large OSS project and finds that participation is mainly driven by developers' group identification, by the possibility of improving their own software, and by their tolerance of the required time investments for contributing to the project [9]. Lakhani and Wolf [10] identify enjoyment-based intrinsic motivation, user need, and learning as the most pervasive drivers of developer participation. In summary, the studies suggest that developers participate in OSSD mainly because of intrinsic factors such as enjoyment and extrinsic factors such as career advancement. However, the motivations identified from these surveys of developers do not explain why developers choose to join one project over other possible similar projects. When deciding whether to join an OSS project, in addition to the previously cited motivational factors, a developer will also be concerned about issues related to coordination and communication with other team members. In general, when forming teams people prefer to work with those with whom they have worked in the past [11]. Familiarity bred from preexisting social relations with others can facilitate the newcomer's socialization process. Hence, we identify and test social ties among developers as a potential driver behind developer joining behavior and project team formation.

2.2   Social Network Analysis

Social network analysis aims to understand the relationships between people, groups, organizations, and other types of social entities [12-14], and has been used extensively in fields such as sociology [13, 15] and management [16-17] among others [18-19]. A social network is modeled as a graph with nodes representing the individual actors in the network and ties representing the relationships between the actors.

In a social network the actors maintain a tie by exchanging either tangible or intangible resources such as information, goods and services, and financial support. The strength of a social tie varies depending on a number of factors. Granovetter [12] distinguishes between strong and weak ties and asserts that tie strength depends on the amount of time, the emotional intensity, the intimacy, and the reciprocal services associated with the relationship. Strong ties are characterized by a sense of special relationship, an interest in frequent interactions, and a sense of mutuality of the relationship [20]. In contrast, weak ties are maintained infrequently or indirectly between the actors who belong to different social clusters. Both strong ties and weak ties play an important and differential role in a social network. Strong ties maintain and promote trust and collaboration whereas weak ties enable actors to access resources and information that are unavailable in their immediate social circles [12, 21].

2.3   Social Network Perspectives of Open Source Software Development

Although it has been recognized early on that OSSD has become a significant social phenomenon and that OSS developers and users form a complex social network via various electronic communication channels on the Internet [22], few researchers have examined this phenomenon from a social network perspective. Madey, Freeh, and Tynan [23] conducted the first empirical investigation of the open source movement by modeling OSS projects as a collaborative social network and found that the OSSD community can be modeled as a self-organizing social network. Others propose the methodology of applying social network analysis to data gathered from CVS code repositories of OSS projects [24]. Xu, Gao, Christley, and Madey [25] explored some social network properties in the open source community to identify patterns of collaborations. However, the works cited above tend to be highly technical and mainly investigate the network properties of the OSSD community, offering limited theoretical and practical contributions. The work most similar to our research is done by Ducheneaut [26] who examined the socialization process of newcomers over time as a learning process and a political process by analyzing the developer activities in a large OSS project.

2.4   Research Hypotheses

Conventionally, project teams are formed by a manager assigning individuals to a team based on certain characteristics such as expertise and personality. An alternative approach is driven by team members' self-selection into teams. As such, in OSSD, some project initiators may formally recruit developers[1] (e.g., by broadcasting position openings and required qualifications to the entire community), or alternatively developers may voluntarily join a project team or be invited to participate in a project team by its existing members. Prior research suggests that people are more likely to work together when they have prior social ties [27-28]. Moreover, teams consisting of individuals with preexisting relationships have been shown to solve complex problems better than teams of strangers because they are able to pool information more efficiently [29]. In the open source software development context in particular, due to the lack of opportunities for face-to-face contact, developers face greater barriers to effective communication and coordination and are thus more likely to be concerned about these issues. Direct social relations with existing members of a project can mitigate concerns regarding communication and coordination difficulties due to the shared context accrued from prior interactions. We propose the following hypothesis with regard to the impact of preexisting social ties on open source software development project team formation:

H1: Projects whose initiators have preexisting social ties with the network are more likely to have other developers join the development team than those whose initiators do not have ties.

Projects can fall into two categories depending on whether or not their initiators have relationship ties in the network. Some projects are initiated by developers who have participated in other projects and formed social relationships with other developers in the community. For this type of project, the more social ties the initiators have, the larger will be the pool of potential developers. Consequently, these projects will be able to attract or invite others into the development team more easily.

---

[1] Interestingly, the extent of recruiting is surprisingly low based on our informal observations. For example, there are only about 200 position openings posted on SourceForge.net. When we consider that there are currently over 100,000 OSS projects are hosted on SourceForge.net, this number is quite inconsequential.

Therefore, we propose the following hypothesis regarding the impact of the amount of preexisting strong ties in a project:

H2: For those projects whose initiators have preexisting social ties with the network, the amount of such ties is positively associated with the probability of having other developers join the project team.

It may not necessarily be the case that projects are initiated by developers who are well connected to the network. Some projects may be initiated by developers who have yet to collaborate with others in the open source software development community even though they may have experience in managing software projects before (i.e., self-developed projects). In such cases, developers with prior open source project experience will have superior knowledge of OSS development and management processes. As a result, projects initiated by developers with prior experience may be more likely to have additional team members than projects initiated by developers with no prior experience. We propose the following hypothesis:

H3: For those projects whose initiators do not have preexisting social ties in the network, the experience of initiators is positively associated with the probability of having other developers join the project team.

3   Results

3.1   Data Collection and Measures

We collected data from open source software projects hosted on SourceForge.net. As the largest repository of open source applications on the Internet, SourceForge.net currently provides free hosting to more than 100,000 projects and more than 1,100,000 subscribers. It also offers a variety of services to hosted projects, including site hosting, mailing lists, bug tracking, message boards, file archiving, and other project management tools. SourceForge.net has been an attractive source of data for many researchers studying open source software mainly due to the abundance of publicly accessible data [30].

We randomly selected 1030 new projects that were registered between September and November in 2005. A web crawler downloaded the HTML files containing project summary data and developer information on the date of registration. We revisited sample projects one month after their respective registration dates to identify those developers who had subsequently joined. This process enables us to distinguish between the initiator and the developers who subsequently join. Further, in order to identify the social ties of the developers, we collected data on other projects that each developer has participated in before to identify their past collaborators. Based on this data, we are able to construct affiliation matrices of developers and projects that depict the existence and strengths of the relationships ties between developers.

The following measures were computed for empirical analysis (see Table 1).

Table 1. Summary of Measures

Variable	Definition
Dependent Variable	
DevelopersJoin	1 if at least one developer joined the project within the first month of project initiation, 0 otherwise.
Independent Variable	
InitiatorHasTies	1 if project initiator(s) have preexisting social ties in the network, 0 otherwise.
InitiatorTiesAmount	The amount of direct ties that the project initiators have prior to project registration calculated as the number of distinct developers who have collaborated with the project initiator(s).
InitiatorExperience	Number of projects that the project initiators have participated in before.
Control Variables	
NumInitiators	Number of project initiators[2].
ProjAmbiguity	Level of ambiguity of project definition (i.e., how ill-defined a project is) calculated as the number of project characteristics left undefined[3].

3.2   Results

The descriptive statistics and pairwise correlations of the measures for the sample are summarized in Table 2. The highest correlation between the independent variables is between *InitiatorHasTies* and *InitiatorTiesAmount* ($\rho = 0.333, p < 0.001$). The sample projects had 1.13 initiators on average. Within the first month 43% of the 1030 projects had at least one developer joining the development team. Most projects (55%) attracted one developer, 170 projects (40%) had added two to five developers, and 20 projects (5%) had more than five additional developers.

---

[2] The granularity of data collection is daily. In other words, we were unable to distinguish between initiators and subsequent joiners if the project registration and the developer's join event happened on the same day. We classified all members that joined on the day of registration as initiators.

[3] On SourceForge.net, project administrators may clarify the details of the project in terms of several characteristics such as development status, database environment, intended audience, license type, operating system, programming language, software category, translations and nature of user interface.

Table 2. Descriptive Statistics

Variable	Descriptive Statistics				Correlations				
	Mean	St. Dev	Min	Max	(1)	(2)	(3)	(4)	(5)
(1) DeveloerJoin	0.43	0.495	0.00	1.00					
(2) InitatorHasTies	0.26	0.441	0.00	1.00	0.06*				
(3) InitiatorTieAmount	4.01	20.149	0.00	330.00	0.09***	0.33***			
(4) InitiatorExperience	1.12	4.708	0.00	81.00	-0.04	0.33***	0.22***		
(5) NumInitiators	1.13	0.510	1.00	9.00	-0.01	0.18***	0.13***	0.30***	
(6) ProjAmbuguity	3.92	3.216	0.00	7.00	-0.22***	-0.05***	-0.05*	0.00	-0.09***

Note: Sample size N = 1030.
Significance Levels: *** $p < 0.01$, ** $p < 0.05$, * $p < 0.1$

Since our dependent measure (i.e., *DevelopersJoin*) is binary, we test the impact of the existence of initiators' prior social ties on developer joining behavior (hypothesis H1) by estimating the parameters for the following logistic regression model:

$$\text{logit}\left(P\left(DevelopersJoin = 1\right)\right) = \alpha + \beta_1 InitiatorHasTies + \beta_2 NumInitiators + \beta_3 InitiatorExperience + \beta_4 ProjAmbiguity + \varepsilon$$

A positive and significant estimate of parameter β_1 would indicate that the probability of other developers becoming members of a project whose initiators have direct social ties is greater than that of a project whose initiators have no direct social ties in the network. The results of the logistic regression are presented in Table 3 (Model 1). The model shows a good fit with the data (likelihood ratio $\chi^2 = 58.428$, $p < 0.01$). The variable *InitiatorHasTies* has a significant positive effect on the likelihood of developers joining ($\beta_1 = 0.389$, $p < 0.05$). The results suggest that projects with initiators who have preexisting ties with the developer network are 47.6% more likely to have at least one additional developer join the project team compared to those with initiators who do not have any preexisting ties with the network (H1 supported).

Next we test the impact of number of prior social ties on developer joining behavior (hypothesis H2) by estimating the parameters for the following logistic regression model:

$$\text{logit}\left(P\left(DevelopersJoin = 1\right)\right) = \alpha + \beta_1 InitiatorTieAmount + \beta_2 NumInitiators + \beta_3 InitiatorExperience + \beta_4 ProjAmbiguity + \varepsilon$$

The results of the logistic regression are presented in Table 3 (Model 2). The model shows good fit with the data (likelihood ratio $\chi^2 = 24.556$, $p < 0.01$). *InitiatorTieAmount* has a significant positive effect on the likelihood of developers joining ($\beta_1 = 0.0145$, $p < 0.05$). The results suggest that an additional tie for an initiator increases the likelihood of at least one developer joining the project team by 1.5%. Given that on average an initiator has had prior relationships with approximately 4 other developers, this would amount to an average increase in the likelihood by 6%. Thus, projects with initiators with more ties with the developer network are more likely to attract additional developers than those with initiators with fewer direct ties (H2 supported).

Finally, we examined the impact of initiators' experience with open source software development projects on developer joining behavior for those projects without preexisting social ties (hypothesis H3). We estimate the parameters for the following logistic regression model:

$$\text{logit}\left(P\left(DevelopersJoin = 1\right)\right) = \alpha + \beta_1 InitiatorExperience + \beta_2 NumInitiators + \beta_3 ProjAmbiguity + \varepsilon$$

Table 3 (Model 3) summarizes the results of the logistic regression. The model shows a good fit with the data (likelihood ratio $\chi^2 = 51.092$, $p < 0.01$). The parameter estimate for *InitiatorExperience* is significant but negative ($\beta_1 = -0.604$, $p < 0.01$), indicating that projects whose initiators have more OSSD experience are less likely to attract additional developers than those whose initiators have less OSSD experience, a result which may seem counter-intuitive. An alternative explanation may be that developers in the OSS community support newcomers by joining their projects and at the same time expand their existing social relationships. Therefore, hypothesis H3 that for those projects without preexisting strong social ties the experience of initiators tend to have a positive impact on the probability of having other developers join the project team was not confirmed by the results.

Table 3. Logistic Regression Results

Variable	Model 1 (H1) Parameter Estimate	Model 1 (H1) Odds Ratio	Model 2 (H2) Parameter Estimate	Model 2 (H2) Odds Ratio	Model 3 (H3) Parameter Estimate	Model 3 (H3) Odds Ratio
Constant	0.2878		0.4896*		0.4986*	
InitiatorHasTies	0.3891**	1.476				
InitatorTieAmount			0.0145**	1.015		
InitiatorExperience	-0.0464	0.955	-0.0363	0.964	-0.6040***	0.547
NumInitiators	-0.0742	0.928	-0.0997	0.905	-0.1787	0.836
ProjAmbiguity	-0.1416***	0.868	-0.1400***	0.869	-0.1432***	0.867
Model Statistics						
Sample Size (N)	1030		271		759	
Likelihood Ratio (χ2)	58.428***		24.556***		51.092***	
Significance levels: *** $p < 0.01$, ** $p < 0.05$, * $p < 0.1$						

6 Conclusion and Discussions

In this study we investigated the role of social ties in OSSD team formation. Specifically, we examined whether the existence of prior social ties impacts the probability of an OSS project to attract more developers. We find that overall the existence of prior social ties does increase the probability that developers join a project. We also find that, for projects with preexisting social ties, the number of such ties has a positive influence on whether additional developers join the project. Interestingly, for projects without preexisting social ties, developers tend to join the project initiated by people with less OSSD experience. This research fills a gap in the open source literature by conducting an empirical investigation of the role of social relations on project team formation behavior. Second, the adoption of social network analysis, which has received little attention in the OSS literature, can yield some interesting results on the interactions among OSS developers.

However, the study has some limitations. For example, we only look at joining behavior within the first month after project registration. The joining behavior may differ during different stages of project development. While controlling for development stage would shed more theoretical insights, practically many newly registered projects do not define their development stages explicitly, which limits our ability to incorporate this factor into the analysis. Moreover, we assume that developers who have collaborated on a project before have developed direct social ties of uniform strength. In reality, the strength of the tie may depend on many factors such as developers' roles, duration of collaboration, and outcome of the collaboration. We hope to distinguish the strength of social ties in a follow-up study. An important extension of this paper is to study the effect of developer joining behavior on the network structural characteristics within project team as well as its performance implications.

REFERENCES

[1] E. S. Raymond and B. Young, *The Cathedral and the Bazaar: Musings on Linux and Open Source by an Accidental Revolutionary* (O'Reilly & Associates, Sebastopol, CA, 2001).

[2] T. O'Reilly, Lessons from Open-Source Software Development, *Comm. ACM.* **42**(4), 33-37 (1999).

[3] E. S. Raymond. The Cathedral and the Bazaar; http://www.4linux.com.br/arquivos/cathedral-bazaar.pdf

[4] J. Lerner and J. Tirole, The Open Source Movement: Key Research Questions, *European Econom. Rev.* **45**(4-6), 819-826 (2001).

[5] W. W. Powell, K. W. Koput, and L. Smith-Doerr, Interorganizational Collaboration and the Locus of Innovation: Networks of Learning in Biotechnology, *Admin. Sci. Quart.* **41**(1), 116-145 (1996).

[6] R. Gulati, Social Structure and Alliance Formation Pattern: A Longitudinal Analysis, *Admin. Sci. Quart.* **40**, 619-652 (1995).

[7] J. Lerner and J. Tirole, Some Simple Economics of Open Source, *J. Industrial Econom.* **50**(2), 197-234 (2002).

[8] A. Hars and S. Qu, Working for Free? Motivations for Participating in Open-Source Projects, *Internat. J. of Electronic Commerce.* **6**(3), 25-39 (2002).

[9] G. Hertel, S. Niedner, and S. Herrmann, Motivation of Software Developers in Open Source Projects: An Internet-Based Survey of Contributors to the Linux Kernel, *Res. Policy.* **32**(7), 1159-1177 (2003).

[10] K. R. Lakhani and R. Wolf, in Perspectives on Free and Open Source Software, edited by J. Feller, B. Fitzgerald, S. Hissam, and K.R. Lakhani (MIT Press: Cambridge, MA. 2005).

[11] P. J. Hinds, K. M. Carley, D. Krackhardt, and D. Wholey, Choosing Work Group Members: Balancing Similarity, Competence, and Familiarity, *Organ. Behavior and Human Decision Processes*. **81**(2), 226-251 (2000).

[12] M. Granovetter, The Strength of Weak Ties, *Amer. J. Sociology*. **78**, 1360–1380 (1973).

[13] S. Wasserman and J. Galaskiewicz, *Advances in Social Network Analysis* (Sage, Thousand Oaks, CA, 1994)

[14] B. Wellman and S. D. Berkowitz, *Social Structures: A Network Approach* (Cambridge University Press, Cambridge, 1998)

[15] K. S. Cook and J. M. Whitmeyer, Two Approaches to Social Structure: Exchange Theory and Network Analysis, *Ann. Rev. Sociology*. **18**, 109-127 (1992).

[16] S. P. Borgatti and P. C. Foster, The Network Paradigm in Organizational Research: A Review and Typology, *J. Management*. **29**(6), 991-1013 (2003).

[17] W. Tsai, Knowledge Transfer in Intraorganizational Networks: Effects of Network Position and Absorptive Capacity on Business Unit Innovation and Performance, *Acad. Management J.* **44**(5), 996-1004 (2001).

[18] J. Singh, Collaborative Networks as Determinants of Knowledge Diffusion Patterns, *Management Sci.* **51**(5), 756-770 (2005).

[19] S. Huang and G. DeSanctis. Mobilizing Informational Social Capital in Cyber Space: Online Social Network Structural Properties and Knowledge Sharing. *Proceedings of the 26th International Conference on Information Systems (ICIS 2005)*. Las Vegas, NV.

[20] J. Walker, S. Wasserman, and B. Wellman, in Advances in Social Network Analysis, edited by S. Wasserman and J. Galaskiewicz (Sage, Thousand Oaks, CA. 1994).

[21] R. Burt, *Structural Holes: The Social Structure of Competition* (Harvard University Press, Cambridge, MA, 1992)

[22] E. von Hippel and G. von Krogh, Open Source Software and the 'Private-Collective' Innovation Model: Issues for Organization Science, *Organ. Sci.* **14**(2), 209-223 (2003).

[23] G. Madey, V. Freeh, and R. Tynan. The Open Source Software Development Phenomenon: An Analysis Based on Social Network Theory. *Proceedings of 8th Americas Conference on Information Systems (AMCIS 2002)*. Dallas, Texas.

[24] L. Lopez-Fernandez, G. Robles, and J. M. Gonzalez-Barahona. Applying Social Network Analysis to the Information in CVS Repositories. *Proceedings of the 1st International Workshop on Mining Software Repositories (MSR 2004)*. Edinburgh, UK.

[25] J. Xu, Y. Gao, S. Christley, and G. madey. A Topological Analysis of the Open Source Software Development Community. *Proceedings of 38th Hawaii International Conference on System Sciences (HICSS 2005)*. Hawaii, HI.

[26] N. Ducheneaut, Socialization in an Open Source Software Community: A Socio-Technical Analysis, *Computer Supported Cooperative Work.* **14**, 323-368 (2005).

[27] D. McClelland, J. Atkinson, R. Clark, and A. Lowell, *The Achievement Motive* (Appleton-Century-Crofts, New York, 1953)

[28] S. Schachter, *The Psychology of Affiliation* (Stanford University Press, Stanford, CA, 1959)

[29] D. H. Gruenfeld, E. A. Mannix, K. Y. Williams, and M. A. Neale, Group Composition and Decision Making: How Member Familiarity and Information Distribution Affect Process and Performance, *Organ. Behavior and Human Decision Processes*. **67**(1), 1-15 (1996).

[30] J. Howison and K. Crowston. The Perils and Pitfalls of Mining Sourceforge. *Proceedings of the 1st International Workshop on Mining Software Repositories (MSR 2004)*. Edinburgh, UK.

Social dynamics of free and open source team communications

James Howison, Keisuke Inoue, and Kevin Crowston

School of Information Studies
Syracuse University
Syracuse, USA
{jhowison,kinoue,crowston}@syr.edu

Abstract[1] This paper furthers inquiry into the social structure of free
and open source software (FLOSS) teams by undertaking social network
analysis across time. Contrary to expectations, we confirmed earlier
findings of a wide distribution of centralizations even when examining
the networks over time. The paper also provides empirical evidence that
while change at the center of FLOSS projects is relatively uncommon,
participation across the project communities is highly skewed, with
many participants appearing for only one period. Surprisingly, large
project teams are not more likely to undergo change at their centers.
*Keywords: Software Development, Human Factors, Dynamic social networks,
FLOSS teams, bug fixing, communications, longitudinal social network analysis*

1 Introduction and Literature Review

Free/Libre Open Source Software (FLOSS[2]) is a broad term used to embrace
software developed and released under an "open source" license allowing inspection, modification and redistribution of the software's source without charge
("free as in beer"). Much though not all of this software is also "free software,"
meaning that derivative works must be made available under the same unre-
strictive license terms ("free as in speech", thus "libre"). We study FLOSS
teams because they are remarkable successful distributed work teams; we are
interested in understanding how these teams organize for success.

In this paper, we investigate the informal social structure of FLOSS development teams by examining the pattern of communications between developers.

---

[1] Acknowledgement: This research was partially supported by NSF Grants 03–41475,
04–14468 and 05–27457. Any opinions, findings, and conclusions or recommendations expressed in this material are those of the authors and do not necessarily
reflect the views of the National Science Foundation

[2] The free software movement and the open source movement are distinct and have
different philosophies but mostly common practices. In recognition of these two
communities, we use the acronym FLOSS, standing for Free/Libre and Open Source
Software.

Please use the following format when citing this chapter:

Howison, J., Inoue, K., and Crowston, K., 2006, in IFIP International Federation for
Information Processing, Volume 203, Open Source Systems, eds. Damiani, E., Fitzgerald,
B., Scacchi, W., Scotto, M., Succi, G., (Boston: Springer), pp. 319-330

We are seeking social patterns reflected in artifacts of project activity, what de Souza *et al* call "an 'archeology' of software development processes" [5]. In this paper, we analyze communication network data over time, using snapshot data, to understand better how social structures in projects are changing over time. We first examine average centralization over time, then we examine change at the center and finally the stability of participation in project communications[3].

White et al [15] introduced the modeling of social structure over time using snapshot data. Our method is similar and their clear comment also applies, we "present no models of processes over time; there are neither predictions of other behavior nor explications of a stochastic process of tie formation and dissolution" (p 732). Rather the analysis below seeks merely to describe the structures as found at different points in time. Analysis of networks over time with attention to causes and predictions from structure and its change, such as preferential attachment, is an active area of research [11, 9] and one that may be fruitful on this data.

Analysis of networks over time is also new to analysis of software development communications. Recently de Souza et al [5] reported their examination of FLOSS project communications for a small number of projects at two points in time; they were able to see the movement of developers between the core and the periphery of the project. The work presented below extends such analysis to a large sample of data using automated analysis techniques.

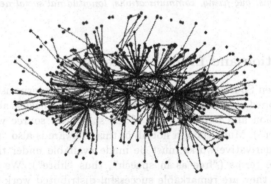

Fig. 1. `squirrelmail` from [4] Modular, or changes at the center over time?

Prior research has shown that FLOSS teams exhibit a wide range of centralizations, counter to both the common image of teams as totally decentralized and the academic expectation of centralization [3, 4]. This work has also shown that centralization scores are negatively correlated with number of participants in the bug report discussions, specifically, that small projects can be centralized

---

[3] A longer version of this paper, that presents full summary statistics and time series of network centralization over time, is available online at http://floss.syr.edu/publications/

or decentralized, but larger projects are decentralized. Figure 1 shows a large decentralized network.

Two explanations have been offered for this finding: first, the fact that in a large project, it is simply not possible for a single individual to be involved in fixing every bug. As projects grow, they have to become more modular, with different people responsible for different modules. In other words, a large project is in fact an aggregate of smaller projects, resulting in what might be described as a "shallot-shaped" structure, with layers around multiple centers.

An alternative explanation is that the larger projects are more likely to have experienced changes in leadership. This seems particularly credible when one considers that participant counts are positively affected by project lifespan. During any given period, the network may be centralized around a current leader, but overlapping the networks from all periods gives a total network with multiple centers and thus an artificially decentralized network.

Accordingly after comparing average centralization over time with the overall centralizations reported in [4], we then examine changes at the center of the communications networks. Stability at the center of a project is likely important to the team's performance. Linus Torvald's position in the Linux project is legendary and there is constant concern that he is being over-stretched [10]. This concern is based, in part, on the knowledge that transition is difficult; central personnel likely hold much tacit knowledge and stability in structure ought to assist coordination through transactive memory.

Finally we examine the frequency of participation in project communications. The ability to attract and retain project participants is an important measure of FLOSS project success, demonstrating the project's viability as well as its ability to satisfy its participants. Repeated involvement, or what we might call tenure, should also serve as a knowledge and skill transmission device. This is particularly important amongst the core team but is also important amongst the periphery of active users, who learn to provide "usable" bug reports as well as how to run the latest development snapshots. Long-term active users may step in as 'newbie wranglers' able to answer the frequency asked questions and thus shielding the core developers, freeing up their time and attention. We examine the frequency of participant's involvement across time and relate it to the patterns of difference in centralizations

2 Data and Method

For this analysis we utilized data collected from the SourceForge bug tracker. The bug fixing process provides a "microcosm of coordination problems" [2] and is a collaborative task in which, as Eric Raymond [12] paraphrases Linus Torvalds: the people finding bugs are different from those that understand the bugs and those that fix the bugs.

We selected projects from SourceForge and downloaded project and bug database data using Web spiders (see [8]). The projects selected were projects that had had more than 100 bugs (open or closed) in the tracker at the time of selection in April 2002 and which had more than seven developers active overall in the discussions. This yielded data on 120 relatively successful projects.

We extracted interaction data from the project bug reports to create interaction matrices. These were analyzed using social network analysis (SNA) [14]. The bug reports contain a thread of discussion (shown elsewhere in Figure 4 of [4]). The initial bug-reporter posts via a web interface, typically triggering a message to a group of developers, or the development mailing list, depending how the project is organized. Replies, often seeking more information or confirmation, are then posted to the bug, being copied to all previous recipients and posted in the public forum.

SNA requires the construction of sociomatrices, depictions of social networks organized around dyads (pairs of senders and receivers). The appropriate dyad in the case of an open forum is an interesting question in its own right. While the origin of the message can be determined from the Sourceforge ID, the message may well be received by all project participants (if the tracker is copied to a mailing list), by all previous posters to the tracker, or merely by the previous poster in the thread. This question is of great importance to studies relying on the information flow characteristics of social networks.

For this reason, we simply coded the interaction as occurring between the sender and the immediately previous poster and calculated outdegree centralization. This was reasonable because our reading of the bug-reports showed that most messages are a reaction to the immediately prior message and because we are primarily interested in contribution, and not information flows per se. Our dyad can be understood as 'was prompted to speak in public by,' an interpretation which is robust with our interpretations below. These 'in-public' dyads mean that it is conceptually difficult to utilize network measures, such as betweenness centrality, which assume that only the recipient has read the message, and that the recipient chooses whether to forward that information onwards.

Outdegree centralization measures inequality in the proportion of the total population spoken to by each node. A network in which a single individual has spoken with all other participants, but where those others have only spoken with that single individual would have very high outdegree centralization (1.0). Conversely a network in which each participant has spoken with every other participant would have very low outdegree centralization (0.0).

Each message has a time-stamp given when the message is received by the tracker system. We used this data to divide the networks into over-lapping snapshots. We sampled the network in 90-day windows, moving the window forward 30 days at a time. This means that a single dyad may be reflected in up to three consecutive snapshots. We chose to use overlapping windows to smooth changes in the network structure and 90 days was chosen so that the majority of the projects contain enough communications to analyze in each time period. The data and analysis scripts for this paper are available through FLOSSmole [7].

3 Findings

3.1 Centralization

Our snapshot data provided an outdegree centralization figure for each project in each frame. Thus we have a time series for project centralization. We hope to explore such patterns in detail using time-series techniques to measure stability and trends across the data set, but at present we describe the series only through their means and variance. The left-hand figure in Figure 2 shows the distribution for the average outdegree centralization over time. Centralization is distributed, with a mean of 0.59, and Median of 0.58 and a standard deviation of 0.15. The right-hand figure in Figure 2 attempts to measure the stability of the centralization scores by examining the standard deviations of the series. Given that centralization is normalized between 0 and 1, it is reasonable to compare the standard deviations. The distribution shows that the majority of centralization scores vary ± 0.2 through their lifetime.

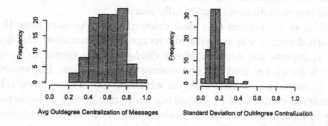

Fig. 2. Average Centralization over time is widely distributed, with moderate internal variance

If the hypothesis expressed in [4] was correct, and changes at the center had artificially reduced the centralization score by collapsing time, the distribution of average centralization ought to be higher overall than the distribution of overall centralization. This was not the case. There was no statistical difference between the distribution of average centralization presented in this paper and overall centralization presented in [4].

Figure 3 shows the differences between the average of our centralization scores computed from the snapshots, and the centralization score obtained by collapsing the network over time. The diagonal line shows equality, and the perpendicular distance from that line shows the difference, either positive (the collapsing of the network has produced an 'artificially' decentralized network) or, somewhat unexpectedly, negative (where the collapsing of the network has produced an 'artificially' centralized network). We can see that the projects with positive and high differences appear to include some of the projects, such

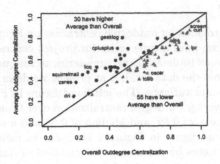

Fig. 3. The effects of collapsing networks over time

as `squirrelmail`, that we anticipated might have undergone change at the center, but the significant number of projects with low negative differences renders the two distributions statistically similar.

To clarify, we considered two ideal cases of networks over time that would produce such differences in overall and average centralizations. The first, shown in Figure 4, depicts the network where change at the center in an otherwise centralized network has lead to lower overall centralization. The second, shown in Figure 5, introduces a new case, in which an otherwise decentralized network is rendered centralized by collapsing over time due to a single participant appearing in each frame, but with entirely different 'partners'. Even in a decentralized network the developer with high 'tenure' appears to form a core, in regular discussion with a transient periphery.

In concrete terms these structures might indicate projects at different stages of their lifecycle (as described in [13]). The first, centralized structure might indicate projects on a growth trajectory driven by the creative vision of their leaders in communication with a group of active alpha testers. The second, decentralized structure might indicate a project in a maintenance mode, being tended to by a few long-timers and a transient group of infrequent bug reporters.

3.2 Changes in central members

We can assess the occurrence of change at the center graphically by examining individual centralities over time. In our data, individual outdegree centrality is a measurement of the number of individuals that a participant has replied to, standardized by the total number of participants (the potential audience). For the projects with the highest positive difference between average and overall centralization, we selected the five nodes with the highest average centralization as candidates for being at the center. We then computed their ranks in each

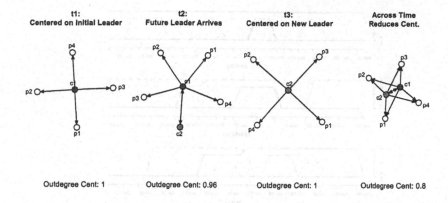

Fig. 4. Ideal Type: Change at the center

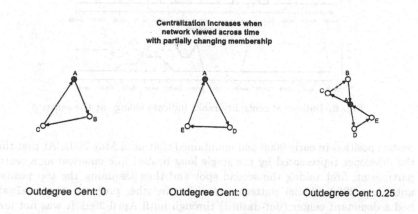

Fig. 5. Ideal Type depicting inequality in tenure

time period and graphed them in Figure 6. When the line ascends to the top (rank 1) it indicates that the node had the highest centralization, on its own, in that period. (Ties were separated by assigning the minimum value for the tied group, so if all lines head down to rank ≤ 5 that indicates that the 'central' position was shared during that period.)

curl is plotted first for comparison; it has not undergone change at the center. Its central node, the solid line, has maintained the top rank in individual centralities throughout the time period, shown by the horizontal line at rank 1. In contrast the four projects with highest differences show clear changes in the developer in the most central position. cplusplus is the clearest of all, we see that the developer represented by the solid line rapidly assumed the

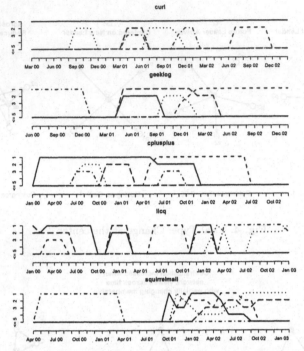

Fig. 6. Individual centrality ranks indicate change at the center

central position in early 2000 and maintained that until May 2001. At that time the developer represented by the single long dashed line emerged as a central participant, first taking the second spot and then assuming the top position until June 2002. Similar patterns are visible in other projects. squirrelmail had a dominant center (dot-dashed) through until April 2001 It was not until January 2002 that another relatively stable center, the solid line, emerged but he was soon replaced by the developer represented by the dashed line who was replaced in turn by the dotted line. The graphical analysis suggests that change at the center is a good explanation for the reduction in centralization that occurs when the networks are flattened across time.

The snapshot data allows a numerical assessment of stability at the center two ways for each project in our sample. First we counted the number of developers ever at the top rank of individual centrality, and second we counted the number of times the top rank position changed (we counted a change if the top ranked developer at $t + 1$ was different than the developer at t). If there are developers alternating in the center then the second figure will be larger than the first. We expected to find that most projects were more similar to curl than to squirrelmail, that the node at the center would be stable through the project, quite possibly the project founder.

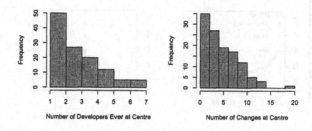

Fig. 7. Change at the center is uncommon

Figure 7 shows the distributions for our two measures of center stability. Among our sample the majority had only ever had one developer ever at the center and seven was the largest count. Leadership changes showed a similar distribution (the measures correlated at $r = 0.73$). This is an interesting finding because it suggests that change at the center of a project is uncommon.

We expected that larger projects, with many more candidates for the center and a greater 'load' on the central participants, would experience more change at the center. However our measures did not show correlation with the number of participants (0.18 and -0.02 respectively); larger projects do not seem more likely to undergo more changes at the center.

The measures of change at the center did show correlation ($r=0.4$) with the difference between average and overall centralization, lending quantitative support to the graphical exploration of change at the center in Figure 6 and to the hypothesis expressed in [4] at least for the cases with positive differences. We now turn to examine the potential of transient peripheries suggested by 5 above.

3.3 Transient Peripheries?

As an heuristic to understand stability in participation, we measured the number of time windows in which each participant posted a message and expressed that as a percentage of the total number of snapshots of the project's lifetime in our data. Figure 8 shows the distribution of this measure for projects where we had data on at least 10 periods. The data show a highly skewed distribution; the majority of participants are active for only between 10 and 20 percent of the periods in which we had data. This reflects the fact that the mode was activity for just a single period. On the other hand there are a number of projects, like lyxbugs, ucsf-nomad and oscar, that had their participants active in half of the periods examined, indicative of a fairly stable team.

While this finding is interesting on its own and would bear further investigation, it showed low correlation with the differences between overall and average

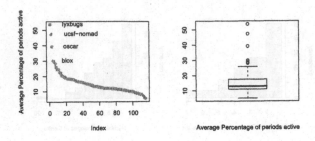

Fig. 8. Most participants are highly transitory

centralization suggesting that the second ideal-type model is not that common amongst our dataset.

4 Discussion

Our initial expectation that a dynamic snapshot analysis would revive our expectation of a pattern of high centralization in FLOSS project communications was not supported. There was no significant difference between the overall and average means and there were a large number of projects that had the opposite reaction, where collapsing the network over time in fact raised their centralization. We found reasonable evidence that changes in leadership played a role in suppressing the expected centralizations but did not find a full explanation for the negative cases.

Nonetheless, our analysis also provides possible insight into project leadership and change. Outdegree centrality in our study is essentially measuring contribution in the bug tracker. Contribution is crucial to leadership of FLOSS projects, partially a result of its self-organization and volunteer nature and partially as a result of its ideological commitment to meritocracy. It is tempting then to make a direct connection between high outdegree centrality and thus a central position, and project leadership.

Caution is called for, however, because this data is only measuring communications contribution, which is controversial as a measure of leadership compared to development contribution. In fact Raymond expects FLOSS leaders to 'speak softly' [12] and Alan Cox provides anecdotal reports of blow-hard 'town councilors' who speak a lot without writing code [1]. On the other hand our data comes from the bug tracker, a place of focused activity, rather than the project mailing lists where 'town councilors' are more likely to be found. Sustained contribution in the bug tracker, answering questions and seeking further information is likely to indicate a participant who is at least important to the project, if not the over-all leader.

An expectation that figures central to a project would be found in the bug tracker is in marked contrast to expectations in proprietary software development teams. Here bug-fixing is likely to be 'grunt work'; a leader in proprietary teams is more likely to be found in an architecting and over-sight role. Empirical work is needed to explore this difference further.

5 Conclusion

This analysis of FLOSS project communications over time has presented three substantive findings:

- We confirmed the finding reported in [4]. Projects vary widely in their social structures between projects even when the networks are analyzed over time. Initial examination of centralization over time within projects also shows substantial variance.
- We found that the majority of projects examined retain a single participant at the center for substantial periods of time, and found that larger projects do not change central participants more often than smaller projects. Perhaps 'Linus' does scale after all (contra McVoy et al [10]), or, more likely, lieutenants face a glass ceiling, collecting below and buffering a still active central actor.
- We provide evidence that a vast majority of project participants are involved for only a very small number of periods, and there is a characteristic power law distribution whereby a very small number are involved for long periods.

This paper, and the longer version available online, also makes a methodological contribution, describing a dynamic analysis of FLOSS project communication and suggesting that collapsing a network over time is not a reliable way to describe social structure as experienced by participants. Finally, the paper also introduces a possible quantitative method for assessing leadership change, a crucial event in virtual team dynamics. The individual centralization rank graphs in Figure 6 identify time periods where qualitative investigation of the project communications would be likely to reveal evidence of leadership change. Thus a dynamic SNA approach can function as a data reduction device. We hope to extend this work by examining the time series, combining it with an analysis of contribution in code repositories and exploring 'concentration' [6], a newly introduced SNA measure of centralization capable of placing a group, rather than an individual at the center of a project

References

1. Alan Cox. Cathedrals, Bazaars and the Town Council. *Slashdot*, 13 October 1998 1998.
2. K. Crowston. A coordination theory approach to organizational process design. *Organization Science*, 8(2):157–175, 1997.

3. Kevin Crowston and James Howison. Hierarchy and centralization in free and open source software team communications. *Knowledge, Technology and Policy*, 18(4), 2005.

4. Kevin Crowston and James Howison. The social structure of open source software development teams. *First Monday*, 10(2), 2005.

5. C. de Souza, J. Froehlich, and P Dourish. Seeking the source: Software source code as a social and technical artifact. In *Proceedings of GROUP '05*, pages 197–206, 2005.

6. Martin Everett and Stephn P Borgatti. Extending centrality. In Peter J Carrington, John Scott, and Stanly Wasserman, editors, *Models and Methods in Social Network Analysis*. Cambridge University Press, 2005.

7. James. Howison, Megan Conklin, and Kevin Crowston. Ossmole: A collaborative repository for floss research data and analyses. In *Proc. of 1st International Conference on Open Source Software*, Genova, Italy, 2005.

8. James Howison and Kevin Crowston. The perils and pitfalls of mining sourceforge. In *Proc. of Workshop on Mining Software Repositories at the International Conference on Software Engineering ICSE*, 2004.

9. M. Huisman and T. A. B. Snijders. Statistical analysis of longitudinal network data with changing composition. *Sociological Methods & Research*, 32(2):253–287, 2003.

10. L. McVoy, E. Raymond, and Others. A solution for growing pains (mailing list thread). email to linux kernal mailing list (30 sep 1998). Available from: http://www.ussg.iu.edu/hypermail/linux/kernel/9809.3/0957.html, 1998.

11. P. Monge and N. Contractor. Emergence of communication networks. In F. Jablin and L Putnam, editors, *New Handbook of Organizational Communication*, pages 440–502. Sage, Newbury Park, CA, 2001.

12. Eric S. Raymond. The Cathedral and the Bazaar. *First Monday*, 3(3), March 1998.

13. Anthony Senyard and Martin Michlmayr. How to have a successful free software project. In *Proceedings of the 11th Asia-Pacific Software Engineering Conference*, pages 84–91, Busan, Korea, 2004. IEEE Computer Society.

14. S. Wasserman and K. Faust. *Social Network Analysis*. Cambridge University Press, Cambridge, 1994.

15. H. C. White, S. A. Boorman, and R. L. Brieger. Social structure from multiple networks I. Blockmodels of roles and positions. *American Journal of Sociology*, 81(4):730–780, 1976.

Part VIII

Posters

How is it possible to profit from innovation in the absence of any appropriability?

Andrea Bonaccorsi[1], Lucia Piscitello[2],Monica Merito[1] ,and Cristina Rossi[2]
1   DSEA-University of Pisa, Via Diotisalvi 2, 56126 Pisa, Italy
{bonaccorsi,merito}@sssup.it,
2   DIG-Politecnico di Milano, Piazza Leonardo da Vinci 32, 20133 Milano,
Italy
{lucia.piscitello,cristina1.rossi}@polimi.it

Abstract. Open Source Software (OSS) represents an "open innovation" paradigm based on knowledge produced and shared by developers and users. New findings from a large survey of European software companies show that: (i) the OSS business model is currently involving almost one third of the industry, although with different intensity; (ii) compared with pure proprietary software producers, OSS firms have a broader product portfolio and are more diversified; moreover, (iii) OSS firms provide more complementary services to their customers; (iv) over time OSS firms increase the share of OS turnover out of the total turnover, becoming more and more OSS oriented; (v) both NOSS and OSS firms do not consider appropriability as a crucial requirement for innovation and do not consider the lack of appropriability as an obstacle to profitability.

Open Source (OS) software is now booming. More and more users are running open programs on their systems, and several OS solutions have turned out to be extremely successful (e.g., the Open Source Web server Apache). Such a bright demand together with the availability of software of good technical quality has stimulated firms' involvement in the OS movement. The new production paradigm has progressively acquired increasing importance within the software industry. Large incumbents like IBM, Hewlett Packard, Compaq, and Sun Microsystems have decided to release their source code to the community [1]. Furthermore, particularly after the drawing up of the Open Source Definition in 1998, many new software firms have entered the market, trying to profit not from traditional license fees but from other software-related services [2]. Bonaccorsi et al. [3] have examined in great detail these companies finding that the large majority of them follow what they call a "hybrid" business model (as opposed to a pure OS model) by mixing products, types of licenses, and sources of revenues. Using a large dataset on software companies (NACE code 72, computer and related activities) based on a field survey in five European countries (Finland, Germany, Italy, Portugal, and Spain), we find strong evidence supporting this view.

The offering profiles of the 769 respondents take place along a continuum ranging from the exclusive provision of proprietary solutions to a product portfolio entirely based on OS. In particular, 66.8% of the firms supply only proprietary products and/or services, whereas only 19 provide just OS solutions. Of the 236 (30.7%) firms supplying both types of software, a large fraction (38.1%) claim to provide open source and proprietary software with no distinction. Among companies supplying also OS based products and services (OSS firms), the proportion of sales generated by open software increases over time. Between 2000 and 2003, the percentage of respondents whose OSS turnover is above 50% has increased from 17.25% to 25.49%, while those who work with OSS without generating revenues out of it have decreased from 33.33% to 10.98%. If the OSS business model were not sustainable, we would not observe such an increase.

Compared with pure proprietary firms, OSS firms have a broader product portfolio, as measured by the number of product areas in which the firms are active. The majority of the firms working with proprietary software are active mainly in management and data management software while no other applications involve more than one third of them. In addition, compared with pure proprietary firms, OSS firms provide more complementary services to customers, as measured using a detailed taxonomy derived form the literature [1]. This corroborates the hypothesis that the increase in the number of product supplied is made possible by the exploitation of the open knowledge base created by the community of developers.

Data also show that, OSS firms do not consider the lack of appropriability as an obstacle to profitability and do not consider appropriability as a crucial requirement for innovation. Both OSS and proprietary firms agree that patents are costly (72.55%), do not constitute a valid barrier to entry (71.70%), and need a too long legal procedure (68.81%). Such negative effects are not compensated by their capacity of providing incentives to innovators (only 32.09%). These results are in line with the literature claiming that patents increase the cost of innovations while the impact on the expected revenues may be dubious [4]. In general, respondents have a more positive attitude towards licenses. However, the percentage of respondents agreeing that licenses are an appropriate mean of marketing products and recovering R&D investments is decreasing with the degree of openness of the firm.

1. Wichmann, T., 2002. Firms' Open Source activities: motivations and policy implications. International Institute of Infonomics, Berlecom Research GmbH, Maastricht.

2. Hawkins, R.E., 2004. The economics of the Open Source Software for a competitive firm. Why give it away for free?. Netnomics 6, 103-117.

3. Bonaccorsi, A., Giannangeli, S., Rossi, C., 2006. Entry strategies under dominant standards. Hybrid business models in the Open Source software industry. Management Science, forthcoming.

4. Levin, R.C., Klevorich, A.K., Nelson, R.R., Winter, S.G., 1987. Appropriating the returns from industrial research and development. Brookings Papers on Economic Activity 3, 783-820.

Producing and Interpreting Debug Texts

An Empirical Study of Distributed, Parallel Debugging in Open Source Software Development

Thomas Østerlie

Norwegian University of Science and Technology
Sem Sælands vei 7-9, 7491 Trondheim, Norway
thomas.osterlie@idi.ntnu.no

Abstract. This paper presents preliminary findings from an ethnographic study of distributed, parallel debugging in an open source software (OSS) community. Focusing on the OSS developers' daily activities, I propose the concept of making software debuggable. In so doing, I see a somewhat different story than common narratives of debugging in current OSS research, which describes distributed, parallel debugging as a set of highly cohesive tasks within loosely couple groups. I find that parallel, distributed debugging is rather a closely coupled collective process of producing and interpreting debug texts with high cohesion between the activities of reporting, finding, and understanding bugs.

1 Introduction

Parallel debugging is identified as one of the key characteristics of OSS development processes [1], and "is the site of claims of effectiveness made for [OSS] projects" [2]. While empirical research show that defects are found and corrected rapidly with parallel debugging [3][4], explanations for these findings remain inconclusive. It has been proposed that OSS is more maintainable than commercial software. However, no difference is found in the maintainability between commercial and OSS software [3]. Another proposed explanation is that successful OSS projects exhibit a specific social structure [5]. Yet, research has shown the structure varies among projects and that different successful OSS projects may exhibit different social structures [2].

In my research I seek to explore an explanation to the success of parallel debugging that lies in the everyday activities of debugging. Existing studies of parallel debugging tells us little about what OSS developers do on a day-to-day basis. The key question raised in my research is therefore: what are OSS developers daily activities in parallel debugging?

My research is based on materials collected during ten months ethnographic studies in the Gentoo OSS community. The Gentoo community develops, maintains, and operates a system for distributing and installing third-party OSS on various Unix variants, along with their own GNU/Linux distribution. Gentoo releases its software for parallel debugging by the community as part of a formalized process.

2 Preliminary findings

Mockus et al. [4] find that "most of the effort in bug fixing is generally in tracking down the source of the problem". I find that tracking down the bug need not be all that simple in practice. It need not be obvious what the bug "really is". Rather, it is subject to interpretation. To make sense of failures reported in bug reports, the developers discuss a number of possible sources for the failure. Of these possible explanations, I find that none are dismissed on conclusive evidence. Instead, alternative explanations for reported failures are made more or less plausible by producing new debug texts, trying to reproduce the bug, and drawing on external texts like installation scripts, source code, documentation, and change logs.

Wherein previous studies seek to explain the success of debugging in OSS as a function of qualities with the software product [3], my observation is that the success of debugging may be found in the daily activities of OSS users and developers. Finding the source of a bug is a process where the person reporting the bug and those trying to understand make the bug debuggable by working together to find relevant pieces of information and producing new debug texts. Making the software debuggable can therefore be interpreted as a collective process including both the person submitting the bug report, those trying to understand and resolve the problem, as well as the tools involved in producing the various debug texts being interpreted. It is by iteratively producing debug texts and extracting pieces of from these texts into meaningful combinations that bugs are made debuggable.

3 References

1. J. Feller and B. Fitzgerald, *Understanding Open Source Software Development* (Pearson Education Limited, Harlow, 2002)
2. K. Crowston and J. Howison, The Social Structure of Free and Open Source Software Development, *First Monday* 10(2), 2005.
3. J.W. Paulson, G. Succi and A. Eberlein,, An Empirical Study of Open Source and Closed-Source Software Products, *IEEE Transactions on Software Engineering* 30(4):246-256 (2004).
4. A. Mockus, R.T. Fielding amd J.D. Herbsleb, Two Case Studies of Open Source Software Development: Apache and Mozilla, *Transactions on Software Engineering and Methodology* 11(3), 309-346 (2002):
5. J.Y. Moon and L. Sproull, The Essence of Distributed Work: The Case of the Linux Kernel, *First Monday* 5(11), 2000.

A graphical installation system for the GNU/Linux Debian distribution

Fiandrotti Attilio[1],Pierluigi Di Nunzio[1], Federico Di Gregorio[1],Angelo Raffaele Meo[1]
1 Politecnico di Torino, Dipartimento Automatica e Informatica,
Centro Primario di Competenza sul Software Libero
Corso Duca degli Abruzzi 24, Torino, Italy
fiandro@initd.org, pierluigi.dinunzio@polito.it,
fog@debian.org, meo@polito.it
WWW home page: http://freesoftware.polito.it/

Abstract. One of the main objectives of the Centro di Competenza sul Software Libero del Politecnico di Torino is to provide custom GNU/Linux distribution to the Public Administration, small and medium enterprise and schools. Debian GNU/Linux was choosen as the base for the custom distributions because of its strong support of free software and its long-standing technical merits: minimalist hardware requirement, the best available packaging system, support for 13 different architectures and a strict set of quality guidelines adopted by all the active Debian developers. The only foreseeable limitation, the Debian default text-based installer, was overriden by restarting the development of the then-abandoned Debian graphical installer. Now the new graphical installer is developed by tens of people and it will be included in the next official Debian release.

1 Custom Debian distributions

One of the main objectives of the Centro di Competenza sul Software Libero del Politecnico di Torino is to provide custom GNU/Linux distributions to the PA and educational world; such distributions will be preconfigured and easily installable to minimize the amount of manual operations required to the final user.

Debian GNU/Linux was deemed to be the perfect distribution to base our custom work on, mainly because of its strong support of free software (as in the Debian Free Software Guidelines), its support for multiple hardware architectures, robust package management system and flexible and easily customizable installation system.

In particular, we needed an installation system with the following characteristics:

1. Released (and releasable) under a free software license (Debian does);
2. With a strong developers base (Debian does);
3. Modular and independent on packages about to be installed (Debian does);
4. Pre-configurable, to reduce the steps needed to install a working system (Debian does);
5. With a state-of-the-art User Interface supporting non-latin wide-char alphabets and a variety of input/output devices.

The only limitation to use the default Debian installer was point (5): when the project was started the Debian installer only supported a text-based front-end; user interaction

Please use the following format when citing this chapter:

Attilio, F., Di Nunzio, P., Di Gregorio, F., and Meo, A.R., 2006, in IFIP International Federation for Information Processing, Volume 203, Open Source Systems, eds. Damiani, E., Fitzgerald, B., Scacchi, W., Scotto, M., Succi, G., (Boston: Springer), pp. 337-338

was poor and support for non-latin alphabets only partially working (mainly because of the limitations of a fixed-size cell-based output device.)

2 The graphical debian-installer

Classical text-based Debian installer supports 13 different architectures (from embedded systems to mainframes) and provides a solid technical base on which to build a graphical installer:

1. It is completely based on independent *back-end* modules (micro-debs or udebs) to which the install procedures (hardware recongition, hard disk partitioning, base system install, ...) are delegated.
2. The *back-end* modules communicates with the *front-end* using a well-defined and well-tested protocol (i.e., the debconf protocol.)
3. It is ready for localization and internationalization (even if the text-based *front-end* cannot render correctly non-latin or complex alphabets.)
4. Can be easily customized by providing package pre-configuration (pre-seeds) and/or custom procedures in the form of extra udebs.

The development of a graphical *front-end* module was based on previous work that used the GTK toolkit and was coordinated on the *debian-boot* mailing list, getting precious feedback and support by the official Debian Installer team. What we wanted was to be able to perform graphical installations even on low-resources machines, so we gave up using an X server and decided to put efforts in reviving the GTK-over-DirectFrameBuffer project. DirectFrameBuffer (DFB) is a small set of libraries designed to be used in embedded Linux systems: the GTK-over-DFB project consists in a GDK backend module for the GTK libraries that allows GTK to run even without an X server. The work on the graphical debian-installer also gave new life to the DFB port of the GTK libraries: some talented developers from other projects put a great deal of efforts in fixing it and making it work with the last releases of GTK.

Hand-crafted prototypes of grapical ISO installations images led to full integration into the standard Debian ISO building system and after about 1 year of work the debian-installer team officially adopted the new codebase and announced the next Debian release will feature the new graphical *front-end*. The prototypes allows optimal rendering of over 70 different languages, included Indic ones, and run on less then 64 megabytes of RAM.

Also, Debian-derived LinEx distribution, developed in Extremadura and whose regional government even sponsored a worksession on the grapgical installer, is going to be the first Debian derived distribution to offer a graphical, native, debian-installer.

The micro-dynamics of open source software development activity

Paul A. David[1], Francesco Rullani[2]
1 Stanford University, Economics Bldg 333
Stanford, California, 94305-6072, United States; and All Souls College,
Oxford, OX1, 4AL, United Kingdom.
2 Sant'Anna School of Advanced Studies, Piazza Martiri della Libertà 33,
56127 Pisa, Italy.
pad@stanford.edu, rullani@sssup.it

Abstract. This study aims to isolate and identify the properties of FLOSS development insofar as these can be revealed by examining the ecology of *SF.net*. It characterizes the contrast between the many "lurkers" and a much smaller core of "entrepreneurial" developers who are responsible for launching new projects, and gives an interpretation of the function of platforms such as *SF.net* as sites that people with a propensity to start open source projects can use to recruit "laborers". It describes the process underpinning the mobility of those who are recruited among the projects that are launched and provides insights on the evolution of developers' level and mode of involvement in FLOSS production.

1. Research Questions

The FLOSS model has given rise to a self-organizing global ecology of atomistic and collective projects that both share and compete for productive resources as well as for final "users". This structure is manifested within the microcosm of the SourceForge.net (*SF.net* henceforth), the largest platform for FLOSS development worldwide. By studying a dataset containing information about the population of 222,835 developers who registered themselves on *SF.net* during an early period in the platform's history (specifically, from September 1, 2000 through October 26, 2001), we have been able to address the following questions.

Is there a stable, distinct typology of actors, e.g. "entrepreneurial" developers who launches many projects, "laborers" who participate as group members of existing projects without launching any projects themselves, and "lurkers", who simply observe or contribute form outside the projects teams? How and one the basis of which characteristics individuals move over time between lurking, laboring, and launching projects?

2. Analysis

We define the following 7 states and assign each developer to one of these for every 30-days period of his/her "life" in *SF.net*:

0=non member and non founder, inactive (i.e. she/ he did not post any bug report,

---

David, P.A., and Rullani, F., 2006, in IFIP International Federation for Information Processing, Volume 203, Open Source Systems, eds. Damiani, E., Fitzgerald, B., Scacchi, W., Scotto, M., Succi, G., (Boston: Springer), pp. 339-340

patch or feature request);
1=non member and non founder, active;
2=member of 1 project and non founder of any project (active or inactive);
3=member of more than 1 projects and non founder of any project (either active or inactive);
4=founder of 1 project and member of 1 project (either active or inactive);
5=founder of 1 project and member of more than 1 projects (either active or inactive);
6=founder of more than 1 project and member of more than 1 projects (either active or inactive).

We study the transitions from one state to the others by applying Markov chain theory to describe how developers' involvement changes over time, obtaining estimates of a series of transition probability matrices pertaining to mutually exclusive sub-samples of developers, spanning the most important characteristics provided in the dataset: developers' *registration date* to *SF.net*; developers' state in *pre-analysis* periods; developers' characteristics such as the *skills* they declare to have, the main *language* they declare to speak, and the provision or not of an *email* address to be directly contacted.

3. Results and Limitations

Comparisons among the obtained strata enable us to better understand the nature of the mechanism triggering the launching of new projects, the participation in existing projects (i.e. the laboring activity) and "passive" participation (i.e. lurking activities).

In particular we have found that early-registered users have higher persistence in their foundation activity, and that developers who send "signals" into the community (e.g. disclosing their skills sets or their email addresses) tend to be, and become over time, more active and "entrepreneurial". The level of pre-analysis activity induces a sort of "role exchange" between the developers, where initially active individuals become inactive, and vice versa. Eventually, languages differences also matter. While English speakers follow the whole population dynamics, European, and even more so Asian, languages speakers enter mainly as lurkers, and then move in a greater proportion to more active states.

The main limitation of the study concerns the focus on the SourceForge population, which is only a sample of the universe of FLOSS projects, and one that does not capture phenomena characteristic of the very large projects. These points to the need, and the opportunities to apply the methodology developed here to the study of other sites, such as Savannah, and FreshMeat.

Development Platforms as a Niche for Software Companies in Open Source Software

Marinette Savonnet[1], Eric Leclercq[2], Marie-Noëlle Terrasse[3], Thierry Grison[4],
George Becker[5], Anne Sophie Farizy[6], and Ludovic Denoyelle[7]

[1] LE2I, Université de Bourgogne, France Marinette.Savonnet@u-bourgogne.fr
[2] LE2I, Université de Bourgogne, France Eric.Leclercq@u-bourgogne.fr
[3] LE2I, Université de Bourgogne, France Marie-Noelle.Terrasse@u-bourgogne.fr
[4] LE2I, Université de Bourgogne, France Thierry.Grison@u-bourgogne.fr
[5] gbecker@nerim.net
[6] ARIST Bourgogne, France
[7] ARIST Bourgogne, France l.denoyelle@bourgogne.cci.fr

As long as information systems do not become overly large and while they address a well-known domain, they can be controlled by engineering staff. Nevertheless, when dealing with large-scale, complex, or innovative information systems, it can be difficult to separate design issues and to formulate a meaningful information system proposal. In such a context, platforms for software engineering appear to be a promising approach. In this paper, we propose to view development platforms as a major opportunity for Open Source Software and Open Formats.

One of the major evolutions in the Open Source world is its integration with the proprietary world. Open Source tools and proprietary tools keep mixing up which each other at various levels: on the same machine, on the same company network, on the Internet and more recently even on the same platform (see, e.g., Eclipse [7]). In terms of business strategies, very large companies or very innovative ones enter consortiums for standard definitions. At the same time, small companies offer Open Source products and sell their competency in customizing their products (e.g., technical support, relevant sets of data, fine tuning of the basic software) to a given business context. In both cases, companies now act as service providers rather than as mere producers.

In such a context, development platforms appear to be a sound basis for engineering of flexible products built on consolidation of computer-based solutions and the know-how of users [2, 3, 5, 6]. In order to develop such platforms as meaningful industrial products, it is necessary to assure that Open Formats soon become more generally accepted, and completed with exchange and descriptive languages (such as XMI and the MOF for MOF-repositories [4, 8]).

Thus, development platforms need to evolve towards the schema depicted in Figure 1: a **description of a business knowledge made available through open formats and plug-ins** (either proprietary or Open Source plug-ins). Such platforms can offer (under Open Source licences) basic business-related

Please use the following format when citing this chapter:

Savonnet, M., Leclercq, E., Terrasse, M.-N., Grison, T., Becker, G., Farizy, A.S., and Denoyelle, L., 2006, in IFIP International Federation for Information Processing, Volume 203, Open Source Systems, eds. Damiani, E., Fitzgerald, B., Scacchi, W., Scotto, M., Succi, G., (Boston: Springer), pp. 341-342

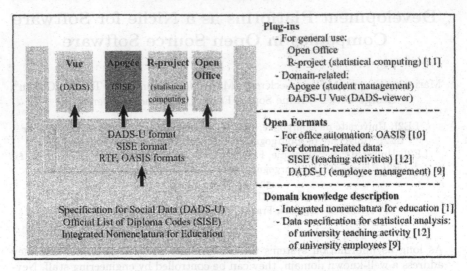

Fig. 1. An example platform for university management

functionalities and can be fine-tuned for specific uses. As an illustration, we describe a platform for education and job market surveys which encompasses: domain knowledge description and specifications, Open Formats, and domain specific plug-ins (Open Source/Format plug-ins are depicted in yellow and proprietary ones in green).

References

1. Nomenclatures intégrées dans FeDoX (*Nomenclatures integrated into FeDoX*). URL http://fedox.irisa.fr/Pages/nomenclature2.htm.
2. ARIST Bourgogne. Résultats d'enquête sur l'usage de l'informatique et des logiciels libres dans les entreprises bourguignonnes. (*Survey Results on the Use of Open Software in Burgundy Companies*)
3. J. Koenig. Seven OS Business Strategies for Competitive Advantage. 2005.
4. Meta Object Facility (MOF) Specification, V. 1.4, 2002. URL www.omg.org.
5. T. O'Reilly. OS Paradigm Shift. In *Proc. of OSBC'04*, 2004.
6. C. Shirky. The Interest Horizons and the Limits of Software Love. 1999.
7. Eclipse Platform. URL http://www.eclipse.org/.
8. XML Metadata Interchange (XMI). URL http://www.omg.org.
9. Déclaration annuelle des données sociales unifiée (DADS-U, *Annual Report of Standardized Social Data*). URL http://www.travail.gouv.fr/dossiers.
10. OASIS Open Document Format for Office Applications.
11. The R-Project for Statistical Computing. URL http://www.r-project.org/.
12. Programme des opérations statistiques et de contrôle de gestion, SISE. (*Program of statistical operations and management inspections*) Official Report of the Department of Education, France, 2000.

Reusable Parser Generation from Open Source Compilers

Kazuaki Maeda

Chubu University
1200 Matsumoto, Kasugai, Aichi 487-8501, JAPAN
kaz@acm.org

Many Open Source Software (called OSS) projects have been proposed and many software developers have contributed to develop software by OSS style. In the OSS development style, the source code is opened to the public and checked by the distributed software developers to improve the quality. The source code is, however, not effectively used to improve the productivity of other software development. This paper describes reusable parser generation from the source code of popular open source compilers.

In construction of code analyzers or reverse engineering tools, the parser development is a time-consuming task. To improve the productivity of the task, a renewal parser generator MJay was developed. MJay generates grammar definitions and some utility programs. It is useful to construct software tools to analyze source code.

Based on my experiences to construct software tools to generate UML diagrams from source code, there are three approaches to develop the parser.

1. To develop a parser from scratch by reading the programming language specification.

   It takes about one week to develop the parser from scratch to the best of my knowledge. There are some cases where it takes more than one week to develop it with high quality because the specification of recently popular programming languages is very complex. It is too long to catch up with the short-term development in the current situation as agile software development grows in popularity.

2. To get grammar definitions from major web sites, or find them using web search engines.

   There are some web sites including collections of public grammar definitions[1]. The collections in the web sites are very useful, but many public grammars contain errors and they provide no sufficient guarantee that they are strictly correct. As a result of this, we must debug them to improve the quality by ourselves with spending much time.

3. To extract source code of the parser from open source compilers.

   There are free open source compilers available with high quality. One of the famous compilers is GNU compiler collection[2]. The other is Mono C# compiler which is an open source implementation of .NET development environment available on major operating systems (e.g. Linux, Mac OS X,

Please use the following format when citing this chapter:

Maeda, K., 2006, in IFIP International Federation for Information Processing, Volume 203, Open Source Systems, eds. Damiani, E., Fitzgerald, B., Scacchi, W., Scotto, M., Succi, G., (Boston: Springer), pp. 343-344

Solaris and Windows) [3]. These compilers, however, were developed with only consideration for generating object code from source code. It is difficult to extract only the parser to reuse for another purpose because it is tightly coupled with other modules in the compiler.

This paper proposes the other approach, that is, to replace the parser generator with a renewal parser generator MJay. If we develop a parser for C#, we can reuse Mono C# compiler[3]. The parser in Mono C# compiler is developed using a parser generator Jay. After the replacement of Jay with MJay, MJay generates grammar definitions for a reusable parser in addition with a commonly used LALR parser. As a result of this, the parser in Mono C# compiler is opened and we can construct software tools quickly.

The development process is the following;

1. MJay reads the grammar definition G, and it generates the parser P1 of the usual C# compiler written in C#, the grammar definition H and some utility programs for the reusable parser.
2. P1 and the related files are compiled, and the special Mono C# compiler is built. The compiler reads C# source code and generates parser behavior in addition with the object code. The parser behavior consists of primitive actions for a typical LALR parser, for instance, shift, reduce, et al.
3. Jay reads the grammar definition H and generates the reusable parser P2 written in C#.
4. P2 and the related files are compiled by the usual Mono C# compiler, and a software tool is built. The reusable parser P2 reads the parser behavior and it takes the same sequence of actions as the parser P1 does.

In summary, this paper describes the motivation and the idea about reusable parser generation from the source code of popular open source compilers using the renewal parser generator MJay. It is based on my hard experiences of constructing reverse engineering tools, by oneself, which extract design information and draw diagrams (e.g. class diagram, communication diagram, et al.) from source code. It took a few weeks to construct it according to traditional parser development. MJay was developed to help me build the parser as soon as possible.

Now another reverse engineering tool for Visual Basic is under construction. It took just only two hours to develop the parser using MJay. I believe that MJay becomes an important tool to construct programming tools using open source compilers.

References

1. Grammar List, *http://www.antlr.org/grammar/list*.
2. Free Software Foundation, GCC Home Page, *http://gcc.gnu.org/* .
3. Main Page - Mono, *http://www.mono-project.com/Main_Page* .
4. jay Homepage, *http://www.informatik.uni-osnabrueck.de/alumni/bernd/jay/* .

Open Source Software Development (OSSD) Based On Software Engineering

Dengya Zhu , Vidyasagar Potdar, and Elizabeth Chang
School of Information Systems, Curtin University of Technology.
GPO Box U1987,Perth WA 6845, Australia
{dengya.zhu, vidyasagar.potdar, elizabeth.chang}@cbs.curtin.edu.au

Abstract. With the advent of Open Source Software (OSS) at the end of last century, many proponents believe that OSS is a new software development process and some even advocate OSS as a revolution for software engineering. The Cathedral and the Bazaar is a typical metaphor of the software development methodologies for the Closed Source Software (CSS) and the OSS. By comparing the phased (namely, requirement analysis, document design and system design, coding, testing and maintenance) software development methodology proposed by Software Engineering (SE), and by studying the management tools provided by SourceForge.net, we believe OSS development method not only follows the phased software development process, but also in return enriches the theory of SE.

"Software engineering: (1) The application of a systematic, disciplined, quantifiable approach to the development, operation, and maintenance of software; that is, the application of engineering t o software. (2) The study of approaches as in (1)" [5]. Software product engineering includes software requirements, design, coding, testing, and software operation and maintenance [2]. Contemporary software development process is also iterative and agile [5]. Frederick and Brooks claim *No Silver Bullet* [1]; Raymond, however, argues that OSS development process is a breakthrough of SE. By comparing the different development phases suggested by SE with the typical development procedure of OSS, the writers try to verify that the OSS development process is not only based on SE, but also in return enriches the SE theory in testing and maintenance phase.

The purpose of requirement analysis is to manifest the exact needs of software and document it unambiguously. It is true that seldom are there formal documents of requirements among OSS development. However, usually there is a mailing list or newsgroup to discuss the requirements [9]; some OSS programmers are themselves user [7]. They can also refer to the existing CSS to get the requirement [3].

Software design concerns with the transformation of requirements into a description of how these requirements are to be implemented. Although lack of formal design documentation, successful OSS project tend to be architected by developers of extraordinary skills and experience; the underlying architecture and implementation often begins as an inheritance from a traditional SE project [3]; mail archives and community chat sites are also sources of relevant documentation.

Construct software components that are identified and described in the design documents is the goal of coding. While coding is only a small percentage within the phased SE, for some OSS developers, software is nothing but coding. Spend a lot

Please use the following format when citing this chapter:

Zhu, D., Potdar, V., and Chang, E., 2006, in IFIP International Federation for Information Processing, Volume 203, Open Source Systems, eds. Damiani, E., Fitzgerald, B., Scacchi, W., Scotto, M., Succi, G., (Boston: Springer), pp. 345-346

time on coding can compensate the lack of sufficiency design document, by "release early, release often, and listen to your customers" [6], this OSS development strategy has been proven results in faster, feasible and economic coding [4].

"Given enough eyeballs, all bugs are shallow" [6]. "By sharing hypotheses and results with a community of peers, the scientist enable many eyes to see what one pair of eyes might miss" [9]. The success of many OSS products has proven that software test productivity scale up as the number of developers helping to debug the software increases [8].

SourveForge.net is the world's largest OSS development web site which provides free hosting and management to OSS development projects (http://sourceforge.net). SourgeForge.net provides a wide range of services, such as web tools for community and project management, file release system, compile farm, version control system, communication tools, publicity, and project web service. These services facilitate the OSS developers to follow the phased development process suggested by SE.

References

1. Frederick, P. and Brooks, Jr. No Silver Bullet: Essence and Accidents of Software Engineering, IEEE Computer 20 (1987), 10-19.
2. Hilburn, T. B. Hirmanpour, I. Khajenoori, S Turner, R. and Qasem, A. A Software Engineering Body of Knowledge, Carnegie Mellon Software Engineering Institute,
3. Massey, B. Where Do Open Source Requirements Come From. In Proceedings of the 2nd Workshop on Open-Source Software Engineering, (Orlando, Florida, May 19-25, 2002).
4. Potdar, V. and Chang, E. 2004, Open Source and Close Source Software Development Methodology. In The 4th Workshop on Open Source Software Engineering, (Edinburgh, Scotland, May 25, 2004). ACM Press, New York, 2004, 105-110.
5. Rressman, R.P. Software Engineering: A Practitioner's Approach, 6th edt. McGraw-Hill, New York, 2005.
6. Raymond, E. S. The Cathedral and the Bazaar: Musings on Linux and Open Source by an Accidental Revolution, O'Reilly, Sebastopol, 1999.
7. Scacchi, W. Software Development Practices in Open Software Development Communities. In Proceedings of the 23rd International Conference on Software Engineering. (Toronto, Canada, May 15, 2001). ACM Press, New York, 2001, 48-51.
8. Schmidt, D. C. and Porter, A. Leveraging Open-Source Communities to Improve the Quality & Performance of Open-Source Software. In Proceedings of the 23rd International Conference on Software Engineering. (Toronto, Canada, May 15, 2001). ACM Press, New York, 2001, 52-56.
9. Vixire, P. Software Engineering. In C. DiBona, S. Ockman & M. Stone(eds), Open Sources: Voices from the Open Source Revolution, O'Reilly Sebastopol, 1999.

Open Source in Web-based Periodicals

Andres Baravalle and Sarah Chambers
Department of Computer Science, University of Sheffield, UK.

email: {andres,sarah}@dcs.shef.ac.uk

Abstract. In this paper we aim to investigate the role of the media in the diffusion of Open Source, analysing three web-based periodicals from Italy, United Kingdom and USA. The influence of the media in our society is wide and we have to look to that direction if we want to seriously investigate the in-depth causes of the different trends. Nevertheless, our results show a picture that may not be familiar to many researchers of the field.

1 Introduction

The starting point for our research was the COSPA project which is investing the use of Open Source (OS) and Open Data Standards in the public administrations in Europe. It quickly became apparent that there was a different perception of Open Source across the different project partners and that OS is more positively perceived in some countries than others.

Decisions to use OS depends on numerous factors, including technical, economical and socio-cultural, but the information that the persons have plays a fundamental role [Lippmann 1950]. A question that arose was: why does OS has such different levels of acceptance and success in different countries, and what are the factors that influence it? We thought that these differences in opinion may be linked to the way that OS had been reported in the media the these countries and this is what we set to to investigate further.

2 Method

For our research, we selected three web-based periodicals The Register (UK); Punto Informatico (Italy) and C-Net News.com (USA). The periodicals are amongst the most read IT periodicals in their respective countries. At present we do not aim to identify global patterns or rules but specifically look at UK, Italy and USA.

To harvest the information from the periodicals, we developed a set of parsers, that can be used though a web interface. Using the parser, we have been able to collect information about more than 13,000 articles on OS, from 1998 until December 2005.

The core analysis is based on almost 500 articles published in the periodicals during November and December 2005. We analysed these articles categorizing them by level of relevance to OS. This was carried out to select the number of articles that

Please use the following format when citing this chapter:

Baravalle, A., and Chambers, S., 2006, in IFIP International Federation for Information Processing, Volume 203, Open Source Systems, eds. Damiani, E., Fitzgerald, B., Scacchi, W., Scotto, M., Succi, G., (Boston: Springer), pp. 347-348

were discussing issues related to OS, compared to the number of articles that had just were just referring to OS in passing. Articles were also classified by the topic of the article, the categories included: software, community and business.

3   Results and Discussion

In all the periodicals OS is well represented. There is not a overload of information, with articles on OS in a ocean of articles on proprietary software. Punto Informatico had a higher percentage of articles related to OS that were actually focused on OS, while both The Register and C-Net News.com had a higher number of OS articles on business aspects. Punto Informatico had a higher ratio of articles on OS compared with the number of articles including the keyword "Microsoft".

However, both The Register and C-Net News.com have been featuring more articles on OS migrations compared with Punto Informatico. Moreover, Punto Informatico has been always the last periodical to report on the migrations.

5   Conclusions

Our experience working on the COSPA project in the UK and the failure in finding suitable test location sites for migrations lead us to consider whether the press in the UK was biased against OS or whether there was a lack of coverage on the ongoing migrations, compared to other countries like Italy. The data of our sample period shows that this is not true, and a more in-depth analysis shows that it is neither true using a longer time frame.

However, according to our research, OS was covered as well in the UK and USA as it was in Italy. In fact, the Italy periodical contained a few less articles on OS migrations.

Future work might focus more on the topics that have been covered in the web-based periodicals and we plan to continue our research investigating different causes, to try to define more clearly which are the significant factors that influence the adoption of OS.

References

Lippmann, W. 1950. *Public opinion.* New York : Macmillan.

Software Patents and Open Source Software in the European Union: Evidences of a Trade-Off?

Francesco Rentocchini[1] and Giuditta De Prato[2]

[1] Department of Economics, University of Bologna, Italy
francesc.rentocchini@studio.unibo.it
[2] Department of Economics, University of Bologna, Italy deprato@spbo.unibo.it

Abstract. The present work aims at giving an account of the patenting behaviour in the software sector, focusing on the European Union and pointing out issues regarding a trade-off which would support a policy attitude in favour of a wider diffusion of the Open Source model.

1 Introduction

It is well known that art. 52 of the European Patent Convention regulates patenting activities within the Union and expressively do not allow software and business methods patentability. This exception is not completely applied in practice. In fact, more than 70,000 patents are found to have been accorded by the European Patent Office in the period 1982-2004. The aim of this paper is threefold: first, economic literature on patents is reviewed concentrating on more recent contributions; second, an original database for the European Union is constructed which links the number of software patents filed at the European Patent Office by European firms with their R&D spending and other relevant variables, and advanced econometric techniques for data counting are applied to find out the most relevant factors affecting the accorded software patents; finally, conclusions are drawn showing that support to Open Source Software (OSS) could help stimulating competition in the ICT sector and increasing the innovation rate, while in fact, on the other side, strategic patenting is confirmed by available data analysis.

2 Recent Developments in the Theoretical Literature

Since a long time, the economic literature has recognised the importance of the patent system in shaping and directing the rate of appropriation of the innovative effort of the firm [1, 6]. In addition to 'classical' contributions, the literature that has been developed to explain the recent trends in worldwide patenting, has relied on Schumpeter's contributions to economic thought [7]. More recently, evolutionary economics [5] has focused on the role of patents in enhancing or hindering innovation depending on sectors where firms compete. Therefore, a number of authors underlines that, depending on appropriability

Please use the following format when citing this chapter:

Rentocchini, F., and De Prato, G., 2006, in IFIP International Federation for Information Processing, Volume 203, Open Source Systems, eds. Damiani, E., Fitzgerald, B., Scacchi, W., Scotto, M., Succi, G., (Boston: Springer), pp. 349-351

conditions of sectors in which they are used, patents might be, or not, a useful institutional mechanism in order to promote the variety of technological solutions and the selection by market forces via competition. In addition, empirical contributions have shown that firms do not always rate patents as effective appropriability mechanisms [3]. Hence, on one side, empirical literature shows how patents are not suitable appropriability mechanisms in a high number of sectors, but, on the other side, we witness an explosion in the number of patents filed in recent years. Why is there such a trade-off? Which factors contribute to explain it? One of the main reason refers to strategic patenting, which is a strategic behaviour of firms aimed at hindering competition, obtain licensing revenues and to have stronger power in negotiations.

3 Data Collection and Econometric Analysis

In order to analyse recent trends in software patenting in the European Union, we relied on the Gauss.ffii database. The subset of data relevant to the present work had been built by extracting and collecting all records regarding patents filed between January, 1st 1995 and December, 31st 2004, thus obtaining a total of 65.536 patent records. After that, a relation has been established between the collected dataset and the 2004 EU Industrial Research Investment Scoreboard. The resulting dataset is composed by 1000 firms both European and non European whose data concerning Research and Development spending, FTSE sectoral classification and geographical classification, number of software patents filed at EPO, net sales, number of employees and operating profit and revenue are available for the period 2000-2003. Hence a panel dataset has been created with information on one thousand firms through a four year long time period (2000-2003). After that, econometric techniques have been applied in order to analyse more in deep the relationship between software patents and other variables in the dataset. Results show that R&D and size contribute to explain the number of software patents filed within this period. A second specification of the model is used to investigate sectoral differences in the number of software patents firms apply for. Results show that, in line with empirical studies conducted in US [2, 4], only electronic and electrical and IT hardware industries are found to be highly significant in explaining the number of software patents filed during the period of consideration. Hence, it seems that software patents are principally filed by firms which do not have software production as primal activity. Electronic and IT hardware firms instead are found to rely disproportionally on software patenting.

4 Which Role for the Open Source Software?

Such conclusions coming from the data analysis are then put in relation to the support in principle accorded by the European Union to the Open Source model and to the fact that OSS demonstrated a potential in stimulating innovation and technological improvement. OSS is perceived as suitable to promote innovation to different extents, because free circulation of software makes progress results fully available and it provides incentives to users to innovate, to freely reveal and to diffuse innovations, making them affordable also to small enterprises. Early surveys showed OSS is likely to promote innovation among SMEs by lowering costs for knowledge appropriation and licences, while lack of information and proprietary innovation delay the process of innovation adoption. Along with similar arguments, the European Union declared a willingness to consolidate a dominant position in the Open Source environment, also in order to find a new role in the software sector. The paper therefore proposes some reflections, which could help to draw policy indications, on the limitations which the analysed patenting system could pose to the role of OSS in diffusing innovation, and on alternative strategies which EU Instititions could push forward to promote alternative methods of intellectual property protection involving -for example- GPLs.

References

1. K. Arrow. Economic welfare and the allocation of resources for invention. In R. Nelson, editor, *The Rate and Direction of Inventive Activity: Economic and Social Factors.* NBER, Princeton University Press, 1962.
2. J. Bessen and R. Hunt. The software patent experiment. In *Patents, Innovation and Economic Performance*, pages 246–263. Organisation for Economic Cooperation and Development (OECD), April 2003.
3. W. Cohen, R. Nelson, and J. Walsh. Protecting their intellectual assets: Appropriability conditions and why U.S. manufacturing firms patent (or not). Working Paper 7552, 2000.
4. B. Hall. Exploring the patent explosion. *Journal of Technology Transfer*, 30(1-2):35–48, 2004.
5. R. Nelson and S. Winter. *An Evolutionary Theory of Economic Change.* Belknap press, 1982.
6. W. Nordhaus. *Invention, Growth and Welfare.* MIT Press, Cambridge Massachussets, 1969.
7. J. Schumpeter. *Capitalism, Socialism and Democracy.* McGraw Hill, 1942.